a MOTHER'S LOVE is a BLESSING

17,498 Days With Alice Marie Kennedy

Daniel J. Kennedy, Sr.

ISBN (Print Edition): 978-1-54397-440-9
ISBN (eBook Edition): 978-1-54397-441-6

DEDICATION

Life doesn't come with a manual; it
comes with a mother (Anon).

To Katie, Patti, Anne Marie, Danny and Jack.
A portrait of your mother, as seen
through the eyes of your father.

TABLE OF CONTENTS

INTRODUCTION

On the 17th day of February in the year of Our Lord, 1968, the marital life of a young girl from western Massachusetts commenced at the Church of Saint Thomas the Apostle in West Springfield, Massachusetts. Throughout the subsequent 17,498 days of jubilation and sadness with her, euphoria concluded on the 13th day of January in the year of Our Lord, 2016, when Alice Marie (Haggerty) Kennedy entered Eternal Life.

This genesis of young Alice's leadership as matriarch of our family began on a golf course in western Massachusetts, transited to Greater Boston with summers on Cape Cod, and culminated in a cemetery in Westfield, Massachusetts. She experienced triumphs and tragedies, joys and sadness, days of happiness and challenges, but through it all she maintained an unwavering faith in Christ. As a young businesswoman in a world of business men, she was on an upward spiral, rivaling expectations of many Ivy League aspirants when divine providence intervened and her ascent in her chosen profession was providentially redirected.

In the exciting world of the Fabulous Fifties and the Seismic Sixties, prospects of attaining corporate advancement did not deter this young woman from fully engaging in numerous recreational activities. She was a prototype All-American girl who loved life, radiated abundant zest, possessed a demonstrable love for cars, athletics, sailing, and horse-back riding and, most of all, relished playing practical jokes on her friends. Manufacturing fun and mischief- making was her priority when, the unintended consequence in accepting an invitation for a casual game of golf sidetracked her corporate expectations. Ultimately, she suspended a promising business career, raised five children, rejuvenated her business career, and then encountered a lengthy illness. During all phases of her life, she was indefatigable; her intense love of the Lord and His people permeated all aspects of her 17,498 days with our family.

In 1947, in the industrial city of Chicopee, Mass., an eight-year-old girl spent every Saturday in the cafeteria of a local school as an active member of the internationally renowned 4-H Club, a youth organization devoted to developing life skills. True to this young girl's propensity for mischief, she typically didn't depart for 4-H meetings until she playfully tantalized the Sisters of Saint Joseph, who resided in a convent adjacent to her home.

One morning, the young maiden strategically placed a mirror on her bedroom window-sill to re-direct the rays of the morning sun into convent rooms. With the sun ricocheting off their Bibles, the Sisters of Saint Joseph were not in the right frame of mind for morning prayer that day!

Many people, including myself, perceive the 4-H Club to be an organization exclusively affiliated with agricultural projects. Although that is of course true, it is much more than an agrarian undertaking. The organization is predicated on instilling developmental and leadership qualities, while, at the same time, acquainting members with an awareness of the need for compassion.

As a dedicated member of the 4-H Club of Chicopee, young Alice participated in canning food and distributing sustenance to homeless shelters. The primary benefit she acquired from this activity was the lifelong adaptation of the four foundational precepts of the 4-H Club—Head, Heart, Hands, and Health. The lessons learned by the little tyke from Chicopee were applied for 17,498 Days.

As a young lady, she engaged her *head* in decision-making, her *heart* in helping others, her *hands* in skillfully utilizing her ever-present toolbox, and dispensed *health* medications to those in need. In addition to the four Hs, she demonstrated two additional "Hs" during her life—*holy* and *harmony*. Through faith, she displayed holiness, and through her efforts in the restoration of relationships, she epitomized harmony.

With determination, vigor and love, this young woman hit the pause button on corporate aspirations quickly, grasping domestic responsibilities and motherhood. Since day one of 17,498 days of our marriage, she became *The Heart of Our Home*, skillfully navigating through the turbulent waters of family life while continually instilling values of compassion and kindness into the hearts of her children.

When Alice was confronted with dementia during the twilight of her life, she always had her family there to assist her. The power of love was omnipresent, as her children displayed the love they acquired from their loving mother. Truly, a mother's love is a never-ending blessing.

Daniel J. Kennedy, Sr.

Feb 17, 2019

PART ONE

THE FIRST DAY

CHAPTER 1

YOU ARE MY SUNSHINE

I have competed well; I have finished the race;
I have kept the Faith. (2 Timothy 4:7)

It was during 2008 or 2009 when I first began to fear that Alice might be experiencing cognition diminishment. Time passed, and by 2010, the lessening of her customary acuities became more concerning. Every night after dinner we sang her favorites in order to stimulate her mind: "I'm Looking Over A Four-Leaf Clover," "My Wild Irish Rose," "A Bicycle Built for Two," "Always," and some others. As further time passed, Alice remembered less and less of the lyrics. However, one of the melodies weathered the storm of failing cognition—she remembered every word of "You Are My Sunshine!"

Alice's memory, which I hoped would never completely die, ultimately faded into obscurity. Although the prognosis for dementia patients was dire, I was hopeful our "Golden Oldie Hour" would keep her brilliant mind clicking for many years. Our evening sing-alongs were grace-filled moments, especially for me. It was thrilling to witness Alice's disabled mind recall the lyrics and tunes from a past era. I couldn't help but paraphrase a Noel Henry song that kept reverberating in my ears: "How Can I Keep from Crying?" Even in the later stages of Alice's illness, when she was no longer able to speak, at the end of the chorus of "You Are My Sunshine," she would lean forward, rub her nose against mine, and somehow enunciate the words "please don't take my sunshine away."

After experiencing the nuances of her illness, I now believe her response to that particular song was a threefold blessing. First, she was so proud of herself that she remembered the lyrics. Secondly, her intellect enabled her to associate me as "her sunshine," and thirdly, she didn't want me to be taken away.

Whenever Alice exhibited—and she did on occasion exhibit—the semblance of recollection, I construed those moments as God's way of communicating through a "non compos mentis" mind. To me, it was an "attaboy" message, a spiritual pat on the back, a sign that Christ was with Alice constantly.

As 2015 slipped away, so too did my "Little Alice Blue Gown." Gone were our nightly songfests, gone was the semblance of a smile on her beautiful face, and gone too was her brilliant, beautiful mind.

On the 13th day of January, in the year of Our Lord, 2016—the 17,498[th] day of our marriage—Alice Marie (Haggerty) Kennedy entered eternal life.

After a restless night, it was consoling for all of us to see that Alice, at long last, was lying peacefully in our living room in Needham, Mass. During the night, Katie, Alice's first born, was in continual contact with the hospice unit of the Visiting Nurse Association (VNA), communicating regular updates on any changes in Alice's condition. In the early morning hours, the restlessness and the rattle in her throat, which had been of concern to all of us during the night, abated and, thankfully, Alice was resting comfortably.

Katie and her husband, Max Collins, spent the night at our home and, along with Patti, Alice's second born, and daughter, Ashley, took turns sitting with Alice during the night. As each of us sat next to her in our own way, our thoughts went back to happier days that we realized were gone forever. When I sat with Alice and said the rosary, I was consumed with the moment, unfortunately, and even though a bottle of Holy Water was on our mantle next to the Belleek Statute of the Blessed Mother, I never thought to make the Sign of the Cross on Alice's forehead with Holy Water, which I had done when my father was dying in 1985.

Alice's serenity in the morning seemed to indicate that she had attained a long-sought calmness, free from the discomfort, which was so disconcerting to all of us to witness. At the VNA hospice nurse's direction, Katie administered another dose of morphine at 4:00 a.m., which seemed to allay her breathing difficulties. Gratefully, and since Alice was resting comfortably, I went to St. Joseph's Parish in Needham to serve at the 6:50 am Mass. After Mass when I returned home, I was pleased that Alice was still sleeping contentedly.

A few days before our son Danny was ordained to the priesthood in 2007, he instructed me to purchase an inexpensive stole at the Sister Disciples of the Divine Master on West Street in Boston, and to give it to him so he could wear it when he heard confession for the first time. Danny informed me he would subsequently return the stole, along with the Sacred Linen the Archbishop of Boston, Cardinal Sean O'Malley, would use to dry his hands of Sacred Chrism oil at his ordination. He charged me with custodial responsibility of both items and gave explicit instructions to secure both items in my safe deposit box. Specifically referring to the Sacred Linen, his instructions continued. "When Mom dies, place the Sacred Linen on her hands when she lies in the casket. When you die, the stole should be placed on your hands," he said. I thought these were interesting instructions since presumably, he would long outlive Alice and me, yet his instructions were unambiguous.

Based on Alice's critical condition, we believed God would come for her sometime during the day. In anticipation of the trauma and complexities that would ensue, I decided to retrieve the Sacred Linen from the safe deposit box as soon as the Needham branch of Santander Bank opened on Wednesday morning. I was the first customer to enter the bank on January 13, 2016.

After obtaining the Sacred Linen, as I was leaving the bank, I had the thought that; most often, people retrieve bonds, jewelry, and deeds etc. from safe deposit boxes, so it must be rare for a customer to retrieve Sacred Linen. Consequently, I had the thought to tell someone in the bank about my mission, so I went back into Santander Bank and shared the story with the branch manager.

The manager, Daniel O'Brien, whom I never met, listened intently and thanked me for sharing the story of the Sacred Linen. Mr. O'Brien assured me he would relate the story with his parents, who, he said, were active in Archdiocese of Boston's Catholic Charities organization. At that point I left the bank and drove directly home.

As soon as I opened the front door of our home, Patti, obviously distraught, informed me that "Mom died." I was stunned and could not believe it to be true. I rushed into the living room and saw that Alice looked completely different than she looked thirty minutes ago; she looked serene. Patti was right, Alice had died and I wasn't with her!

It is impossible for me to describe how disappointed I felt that Alice died without me by her side. For the past six years, I had been with her 24/7, yet while I was at the bank retrieving the Sacred Linen, entrusted to me by her son, she passed. Alice was *The Heart of Our Home* and, as she lay so peacefully in our living room I knew; *The Heart of Our Home* was gone; gone home to God!

We were blessed Alice died in our living room with our Kennedy family manger and her favorite Belleek Figurine of the Blessed Mother holding the infant Jesus prominently displayed on our mantle, looking down, protectively, at Alice. The prior home for the Belleek Figurine of the Blessed Mother was on Alice's bureau, looking directly across to Alice on her side of the bed. Several years ago, when cleaning the statue, the left arm of the Blessed Mother broke. Alice always planned on having the arm reattached but did not accomplish the mission. In the interim, for safekeeping, she put it securely in a small plastic container. Before she could have the arm reattached, her cognitive skills began to erode and the detached arm remained in the plastic container. Just before Christmas, I took the figurine and the detached arm to a jeweler in Needham. My final Christmas present to Alice was the figurine of the Blessed Mother with a reattached left arm. On Christmas day, I placed the restored figurine on our living room mantle so Alice could see Mary every day.

As Alice lay in her living room bed, she was facing a crucifix on the wall, which was given to Danny on the day of his Baptism on February 17, 1974, and an illuminated Christmas tree figurine, which was our gift to him on his first Christmas as a priest.

Directly above where she lay was the Della Robbia Christmas Wreath Alice had constructed for our family, shortly after we were married. During the Renaissance period, Luca Della Robbia, an Italian Sculptor, was noted for his brilliantly colored terracotta statuary often depicting seasonal fruits and vegetables. Years later, the Della Robbia techniques were applied to what had formerly been solid evergreen Christmas wreaths, thus, the Della Robbia Christmas Wreath! As I stood, still in shock, staring at Alice's motionless body, I realized she was wearing my recently blessed Brown Scapular.

On Monday morning, January 11, after the 6:50 am mass at St. Joseph, I had asked our local priest, Father Peter Stamm, to bless a scapular of Our Lady of Mount Carmel, a.k.a. brown scapular, for me. For many years, I have worn a brown scapular and, over time, they eventually become torn and tattered. The brown scapular I had been wearing was no exception. The cord had been pieced together so many times it was an amalgamation of knots and I could barely fit it over my head. Replacing the scapular was long overdue.

Father Peter went to the upstairs church and returned to the downstairs sacristy with a large book, which contained the Rite for Blessing and Investiture of the Scapular of Our Lady of Mount Carmel. After blessing the brown scapular, he placed it around my neck and I went home to check on Alice.

When Alice was trying to consume a few sips of watermelon juice, the thought crossed my mind that I should tell Alice I was wearing a new scapular. Instantaneously, I had another thought: to give the recently blessed brown scapular to Alice. In Alice's adult life, she never wore a scapular. So, as I placed the brown scapular around Alice's neck and told her the Blessed Mother would give her special protection, she looked at me with no appreciable change in her face. She was expressionless. Now, just two days later, Alice Marie Kennedy died wearing the brown scapular of Our Lady of Mount Carmel.

Alice died on the thirteenth day of the month, in January, 2016. At Fatima, Portugal in 1917, the Blessed Mother appeared on the thirteenth day of several consecutive months. During one of those monthly apparitions, the Blessed Mother was holding a brown scapular of Our Lady of Mount Carmel.

After Alice's Funeral, Anne Marie said to me, "Dave (David F. Russell, her husband and Funeral Director) is afraid you will be upset because when he retrieved Mom's jewelry and rosary beads prior to the burial, he forgot to repossess her brown scapular." I have come to learn that during traumatic times, it is not unusual to experience other unexpected traumatic events, which I presume to also be in God's plan. Consequently, I was not disturbed that Alice was buried wearing the brown scapular of Our Lady of Mount Carmel.

A week or two later I was having breakfast with a longtime friend who we met after moving to Needham, Father John McLaughlin, and I told him I put a brown scapular on Alice two days before she died. Immediately, he asked if she was buried with the scapular. I told him, "Inadvertently, she was buried wearing the scapular. In the stress of the moment, my son-in-law forgot to retrieve it."

"That's a good thing, that's a very good thing," Father McLaughlin responded. He proceeded to explain, "The scapular is supposed to remain on the person after death." He continued, "Ideally, a scapular should be placed around the recipient's neck by another person and, at the time of death, the deceased should be buried wearing the brown scapular!"

Father Matt Westcott, one of Danny's seminary classmates, had planned on visiting Alice the morning she passed away. Soon he was standing alongside us in our living room as we lamented and tried to grasp the reality that Alice—wife, mother, grandmother, and friend to so many—was no longer with us. Now, for all eternity, Alice was with Jesus and His Blessed Mother.

As we reminisced about various moments in Alice's life, her face appeared to take on a beauty that was not previously discernible. Perhaps in the 17,498 days of our marriage I became conditioned to her appearance or, quite possibly, the beauty of her face became more pronounced as the neurodegenerative disease of dementia progressed. To those of us blessed to be with her in our living room, the beauty of Alice's face appeared to reflect a transcendent tranquility. At this point, to give full view of her beautiful face, and wrinkle-free at that, I decided she would look better without her beloved baseball cap. Plus, she no longer needed the security of her cap; she now knew of true and everlasting security—she knows Jesus!

Alice loved to wear baseball caps. It was an obsession for her to accumulate numerous baseball caps. With that in mind, during the past few years I always placed a cap on her head day and night. Especially in the winter months, I placed a cap on her head when she went to bed. In my mind, the cap would serve a dual purpose: first, it would provide a sense of security during long and lonely nights of bewilderment; and secondly, it would keep any draft off her head during cold winter nights. She wore one of her prized baseball caps 24/7!

The cap that adorned her head the past few weeks was a black Catholic Memorial High School hockey cap designed to reflect the logo of the Montreal Canadians. I think she would be pleased with that cap as it represented two of her most precious loves—Danny's alma mater and her intense interest in hockey.

The day Alice entered Eternal Life, January 13, 2016, was a re-enactment of Danny's spontaneous living room wake. So many people were so thoughtful. As Alice lay there in peace and quiet, the doorbell never stopped ringing. Neighbors arrived bearing coffee cakes and casseroles, priests with their priestly blessings, florists with beautiful flowers, and not to be overlooked, hugs galore!

Later that day, our Archbishop, Cardinal Sean P. O'Malley, called to express his sympathies, and I shared with him that the beauty on Alice's face reminded me of the biblical description of Saint Stephen, "His face was like that of an Angel." (Acts: 6-15)

I also mentioned to Cardinal Sean that I recall hearing him discuss what he deemed to be 'Irish Alzheimer's—when a person of Irish Heritage is afflicted with Alzheimer's, the person forgets everything except grudges! I told him that observation certainly has a degree of validity. Yes, Alice was of Irish Heritage and, yes, she was afflicted with a form of Alzheimer's but contrary to Irish Alzheimer's, Alice never held any grudges!

A TIME OF SADNESS

Many people at Alice's wake commented on how beautiful she looked—which of course was an accurate assessment. In a sense, even those who said "she looks like an angel" was a credible remark, but in fact, the radiance of her beautiful face was apparent to those of us in our living room on the day she died. Yes, she seemed to reflect an aura of angelic appearance.

Alice was gifted in the sense that she got along with everyone she met. If there is such a thing as the gift of getting along with people, Alice was blessed with that gift. "Never did Alice return evil for evil or insult for insult; revenge was not in her vocabulary. Alice always sought the positive," said cousin Bill St. Lawrence, in recalling her childhood days.

Alice was feisty. She certainly did get her "Irish-Up" from time to time. She wasn't bashful in confronting the perpetrator of an injustice and, if necessary, she would have no qualms in taking remedial action after which, at least in her mind, the issue was over and forgotten. No matter what the injustice, no matter what the issue, Alice never expressed any recrimination toward the person nor did she ever harbor a grudge. Forgiveness was in the depth of her soul. In fact, Alice actively promoted the gift of forgiveness! Whenever a contentious family issue occurred, Alice put on her "peace-maker cap" and, even if it took years, she did everything within her power to generate a peaceful resolution.

If an individual was an anathema to others and non-gratis to many, as far as Alice was concerned, they just needed a friend. So, she became their friend. She approached the unapproachable with genuine concern and love and, invariably, she was able to bridge the hostility gap with love.

"I never heard Alice say a negative word about anyone. She loved to have fun and she was mischievous, but most of all she was kind and virtuous," said her cousin Bill St. Lawrence when recounting Alice as a young woman. Bill, in continuing his heart-felt recollections; "Alice was a 'controlled rascal' always looking to have fun, but she knew the boundaries, she never went too far in 'needling' her friends."

Katie's good friend, Neasa, from Ireland, called when she received news of Alice's death and consoled Katie with an Irish expression; "Fuair si Cuireadh na Nollag" (meaning—chosen to pass at such a Holy Time).

Several years ago, Alice and I enjoyed tea with Neasa and her parents in Burnham West, County Kerry, Ireland.

A TIME FOR HEALING

As occasionally happens in our family, and seemingly within seconds, minor disagreements between siblings can escalate into major confrontations. Such an incident occurred shortly before Christmas 2015, when our daughters Patti and Ann Marie had a disagreement. Unfortunately, I couldn't resolve the breach and animosities continued to fester.

All of us were distraught that Alice died but Patti was particularly downcast as she was the only one present at the time. I sensed that even though Patti was deeply impacted by Alice's death, to an extent she felt honored to be the only person with her when she died.

The date of Alice's death also coincided with the birth date of our third-born daughter, Anne Marie. Even in the depth of sadness, she too felt honored; honored in that her mother died on her birthday. Both Patti and Anne Marie were uniquely affiliated with their mother's death; a death-bed blessing from their loving mother. Resultantly, the seemingly unresolvable breach between two of Alice's daughters was immediately defused; anger melted away, love prevailed and, once again peace reigned in the Kennedy family. Deo Gratias! (Thank God!)

Alice continually emphasized the importance of compatibility within her family and within her extended family and friends. It is fitting that her love for others was still in evidence at the time of her entry into eternal life. Alice must be pleased; Heaven must have presented her with a "peace-maker cap."

A mother's love for her children is eternal, she never stops caring for her children!

<u>Intriguing Intergenerational Associations</u>:

- Alice loved to share her joy with others, and she delighted in receiving reciprocal joy from others!

- Alice shared her birthday, August 22nd, The Queenship of Mary, with her daughter Katie.

- Alice shared her first name with her mother Alice (McCarthy) Haggerty.

- Alice shared the day of her death with her daughter Patti, who was the only person present at the hour of her entry into Eternal Life.

- Alice shared the date of her death with the birthdate of her daughter Anne Marie.

TOUGHEN-UP, DAN

After a long and difficult day, with several more stressful days on the horizon, I could almost hear Alice say, "When it gets tough, it's time to toughen-up Dan." I must admit, I didn't feel "tough." I looked forward to peaceful night's sleep; unfortunately, I couldn't sleep. I continued to weep. The marital lamp that burned brightly for 17,498 days was extinguished.

The following day, Anne Marie's husband, David Francis Russell—the proprietor of the Russell-Pica Funeral Home in Brockton—discussed the arrangements for Alice's funeral. Dave suggested leasing a local funeral home in Needham with the proviso that he and his staff would oversee the services. I concurred and we agreed to hold Alice's wake at the Eaton Funeral Home on Highland Avenue in Needham, conveniently located directly across the street from the Church of St. Joseph, our local parish.

Alice shared many mutual interests with her father, Charles Joseph Haggerty, a funeral director in Chicopee. One of their pet peeves was the importance of a quality casket. Whenever Alice and I attended a wake or a funeral, Alice not only commiserated with the grieving family, but also commended them on their choice of a casket. If the deceased was adorned in a top-of-the-line casket, Alice typically commended on their exquisite choice of a casket." She and her mother Alice would have been pleased. She and her mother, Alice Helen Haggerty, would be delighted to know that she was adorned in an azure blue dress befitting the song they both loved so much: "Alice Blue Gown."

In accord with her son, Father Daniel J. Kennedy's request, the Sacred Linen that Archbishop Cardinal Sean O'Malley used to dry Danny's hands of the Holy Chrism on his ordination day (May 26, 2007) was placed on Alice's hands as she lay in a mahogany coffin she would have loved. Also, consolably draped on her hands were the sterling silver Rosary Beads she received on the day of her First Communion from her godfather, Melvin O'Leary.

In testament to the high esteem in which Alice was held, many of her friends from the Boston area, Cape Cod, and western Massachusetts visited the Eaton Funeral Home to pay their respects to Alice on Sunday, January 17, 2016. Our entire family was gratified to see so many people commenting on how beautiful Alice looked. Although their assessment was acutely accurate, I knew the beautiful look of serenity occurred as she lay in our living room on the thirteenth day of January.

On the 18th day of January 2016, a funeral Mass for Alice Marie (Haggerty) Kennedy was held at St. Joseph's Church in Needham. My mind reverted back to the 17th day of February 1968, at St. Thomas the Apostle Church in West Springfield—our wedding day. Alice's father was hospitalized with a heart malfunction and was unable to attend her wedding, thus he was unavailable to walk Alice down the aisle. Each of Alice's two brothers-in-law, Lowell Harlow and Emil Masi, offered to stand in for Mr. Haggerty but Alice was adamant. If her father, though living, was unable to walk her down the aisle, she was determined to walk alone. Cognizant of Alice's determination to walk alone on her wedding day almost 48 years ago, in tribute to Alice, I was determined to walk alone at her Funeral Mass in 2016.

Danny's close friend, Father Matthew J. Westcott, celebrated Alice's funeral Mass. Numerous priest friends of Danny, as well as Bishop Arthur L. Kennedy, the Auxiliary Bishop of Boston, and Very Reverend James Flavin, Episcopal Vicar, officiated. Alice's children were pleased to participate in various aspects of the Liturgy. Patti proclaimed the first reading from Proverbs 31:10-1. Katie proclaimed the second reading from 1 Corinthians 13:1-8. Anne Marie and Ashley offered the prayers of the faithful, and The Harlow and Masi families presented the gifts. After the conclusion of the Mass, our youngest child, John Francis (Jackie), offered words of remembrance and Bishop Arthur L. Kennedy offered the prayer of commendation.

INTERESTING EPILOGUES

(1) Chalice. The chalice Alice and I gave Danny at his ordination has been used numerous times since his death. Danny's chalice was available for family and friends to use on special spiritual occasions, such as weddings, funerals, and baptisms etc. It was at the consecration when I realized I forgot to provide Danny's chalice for Alice's Funeral Mass! I was absolutely shocked to see Father Matt Westcott using another chalice. I will never understand why I forgot to offer Danny's chalice. In God's divine providence, there must be a reason for my flagrant omission, which is known only to God and not to me.

(2) Reading citations. Coincidentally, both the readings had recurring numerals 1 and 3. Alice died on January 13th (1-13).

(3) Words of Remembrance. In Jackie's words of remembrance, he cited the comment Alice offered when Danny died. "Just think he

is with Our Blessed Mother," then Jack added, "Now my mother is also with Our Blessed Mother."

(4) Celebrants named Kennedy. Father Francis M. Kennedy (no relation) officiated at our Sacrament of Marriage in 1968 and baptized all five of our children. The bishop presiding at Alice's Funeral Mass in 2016 was also a Kennedy—Bishop Arthur L. Kennedy (also no relation).

After the Funeral Mass, our family invited everyone in attendance to join us at one of Alice's favorite restaurants—The Sherborn Inn in Sherborn, MA. It was truly a joyful occasion as everyone reflected on Alice, her effervescent personality, her innate goodness, her keen sense of humor, and especially, her love for people.

The following day, January 19, 2016—which would have been the birthday of Tom McGill, our good friend from Cleveland, Ohio, who Danny greatly admired—Alice's mortal remains were interred in the same burial site in Needham's Saint Mary's Cemetery as her priest son. Danny's good friend, Father Matt Westcott, officiated at the Committal Service for Alice. Our entire family was grateful to see such a large group of western Mass friends attend the committal service, many of whom were unable to attend the wake or the funeral Mass in Needham.

After the committal service, we invited the western Mass entourage to join us at a gathering at the Storrowton Tavern in West Springfield. I presumed our luncheon would be in the Storrowton Tavern's Carriage Room where our wedding reception was held in 1968; the same room where Danny's after-committal reception was held in 2008.

Upon arriving at Storrowton Inn, we disappointedly learned that the carriage house we had requested was reserved for the Kiwanis Club, so we were to receive guests in the Connecticut room. Initially, I was disheartened.

However, it wasn't long before I commenced to realize this too might have been providential!

Upon further reflection, I realized the Connecticut room had no particular significance to anyone except me. When Alice and I were in the initial discernment stages of our acquaintanceship, I invited Miss Alice Haggerty to dinner at a popular restaurant that displayed a pronounced colonial atmosphere—the Storrowton Inn, on the grounds of the Eastern States Exposition, and the Hostess graciously seated us in the prestigious Connecticut Room.

There was an unquestionable Colonial Era atmosphere that encompassed all aspects of the dining experience—the wait staff was clothed in long dresses with fashionable caps common to that era, and food was served family style. In order to impress Alice, I—as debonair as possible with pewter-serving pieces provided for the patrons—proceeded to adroitly place peas onto Alice's dinner plate. Unfortunately, I failed to compensate for a small colonial candle, illuminating the center of our table. As I suavely proceeded to place a spoonful of peas on Alice's plate from the pewter bowl, suddenly, the back of my hand was synched by the flame of the candle compelling me to drop the perter bowl of peas; yes, small green peas spilled all over Alice's beautiful pale blue print dress!

As the wait-staff scurried around picking peas off rustic pine planks of the Connecticut Room floor, I was concerned the flame from a small colonial candle may have extinguished emerging enchantment. As Kennedy family history clearly demonstrates, my fears of an aborted affiliation were grossly exaggerated.

Despite the absence of peas rolling uncontrollably on rustic pine planks, the 2016 wait staff was just as attentive in 2016 as they were in 1967. They were extraordinarily solicitous to Alice's many western Mass friends, especially her high school chums who boisterously reminisced about memorable "Alice Blue Gown" moments.

MEMORIES, MEMORIES....

There were many recollections: Do you remember when Alice drove her MG convertible in West Springfield's 4th of July Parade? Do you remember when Alice cut off the rubber band on a girl's hair during a concert? Do you remember Alice galloped down Northwood Avenue on her boyfriend's horse, which proceeded to then deposit his calling card on her father's driveway? Do you remember...Do you remember?

Katie recalled a remark Alice made to her: "In over 40 years, your father and I haven't had many disagreements; whenever we did disagree, your father was always right." I was shocked to hear Katie's recollection as Alice never expressed those sentiments to me. She could not have known how much that reflection impacted me, particularly to hear it at the time of her death.

Alice was competent and capable in every imaginable aspect and I had absolute, unconditional, confidence in her judgement. I didn't necessarily concur with all her conclusions, but by virtue of her extensive abilities I deferred to her decisions. Apparently, she was under the impression that the absence of a dissenting perspective was tantamount to concurrence, where, in fact, it was my absolute trust in her ability and not necessarily my affirmation. On the few occasions when I did voice a dissenting opinion, she would vehemently express her consternation and drag out her favorite weapon—the Kirby vacuum cleaner. Wherever I may have been—watching a baseball game in the family room or sitting at the computer—the deafening sound of the Kirby vacuum cleaner was relentless as it banged against chairs and tables, clearly conveying Alice's consternation.

At that point, I often felt compelled to quench an insatiable desire to sip a cup of freshly brewed Green Mountain Coffee at Bagel's Best Café in Needham Center. An hour or two later, when I returned, thankfully the storm clouds that had gathered over our Woodlawn Ave abode had dissipated and, *The Heart of Our Home* was once again, her happy, upbeat self.

In reality, and perhaps unwittingly, both Alice and I were expressing true marital love. When I did not question her proposals, I was putting her interest first and, when I occasionally offered a dissenting point of view, ultimately Alice gave precedence to my perspective.

"Alice was such a happy person; never a frown on her face," opined longtime friend John Hooben. "She was always full of fun." Then, to lighten up the atmosphere, he added, "When I first met Alice at Shaker Farms Country Club, I knew she was the perfect girl for a sour-puss like you Dan." John's remark provoked a few laughs, which obviously underscored truth in his assessment.

Contemplating the Connecticut room at Storrowton Inn in 1967 was nostalgic and indelibly imprinted on my mind, but truth be told, the forum in which the seed of love was planted on rich and fertile soil—green enough to nurture a lifelong relationship—was in fact planted five years earlier.

In the spring of 1962, Francis X. (Frank) Tierney, who had previously interceded for me in obtaining an employment interview at the Springfield branch office of the General Accident Fire and Life Assurance Company Ltd., suggested that I consider joining a golf club. A good friend of Frank's had recently purchased a plot of land on Shaker Road in Westfield, Mass. and developed Shaker Farms Country Club. Frank assured me I would receive an attractive proposal if I was interested in applying for club membership.

I mentioned Frank's suggestion to John Hooben, a classmate of mine at Cathedral High School as well as St. Michael's College. John, a former caddy at Springfield Country Club, was an accomplished golfer, I was not. Without hesitation, John urged me to pursue memberships for both of us. and, in the spring of 1962, John and I became Charter Members of Shaker Farms Country Club.

At that time, the teaching professional at "Shaker" was Johnny Banks, a Scotsman replete with a distinctive Scottish burr. Johnny was an older gentleman and well-fortified with the intricacies of the game. He assisted John and I immeasurably in developing golf proficiency.

Several years later, in 1967, I noticed several new Shaker Farms members were female, one of whom was a cute little blond. I inquired about the young lady and was informed she and a friend of hers were former members of Edgewood Country Club in Southwick, Mass. Speculation was she might be a nurse at a hospital in Springfield and her friend was rumored to be employed by Stanley Home Products in Westfield. It wasn't until a month or so later that an opportunity presented itself for me to speak with the purported nurse.

After playing eighteen holes of golf on a hot humid July afternoon as was our custom John and two other members of our foursome paused for a brief respite at the nineteenth hole to lament our golfing struggles and to embellish our accomplishments. When I went to the bar to order a round of drinks, I discovered I was standing next to a new member—the cute little blonde from Edgewood Country Club who was also waiting to order a beverage.

Clumsily, I offered to buy the young lady a drink; politely, she declined. I persisted but she continued to reject my offer. Not to be deterred, when the bartender, Bill Lacey, a good friend of John and mine, came over to take my order once again, I offered to purchase a drink for the young lady but again she protested. Bill hesitated a moment as I attempted to persuade her. Thankfully, she acquiesced and ordered Ballantine on the Rocks. At that time, two of the more popular beers were Schaffer beer and Ballantine beer. After a day playing golf on a hot summer afternoon, I wanted an extremely cold glass of liquid so I customarily ordered a glass of ice with my bottle of Schaffer. Coincidentally, I was thrilled to hear the young lady order Ballantine on the Rocks. I presumed I had met a young girl who also preferred beer on ice after a round of golf; I was wrong.

While we waited for Bartender Bill to return, I introduced myself and learned the young lady's name was Alice Haggerty. When Bill returned with a bottle of Schaefer beer with a large glass of ice cubes for me and a smaller glass of ice cubes immersed in an amber liquid for the young lady I was in shock. I soon discovered the amber liquid was Ballantine Scotch (not Ballantine Beer). Scotch was considerably more expensive than a thirty-five-cent bottle of beer!

As soon as Alice received her glass of Ballantine on the Rocks, she politely thanked me and left to join the three girls who played in her foursome. I stood there with my glass of ice cubes, my mouth wide open and a pocket much lighter than anticipated. To say things did not work out as well as I hoped would be an understatement! It cost me more money than I anticipated and, the cute young blonde was long gone.

Eventually, I met Alice's golfing companions: Mary Toohey—an administrative aid to the chief operating officer of Stanley Home Products in Westfield—and Peg (Murphy) Bradley, who was employed by Blue Cross and Blue Shield in the same office building as General Accident. Other members of Alice's foursome were Muriel Koehler from Holyoke, who was the granddaughter of the nationally known Koehler Plumbing Supply Magnet.

A few weeks later, as I was leaving the Shaker Farms' parking lot on my way home to Penacook Street in the Irish section of Springfield called Hungry Hill, Alice Haggerty pulled out of the Shaker Farms parking lot directly in front of me. Driving a white convertible sports car on a hot Saturday afternoon, blonde hair blowing in the breeze, passing car after car, Alice was an obvious eye-catcher. Coincidentally, both of us were traveling in the same direction, east on Route 20 from Westfield toward Springfield. As both vehicles proceeded through West Springfield, the white convertible, moving at a fast pace, suddenly took a sharp left-hand turn from Westfield

Street onto a side street immediately preceding Rogers Avenue, while I continued toward my parents' home in Hungry Hill.

Not only did she drive speedily, as I learned later, she also lived a rapidly paced life—multi-tasking, quick thinking, walked rapidly and perceptively assessed needs of the disadvantaged.

The following weekend, on my way home from Shaker Farms, I decided to take that same left-hand turn onto the side street, Northwood Avenue, to see if I could spot Alice's white convertible. What a revolting development, much to my chagrin. Northwood Avenue was a dead-end street! Consequently, at the end of the dead-end street, I was compelled to turn around. As I proceeded back toward Westfield Street at a normal pace, I spotted the white convertible parked in a driveway, so I was able to identify Alice's house.

In the later part of July, Shaker Farms sponsored a Scotch Foursome Tournament, which partners teams comprised of a man paired with a woman playing as a unit, with each alternating golf shots. I had never participated in a Scotch Foursome, so if I could locate a female partner this would be my first Scotch Foursome.

Eventually, summoning all the nerve I could muster, I called Alice to see if she was interested in being my partner in the Shaker Farms Scotch-Foursome Tournament. When I called Alice's house, her mother answered and informed me that "Al Marie" (i.e., Alice) and a friend of hers were on a cruise to Prince Edward Island (PEI) and wouldn't be back for a few days. Mrs. Haggerty kept talking, and talking, and talking about all kinds of various things. I later learned that Mrs. Haggerty was not accustomed to conversing with people who called to speak with Alice. Subsequently, I learned that Mrs. Haggerty's first name was also Alice (Alice Helen) so to differentiate between both, Mrs. Haggerty referred to her daughter as Al Marie.

For what seemed like an eternity, Mrs. Haggerty went to great lengths in discussing Alice's interests—cars, cruises, and Prince Edward Island, where she was currently enjoying a brief vacation. She further explained Alice possessed an intense interest in the Springfield Kings hockey team of the American Hockey League, which played its home games at The Coliseum in West Springfield and were the primary farm team of the National Hockey League's Los Angeles Kings.

The Springfield Kings, formerly known as the Springfield Indians, were previously owned by a former Boston Bruin and National Hockey League Hall of Famer, Eddie Shore, who had recently sold the team to Jack Kent Cooke, owner of the Los Angeles Kings. Surprisingly, Mrs. Haggerty spoke extensively and quite knowledgeably about the owner and his business interests.

As Mrs. Haggerty continued speaking, she volunteered that every weekend during the winter months, her daughter Alice and her friend Joan Daubitz were at center ice for all the Springfield Indians hockey games. The Coliseum was on the grounds of the Eastern States Exposition, which is adjacent to the Storrowton Tavern on Memorial Ave in West Springfield. Evidently, everyone in West Springfield, including Mrs. Haggerty, was aware, if not a fan of the Springfield Indians. At that time, The Coliseum was the only indoor ice-skating rink in western Massachusetts.

When I was a young boy, I did play hockey on the Van Horn Park pond, but it wasn't organized hockey and nothing like the brand of hockey played by kids who had the privilege of living near The Coliseum. Even though I could skate well and played pond hockey, my winter interest was focused on basketball. Hockey was, at best, secondary.

Talkative Mrs. Haggerty continued, informing me that she was a regular patron of Storrowton Tavern, a dining facility adjacent to The Coliseum. Evidently, the Cavanaugh Family, owners of Storrowton Tavern, and Mrs. Haggerty were originally from Holyoke and they had been friends for years.

Storrowton Tavern was initially comprised of two antique buildings that were relocated to West Springfield in the late 1800s. One from Southwick, Ma, and the other from Prescott, Ma. Later, after World War II, the Storrowton Carriage House, a banquet facility, was constructed. Incidentally, the town of Prescott was one of the four towns in Hampshire County that, in 1938, were confiscated by eminent domain, subsequently flooded to form the Quabbin Reservoir and supply drinking water for the city of Boston.

I later learned from Al Marie that she had been calling home from Prince Edward Island (PEI) and the line was continually "busy" and she couldn't understand to whom her mother was speaking with for such a prolonged period. When she finally contacted her mother, she informed her that she just had the most enjoyable conversation with Dan Kennedy. Alice later told me that it was unusual for her mother to have a conversation with someone calling for her. Generally, it was, "Give me your number and I will pass it along."

In 1967, which ultimately became known as the Impossible Dream year, the Red Sox reversed their former inept performance and became a genuine American League Pennant contender. When I could secure tickets, I spent much of my free time driving down the Mass Pike from Springfield to Fenway Park to watch the exciting Sox. After years in the doldrums with little or no fan interest, tickets to Fenway Park all of a sudden were at a premium in 1967. After finishing in last place in 1966, fan interest accelerated in the year of the Impossible Dream. To spark the radical change in proficiency, during the winter, the Red Sox hired a relatively unknown manager, Dick Williams, (no relation to Hall of Famer Ted Williams) and he proved to be an outstanding manager.

Fortunately, George Pumphret ("Pump"), manager of General Accident's Boston Branch Office, possessed many contacts in Boston business circles, including Boston professional sports teams. Mr. Pumphret was able to secure excellent tickets for me at Boston Celtics and Boston Bruin playoff games, and for the Boston Red Sox. Thanks to Pump, I spent much of my time driving to Boston to see basketball games, hockey games and, during the exciting summer of 1967, the Red Sox.

Among Mr. Pumphret's numerous contacts was Dick O'Connell, general manager of the Red Sox. Other sources for tickets were Bernie Baldwin, the owner of a large insurance agency—Kaler, Carney, and Liffler Inc (KCL); Gene Shedd, a Boston branch underwriter, and Paul Dunn, a former General Accident (GA) employee who had recently founded his own insurance agency in downtown Boston, and who was a close friend of several people in the inner circle of Boston sporting activities.

After Alice Haggerty's scheduled return from PEI, I called again and this time she was home when I called. Thankfully, she was receptive to playing in the Shaker Farms Scotch Foursome Tournament!

Prior to the tournament, as the golfers practiced their putting on the Shaker Farms putting green, Al Marie circulated among the other players, introducing me to her friends enthusiastically, looking forward to an exciting day of golf. I couldn't have been more impressed with my Scotch Foursome partner, not because of her putting prowess, but her personality. Alice greeted all golfers with genuine gladness. Her gregarious and upbeat personality was infectious. It permeated joy on the putting green.

Prior to teeing-off, Alice and I, along with two other tournament contenders, were approaching the first tee when a bee flew down Alice's print blouse and she became flustered. Before the bee could sting her, with the speed of Roger Bannister, she made a *bee-line* to the ladies locker-room. The foursome behind us wasn't particularly sympathetic to the plight of Alice's bee attack, but the three remaining members of our foursome patiently waited—patiently may not be the correct word—for Alice's return. When she did return, Alice was relieved to inform us the bee did not sting her nor was she able to locate it. Apparently, the bee extricated itself from close confinement on Alice's rush to the locker room. Disaster was averted. Eventually, Alice and I did tee-off at the Shaker Farms Scotch Foursome Tournament and, we did hit-it-off, not only our first shots on the first tee, but for 17,498 days!

During our round of golf, Alice asked me if I had ever driven down Northwood Ave in West Springfield. I was shocked when she asked that question. Immediately, I realized she knew the answer to the question which she posed. Sheepishly, I admitted, "Yes, I did drive down the street where you live." It was beginning to sound like the song from My Fair Lady.... "On the Street Where You Live."

Alice explained, "I was upstairs in my bedroom and noticed a car that resembled your burgundy Chevy drive down the street, so I ran downstairs and looked out the front door, waiting to see if the car would proceed back up Northwood Ave. It did and you were driving." Yes, I was caught red-handed. Apparently, it doesn't pay to be a sneak. On the other hand, in this case, perhaps it did pay to be a sneak.

In a Scotch-Foursome tournament, the two partners alternate hitting shots. After the first player hits, they select the better of the two shots and both players from that better of those two locations. On the second hole, a par four, on our second shot we selected Alice's ball which was within two feet of the cup. Each of us had the opportunity to sink a relatively easy two-foot birdie putt; however, neither of us made the easy putt.

Missing that two-foot putt was a prognostication of our Scotch-Foursome golfing venture. Although that alone didn't cost us the tournament; we missed many other putts as well. Golf is a great means of enjoyment. The concept of winning in golf is admirable but for Alice and me it was unattainable; camaraderie is attainable and, in this instance, we accomplished that facet of the game of golf.

Although we didn't have many opportunities to play golf during the subsequent 17,498 days of our marriage, whenever we did find time to play golf together it was always a wonderful time. Shaker Farms' Scotch Foursome, our first-time playing golf together, was the bellwether for many happy occasions on the links. I always said I would much rather play golf with Alice than with my golfing pals. For me, the joy of playing golf with Alice truly transcended the game itself.

ADVICE AND CONSENT

Revere your mother. (Leviticus 19:3)

At the end of an enjoyable round of the Scotch Foursome Golf Tournament, the players relaxed and recounted the day at the nineteenth hole, Alice with her Ballantine on the rocks and me with my iced Schaefer beer. After playing, it was easy to see that the men and woman with whom we played were also grateful for Alice's spirit.

During our respite from an inept impersonation, would-be golfers Alice and I spent a few "getting-to-know-you" minutes. For whatever reason, we seemed to cover a multitude of topics in probably not such a short period. Shortly after we sat down, Alice shared with me that she had been previously engaged and broke off the relationship on the advice of her mother. I have absolutely no idea what prompted Alice to relate such a personal story to me, especially when we hardly knew each other.

From my perspective, her voluntary revelation was, to me, profound:

(1) I viewed Alice's respect for her mother's advice as an act of humility.

(2) Intelligent as she was, Alice realized she did not have all the answers and was willing to listen to others.

(3) The fact she voluntarily shared such a personally sensitive topic with a total stranger was an insight into the depth of goodness within her soul.

I concluded Alice was much more than an attractive wannabe golfer; she was an upbeat, happy, joyful, young girl full of gladness and glee! She was not only a happy person, she was forthright and wholesome. The personification of perfection, in my mind.

Speculation at Shaker Farms that Alice was in the medical profession proved to be erroneous. Contrary to general opinion, Alice was not a nurse and she was not a dental technician. She was an executive with Carborundum Corporation, an abrasives manufacturer headquartered in Niagara Falls, New York. Carborundum Corporation distributed products such as grinding wheels, commercial wire brushes and sandpaper products from various distribution centers throughout the country.

Alice and I had an enjoyable chat after the Scotch Foursome Tournament, but that was not a date, per se. It was, more or less, a meeting of convenience. In order to participate in a Scotch Foursome, a male must be matched with a female. The compatibility and pleasantries we exchanged during the day of the tournament empowered me to contemplate asking Alice for an official first date.

The following week, as I was walking toward my car after a round of golf, I noticed that my Scotch Foursome partner, Alice Haggerty, was about to drive away in her convertible. I stopped to speak with her. During our brief conversation, I decided this was the opportunity to take a leap of faith and ask Alice if she would like to go out.

I was, of course, nervous and fearful that she would tell me she was busy, or that she was going on another trip, so after summonsing every bit of courage I could muster, I said, "Would you like to go out to dinner sometime?" She responded, in what I construed to be a less than enthusiastic response, "That would be nice." After uttering something nebulous, an off-topic remark, I repeated my initial question and she responded again with her initial response.

More nebulous and nonsensical comments continued and, periodically, I would inject, "Perhaps you would like to go out to dinner sometime?" With consistency, Alice responded, "That would be nice." I guess I was hoping to hear a monosyllabic response "yes," and in absence of a one-word answer, I repeated the same question.

Every time I posed the same question, the verbal jousting continued; Alice volleyed back the same answer, back and forth, back and forth we went; a virtual tennis match of words. Eventually, as Alice continued to patiently sit in her convertible and I stood timorously next to her car, hoping for an indication of positivity, it dawned on me. *Be specific Dumbo! Suggest a day.* "Saturday?" I suggested. Thankfully, petite little Alice concurred, concluding our improvised litany of words. At long last, both of us could declare victory. ALLELUIA!

Alice undoubtedly realized I was nervous, and took pity on my pathetic performance. Her *sixth sense of compassion* must have kicked in and she saw me in need of help—my self-confidence needed to be strengthened.

CHAPTER 2

ALICE BLUE GOWN

Women should adorn themselves with
modesty. (1 Timothy 2:9)

Without mentioning to Alice where I intended to make dinner reservations, I called The Federal Hill Club on Cooper Street in Agawam and made reservations. If I recall correctly, it was the first Saturday in August. I had great expectations. The Federal Hill Club, an elegant and plush private dining experience, would impress Alice. I assumed that an attractive young girl like Alice, the object of many suitors, would have dined there in the past. Surprisingly, she had not.

When I arrived at her home, she was wearing an azure blue floral print dress; dignity personified. Immediately, I associated Alice with a song that was popularized by Joni James when I was a senior in college: "Alice Blue Gown." Her dress was pale blue and her name was Alice! Ultimately, I learned that floral prints, especially light blue or pink, were Alice's favorites.

I also met Alice's mother, who was ebullient and most welcoming, just as depicted on our prolonged telephone conversation. On the other hand, meeting Mr. Haggerty was, you might say, a casual encounter. He was preoccupied with mowing the lawn. Not to be deterred from the task at hand he merely waved and kept right on mowing.

As we pulled into The Federal Hill Club, Alice was obviously impressed. "I've always wanted to come here for dinner," she said. "This is a great idea." The Federal Hill Club was an elegant restaurant owned and operated by the Morelli family. A staple of their ambiance was the Morelli family's personal touch: a member of the family would sit with the guests in the cocktail lounge and personally recite the evening entrees. After a patron selected an entree, the Morelli family member recommended an appropriate wine to accompany the dinner.

After this unique and debonair recitation of the menu, Alice and I enjoyed a cocktail in the well-appointed lounge at which point, the maître-de escorted us to our table in the dining room, which had been set-up for us with appetizers appropriately placed on a candle-lit table.

As Alice and I dined and sipped the Morelli family wine, we learned more about each other. I noted that Alice had a rather distinctive voice, seemingly at a deeper pitch than most young women, distinguishing and mellifluous. Dining at The Federal Hill Club proved to be a first-class experience for Alice Marie Haggerty. She was duly impressed! As Alice and I became better acquainted, she shared with me that a close friend of hers, Betsy Provencher, moved to Atlanta, Ga., and unfortunately, became afflicted with multiple sclerosis. When Alice heard that news, she took a week's vacation and flew down to Georgia to spend a week taking care of her friend (FOA—Friends of Alice). After Betsy Provencher died, Alice made it a point to regularly visit with Betsy's mother, Mrs. Hellstein, who resided on Tatham Hill Road in West Springfield. The concern and compassion Alice demonstrated for her friend and for her friend's mother gave me greater insight into the innate goodness of Alice's heart.

Alice also informed me that, concomitant with her graduation from West Springfield High School and Carborundum Corporation's relocation from South Boston to West Springfield, she has been affiliated with that organization. Alice was seeking full-time employment and they were seeking local employees to integrate with longtime company personnel. Alice empathized with the difficult adjustments her Carborundum colleagues were experiencing in relocating from the big city to "the sticks," so she dedicated herself to facilitating their transition.

The general manager of Carborundum Corporation, Edward (Ted) Mulkerin, his wife and four children, relocated from the Boston area to Longmeadow. Support personnel, Regina (Jeannie) McGraft, resided in an apartment on Mercury Court in West Springfield, as well as Lucy Kerins resided in Springfield. Alice knew that relocation would be especially difficult for elderly employees like Jeannie and Lucy. Neither was married and both lived alone, so she took them under her wing.

In Alice's mind, Jeannie and Lucy were not just colleagues; they were dear friends and she introduced them to her friends and facilitated memberships in various civic and parish organizations. (FOA—Friends of Alice).

Carborundum constructed a building on River Road in West Springfield and Alice was among the first western Massachusetts hires. Her intuitive interest in machinery and mechanics ideally suited her well in the world of abrasive manufacturing. With Alice's astute mind, she quickly mastered the intricacies of all company products, grits, speed of wheels, etc. and became one of the premier representatives in the New England distribution center. A few years later, Alice was promoted to assistant general manager, reporting directly to Edward (Ted) Mulkerin, regional general manager. Alice's responsibilities necessitated frequent trips to corporate headquarters in Niagara Falls, New York.

Apparently, the executives in Carborundum's Niagara Falls headquarters recognized Alice's unique abilities; shortly before we met, she was offered the position of general manager in Carborundum's Chicago distribution center. After several days of anguish, for whatever reason, she declined the offer. Her decision proved to be fortuitous; we met one month after she declined the managerial opportunity in Chicago.

"Alice was exceptionally bright, graduating with honors at West Springfield High School, so it wasn't a surprise that she was offered a position at Carborundum," noted Mary Beth (Browne) Ashe, at the Storrowton reception. "Her abilities were soon recognized, and in a few years she became the first female officer in the entire organization."

"Alice held an executive position at Carborundum and, in those days, the position she held was considered to be a man's job," her sister Eleanor said, as she reminisced at the Storrowton reception. "Ali was a hard worker and she earned an excellent salary, which enabled her to purchase sports cars. She absolutely loved driving those convertibles up and down the highways and byways of western Massachusetts and the coast of Maine."

"'Al Hag,' as her West Springfield friends called her, was a straight shooter. She didn't mince words; you always knew where you stood with Alice," added Mary Beth, her longtime friend. "She was extremely smart, loved to laugh and most of all, she was, in the good sense of the word, mischievous. Alice was fun to be with."

Mary Beth's recollection of Alice's intellect and mischievousness is without a doubt, extraordinarily perceptive. Whether it was a mathematical or mechanical problem, Alice was determined to find the solution. She had such an inquisitive mind. She was not content that a particular item functioned as advertised; she wanted to know what made it function. Whatever the device, the first thing she did was to take it apart to see how it worked. Alice was focused on the task at hand but never too busy to create opportunities to make people laugh. She loved to have fun. Alice worked hard and played hard; she loved life!

It was truly unfortunate that Alice's parents persuaded her to transfer out of the college preparatory course at West Springfield High School and enroll in the commercial course. Alice was extremely bright; there was no telling what she might have accomplished with an undergraduate and graduate degree.

"Al Marie was devastated when Daddy told her that he didn't believe in girls going to college so she would not be going," exclaimed her sister, Eleanor. "His explanation that girls eventually marry and have children, thus money spent on college would be wasted, didn't console heart-broken Ali."

As I mentioned earlier, throughout her entire life Alice seemed to have a sixth sense when it came to identifying people in need of a friend. She was particularly empathetic to her Carborundum colleague Jeannie McGrath's frailty and her obvious need for assistance. As time progressed, Jeannie, who did not drive and was becoming increasingly frail, was a frequent guest at our home on Falley Drive in Westfield, as well as a regular guest on Ferncliff Road in Dennisport. Alice considered Jeannie a member of our family and she was always present at every Kennedy family function.

ARTICULATION AND FOREBEARANCE

In what was clearly unique, both Alice and I pronounced the first vowel (second letter) in each other's name incorrectly. I pronounced her surname as my paternal Irish grandfather pronounced the name: "Heh-garty," instead of "Ha-ggerty." Alice pronounced the second letter in my first name as if it were an "i," as in "Dinny," and not "Danny." Correcting our mispronunciations proved to be a daunting task.

It wasn't until Danny was born that Alice learned to pronounce the "a" in Danny correctly and I must admit I never acquired the ability to properly pronounce the short-sounding vowel "a" in her surname.

On one of our first August 1967 dates, we stopped for a cocktail at Club 21 on the corner of Elm Street and Riverdale Street in West Springfield. The restaurant was a popular spot for almost everyone in the Springfield area. Perhaps it was the personal attention afforded by the gregarious owner, John O'Brien, whose father was the chief of police in West Springfield.

During a casual and relaxing time at Club 21, Alice abruptly said, "So far we have had some fun but, just so you know, I don't want to get involved."

I responded, "We are on the same page, neither do I."

Amazing. We hardly knew each other, and we were in complete agreement in denouncing the possibility of a serious relationship. I'm certain Alice was pleased she enunciated her expectations, or lack thereof, so we could continue to enjoy each other's company without any perceived encumbrance impacting our friendship.

The best laid plans of mice and men... surprise, surprise. Six months later, we were involved—and married! When both parties are in complete agreement and unequivocally committed to an agreed course of action and, within a relatively short time, proceed in the exact opposite direction, there must be third-party intervention. Providential? Praise the Lord. "Hopefully, spending 17,498 days with Alice will corroborate that it is the Lord who knows best."

At some point, a friend of mine asked if I was dating a girl who owned a white Mercedes convertible. I said, "Yes, I am dating a girl who owns a white convertible but, what's a Mercedes?" He was appalled. "You are an underwriter for an insurance company that insures motor vehicles and you don't recognize a Mercedes?" he asked.

In the spirit of full disclosure, my friend didn't realize that I was not an automobile underwriter; I was a property and casualty underwriter. My friend was not to be deterred. He proceeded to explain that a Mercedes-Benz was a high-end motor vehicle manufactured in Germany. He concluded his chastisement with words that proved to be totally inaccurate, "You've hit the jackpot. She must be wealthy."

In addition to my unfamiliarity with automobile underwriting, I never had any particular interest in automobiles, per se. To me, the manufacturer of an automobile was irrelevant. Alice's Mercedes 190-SL didn't impress me nor was she wealthy. She was, however, extremely bright and she was enterprising!

Alice believed in putting her substantial Carborundum salary to work and, after acquiring an interest in sports cars, she found a bargain: a 1953 black MG. Several years later, enterprising Alice located an automobile that she perceived to be another bargain: a 1963 190-SL Mercedes-Benz, in need of much repair. Within a flash, it was hello Mercedes and good-bye MG. Alice was confident a foreign car mechanic she knew could put the neglected 190-SL in top-flight condition, and she was right.

Not surprisingly, this petite blonde was soon displaying her 190-SL as a member of the Sports Car Club of Western Massachusetts. Every month, she participated in Sports Car meets, competing on challenging routes through the hills and valleys of western Massachusetts and western Connecticut. As a member of the Sports Club, she was equipped and well prepared to deal with any weekend meet emergency. As a consequence, for the rest of her life she never left home without her cherished canvas bag of foreign-car tools neatly packed in the trunk of every car she owned.

Alice Haggerty sits proudly behind the wheel of her treasured MG, circa 1962.

In addition to her ever-present canvas bag, she also carried jumper-cables in the trunk of her car and for the next forty years, both the canvas bag and jumper-cables were transferred into the trunk of every car she owned. Alice was always on the look-out for a stranded motorist on the side of the road with the hood of their car raised. If she spotted a beleaguered motorist, she would stop delightedly, pull out her jumper-cables and jump-start the stranger's car. In today's world, it is uncommon to see a stranded motorist but in the 1960s that was not at all unusual. Even as a young girl, Alice was always on the look-out to help stranded motorists as well as anyone who appeared to be in need.

It seems as if everyone who ever met Alice was captivated by her effervescent personality and genuine goodness; her innate mischievousness was also an attribute. "Alice was so much fun to be with. She loved to laugh. She loved to have a good time, and she really, really, loved to zip around in her black MG," said Mary Beth Ashe.

It wasn't long before Alice realized I wasn't particularly interested in cars, yet she began to give me instructions on how to drive a sports car. Her first instruction was to explain the proper means of slowing down a sports car without applying the brakes. In the world of sports cars, there was a "stick shift" to the right side of the steering wheel, perpendicular to the floorboard of the car, which, with the clutch pedal engaged, regulated the torque transfer from the engine to the transmission. I often remembered what she said, using her "down-shifting" mechanism, but it made no sense to me. I preferred using the brake to slow down the momentum of the car. In addition to Alice's rationalization that down-shifting preserved the brakes, she seemed to get a real thrill out of "down-shifting" and "banking the car" when she turned corners.

Alice could not only appraise automobiles and negotiate with sales people, she could also change the oil, replace spark plugs, fix malfunctioning windshield wipers, and lubricate squeaks. A strong advocate for preventative maintenance, she was always listening and diagnosing any unusual engine sound, and continually picking the minds of foreign-car mechanics so she could perform basic repairs herself. To say Alice was resourceful would be an understatement!

I knew Alice possessed her own toolbox and jumper-cables. What I didn't know until later was that she also carried several cans of motor oil, a funnel, and a pipe wrench as well. In Alice's mind, if a person owned a motor vehicle, tools were as essential as the Standard Operating Procedure (SOP) manual. General Accident Insurance Company provided me with a company-owned vehicle, and Alice applied pressure on me to convince General Accident Management to equip all of their vehicles with emergency repair kits. "For safety reasons, all General Accident Insurance Company owned vehicles should carry the same equipment I carry in the trunk of my car," she said. Alice had yet to realize between my mechanical limitations and my obvious disinterest in mastering the technique of using jumper-cables, support for her admonitions was non-existent.

MUTUAL INTERESTS TO THE FOREFRONT!

As the American League Pennant race intensified during the summer of 1967, the Boston Red Sox played to capacity crowds and tickets were difficult to procure. Fortunately, our Boston branch manager, George Pumphret, was able to secure premier seats for Alice and I, directly behind home plate, for an August 18th Friday night game with the California Angels.

Alice and I left West Springfield early Friday afternoon so we could have a leisurely dinner at one of Boston's most prestigious restaurants, Jimmy's Harborside, on the Northern Ave pier with a fantastic view of Boston Harbor. The proximity to the harbor emitted a pronounced aroma of the sea, which was pleasing for most people. But for nautical-minded Alice, it was the ultimate! It didn't take long for me to realize how much Alice loved a water view, so I knew this particular one would be unsurpassed.

Traversing the ebb and flow of the soft and gentle wavelets on the beautiful blue water were ships of all sizes: rowboats, yachts, tugboats, and ocean-liners. All were in full view from our table by the window looking out on Boston "Hah-bah!"

We commenced our dining experience, "din-nah on the hah-bah," with a cocktail and Jimmy's Harborside's famous broiled scallops hors d'oeuvres! Once we finished our scrumptious dinner, we were off to Fenway Park to watch a major league baseball game in the height of the 1967 American League Pennant race between the Boston Red Sox and California Angels.

The seats George Pumphret procured were even better than I anticipated. They were not only directly behind home plate; they were only a few rows from the field. We had a close-up and personal view of all the pitches, curves, sliders and, of course, fastballs. We were anxious to see

Red Sox star players, especially Carl Yastrzemski—who shared his birthday with Alice—and a local boy from Medford, MA—young Tony Conigliaro known as "Tony C", who, at the time, was a premier Major League Baseball phenom. Tony hit more home runs at his young age than any other player in baseball history.

Unfortunately, on this day of our "din-nah" date, one of the fastballs from California Angels' pitcher Jack Hamilton struck Tony Conigliaro in the face! What a horrible incident to watch. As Tony C lay on the ground with Red Sox players and doctors milling around him, Carl Yastrzemski, in frustration, was pacing up and down the first base line. A pregnant hush encompassed the entire ballpark and everyone in attendance was sick to our stomachs.

Tony survived the grotesque injury, but he never again attained the hitting prowess he possessed as the premier player he was in 1967. Ultimately, the beaning on the night of August 18, 1967 compelled him to retire from baseball, and he succumbed to an early death.

At some point in September, I brought Alice to our Penacook Street home to meet my mother and father. With a mother's God-given intuition, I am certain that, in bringing Alice home to meet them, it conveyed tacit import to the occasion; seldom did I bring a girl home to meet them. Certainly, my mother's maternal instinct must have alerted her that Alice was, in my mind, a special person. Deep indeed is the wisdom of the maternal heart.

Alice was one of three daughters born to Charles Joseph Haggerty and Alice Helen McCarthy. Betsy was the first born; three years later came Alice and, in another three years, Eleanor. As is the case in most three-children families, the first born seems to hold a distinctive status by virtue of being number one, the third-born enjoys the unique status of forever being the cute little baby. Thus, oftentimes, the second child doesn't have the uniqueness of the other two and fights for recognition.

Alice certainly represented that characterization. She wanted to establish her individuality. Not only was she feisty, she was athletic and, unlike most young girls, Ali wanted to know "how and why" mechanical things worked. Resultantly, she gravitated toward her father and developed interests in things generally associated with boys. Her father, of course, was delighted to have a daughter who liked to throw a baseball, go fishing, fuss with cars or even do mischievous things.

After Alice died, in speaking with one of Alice's childhood friends from Chicopee, her sister Betsy mentioned to Ceil (Dooley) Clune, that Alice looked so peaceful in the mahogany casket. As Betsy continued to describe the casket and the radiant beauty on Alice's face she said, "Alice's face was so beautiful, she looked like an angel."

Without hesitation Ceil responded, "Betsy, you and I both know Alice was no angel! Don't you remember the time in your backyard in Chicopee? Alice was so irate she was going to hit you over the head with a milk bottle and your father had to intervene and say, 'Ali, you can't do that, give me that milk bottle'."

Mr. Haggerty formerly owned and operated the Charles J. Haggerty Funeral Home at 333 Springfield Street in Chicopee, adjacent to the College of Our Lady of the Elms. I thought it was cool that Alice's father was a funeral director. As a young boy, my ambition was different from most young boys—I didn't aspire to be a fire fighter or a policeman or a doctor. My childhood aspiration was to be an undertaker, so I was delighted to learn of Mr. Haggerty's prior occupation.

When we were young, my sister Judy, who loved to play with dolls, was delighted one Christmas when she received a beautiful doll with a variety of doll clothes. I didn't view Judy's doll with admiration; I viewed its destination. When spring came, I suggested to Judy it would be nice to give her precious doll a ride in the red wagon I received for Christmas. She concurred.

With Judy's doll appropriately covered with a blanket, reclining comfortably and with dignity befitting a solemn occasion, I slowly pulled the wagon in regal procession. Judy thought her doll was the Queen of England on her way to Buckingham Palace; I viewed the doll as Betsy Ross on her way to Arlington National Cemetery.

Slowly and with the utmost care, I solemnly pulled the Little Red Wagon into Van Horn Park where I promptly proceeded to dig a hole and bury Betsy Ross. It wasn't until bedtime when Judy didn't have her doll that the burial, pardon the pun, was uncovered! My mother, in what I perceived to be an irrational reaction, directed me to exhume Betsy Ross!

Mr. Haggerty and I had a common bond—interment!

The Haggerty family resided on the second floor of the Charles J. Haggerty Funeral Home, which was, in a sense, good but not ideal. Between his business and his family, Mr. Haggerty was on-site, twenty-four seven. At times that arrangement was beneficial but on occasion, also challenging, especially with respect to mischievous daughter number two.

Alice informed me that as the deceased family and friends mourned in the downstairs parlor, her father would play soft mirthless music from the upstairs family record player. During one of those dire occasions, Alice told me, as solemn music permeated the parlor and somber sympathizers sobbed sorrowfully in hopes of brightening the dour mood of the mourners, she replaced the depressing funeral recording with another record—the uptempo McNamara's Band!

"My father was not a happy camper," said unregretful daughter No. 2. "He bounded upstairs, two treads at a time, simultaneously yelling at me as he ripped the McNamara's Band record off the record player." Similar infractions and blatant disregard for funeral protocol were unquestionably considerations in Mr. Haggerty's decision to entertain offers to sell the Haggerty Funeral Home.

Whether little Alice's proclivity to replace "Nearer My God to Thee" with "McNamara's Band" was the primary consideration or not I don't know, but in 1952, Mr. Haggerty sold the Charles J. Haggerty Funeral Home and relocated his family to 23 Northwood Ave in West Springfield.

Mischievous though Alice was, she was also a source of endearment for her father. Alice wasn't the conventional doll-loving little girl. She was more of a rough and ready type of child. Alice loved the same things her father loved—cars, mechanics, sports, gardening and Irish music. Alice was the boy her father never had. I, of course, was thrilled to have met a girl with similar interests to me, especially a love of sports.

In January of 1967, General Accident Fire and Life Assurance Ltd. appointed me assistant branch manager of their Springfield office. The appointment was to allow me sufficient time to garner first-hand managerial experience under the tutelage of the branch manager, William E. Toner, with the right of succession upon his retirement in January 1968. Resultantly, as the heir apparent to Mr. Toner, I was invited to accompany him to the General Accident Branch Managers Annual Meeting at the Tides Inn, in Irvington, Virginia, in September of 1967.

Mr. Toner drove the two of us to the meeting in Irvington, Virginia, interrupted only for dinner at Duffy's Restaurant in Berwyn, Pa., with General Accident home office executives. Among those present at the dinner were Executive Vice President Jack Orr and his wife Ruth, and Senior Vice-President Jim Corcoran and his wife Rosemary. George Pumphret, the Boston branch manager who flew directly from Boston to Philadelphia, joined our group for dinner.

Prior to the dinner, we visited with Jim and his wife Rosemary at their home in Berwyn, Pa. Both Jim and Rosemary were from Brockton, Ma., and Jack Orr and Ruth were originally from Dorchester, Ma. Thus, it was natural for the Massachusetts contingent in the GA home office to band together. During dinner, when Rosemary Corcoran learned I was not married, she proceeded to tell me she knew of a lovely young girl in the Philadelphia area she would like me to meet.

In order to parry Rosemary's persistent suggestions while not divulging that I just met Alice in July, I quickly informed her I was currently interested in a young lady from West Springfield; purposely embellishing our fledgling friendship to deflect Rosemary's maternal match-making machinations. Little did I know, my evasive explanation would prove to be prophetic.

As a *newbie* at the General Accident Manager's Annual Meeting, I attentively watched, listened and observed the wholesome interaction among company personnel. It was evident in this forum of business decorum that a genuine sense of camaraderie permeated the week-long meeting, and I would attempt to emulate in years to come. The meeting at the Tides Inn allowed me to develop lifelong friendships with branch managers and many Home Office personages.

On our return trip from Virginia, Mr. Toner stopped in Georgetown to visit with his brother-in-law, Father Vincent Beatty, SJ, the former president of Loyola University in Baltimore and, at that time, president of Georgetown Prep. While in Georgetown, I went shopping on Wisconsin Ave to purchase a gift for the lady from West Springfield—cameo earrings.

When I was a student at St. Michael's College, I developed fervor for soups and went to great extremes to purchase soups. It wasn't until I spent time considerable time in Philadelphia at General Accident training programs that I was introduced to a soup indigenous to Philadelphia—Snapper Soup (as in snapping turtles). As Mr. Toner and I continued our northward trek, I suggested we take a slight detour and stop at the home of the indigenous Snapper Soup: Bookbinders Restaurant in Philadelphia—so I could purchase some to go. We filled the backseat of Mr. Toner's car with two cases of Snapper Soup—one case for Alice Marie Haggerty and the other for her Scotch Foursome Partner!

Snapper Soup from Bookbinders in Philadelphia was by far my favorite soup, followed closely by black bean soup, a specialty item produced by S. S. Pierce Company in Boston. Regularly, I purchased S. S. Pierce's specialty soups from Forbes and Wallace, Inc. in downtown Springfield. Unbeknownst to me at the time, while in high school, Alice was a part-time employee at Forbes and Wallace. Conceivably, long before I purchased Bookbinders Snapper Soup for Alice in Philadelphia, she may have been the clerk who sold me S. S. Pierce black bean soup at Forbes and Wallace in Springfield.

UNINTENDED CONSEQUENCES

As soon as Mr. Toner and I returned from our week-long sojourn to the southeastern coast, anxiously, I went to West Springfield to present Alice with gifts from Washington and Philadelphia. Both Alice and her mother were standing at the front door when I arrived with the case of soup. As I placed the case of soup on a chair in the dining room, Alice and her mother looked quizzically at the soup. Alice subsequently said, "What's this?" With a grin from ear to ear, I gleefully proclaimed, "It's Snapper Soup, a specialty soup from Philadelphia. You will absolutely love this soup! Its indigenous to the City of Brotherly Love, just as clams are indigenous to Baltimore." Both mother and daughter were obviously bewildered as they stared speechlessly at the case of soup; unquestionably, they were at a loss for words. Even Alice's dog Jacques looked at me quizzically. Mrs. Haggerty was particularly aghast; as for Alice, she feigned interest. But it was obvious that she was deeply puzzled by "Hungry Hill" Dan's unique gift.

In order to disperse the disappointment of the moment, I reached into my pocket and presented Alice with a small gift box containing the cameo earrings I purchased in Georgetown.

Murphy's Law? Yes, Murphy's Law was prevalent: "If something can possibly go wrong, it will go wrong!" I was on a roll, a backward roll, the cameo earrings gift was the second in a succession of fiascos. As Alice excitedly opened the small gift box, initially she manifested elation but as she examined the earrings she said, "I love cameo and these are particularly beautiful earrings, but I won't be able to wear them. I don't have pierced ears."

In 1967, it was not commonplace for women to have their ears pierced and Alice was certainly in the majority with unpierced ears. I was, of course, oblivious and purchased the wrong earrings. I was what might be called "a two-time loser"—the soup was a bust and Alice couldn't wear the earrings! I repossessed the earrings, assuring Alice I would remedy my mistake, but I left the Snapper Soup. I can only imagine the conversation between mother and daughter after I left 23 Northwood Ave.... *where in the world did you find that goofball, Alice?*

Fortunately, the Snapper Soup saga and the pierced earrings fiasco didn't derail the fledging courtship. Alice invited me to the annual Carborundum Corporation outing at Riverside Park in Agawam on Sunday, September 24, 1967. I enjoyed meeting Alice's colleagues. Her boss whom she really admired, Ted Mulkerin, was a fine man who appeared to be pleased to meet me. In his exuberance to shake my hand, Ted tripped over the picnic table bench and fell; fortunately, he was not injured. I construed that to be a good sign; not the fall, but rather his interest in shaking my hand. Alice informed me later that she had never invited a male friend to a Carborundum outing so perhaps Ted was not so much pleased to meet me as he was to welcome a male friend of Alice's.

At the conclusion of the Carborundum outing, Jack Moriarty, a colleague of Alice's in the sales department, and his wife Jeannette hosted a company get-together at their home on Highland Ave in West Springfield. Upon conclusion of the convivial gathering, I drove Alice back to her Northwood

Ave home. It was a fine day—I enjoyed meeting Alice's colleagues and she seemed to think her friends were pleased I was in attendance.

As we pulled in front of Alice's home, without any pre-conceived plan and certainly with no prior contemplation, much to my surprise, I found myself suggesting we might want to consider getting married. I have absolutely no idea what possessed me to express that proposition and it certainly seemed as perplexing and shocking to Alice as well.

Absolute silence reigned! Without a doubt, both of us were caught completely off-guard as we attempted to comprehend the concept. A prolonged pause permeated the atmosphere, with no apparent reflex response in the offing—definitely not a propitious sign. It wasn't a categorical rejection, but one certainly devoid of optimism. Yet persistence prevailed and I pursued the prospect. After what appeared to be an eternity, Alice replied, "Yes, I think that's a good idea!"

Without an iota of doubt this was Divine Providence in action. Neither Alice nor I had foreseen the possibility of this occurrence. If it were even remotely on our radar, both of us would have been pre-programed with negativity. *"My ways are not your ways." (Isaiah 55:8)*

As I drove back to my Penacook Street home on Hungry Hill, reality set in; *"What in the world possessed me to pose that question?"* Without hesitation, I assured myself, although I may have had one too many glasses of Shaefer beer at Jack Moriarty's home, Alice consumed at least as much single malt Scotch consequently, I thought; "In the morning, all will be forgotten; Alice will never recall our conversation."

On Monday morning, as soon as I sat down at my General Accident office desk, the telephone rang; it was Alice excitedly saying, "My mother is thrilled!" Thankfully, before I could respond "Thrilled about what?" I quickly processed that Alice's recollection of the previous evening conversation had not, as I had anticipated, been eradicated! Instantly, I realized for some unexplainable reason, both of us were 180 degrees from our previously declared pact—"Don't get involved, maintain status quo."

A few days later, on Friday, September 29th, coincidently the Feast Day of St. Michael, Mrs. Haggerty hosted a dinner at the Haggerty family homestead. Alice, her parents, even her French poodle Jacque, greeted me at the front door. It must have been apparent to them that this was a nerve-racking experience for me, so they were more than gracious and certainly did their best to make me feel at ease. I was most appreciative.

Prior to sitting down for dinner, Alice's father invited me to sit with him in the living room. Without any procrastination, I requested Mr. Haggerty's approval to "share Alice with them." Out of the corner of my eye, I detected Mrs. Haggerty peering in from the kitchen doorway, intently listening for Mr. Haggerty's response.

Without hesitation, Mr. Haggerty responded, "Yes!" and he elaborated, "I always prayed that God would send a good man for each of my three daughters and, after He sent a good man for Betsy and a good man for Eleanor, I didn't know whether He would deliver another good man, but He did. Welcome."

At that point, out of the corner of my eye, I noticed Mrs. Haggerty once again, now with tears in her eyes, still peering in from the kitchen doorway. Alice was presumably in the kitchen or perhaps in the dining room, undoubtedly, doing her share of eaves dropping as well.

At this point in our conversation, Mr. Haggerty added an admonition, "Dan, I want you to know there is a history of alcoholism in this family, so you will have to closely monitor consumption." I assured him that I would be vigilant, "You don't have to worry Mr. Haggerty, I will take care of Alice." Then on a lighter note, he added, "It won't take much to make Ali happy; all she likes to eat is ravioli and tortellini."

On special occasions, and that visit certainly qualified as a special occasion, Alice and her mother have demonstrated an insatiable appetite for lobster. That evening, all four of us sat down at the Haggerty dining room table for a Lobster Newburg dinner. Even though I was not a lobster aficionado, I did enjoy the pleasant conversation and, surprisingly, I did enjoy the Lobster Newburg. Alice and her mother's obvious enthusiasm in discussing impending arrangements certainly contributed to promoting an informal and positive atmosphere.

After Alice's father sold the Charles J. Haggerty Funeral Home in Chicopee, he accepted a position in the security department of the nationally known John H. Breck Shampoo Corporation. We learned later that Mr. Haggerty had inquired from his Breck colleagues who resided in Hungry Hill, the Irish enclave of Springfield, if they knew Dan Kennedy. Mr. Haggerty, doing due diligence as a father, vetted his prospective Hungry Hill son-in-law. Evidently, nothing was gleaned from his investigation to negatively impact the prospects of acquiring a son-in-law from Hungry Hill.

Following Mr. Haggerty's parental approval of my request and after the Lobster Newburg dinner served by Mrs. Haggerty, Alice and I went to Penacook Street to inform my parents of our plans. My father seemed obviously pleased, but my mother was more than pleased. She was ecstatic!

Alice and I were seated on the living room couch when my traditionally unemotional, mother jumped up from her chair and gave Alice a big hug, which was unlike tradition in her Burke family, a group that was customarily ultra-reserved. Shortly, she left the room and returned with a set of dishes—a set she recently purchased for herself but spontaneously decided to present them to Alice as an engagement gift. My mother's heartfelt gesture certainly touched Alice's heart, and from that point on a bond of immense love was established between them. Deo Gratias!

Later that evening, after I brought Alice back to her home my father told me, "Alice is just what you need; she will open doors for you and improve your despicable personality!" That was a ringing endorsement if I ever heard one.

On Sunday, October 1, 1967, Alice started introducing me to her family. Our first stop was on Gooseberry Lane to meet Alice's sister Eleanor and her husband Emil Masi, as well as their one-year-old baby Scottie. It was a real upbeat occasion, not so much because the Masis were pleased with our news, although of course they were pleased. The exhilaration was because the Boston Red Sox had just shocked the baseball world when they defeated the Minnesota Twins, completing "The Impossible Dream" season and winning the American League Pennant!

Jim Lonborg, who years later would become a friend of our son Danny when he was assigned to St. Mary of the Nativity Parish in Scituate, pitched the Red Sox to the American League Pennant on Sunday afternoon at Fenway Park. It was the first pennant in the City of Boston since the Boston Braves won the National League Pennant in 1948.

During our conversation with Eleanor and Emil, I mentioned that a friend of mine promised me two tickets to the World Series so Alice and I will be at one of the games. "Open mouth, insert foot." There was so much demand for the tickets, Mr. Pumphret never came through with his promise. Obviously, I was embarrassed. In the eyes of the Haggerty family, I was the new kid on the block. They didn't really know me. Why would Alice and her family not view me as a big-mouth phony? Thankfully, they were more tolerant than I would have been; they overlooked my failure to produce the promised tickets to the 1967 World Series.

When Alice and I discussed an engagement ring, she told me she liked surprises but if she were selecting the engagement ring, she would opt for an opal shaped diamond ring.

Jim Sullivan, a close friend, knew of a diamond merchant from whom he purchased a diamond for his wife Janet. Jim assured me that many of his Hungry Hill friends purchased rings from that diamond merchant and they were pleased with the rings and, most importantly, the price of the rings was reasonable. Alice would have liked him; the price was right. Jim and I visited him at his Mayfair Street home, and he assured me he could procure an opal and it would be available in two weeks.

The projected date of the arrival of the ring was a week prior to the Feast Day of St. Jude, the Patron Saint of Hopeless Cases, October 28th. Since my sophomore year at St. Michael's College, when I had difficulty with metaphysics and epistemology, I acquired a devotion to the intercessory power of St. Jude. Consequently, I purposely planned to present the precious ring to Alice on Saturday evening, October 28, 1967. I reserved a table for two in the elegant dining room of the newly constructed and state-of-the-art Hotel Sonesta on Constitution Plaza in Hartford, Conn.

The main tributary in the Nutmeg State, the Connecticut River, was a short distance from the hotel and was illuminated. Thus, Alice's much-desired water view contributed to the spectacular ambiance. My hope was to impress Alice just as she had been impressed with the Federal Hill Club in Agawam. She was pleased.

After a celebratory cocktail, we ordered Chateaubriand for two, along with a bottle of the best of Bordeaux wines. As we sipped our glasses of wine, I presented Alice with a small gift-wrapped box. With bated breath and much anticipation, she excitedly opened the package but, disappointedly, it was not an engagement ring...it was the replacement cameo earrings for her unpierced ears. I thought it would be a comical moment, but the look on her face communicated annoyance. My corny attempt at a light-hearted moment was disastrous. Idle thought: all things considered, I obviously affirmed Alice's perception that I was indeed a "hopeless case."

Quickly, and I mean quickly, I presented Alice with another gift-wrapped box which did contain an oval-shaped diamond engagement ring. Alice's expression changed immediately. She was truly thrilled. She absolutely loved the ring. I will never forget the radiance on her face! So much JOY!

After our dinner, I presented Alice with a third gift-wrapped box. I wanted her to have something in addition to the engagement ring. As she opened the box, I knew she was uncertain if this was another one of my stupid attempts at humor; it was not. The box contained a gold charm bracelet with one gold charm. The charm was inscribed with the date of our engagement—October 28, 1967—and on the other side, in French were words denoting love... Qu'hier moins que demain...meaning: "I love you more today than yesterday; less than tomorrow." Alice was happy!

I didn't recognize the profundity of those words of wisdom until forty years later, when in 2007, Alice was afflicted with a debilitating illness. My love for Alice increased exponentially, in "the tomorrow" of her cognition challenge. Selfishly, caring for Alice brought more joy to me than any benefit she may have derived from my inept efforts. Truly, as much love as I had for Alice on October 28, 1967, it was considerably less than "the tomorrow" of her dementia years. *When one finds a worthy wife, her husband has an unfailing prize. (Proverbs 32:10)*

On special occasions through the course of our marital years, I would augment her bracelet with additional charms depicting the family she loved and places she enjoyed. After each baby was born, I gave her a gold charm with the date of birth and the name of her new baby. In addition, in recognition of her love for Ireland and her love for Cape Cod, she also had gold charms depicting those joyous interests as well.

Alice, an organizer par excellence, meticulously arranged all aspects of our wedding and honeymoon. Her first order of business was to meet with a priest at St. Thomas the Apostle Church in West Springfield and establish a date for the wedding. In order to comply with canonical guidelines, it was specified that the sacrament of marriage should be scheduled before or after Lent. In 1968, Ash Wednesday fell on the 28th of February. Consequently, Alice selected the 17th day of February in 1968 as the date for her wedding.

Alice and Mrs. Haggerty were foisted into an immediate action mode and, in a relatively short period of time, they skillfully managed a multitude of marital arrangements. I was oblivious to the tremendous amount of work they accomplished in coordinating so many divergent aspects of wedding arrangements. Their efforts certainly culminated with a picture-perfect wedding on February 17, 1968. It was an exciting time, as both Alice and I anticipated commencing our lifelong process of navigating the unchartered waters of life.

As Alice and her mother proceeded to formulate wedding plans, I was periodically invited for dinner at the Haggerty house so we could collectively review the prospective arrangements. Although Mr. Haggerty was present at the dinners, neither he nor I were active participants in the decision-making process. Mrs. Haggerty was obviously the Haggerty family spokesperson.

At another evening dinner, Mrs. Haggerty departed from her signature entree of Lobster Newburg and she served a pot roast dinner, which I absolutely loved. Perhaps I was more relaxed than I was at the initial Lobster Newburg dinner, but the pot roast was unforgettably good. I always told Alice my benchmark for a quality pot roast dinner was the dinner her mother served on Northwood Ave.

Mrs. Haggerty was excited to host the reception at her favorite restaurant, Storrowton Tavern, and suggested that Alice and I select the menu as well as the music. But she did stipulate that the band play her favorite song "Alice Blue Gown."

After our engagement announcement, it seemed as if every night we were on-the-road-again meeting relatives and displaying Alice's engagement ring. Alice was hopeful that her aunts, uncles, and cousins would put a stamp of approval on her new friend. Thankfully, at least to my knowledge and at least superficially, they appeared to approve.

As I learned while visiting with Alice's friends and relatives domiciled in Holyoke, Ma., Alice was full of fun, the "life of the party" and most importantly, she loved to laugh. I also learned that as a teenager, many people thought Alice looked like Dorothy Collins, the blonde singer of the popular Saturday evening TV program "Your Hit Parade." Although no one inferred Alice was a singer, in my mind, the physical similarity to Dorothy Collins was indeed correct; both were adorable little blondes.

The most memorable of relatives I met was Alice's great aunt, Scotland born Jessie (Cameron) Bradley. Aunt Jessie was the sister of Alice's deceased maternal grandmother, Elizabeth Cameron McCarthy. Aunt Jessie resided with her husband Henry Bradley, and their two daughters, Alice and Eleanor Bradley on Dartmouth Street, in an upscale section of Holyoke. "Aunt Jessie" the possessor of a thick Scottish Burr, was a tall, regal, meticulously dressed woman, extremely welcoming and obviously enamored with her grandniece Alice Haggerty. Unquestionably, Aunt Jessie was the power-broker on Alice's maternal side; nothing was a "fait accompli" without Aunt Jessie's acquiescence; fortunately, I passed Scottish scrutiny.

Alice's aunts and my aunts couldn't wait to arrange bridal showers for Alice. It seemed as if Alice was off to a shower on a weekly basis. Alice was not the girlie type. She wasn't particularly interested in domestic things. Even though she attended showers for her close friends, she was uncomfortable at those events. She was truly embarrassed at the prospect of being the center of attention. As I learned, Alice was all about putting the other person first; she preferred to be a supporting player and not the primary focus.

Alice's introductory tour meeting my relatives also went well; everyone was absolutely thrilled to meet Alice. I'm certain, with my contrarian personality, no one in my maternal or paternal family thought they would see the day when I would be introducing a fiancé. Perhaps they were happy to peddle me off to an unsuspecting young lady, but little did they know Alice was the last thing from an unsuspecting young lady. She was, as my father realized, "the best thing in the world for you."

PRE-MARRIGE STRESS NECESSITATES COMEDIC RELIEF

One Sunday night, as I was upstairs talking to Alice on the family telephone extension, I informed Alice that my mother, and her sister, my aunt Helen (Burke), were downstairs discussing plans for a bridal shower. As Helen and my mother discussed possible locations for the event, Helen asked her long-time friend Henry Gareau if he would telephone the Log Cabin Restaurant to determine what days it would be available to host a bridal shower.

Dutiful Henry complied and, without listening for a dial tone, picked up the downstairs phone and proceeded to dial a number, at which point Alice, on the line with me, responded; "Willow Glen Restaurant."

To which Henry said, "I didn't dial The Willow Glen, I dialed the Log Cabin."

Alice politely responded, "I'm sorry sir; this is The Willow Glen."

In disgust, Henry slammed the phone down and accused Helen of purposely giving him the wrong number!

Helen provided Henry with the telephone number of the Log Cabin Restaurant and asked Henry to re-dial the number. Again, without listening for the dial tone, Henry dialed the number for a second time.

This time, Alice responded, "Mountain Laurel Restaurant."

Exasperated, Henry emphatically said, "I'm not calling the Mountain Laurel. I'm calling the Log Cabin Restaurant."

Alice replied, "I'm sorry sir, this is not the "Log Cabin. This is the Mountain Laurel Restaurant."

I, of course, could hear the hysterical reaction from my mother and Helen as, in unison, they said, "Damn you Henry, you're dialing the wrong number!"

Yes, the two maternal shower organizers convinced Henry to dial the number a third time. This time, when he dialed the number, Alice answered, "Log Cabin Restaurant."

Henry replied, "It's about time you answered, this is the third time I dialed this same number!"

Henry proceeded to request available dates for bridal showers and Alice responded, "What is the name of the bride-to-be sir?"

Henry responded, "Alice Haggerty."

Alice replied in a perturbed tone of voice, stating, "Sir, Alice Haggerty is nothing but trouble. She and her friends have been banned from dining at the Log Cabin Restaurant. Goodbye!"

Of course, I had a ring-side seat as both my mother and my aunt berated Henrys incompetence and were perplexed to hear that Alice was banned from the Log Cabin Restaurant.

At this point, I concluded my conversation with Alice the Ventriloquist, went downstairs and exonerated the unfairly excoriated booking agent, Henry. I revealed that Henry was innocent; Alice was the culprit. They were delighted that a fun person like Alice would soon become a member of the Kennedy family.

BUILDING FOR TOMORROW

The wise woman builds her house... (Proverbs 14:1)

A classmate of mine at Cathedral High School and at St. Michael's College, Roger Chapdelaine, joined his father in the family business, the Joseph Chapdelaine Construction Company—one of the premier construction companies in the Greater Springfield area. At the time, the company was developing a sub-division in Westfield not far from Shaker Farms Country Club. The City of Westfield, a suburb of the City of Springfield, was known primarily for manufacturing bicycles. However, in the past, Westfield was widely recognized for manufacturing whips, an essential component during the horse-and-buggy days of transportation. Consequently, Westfield was forever known as The Whip City.

Alice and I met with Roger and we agreed to purchase a home, currently under construction, at 296 Falley Drive in the Shaker Heights subdivision. At the time of our agreement with Chapdelaine Construction, Alice and I were not married, so the property was deeded to Alice M Haggerty and Daniel J Kennedy. After February 17, the deed was reconstructed and Chapdelaine Construction granted ownership to Daniel J Kennedy and Alice M Kennedy.

Alice, with her immense knowledge of trade associations, as well as her real estate and business acumen, put on her negotiating hat and proposed that Chapdelaine Construction Company leave the light work to us which, resultantly, would reduce the sales price. Roger concurred and Alice and I agreed to tackle painting, wall-papering, and landscaping as we prepared to become residents of The Whip City. At this early point in our relationship I saw, firsthand, that Alice personified ingenuity in her true nature.

One Sunday, as I was painting the back of the house and Alice was painting the front of house, unbeknown to me, a neighborhood gentleman, Ed Baraka, who lived on Steiger Drive, the parallel street to Falley Drive, stopped and interviewed Alice for the neighborhood, Shaker Heights Newspaper. Alice identified herself as Alice Haggerty and told him she worked in West Springfield and would be moving to Falley Drive at the end of February.

As I came from behind the house, paint brush in hand, the interview was concluding and Mr. Baraka greeted me, "Welcome to Shaker Heights, Mr. Haggerty, it's nice to know we will be having Haggertys in the neighborhood." I introduced myself as Dan Kennedy. Summarily, Ed Baraka's mouth dropped in utter shock as he quickly stammered, "Well, I guess it's nice to know we will be having Haggertys and Kennedys in our neighborhood."

At that time in our culture, it was unheard of for any unmarried couple residing jointly. Before Alice and I scandalized the Shaker Heights neighborhood, I felt 'Reporter Ed' was entitled to a clarification. "In two months, before occupancy, we will be married, and we will both bear the name Kennedy," I said.

My laid-back nature was foreign to Alice. She was, by nature, a trailblazer with no inhibitions; she could walk up to a total stranger, introduce herself and immediately become best of friends. It wasn't long after we commenced painting projects that Alice was on a first name basis with the Shaker Heights to be.

The property at 296 Falley Drive abutted the Springfield Water Department pipeline, which ran from Provin Mountain in Russell, directly behind our house in Westfield in-route to the City of Springfield. The pipeline was located between Falley Drive and the final 200 yards of the dog-leg left, 600-yard par 5, 6th hole at Shaker Farms Country Club. There was a dingle or wooden area between the fairway and pipeline, which was ultimately beneficial. It was the ideal location for me to dispose of autumn leaves!

After Alice finished her work day at Carborumdum Corporation in West Springfield, she customarily drove directly to Falley Drive to monitor progress on her home to-be. One night in December as the sun was setting, Alice was driving up Falley Drive Alice and noticed what appeared to be a canvas bag on the side of the road. Even though it appeared to be a bag, something compelled Alice to stop the car and walk back to where the object was laying. When she approached the object on the side of the road, she discovered it was a young boy who apparently was struck by a passing motor vehicle. She took her coat off and covered the boy and ran to a nearby house and asked them to call for an ambulance. The EMT covered the young boy with warm blankets and returned Alice's coat.

After returning to her Northwood Ave home, with a trembling voice, she called me to inform me of the tragic incident, adding that she would call Noble Hospital in Westfield for periodic updates on the boy's prognosis.

It was after 10 pm when she called with an update, and it was devastating news; eight-year-old Stephen Huffmire had succumbed to his injuries. Alice later discovered the driver of the car that struck Stephen lived further down Falley Drive, and she allegedly did not know she struck the boy.

As a result of the tragedy, out of respect for the tragic death of Stephen Huffmire, the Annual Shaker Heights Neighborhood Kids Christmas Party was canceled in 1967. After Alice and I were settled in the community, we met Stephen's parents. They lived on a street directly off Falley Drive.

Often, I would suggest to Alice that the Huffmire Family might like to know she was the person who put her coat over Stephen as he lay on the Falley Drive pavement on that cold winter night, but she did not concur. "There is no point in drudging up painful memories for those poor parents who lost a child." Alice did not want any recognition, so the Huffmires never learned Alice was their son Stephen's "Good Samaritan."

Interesting; Alice didn't want any recognition for a good deed and, she didn't want "to drudge up painful memories" for grieving parents, characteristics that would be prevalent during her lifetime—humility and the suppression of painful memories.

CERTAINTY IS ILLUSIVE; TRUST NEVER FAILS

As the wedding date loomed closer, and as stressful situations increased, forbearance decreased. Later Alice informed me that when our wedding invitations were to be mailed, she became hesitant, which was not unusual given our relative short acquaintance. In retrospect, both Alice and I experienced periods of demurral; I after the proposal and Alice before mailing invitations. Fortunately, each of us were receptive to God's grace and trusted in the Holy Spirit.

On the 17th day of February in the nineteenth hundred and sixty-eighth Year of the Lord, Alice Marie Haggerty and Daniel Joseph Kennedy received the Sacrament of Matrimony in Saint Thomas the Apostle Church in West Springfield. A close friend, Father Francis M. Kennedy, from the husband's side of the family (Anna Sayers, Dingle, County Kerry circa 1900—definition: a country cousin) officiated at the Sacrament of Matrimony.

When one finds a worthy wife, her value is beyond pearls. Her husband, entrusting his heart to her has an enduring prize. She brings him good and not evil, all the days of her life. She reaches out her hands to the poor and extends her arms to the needy. (Proverbs 31:10-13)

WEDDING PLANS

Even though Alice and I were members of Shaker Farms Country Club, Mrs. Haggerty's preference was the dining facility she loved, Storrowton Tavern in West Springfield. Storrowton Tavern provided a separate facility for banquets, where Mrs. Haggerty reserved accommodation: The Carriage House at Storrowton Inn on the grounds of the Eastern States Exposition.

Prior to February 17th, Al Marie and I selected furniture and made arrangements for it to be delivered to our new home in Westfield before we returned from Jamaica. Most of our furniture was from the Kavanagh Furniture Store (no relation to the Storrowton Kavanagh's) on upper State Street in Springfield and adjacent to Commerce High School. Kavanagh Furniture was an "employee owned" enterprise. One of the employee owners, Joe Maher, was a parishioner at Our Lady of Hope Church and a friend of my parents, which automatically qualified Alice and I as recipients of a "family discount."

Alice and I discussed items we would be bringing to Falley Drive from our respective homes. With Alice's love for dogs, I assumed she would bring her miniature French Poodle, Jacques, but surprisingly she responded, "Jacques is not coming to Westfield; he will be staying on Northwood Ave." Although she didn't elaborate, it was obvious to me that, in spite of her love for Jacques, she didn't want her parents—who she knew would lament her departure—to also be denied the companionship of her dog. It was classic Alice, *always putting of other people first!*

ALICE'S WHITE (NOT BLUE) GOWN

When one finds a worthy wife, her value is far beyond pearls. Her husband has an unfailing prize. (Proverbs 31:10-11)

Shortly before the wedding, Alice's father, who previously had open-heart surgery at Massachusetts General Hospital in Boston, was concerned that he might be experiencing a heart attack, so he checked himself into the Mercy Hospital in Springfield. Mr. Haggerty had previous instructions from his primary care physician that, in the event he experienced unusual heart palpitations, to immediately go the emergency room. In accord with the doctor's instructions a few days prior to the wedding, he purportedly experienced pain in his chest and was admitted to Mercy Hospital. Conveniently or inconveniently, Mr. Haggerty was unable to attend his daughter's wedding.

Alice's two brothers-in-law, Lowell Harlow and Emil Masi, offered to walk Alice down the aisle at St. Thomas the Apostle Church. But she refused. As long as her father was alive, albeit unavailable, she intended to walk alone and that is precisely what she did.

When Alice arrived in the limo at St. Thomas the Apostle Church, the sun was shining brightly. However, after the Sacrament of Marriage, we exited the church and walked into a blinding snow squall! It was over in a matter of minutes, and nothing we couldn't handle. Both of us speculated this might be a prelude to marital life; could we handle an occasional snow squall in years to come? Could we handle the storms of life? At that point in time, after receiving the Sacrament of Marriage, and with God as our strength, we believed that whatever snow squalls we might encounter, we would trust that God would provide us with sufficient grace.

After our wedding and prior to attending our wedding reception at Storrowton Tavern, Alice and I stopped at Mercy Hospital in Springfield to visit with her father. Alice wanted her father to see his daughter in her wedding gown. When we arrived, Mr. Haggerty was seated comfortably in the solarium, conversing with other patients and exhibiting no perceptible discomfort. A rather- matter-of-fact, Mr. Haggerty, didn't comment on Alice's beautiful wedding gown. He merely asked, "How did things go, Ali?" Could Mr. Haggerty's blasé demeanor, along with an apparent lack of remorse for not being in attendance at his daughter's wedding, be affirmation that an "impending heart attack" may have been a figment of his imagination to avoid what he perceived to be, for him, an emotionally stressful day?

A line from an old-time comical radio program came to my mind. The principal character reacted to skeptical queries posed by other characters with the response, "Were you there Charlie?" That line became so popular that most every family in the country would upon occasion repeat the phrase whenever expressions of doubt arose.

When I saw Mr. Haggerty sitting so serenely in the solarium at Mercy Hospital, I thought of paraphrasing the popular radio adage with, "Why, weren't you there, Charlie?"

WAVES AND WATER; SUN AND FUN

After a wonderful wedding reception at Storrowton Tavern on Saturday evening, Alice and I departed snowy New England and we drove to New

York City, stayed overnight at the New York Hilton, and on Sunday morning, departed on a plane from John F. Kennedy International Airport for our flight to Montego Bay, Jamaica. Interesting, we flew from the Long Island neighborhood of "Jamaica," to the Caribbean country of Jamaica.

Upon landing at Montego Bay Airport, we proceeded to the rental car kiosk, at which point Alice, in spite of her love for cars, suggested that I sign as the custodial-operator. I knew, as an avid Motorcar Club aficionado, she would obviously have preferred to be the driver-of-record yet, in the magnanimity of her heart of hearts and, at great personal sacrifice, she provided me with the thrill she would have loved to experience herself. Classic Alice.

As might be expected, Alice's close friend at Springfield's Sheraton Travel Agency provided luxurious accommodations. The Gloucester House at Montego Bay was spectacular and directly across the street from Jamaica's famous Doctor's Cove Beach. The rental car we procured at the airport would enable us to transverse the hills and dales of Jamaica. The accommodations were fantastic, and we had a wonderful time.

As soon as we unpacked our bags, Alice went straight to the beach. Before we stopped at the refreshment kiosk, we had rented two plastic inflatable rafts and, with raft in hand, Alice headed directly into the beautiful blue water in Doctor's Cove. A good swimmer, Alice enthusiastically paddled away on her raft while I, a non-swimmer, timorously boarded the other inflatable raft. In noting my reticence, Alice paddled over to me, presumably with sage advice on basic aquatic techniques but, much to my surprise, and shock, she said, "Now you're going to learn to swim," and mischievously pretended to pull the plug on my raft. Inadvertently, with her comedic ploy in full gear, the plug dislodged and, much to Alice's surprise and to my horror, the air immediately began to dissipate from the rapidly deflating raft as I began to sink into the depths of the beautiful blue Doctor's Cove water. Fortunately, the depth of the water was only four or five feet, but nonetheless it was a momentarily harrowing experience.

After her aborted attempt to inspire me to swim backfired, both of us recognized the incident as humorous. Unwittingly, Alice provided me with a lifetime of comedic mileage, embellishing her *attempt to drown me in Jamaica.* No, she did not think my embellishment was particularly humorous; nevertheless, she was content to allow me moments of self-deprecating enjoyment.

Alice and I put considerable mileage on our Montego Bay rental car. One day we drove three-hours east of Montego Bay to the sleepy tourist town of Ocho Rios. If for no other reason, the sight-seeing on the tortuous drive was worth the venture. As a bonus, while shopping in Ocho Rios, Alice was thrilled to find a *serving dish* for her rose-centered, fine-china place-settings.

After her unexpected "find," we stopped at the primary tourist attraction in the quaint little resort town of Dunn River Falls. The "shtick" of Dunn River Falls is to climb, from the sandy beach, up a steep hill comprised of numerous slimy slippery rocks as torrents of water cascaded down (the term "rocks" is a misnomer, they were more like boulders than rocks). At any rate, negotiating the rocks/boulders that were precariously placed in perilous positions extending to the precipice of the hill, was a challenging exercise. From my childhood, I had acquired a fear of water so, in my mind, one mis-step and, conceivably, I could be swept up by the rushing water into blue lagoon below.

Thankfully, Alice empathized with my plight and guided me from slippery rock to slippery rock, assuring me that as long as I followed her advice, I wouldn't slip. She was right; both of us made it safely unscathed to the top of the hill. If I hadn't realized it before, I realized it then: Alice the Adventurist would become the "the rock" of our family. Whether it was my years as an insurance underwriter assessing hazards and risks or whether it was my reticent nature, I was much more cautious than Daredevil Alice.

When we returned to our Gloucester House accommodations in Montego Bay, we relaxed on our balcony and watched Jamaican men and women return from the fields carrying huge baskets of bananas *on their heads*—bananas that would undoubtedly be on the Gloucester House breakfast table the following morning. The fresh fruit on daily display was phenomenal; I didn't know so many delicious fruits existed! The coffee, however, was much too strong for me.

After our evening dinner, we came to enjoy a glass of Jamaican Gold Rum—an island necessity. Candlelight dinner was of course the highlight of the day at the Gloucester House. There was always a variety of seafood on the menu and it was prepared exceptionally well by the chef and served in an elegant manner by the waitstaff. With their attractive island accent, the waitstaff repetitively offered, "Buns please?"

Upon our return from hot and humid Jamaica, it was a rude awakening to confront a cold and snowy day in the city of Westfield; thankfully, 296 Falley Drive was warm and welcoming. As anticipated, Kavanaugh Furniture Company made their delivery, family and friends hung curtains and drapes and, most importantly, the heating system was obviously functioning; it was hot! Although our new home was only sparsely furnished, it was Home Sweet Home!

For the next several weeks, we made frequent trips to Northwood Ave and Penacook Street to retrieve various personal items. Alice brought her sterling silver rosary beads that her godfather, Melvin O'Leary, gave her when she made her First Holy Communion at the Holy Name of Jesus Church in Chicopee, on December 22, 1946. She also brought two pictures of the Sacred Heart of Jesus, one of which she put on the wall and the other on her bureau. Me? I brought rosary beads to place under my pillow. It is safe to say we were entrusting our marriage to the Lord.

ADJUSTMENTS AND, MORE ADJUSTMENTS

As we continued the process of settling in to our new home, Alice frequently said, "Our dining furniture looks beautiful, but it is 'crying' for an oriental rug to show off the grain of the wood and the beautiful new hardwood floor."

It wasn't long before Alice introduced me to Toros Omartian of Omartian Oriental Rugs Inc., on lower Bridge Street in Springfield. She was convinced that an oriental rug would go well with the new dining room set and would enhance our beautiful hardwood floors.

After expressing my preference for wall-to-wall carpeting, I uttered, what ultimately would become, one of my many, many stupid remarks. "If we have oriental rugs on Falley Drive, it will be over my dead body." I, of course, was ignorant. I didn't know anything but wall-to-wall carpeting and vividly recalled my father saying that we were aristocrats! On the other hand, Alice's father knew oriental rugs enhanced the décor of funeral homes so the Haggerty family was accustomed in having beautiful oriental rugs in the parlor of the Charles J. Haggerty Funeral Home.

Eventually, Alice persuaded me to accompany her to Toros Omartian Oriental Rugs. How do you say "no way" to one small oriental rug when someone is as crazy about oriental rugs as was Alice? Shortly afterward, our dining room was not only adorned with a beautiful dining room set from Kavanagh's Furniture, the quality of the hardwood floor was accentuated by an oriental rug from Omartian's. Just as Alice had scripted, eventually I learned to appreciate and to love oriental rugs!

As summer of 1968 arrived and living room furniture was acquired, once again Alice was singing a familiar tune. "The living room floor is begging for an oriental rug," she said. It wasn't long before we were walking through the door of Charles Yenian's Oriental Rug Inc. on Appremont Triangle in Springfield. Surprise, surprise; Alice negotiated acquisition of a beautiful 10' x 20' Kasvin Rug, which beautified our hardwood living room floor.

Alice also scheduled a vacuum cleaner salesman, Ron Pudlo, to visit our home and demonstrate a Kirby vacuum cleaner. Alice wanted me to see, firsthand, the effectiveness of a Kirby model.

Again, my contrarian nature was on display. I couldn't understand why we needed to listen to a vacuum cleaner pitchman when we paid Roger Chapdelaine to install a central vacuum system in our newly constructed home. Roger's system was housed in the cellar and, when we vacuumed, all we needed to do was plug a portable hose into one of the wall outlets strategically positioned throughout the house.

After Ron Kudlo's 45-minute presentation, I realized Alice's enthusiasm knew no bounds; a Kirby vacuum was of such over-riding significance to her I retracted my objections and, at a cost of $175, which included a lifetime warranty, we purchased a Kirby vacuum cleaner. Regardless of what might happen to the vacuum, all we needed to do was package it, and mail it back to Kirby's factory in Cleveland, Ohio plant and, at no charge, they would replace it with a brand-new Kirby vacuum.

Obviously, both Alice and I needed to integrate our prior individualism to a commonality of purpose. Although we were striving to make progress in uniting, considerable opportunities to reinvent our lives remained.

One typical weekday morning at 7:00 am, as I stood at the doorway of our den preparing for work, Alice chided, "I hope when you come home you will put the cap back-on the toothpaste, your razor back in your toiletry bag, and your shoes in the closet." I turned around and with the most genuine expression I could muster, displaying absolutely no rancor, I said, "When I woke-up this morning I asked myself, 'what can I do today to aggravate Alice?' Now, just 45 minutes later, everything has worked!" It only took Alice a second or two to process my factual yet humoristic phraseology; a slight smile crossed her face as she began to see *my purported egregious offenses from* a different perspective.

We continued to merge our lives together while at the same time maintaining previous friendships. On weekends I would play golf with my usual foursome, while Alice would play golf with her usual foursome.

One sunny Sunday morning in August, a typical hot and humid summer day, Alice played golf with her close friend Mary Toohey in a tournament at the Whippernon Golf Club on Route 20 in Russell, Mass. As was customary, I played a round at Shaker Farms with my usual foursome.

When I returned home around 5:00 p.m., I was anxious to discuss how Alice and Mary played in the Whippernon tournament, but Alice and Mary had not yet arrived home. I wasn't particularly disappointed by their absence. After an hour passed and they weren't home, I started to become anxious. My redheaded disposition seemed to become more and more inflamed as I continued to wait, and when the sky began to darken around 8:00 p.m. and they were still not home, my patience expired. I decided to take remedial action.

It was completely dark when I pulled the car into Whippernon Golf Club parking lot in Russell. As I entered the clubhouse, the gaiety of socializing golfers clustering around the 19th Hole, a.k.a. 'the bar,' drew ominously silent; the raucous atmosphere suddenly subsided. The socializing golfers' merriment was muted as I stridently walked toward the now voiceless joy-makers as a stunned silence permeated the clubhouse lounge.

Alice, along with Mary, was seated at the bar amidst the revelers. "Alice, you're out of here," as I affirmatively took her by the arm. I turned to Mary and said, "You're out of here as well; come with me." There were no objections from either of them and no one else dared to utter a word as I walked out with Alice on one side and Mary on the other side.

Both Alice and Mary appeared capable of driving, so I concluded it was permissible for Mary to drive her own car provided she followed our car.

As we proceeded back to Westfield, Alice sat silently in the front seat; not a single word was spoken during our half-hour ride back to Falley Drive. Most of the time it is beneficial for me to hit "the pause button" before verbalizing what is on the mind. At that moment, the seven-mile ride was the ideal pause button.

It wasn't until we entered the house that I spoke. I was not interested in dialogue nor did I intend to enter into an explanatory conversation – I had a message to convey. As Alice stood with her back against the kitchen sink, I said, "Alice, marital obligations pre-empt much of the fun and frolic with which we were formerly accustomed. It is fine to play golf with our friends but playing golf is secondary, marital obligations are primary. I intend to prioritize my marital obligations and I expect you to prioritize yours. After a long day golfing, a clubhouse atmosphere can be toxic and, it is unacceptable for a married woman to remain in that type of environment for a prolonged period of time. You used poor judgment in not coming home after playing golf today. I never thought I would say this Alice, but tonight, I was ashamed to see you in that alehouse atmosphere."

Immediately, Alice, who never cried, started to bawl her eyes out. I made no effort to console her nor recognize her tears. I turned and went upstairs to bed. I never knew what prompted her to cry; I could only speculate. Was she crying because of what I said to her? I don't know. Was she crying because she herself was disappointed that she over-extended her time at a golf tournament? I don't know. Was she crying because of the encumbrances of married life? I don't know. Was she was crying because she was embarrassed in front of her friends or did she regret being married to what at that time might be construed to be, "a tyrant?" I don't know and I never asked. I verbalized my perspective on the event and never mentioned the incident again. On that hot summer night—which may have been transformational—both of us needed to make a greater effort to integrate our lives.

At that time in our culture, people tended to be married in their early twenties. Since Alice and I were older than the norm, we were more entrenched with our own independence, necessitating significant sacrificial adjustments.

One day in August Alice said, "We've been married for six months, and in a few weeks, I will be 29 years old and I'm still not pregnant." I responded, "I think God wants us to be more tolerant of each other before he entrusts us with another life; let's work harder on compatibility." Alice concurred, at which point I suggested, "Why don't we celebrate your birthday in Maine?" Enough said, Alice put plans in place to spend a week on the coast of Maine.

ALTRUISTIC ALICE

After packing Alice's beloved Mercedes 190-SL white convertible, she handed me the keys and I pointed her car toward the rock-bound coast. Once again, here was Altruistic Alice— always thinking of others. As much as Alice loved driving her Mercedes, she wanted me to enjoy the thrill of driving her car but not before she gave me explicit instructions.

First, she instructed me on how to use a floor shift on a foreign auto. She told me the method of slowing down the car is not by using the brake it is by *downshifting* to a lower gear, which curtails the power. Only when it is necessary to come to a complete stop, should the brake be used. Imagine the trust she must have summonsed from her inner-most being to allow an automobile no-nothing like me drive her pride and joy. It was an explicit example of the innate goodness she reflected so often. She was willing to deprive herself of the pleasure of driving the car she loved so I, who had little interest in cars, could experience enjoyment in driving her car.

I must admit I did enjoy zipping down the Mass Pike and up Interstate 95 in a white Mercedes 190-SL convertible. My enthusiasm must have resonated with Alice because she seemed to enjoy my positive reaction to driving her car. Alice's joy was obvious, and she observed that I enjoyed driving her Mercedes. As we approached the town of Ogunquit, Alice detected a foreboding sound emitting from the engine. I, of course, was oblivious but she, an avid motorcar connoisseur, was concerned and urged me to drive to the gas station in the center of Ogunquit.

After appraising the car, the mechanic informed us that a vital engine component needed to be replaced (I think it was the fuel pump) The mechanic said it would take a day to complete the work. Fortunately, the repair shop was in the proximity to the Betty Doone Motel, where Alice made our room reservations.

Even the repair work on her car didn't dampen her enjoyment, as she gave me a walking tour on the famous Marginal Way, culminating with lunch at Barnacle Billy's on Perkin's Cove. Alice's family always spent their summer vacations in Ogunquit and their three daughters acquired a love for Maine. Alice couldn't wait to share that love with me.

Within a few days, Alice's car was repaired, thus I received a more extensive tour of the rocky coastline of Maine. She loved showing me all the sentimental spots where her family spent so many happy times. On our final day in Maine, after watching young college students make salt water taffy at the Goldenrod in York Beach, Alice suggested that we have dinner at Taylor's Restaurant in nearby York Harbor, officially called Taylor's By the Sea. The food was wonderful and the nautical water view was impeccable. Alice was delighted and so was I. With the exception of the frigid water, I thoroughly enjoyed Alice's birthday week in Maine.

THE FIRST OF MANY SCOTTISH VISITORS

In October of 1968, my boss, Executive Vice-President Charles L. Niles, informed me that the chairman of the General Accident Fire and Life

Assurance Corp Ltd's Board of Directors, Sir Henry Stuart-Black, and his wife were visiting from Perthshire, Scotland, and Springfield would be on his itinerary.

I was further informed that Sir Stuart-Black's wished to host a banquet for our more prestigious independent insurance agents and it was expected that I would make suitable arrangements. For the next two months, preparing for this prestigious event became an all-consuming task.

Since the Highland Hotel and the Kimball Hotel, two four-star Springfield hotels, closed in the 1960's, Springfield was without a downtown hotel. Fortunately, the governmental agency that refurbished downtown areas had subsidized the construction of a first-class Marriott hotel in the city of Springfield. In addition to the hotel, the urban renewal complex included specialty retail shops, an office tower which was identified as Bay State West located on a plot of land situated on the corner of Main Street and Vernon Street, overlooking the eastern shore of the Connecticut River.

As might be expected, our organizationally proficient phenom, Alice, was the primary producer of precise preparations for prominent guests from the United Kingdom. Alice not only selected personal gifts for the Stuart-Blacks, she also selected the bill of fare as well as a top of the line wine.

Alice presumed Lady Stuart-Black might like to have her hair groomed prior to the dinner, so she took it upon herself to made reservations at a beauty boutique in Bay State West aptly named, "Lords and Ladies!" Lady Stuart-Black was, as Alice anticipated, pleased. Again, it was Organizational Alice, at her best.

The visit of Sir Henry Stuart-Black and his wife was just the forerunner of numerous visits from our Worldwide Headquarters in Perth, Scotland. It seemed that, year-in and year-out, in Westfield and in Needham, Alice and I hosted Scottish dignitaries.

Apparently, the Stuart-Blacks were pleased with their visit to Springfield, as it wasn't long before Mr. Niles informed me that Deputy General Attorney

Charles Heath and his wife would also be visiting the Springfield branch office. The term General Attorney is not necessarily associated with legal matters; in the United Kingdom (UK) it signified the senior executive officer In Mr. Heath's case, he was second in command.

With the prospect of entertaining independent insurance agents as well as occasional visitors from Scotland, Mr. Niles reasoned it would be advisable if I, on behalf of the Springfield branch, applied for membership in a private business club in downtown Springfield. In his opinion, General Accident Insurance should provide our producers and out-of-town guests with a private "club-like" atmosphere, comparable to European patrician custom.

After discussing Mr. Niles suggestion with the Springfield branch's legal counsel, Attorney James P. Moriarty, he offered to sponsor me as a prospective member of the prestigious Colony Club of Springfield. Attorney Moriarty introduced me to the president of the club, who accompanied me on a series of interviews with the board of governors and past presidents of the club. Ultimately, my application was approved and I became a member of the Colony Club of Springfield. Jim Moriarty and his wife, Maude Tait Moriarty, were loyal longtime affiliates of General Accident Insurance and soon they became close friends of Alice and mine.

In August of 1968, Alice and I decided to take a trip to Washington DC. We had a great time visiting historic sites in Washington and in Arlington, Va. We were based at the Iwo Jima Motel in Arlington, across the Potomac River from the Capitol. This enabled us to visit the various historical sites in Washington and Arlington.

While we were in Washington, we dined one of my former golfing partners at Shaker Farms Country Club, Art Willett and his wife Nancy, neither of whom met had Alice. Art was recently transferred by his employer, Phoenix Mutual Life Insurance Company, from its Springfield office to the Washington, DC office. I was particularly anxious for Alice to meet Art, as his administrative assistant in Springfield was Alice's cousin, Ruth Haggerty.

WINDING OUR WAY BACK TO THE WHIP CITY

On the morning of our departure from Arlington on the way back to Westfield, I thought it would be nice to take a slight detour and visit the United States Naval Academy in Annapolis, Maryland. Our brief venture on the grounds of the Naval Academy was another wonderful experience.

As we exited the grounds of the United States Naval Academy and began our return trek to New England, I noticed a street sign: "Chesapeake Bay Bridge and Tunnel," with an arrow pointing in the general direction we were heading. I recalled reading an article of the recently dedicated 17-mile bridge/tunnel, an engineering marvel, so I decided to continue on that route. Yes, you are light years ahead of me: my decision proved to be a BIG MISTAKE! A fiasco of unimaginable consequences.

We drove and we drove and we drove. I kept looking for another sign affirming that we were approaching the Chesapeake Bay Bridge and Tunnel, but we never did we see another sign for the Chesapeake Bay Bridge Tunnel. Pride was always in the forefront of my mind, especially when traveling; I would never stop and ask for directions. As far as I was concerned, my sense of direction was beyond reproach. In this instance, that was an absolutely incorrect premise! Mea culpa, mea culpa, mea maxima culpa!

We were neither heading south to the tunnel nor north to Baltimore. We were, in fact, traveling toward Cambridge, Maryland and the confluence of the Delaware River and the Atlantic Ocean. When I finally realized my mistake, we were beyond the point of no return. There was no benefit in reversing our course, so we continued heading toward Cambridge, Maryland.

Eventually, and I mean, eventually, we rendezvoused with Interstate 95 in Dover, Delaware, resulting in one hundred and fifty miles of unnecessary travel. Alice's willingness to tolerate my inept navigational ability was truly amazing. She had every right to be furious, but she was not; truly, her compassion was an insight to her virtuousness. From morning to night, never did she utter a condemnatory word; she was the personification of forgiveness. Hours later, as dinner time approached and we were nearing New York City, I suggested stopping at a well-known Irish Restaurant in Yonkers—Patricia Murphy's; Affable Alice concurred.

Dinner at Patricia Murphy's was, in every sense of the word, superb. Irish music, great food and of course, an evening of craic. Now that our fortunes appeared to improve, why not another imaginative suggestion? Instead of taking the mundane Merritt Parkway through Connecticut, why not drive due north on the scenic Taconic Parkway, which paralleled the Hudson River and the Adirondack Mountains? Agreeable Alice could see I was attempting to redeem myself from my morning fiasco and obligingly said, "Good idea. We can see the sunset behind the Adirondacks!"

The Taconic Parkway is on the east side of Hudson River so we would be able to see the sunset as we passed the United States Military Academy at West Point. Neat. In one day, we will have viewed both the United States Naval Academy and the United States Military Academy.

Initially, as we commenced our drive north on the Taconic Parkway looking west, beyond the Hudson River, toward Bear Mountain in the Adirondack Mountain Range, we witnessed a spectacular sunset. Although there were ominous clouds rolling in, we were also able to see a glimpse of the United States Military Academy in West Point, New York.

Shortly after watching the beautiful sunset (Alice really enjoyed sunsets), a dense fog rolled in, lodging between the Hudson River to the west and the Taconic Mountain Range to the east. Within a matter of minutes, the fog was so thick that we literally could not see the emblem on the hood of Alice's 190-SL! Visibility: nonexistent!

I don't think we exceeded 20 mph during that 100-mile junket from Yonkers, NY to Stockbridge, Mass—not a word was uttered. Silence prevailed. It was an absolutely frightening experience, a treacherous trip on the Taconic Parkway. Lamentations and recriminations were non-existent; prayers were on our lips and in our hearts!

Thank God. After what seemed to be an eternity, the fog dissipated and we reached the Massachusetts border and the entrance of the Mass Turnpike in Stockbridge; thankfully, it was fog free! Gratefully, we pulled into our driveway shortly before midnight. Mentally and, physically depleted, we were too exhausted to speak other than to say, THANK YOU JESUS!

The tolerance and forbearance demonstrated by Alice during a needless eighteen-hour ride from Washington, DC to Westfield, Mass was indeed extraordinary. Never did she display a disparaging glance or a recriminatory word. As I would discover in future years, whenever Alice perceived people to be in need, she exhibited empathy; undoubtedly, she caste me in that category.

In situation after situation, challenge after challenge, trial after trial, Alice reflected an in-depth spiritual dimension—Faith (perhaps misplaced on this trip), Hope, (in this instance, that we would eventually arrive home), and Love (for a non-compos mentis tour director). And the Greatest of these is...LOVE.

Every day of her life, in the truest sense of the word, Alice radiated an intense LOVE for others!

CHAPTER 3

ALICE IN WONDERLAND

How numerous O Lord you have made
your wondrous deeds! (Psalm 40:6)

On a cold winter day in February 1969, after a typical day at the office of General Accident Insurance Company and upon arrival home at 296 Falley Drive, Alice opened the door to our family room to greet me with a grin, which was beaming from ear-to-ear. Before I could say a word, she blurted out, "I'm going to have a baby!" She was elated, she couldn't wait for me to return home from the office to tell me her exciting news. ALICE was, truly in WONDERLAND!!!

Yes, Alice Marie Kennedy was delighted. Delighted beyond description. Delighted to proclaim the magnificent *gift of motherhood!* Hallelujah! I can still envision Alice standing just inside the door of our family room, adjacent to the kitchen countertop island that jutted from the back wall of the house to the entrance of the den doorway. As I stood on the green-carpeted den floor, we hugged and thanked God for blessing Alice with pregnancy. Alice's excitement was thrilling to observe, she was, so, so happy! As for me, I was in total shock, as I had not been prepared for the prospects of pregnancy. (On four subsequent occasions, Alice notified me with similar good news of an impending birth as I entered den door.)

That evening our "happy hour" was truly happy. Alice had the foresight to fortify us with shrimp cocktail and broiled scallop hors d'oeuvres (just like those served at Jimmy's Harborside on Boston Harbor's Fish Pier.)

To say Alice was in "Wonderland" would be an understatement; she absolutely loved the concept of being a mother in God's plan for creation, the first of which would be five wonderful opportunities to bear God's children. It is a given that mothers devote their lives to their children, but few mothers could possibly enjoy motherhood more than Alice.

The Kennedy Kids were indeed blessed to have Alice for their mother and, she LOVED being their mother! Willingly, she sacrificed promising professional aspirations and subjugated personal ambitions to secondary status. She devoted 100% of her ability to be the best possible mother she could be and, she succeeded; Alice was the BEST OF THE BEST!

Not only did excitement reign on Falley Drive in Westfield, grandparents to-be were also thrilled, especially my mother and father, who were yet to experience having a grandchild. Alice's parents, who were accustomed to the world of grandparenting, were also delighted. In the winter of 1969, everyone was anxiously looking forward to the summer of August 1969.

LET THE CELEBRATION BEGIN

Each year on March 17, the city of Holyoke holds an elaborate and festive St. Patrick's Day Parade, at which time it is customary to present the "Irishman of the Year" Award, to a notable person of Irish descent. In 1958, the first person so honored was United States Senator John F. Kennedy of the Commonwealth of Massachusetts. In 1964, in honor of the award's first recipient, the 35th President of the United States, the award was renamed the President John F. Kennedy Award.

In 1969, at the conclusion of the Saint Patrick's Weekend Mass at Saint Jerome's Church in Holyoke, the President John F. Kennedy Irishman of the Year Award was to be presented by Christopher J. Weldon, Bishop of Springfield to the Cardinal-Archbishop of Boston, Richard Cardinal Cushing, a close friend of President Kennedy.

Our good friends, Frank and Eleanor Tierney, invited Alice and me to join them at the Saturday evening Mass. Obviously Alice and I were thrilled to be invited to the Saint Patrick's Weekend Mass, as both of us were ardent admirers of Cardinal Cushing.

As a matter of fact, one of the most memorable events in my life occurred in August of 1959. In conjunction with the Massachusetts National Guard, commonly known as the Yankee Division, the United States Army Reserves, of which I was a member, were deployed for Active Duty maneuvers at Camp Drum, New York.

On Sunday afternoon, during those two weeks, a special visitor celebrated Mass for the troops of the Yankee Division and the Army Reserves it was the Cardinal-Archbishop of Boston, Richard Cardinal Cushing! After the Mass, the Cardinal-Archbishop circulated among the troops. Fortunately, I was able to shake his hand and kiss his episcopal ring, marveling at his down to earth demeanor with the soldiers. In the pre-Vatican II world, the Cardinal-Archbishop was adorned with the customary brilliant red biretta, bright red vestments, and bright red shoes. In spite of the unique attire of a Cardinal of the Church, Cardinal Cushing was down-to-earth and seemingly unassuming.

In 1969, all of Vatican II's revisions hadn't been fully implemented and, in accord with customary practice, Communicants received Holy Communion while kneeling at the altar rail that extended across the breath of the Sanctuary. As Alice and I knelt at the left end of the altar rail (facing the altar), Cardinal Cushing distributed Holy Communion as he walked parallel to the rail, from the right to the left side of the rail.

As the Cardinal-Archbishop came toward Alice, who was kneeling to my right, I was exhilarated to think an expectant mother would receive

Holy Communion from the Cardinal-Archbishop of Boston. Suddenly, after distributing Communion to the person to the right of Alice, Cardinal Cushing abruptly turned and walked back to the opposite end of the altar rail and resumed the distribution process. I was devastated!

Years later, Alice, blessed to be the mother of a priest, would not only receive Holy Communion from the Cardinal-Archbishop of Boston, Sean Patrick O'Malley, he would know her as, "ALICE" and, on the day of her death, the Cardinal-Archbishop of Boston would make a personal telephone call to our home offering condolences and, most importantly, his prayers for repose of Alice's immortal soul! DEO GRATIAS!

In 1969, the Liturgical Secretary to the Cardinal-Archbishop of Boston was Msgr. Joseph F. Maguire, future Bishop of Springfield. Undoubtedly, he was present in the Sanctuary of St. Jerome's Church and, quite possibly, he was the priest who distributed Communion to expectant Alice.

TIME TO RETIRE

In order to prepare for the birth of her first child, on June 13, 1969, Alice resigned from her twelve-year tenure with Carborundum Corporation. Coincidentally, June 13th would have been my deceased brother, John Barrett Kennedy's, 35th birthday.

Shortly after Alice, resigned her position at Carborundum, the two of us took another trip to her favorite "home away from home," Ogunquit, Maine. Massachusetts was in the throes of a brutal heat wave so we sought a cool breeze in Maine. Wrong! The heat wave didn't spare the state of Maine; it was abominably HOT and, HUMID!

As soon as we arrived, we went to Ogunquit beach so Alice could find relief from the oppressive heat. The water temperature at Ogunquit Beach is posted and, on a boiling hot day in the month of June, the water temperature was 58 degrees—40 degrees cooler than the air temperature!

During those years, few coastal motels provided air conditioning. So not only was it brutally hot during the day, but it was also oppressively hot and humid at night. Alice was sweating profusely and couldn't sleep. She was unable to find a cool spot, so as soon as the sun began to rise, we were off to Ogunquit Beach, where the 55-degree water temperature was refreshing! As the beach began to fill with weary sun worshipers, Alice and I played football on the spacious beach; she the receiver and I, the quarterback! People on the beach couldn't believe a woman who was eight months pregnant could run, cut, and catch a football in such brutally hot weather. No matter how warm it has been in any subsequent summer in New England, I don't believe we experienced any heat wave that could rival the intensity of the heat we endured that week in June 1969!

I can still see Alice sitting on a bench, sweltering in the oppressive heat as she tried to appreciate the beauty of the Nubble Light and Short Sands Beach in York, Maine. Obviously, Alice was experiencing excruciating discomfort, but didn't complain, Alice never complained. Furthermore she didn't want any extraordinary attention, suffering silently in the sultry summer sun. As much as Alice loved the rock-bound coast of Maine, she did not lament a return trip to Westfield in her white convertible as cool breezes were flowing through her hair.

It was truly a coincidence (Divine Providence?) that Alice selected Dr. Siragusa to deliver our first child. She did not know that I met Dr. Siragusa at a Cursillo in 1966 and, initially, I didn't particularly enjoy meeting him. However, as the Cursillo evolved, I came to recognize his goodness.

When Alice went for her periodic check-up in July, Dr. Siragusa informed Alice that unless the baby changed position, it would be a breach birth; the longer the baby remained in the womb, the more difficult the delivery. He assured Alice there was a good chance the baby will change position, so she should not be overly concerned.

When the estimated time of arrival for our August bambino, initially projected to be August 8th, had passed, I set my sights on August 15th—the Feast of the Assumption of the Blessed Mother. But that didn't occur either.

On August 16, I decided to start a Novena to Saint Jude in hopes the baby would soon be born. Five minutes after midnight, on the ninth day of the Novena, August 22, Alice's birthday, she experienced the first sign of labor. I immediately rushed her to Providence Hospital and purposely did not inform anyone that Alice was in the hospital.

After spending time between the Providence Hospital Chapel and the maternity floor, as I was pacing the floor in the waiting room the elevator door opened and in walked Alice's father. I was shocked. I felt it was my responsibility as her husband to be waiting expectedly.

As I learned later, the switchboard operator at Providence Hospital was Mr. Haggerty's cousin and he instructed her to call him when Alice was admitted. Yes, the same Mr. Haggerty who alleged had a heart issue so he wouldn't have to endure the emotional strain of attending his daughter's wedding, was now pacing back and forth on the Providence Hospital maternity floor with me.

Perhaps Mr. Haggerty was an undercover CIA agent? First, he vetted me before we were married, and now he managed to acquire critical inside information on Alice's admittance to Providence Hospital. Soon, Dr. Siragusa came out of the Maternity area to provide me with an update. I introduced him to Alice's father, and he said, "I know the baby is a girl, but it will be 45 minutes before I know whether we can complete the delivery."

Dr. Siragusa must have noticed the blood drain from Mr. Haggerty's face because, looking directly at Alice's father he said, "You do know Mr. Haggerty, this is a breach-birth, thus the uncertainty." Alice and I never informed anyone else about this issue, so this news came as a complete surprise for the grandfather-to-be.

Forty-five minutes later, Dr. Siragusa came out of the operating room obviously pleased to announce Alice delivered a beautiful baby girl! Praise the Lord! After a brutally hot and humid summer, replete with anxiety and stress, on Alice Marie Haggerty Kennedy's 30th birthday, August 22, 1969, she gave birth to her first child—Kathleen Marie Kennedy, the first born of Alice's five children! Alice suggested, and I agreed, that we call our new baby Katie.

On September 8, 1969, the birthday of the Blessed Mother, at St. Mary's Church in Westfield, Father Francis M. Kennedy baptized Kathleen Marie Kennedy while godparents James J. Sullivan and Judith E. Kennedy witnessed. In the event our new born baby was a boy, his name would have been Kevin Michael Kennedy. For whatever reason, we seemed committed to the initials (KMK).

Alice was never the stereotype little girl who was interested in dolls, doll houses, cooking, clothes, shopping, etc. Alice was interested in cars, knives, guns, and sports. "I want a switch-blade knife and a rifle with a bayonet for Christmas," was seven-year old Alice Haggerty's response to cousin Marilyn Marshall when, in 1946, she asked, "What do you want for Christmas, Ali?"

In a complete change of heart from her childhood ambivalence for dolls and girlie things, Alice manifested an amazing role reversal! From the day she resigned her position at Carborundum Corporation, Alice devoted every minute of every day in taking extraordinary care of her five children. She relished caring for God's gifts to her.

It was amazing to see this fun-loving, mischievous young girl transition from what she had gravitated toward her whole life—cars, tools, footballs, marbles, guns, and knives—to a 24/7 domestic existence. Now rough and tumble Alice was cuddling with a newborn baby, changing diapers, preparing meals, etc. A seamless transition for multi-talented Al Marie. Without a doubt, she became a truly fantastic mother. Alice alone was solely responsible, day in and day out, morning, noon and night—single handedly, for bringing up our five children to be fine and respectable adults. She instructed them in every aspect of life and she did it with kindness, firmness, and most of all, with unrequited maternal love!

A DAY UNLIKE ANY OTHER DAY: MOTHER'S DAY 1970

On Mother's Day in May 1970, Alice's first Mother's Day as a mother, her brother-in-law Emil Masi hosted a Mother's Day Brunch at the Masi home in West Springfield. It was a great day. Alice, her sisters Betsy and Eleanor and their mother Alice Helen Haggerty, were the honored guests. Our nine-month-old daughter Katie joined the Masi and Harlow Families in the Mother's Day revelry.

In spite of the auspicious occasion, most male family members, including the Haggerty Family's most avid female hockey fan, Alice, were glued to the TV as the Boston Bruins played the Saint Louis Blues in the Stanley Cup Finals at the Boston Garden. Although I was interested in all Boston's sports teams, I was not, as was Alice, a hockey fanatic; I preferred to be in the Masi family's backyard playing baseball with the Harlow kids.

Yes, I missed seeing one of the most famous incidents in sports history; Bobby Orr "flying" famously through the air as he scored the Stanley-Cup-winning goal! After Bobby Orr received a pass from Derek Sanderson, a Needham resident residing a few streets from us, he snapped the puck into the net as he simultaneously "flew through the air." On Alice's first Mother's Day as a mother, she watched the most famous goal ever scored!

Later that day, Alice suggested, "Wouldn't it be nice if Katie had a little puppy?" I was somewhat surprised by Alice's suggestion, but the more I thought about having a puppy, the more I agreed. When I was a young boy, we always had a dog in our house.

Like everything else, Alice did extensive research and discovered that West Highland Terriers were particularly good with kids. Additionally, she had a plan and the plan was to convince me that it would be a piece of cake for me to train a little puppy. She would provide the food, place the leash near the door, and all I had to do was take the puppy for a short walk before I left for the office! I agreed, and within a few days, Shannon, a two-month old West Highland Terrier, was domiciled in our Falley Drive home.

In the summer of 1970, Alice's cousin, Georgie Haggerty, a captain on the City of Chicopee Police Department, called and invited us for a ride on a new boat he purchased and berthed in Essex, Connecticut. Alice, who loved boats, was thrilled. I was not particularly over-joyed. Alice was so excited, not only did she have an opportunity for a boat ride on the Connecticut River, but she could also show-off baby Katie.

Georgie Haggerty was a typical sailor, tough, determined and in his glory on the water. As I held Katie, Georgie Haggerty and his wife, also Alice Haggerty, navigated their boat down the Connecticut River to Long Island Sound. As we approached the mouth of the river at every toss and turn, lurch and heave, I was petrified. I was concerned the rough seas might whip Katie out of my arms into the depths of the river. Thankfully, my fears were unfounded; we returned safely to the berth in Essex!

Alice knew no fear; she had a fantastic time *cruising down the river.* Silently, I told myself this would be the last time Alice would convince me to abdicate terra-firma for a cruise. In 17,498 days, I made many such declarative statements; seldom were they enacted. Case in point; spending summers at Cape Cod empowered Alice to persuade me to, on occasion, to venture out onto the high sea.

PREPARATION IS ESSENTIAL

In the fall of 1970, with winter on the horizon, Alice wanted to fortify our home with sufficient firewood for a long winter. In accord with her organizational ability, she solicited quotes from several different foresters. Eventually, after considerable negotiations, Alice accepted the proposal to purchase a cord of firewood from Pitu, the proprietor of a South Hadley firewood company.

Even though Alice anticipated the birth of a second child in December, she was still overflowing with energy; she did not know how to relax or sit still, she was always in perpetual motion. Eight-months pregnant, with a one-year-old baby and a little puppy to occupy her time on a cold November day, she stacked an entire cord of firewood in our garage! Subsequent to stacking the firewood, she questioned whether she received a full cord of firewood. To satisfy her misgivings, she contacted the Commonwealth of Massachusetts' Bureau of Weights and Measurements (DWM).

Based on Alice's measurements—8 feet by 4 feet by 4 feet—the Bureau of Weights and Measurement confirmed she did not receive a full cord of firewood. Armed with official information, she was duly armed and fully loaded for combat! In a matter of minutes, she was on the phone contesting the firewood company. Within a day, Pitu returned with another truckload of firewood, which she also stacked! Alice was nobody's fool.

It was another victory for Alice. She was happy and she took a great deal of pleasure in stacking another cord of firewood. Between the first partial delivery and the subsequent supplemental delivery, eight-months-pregnant Alice stacked close to a cord and a half of firewood. She was happy!

On December 13, 1970, two weeks prior to the ETA (expected time of arrival) of our second child, Alice gave birth once again. In view of the early arrival, we had not thoroughly discussed potential names if it were a boy. I was leaning toward my father's name, Patrick Joseph. Alice, like my mother, was not particularly partial to the name Patrick so, when the baby was a girl, Alice seized the opportunity to resolve any future consideration of the name Patrick; she proposed naming the new baby Patricia Anne—the genesis of which I don't recall. In any event, now that we had a child named Patricia, the name Patrick would be forever mute.

We were thrilled when beautiful blonde Patricia Anne joined the Kennedy Family just in time to celebrate Christmas in 1970. Everyone in the Haggerty, Kennedy, Harlow, and Masi family rejoiced with our little baby Patti comfortably nestled in the Kennedy Family Cradle under our Christmas tree. Big sister Katie loved to rock our new baby in the Kennedy Family Cradle, purchased circa 1897 at the time of the birth of my paternal grandparent's first child, Mary Margaret (Mae) Kennedy.

On January 6, 1971, the Feast of the Epiphany, Father Francis M. Kennedy, in the presence of her godparents, Eleanor Haggerty Masi and John J. Hooben, baptized Patricia Anne at Saint Mary's Church in Westfield.

FINI TO WESTFIELD WINTER WEATHER

As the days grew longer and snow piles disappeared, signs of spring were beginning to germinate and, rock-salt corrosion on Alice's Mercedes was, once again, a springtime concern. Due to the lack of a protective under-coating on German-manufactured automobiles, rocker-panel corrosion was not an uncommon occurrence in New England.

In the first few years of our married life, I objected to three items Alice loved dearly: first, oriental rugs; then a Kirby vacuum cleaner; and now I was exasperated with the annual bodywork costs on her Mercedes 190-SL. After in-depth personal introspection, I opted to live with that annual rock-er-panel decadence and remain silent until our family expansion. I concluded it would behoove me more to embrace the love of Alice's life, her white 190-SL Mercedes convertible, than object to springtime autobody costs!

When the summer rolled along, it became all too obvious her car wouldn't accommodate the four of us, so she agreed to trade her 190-SL Mercedes sports car for a larger car. Not only did Alice willingly agree to trade-in her Mercedes, the both of us decided to discontinue our memberships at Shaker Farms Country Club so we could devote our leisure time to the kids.

Alice was all about ignoring her own desires, as is the case for many mothers. Her focus was exclusively on her children; their interests pre-empted her own interests. The prospect of trading her beloved 190-SL must have been exceedingly difficult for Alice, but she never batted an eye, as she knew it was for the betterment of her family—her primary focus.

Alice's parents suggested contacting Jimmy Muldoon, the son of their close friends, the Muldoon family, from Fairview Ave in Chicopee. Jimmy, who was a classmate of mine at Cathedral High School, recently accepted a sales position at Cartelli Motors on High Street in Holyoke, so we stopped by the dealership to see Jimmy Muldoon. In exchange for a Pontiac Firebird sedan, Jim allowed Alice $2,000 for her 190-SL. In retrospect, this proved to be another major mistake on my part. If only we put Alice's 190-SL on blocks; 40 years later the car would be valued at over $200,000!

The following year on January 13, 1972, Alice gave birth to our third daughter. We were now proud of our Irish triplet's—three children within three years. While recuperating in the maternity room, Alice suggested using/applying the middle names of her older sisters, Anne and Marie. Our first redheaded baby was baptized Anne Marie Kennedy by Father Francis M. Kennedy on February 9, 1972, at Saint Mary's Church in Westfield. The baptism was witnessed by godparents John Francis Burke and Elizabeth Haggerty Harlow.

As we prepared for life with our rapidly growing family, it was obvious that our ownership of the Pontiac Firebird was short lived; a compact car would not accommodate three children, strollers and toys, so we purchased our first Chevrolet station wagon.

ALL WORK AND ALL PLAY

Our next-door neighbors, Dick and Janice Butcher were parents of comparable-aged children, so it was a natural that Alice and Janice would become close friends. Janice's husband, Richard, was an employee of the Warren Teed Pharmaceutical Corporation and worked out of his Falley Drive home. Consequently, corporate packages were delivered to his Falley Drive address and deposited at his front door.

Although Richard was a fun-loving guy, he had an aversion to dogs; he was concerned that neighborhood dogs were attracted to his pharmaceutical packages. If a dog infiltrated his property and left a "deposit," he felt it was a capital offense.

At some point when Alice was shopping at a local novelty store, she noticed an authentic replica of dog feces and couldn't resist the urge; she purchased the imitation feces and awaited an opportune time to display her acquisition. Such an opportunity presented itself when the Warren Teed delivery man left several cardboard boxes of pharmaceuticals on Mr. Butcher's front stoop.

As soon as the delivery man departed, she sprang into action. With the fake dog feces in hand, she went to the Butcher house stoop and strategically placed the imitation dog feces on top of one of the Warren Teed cartons and returned home to watch for Mr. Butcher's reaction when he picked up the delivery.

Later in the afternoon, Richard and Janice arrived home with Janice's parents in the back seat of his car. As all four exited the car and approached the front door, Richard spotted the "dog feces" on top of a Warren Teed carton, and he went ballistic; he was absolutely livid!

As Janice and her parents watched in horror, Mr. Butcher's fury reached unbridled ferociousness. With venom spewing, he picked up the Warren Teed carton and stormed across the street to the Clemens' house, who had a dog that he considered to be the guilty party. While this scene was playing out, Alice was watching from the secure confines of our dining room.

After arriving at Clemens front door with the purported dog feces prominently deposited on top of the Warren Teed carton, Richard belligerently snapped the carton so the feces would land on Mrs. Clemens' doorstep; unexpectedly, the purported dog feces bounced!

Bewilderedly, Richard yelled across the street to Janice, "Jan, the damn thing is a fake." As Mr. Butcher sheepishly proceeded back across the street to his house, he shouted, "Alice Kennedy must have done this!" At that point, Alice came out from behind the dining room curtains to share in the hilarity. Alice's keen sense of humor was a known commodity to everyone who knew her, especially Falley Drive neighbors.

ACQUISITIONS KEEP COMING

In spite of Alice's full-time maternal responsibilities, she was always thinking, always ahead of the proverbial curve. As summer approached, she decided it was time to introduce Katie, Patti, and Anne Marie to the world of sand and salt-water, and she suggested purchasing a summer cottage on Cape Cod. The plan was to acquire a small cottage that would provide rental income and, if not rented, a vacation for the five of us. In November of 1972, we bought a small cottage on Ferncliff Road in Dennisport, Mass!

As 1972 drew to a close, Alice and I agreed: 1972 was a good year for the Kennedys of Westfield. It was not only a good year it was *a special year!* Within 12 months, we were blessed with another baby, we acquired a new car and, we purchased a Cape Cod cottage. Alice and I aptly described 1972 as the; "Kid, Kar, and Kape year."

In 1973 we took a break, it wasn't until 1974 that Alice and I visited the Providence Hospital maternity floor for another Kennedy Family Blessing. In discussing possible names, I suggested we consider, for a girl, Eileen—my mother's name—and she didn't object. In the event it was a boy, I continued to opt for Kevin Michael, a name that had been on top of the boy-list since 1969.

On the afternoon of January 16, as the nurse wheeled the baby basket from the maternity ward into the waiting room, I was oblivious to the *blue and white blanket* as the nurse said, "Mr. Kennedy, this is you new son." Although I was accustomed to hearing, "Mr. Kennedy this is your new daughter," my reaction was no different when I heard "this is your new son." I was simply relieved the baby was born and Alice's ordeal was over.

When I was permitted to visit Alice in the recovery room, amid my customary tears, Alice said, "What's wrong? Is the baby all right?"

I explained, "Yes, the baby is fine; don't be concerned. I'm just relieved the delivery is over and you are all right. I just saw Kevin Michael and he looks great."

Immediately, she retorted, "No, he is not "Kevin Michael," he will be named after his father, Daniel Joseph." I truly planned on the name Kevin Michael, but in truth, I didn't offer much opposition to Alice's maternity room pronouncement.

Prior to Danny's anticipated winter arrival, Alice arranged to engage a highly recommended, retired woman, Mrs. Pignatare, to watch the kids during the day while she was recovering in the hospital. Mrs. Pignatare, a mother of several adult children and a retired schoolteacher, came highly recommended by several of Alice's friends. The plan was for me to stay home until the kids boarded the school bus in the morning and Mrs. Pignatare would be on sight when the school bus dropped the kids off at 3:00 p.m. I would relieve her at 6:00 p.m.

The first day Mrs. Pignatare was on duty, the kids were seated at the kitchen table devouring their afternoon snacks, while Mrs. Pignatare opened the sliding glass door in the den to hook Shannon to his backyard leash. As soon as Mrs. Pignatare left to hook-up Shannon, one of our three lovelies decided it would be a good idea to lock the door behind her!

On a cold winter day, in the middle of January, elderly and coatless Mrs. Pignatare was locked out of the house. Desperately, she pleaded with the lovelies to unlock the door, but they thought it hysterical as they stood inside and laughed and laughed. Without a coat or boots, the frightened elderly woman trudged through a foot of snow to Janice Butcher's house and pleaded with her for help. The lovelies were petrified when they heard Mrs. Butcher pounding on our front door as a shivering Mrs. Pignatare stood sheepishly at her side; yes, they finally opened the door! We learned at that moment that the Kennedy children were indeed Alice's offspring. Thankfully, Mrs. Pignatare did not experience similar disobedience during the next few days.

On January 19, Alice brought her newborn son into our Falley Drive home and, as she did with her three daughters, she immediately placed baby Danny in the Kennedy Family Cradle as she sang the well-known lullaby; "Rock-a-bye Baby, on the tree top; when the wind blows the cradle will rock..."

On February 17, 1974, at Saint Mary's Church, the 6th Anniversary of our Marriage, in the presence of our new babies' godparents, William Golden and Brenda Harlow, Daniel Joseph Kennedy was gifted with the Sacrament of Baptism, administered by Father Francis M. Kennedy. At the conclusion of the baptism, as was our baptismal day custom, the entire family returned to our Falley Drive home where Father Francis M. Kennedy, assisted by altar server John Hooben, celebrated a Mass of Thanksgiving for the gift of Daniel Joseph, who was destined to share in the priesthood of Jesus Christ. During the subsequent happy repartee, everyone had an opportunity to rock Daniel Joseph in the historic Kennedy Family Cradle.

Danny, like his sisters Katie, Patti, and Anne Marie before him, spent his first day in our Falley Drive home sleeping comfortably in the Kennedy Family Cradle while his father, mother, sister and maternal grandfather observed.

RESOURCEFULNESS RUNS IN THE FAMILY

In the summer 1974, the General Accident Springfield branch office lease with Alfred Bettigole Realty Trust at 333 Maple Street was due to expire.

With a dual interest in mind, I recommended to our home office executives that we consider relocating, at a considerably lower per square foot rate, to West Springfield, MA. Most importantly, the West Springfield location was much closer to Westfield, and, in the event of an emergency I was within minutes of Falley Drive.

I didn't have to expend much energy in persuading my boss, Charlie Niles; he was enamored with the prospect of a considerable rate reduction. In October of 1974, the Springfield branch of the General Accident Insurance Company relocated from Maple Street in Springfield to Park Ave in West Springfield. Although I didn't realize it at the time, the proximity to a Catholic chapel for a noontime Mass, which I customarily attended, unfortunately was not offered in the proximity of the West Springfield location.

MARITAL BLISS NECESSITATES INNOVATIVE STRATEGY

A gentle answer turns away wrath. (Proverbs 15:1)

As our family continued to expand, my primary concern was to be available as much as possible to provide support for Alice. Actually, her instinctive and God-given abilities rendered my assistance superfluous, but nonetheless during the week (and always on weekends) I occasionally devised places to take the kids so Alice's weekends would be free. I also realized Alice's feisty disposition warranted an outlet for her to blow off steam. My strategy was to point out opportunities for Alice to expend her intensity, preferably on a cause unrelated to me.

It wasn't long before I discovered an ideal opportunity for Alice to release her tremendous energy was in area of academia; the Church of Atonement Nursery School, the Westfield School System, and Saint Mary's School were prime venues. Alice was no shrinking violet and she certainly didn't need any prodding from me. However, I thought subtle suggestions might *"prime the pump."*

If an incident of any sort occurred at school, I urged her to express indignation over what appeared to be an overreaction to a baseball that came crashing through her window. If an incident with a neighbor developed, I urged her express surprise and indignation with a neighbor's over-reaction, even if it be a baseball crashing through the window. I admit it wasn't necessary for me to sell this concept to a strident and self-confident Alice, but I didn't think encouragement would hurt.

It was not unusual for Alice to recount these *discussions,* or as some might call them, *confrontations*, with me, which was also a supplemental outlet to expend pent-up energy. Often after she made known her point of view, she made a new friend. A win-win—problem resolved—new friend acquired, and excess energy expended. With the added bonus, Alice was enervated and much too exhausted to engage me in combat!

Alice's feisty disposition was that of a *maternal warrior,* one that was always ready, willing and able to fight for her children. Her feistiness epitomized inherent self-confidence and in no way was pugnaciousness; she is probably more aptly described as courageous. Her self-confidence emanated from, and was perpetuated by, an in-depth and thorough knowledge of almost every topic. Though Alice was self-confident and spoke her mind, she was never brash nor rude nor garrulous; she was concise, candid, and most of all, genuinely convincing.

Intense preparation provided Alice with persuasive proposals that enabled her to present arguments worthy of an accomplished attorney, reflective of irrefutable logic. Any defense in opposition to Alice's logical and well-prepared propositions were generally rejected; inevitably, her perspective prevailed.

If a problem presented itself at school, Alice was there. If the kids demonstrated unacceptable behavior in the neighborhood requiring remedial action, Alice offered an appropriate punishment. If injuries occurred, she was readily equipped with her omnipresent yellow bag. The yellow bag was a depository of every medication prescribed by pediatricians and/or primary care doctors since the birth of our daughter Katie. Never did Alice venture far without her yellow bag in tow. For years and years, she continued to dispense long-expired, hoarded prescription bottles, medicating anyone and everyone in need of first-aid.

To my knowledge, Alice never documented the various illnesses of the kids nor the medication prescribed to remedy the malady. All that data was retained in her reservoir of recollections. She knew instantaneously who had which illnesses and what medications had been prescribed. All medications, and I mean *all medications*, were preserved in her ever-present yellow bag. In a sense, she was comparable to the Presidential aide who accompanies the President of the United States carrying the emergency satchel, a.k.a. nuclear football, which is available to the President of the United States 24/7!

It would fallacious to conclude that Alice was practicing medicine—she was not. She was, however, cognizant of vital signs indicating medical conditions and the medications that had previously been prescribed for them. On more than one occasion, in public, Alice approached the mother of the whaling infant, suggesting that she have the baby's ears checked by the pediatrician because Alice recognized the abhorrent cry as an indication of an ear infection. She was attuned to the excruciating cry because our kids incurred middle ear infections, which required the insertion of a stent in the baby's ear canal in order to relieve pressure. Alice's medical bailiwick of solutions doesn't adequately portray her ability to provide solutions for a multitude of issues.

Alice was uniquely observant. She could anticipate problems; her mind was always operating at top speed, and generally for the betterment of others. One day, after a Saint Mary's Parent Teacher Organization (PTO) meeting, Alice offered to give Tom and Connie Lane a ride home; as the

Lanes were exiting her car, Alice inquired, "Does water leak through your upstairs bedroom window?" Both Tom and Connie were flabbergasted with her remark, as they replied in unison, "Yes, how did you know?" Alice replied, "The upper portion of the storm window should be mounted on the outside track and not the inside track. Change the tracks and your water problem will be resolved."

Alice was so acutely aware of the needs of other people that her middle name should have been "observer." If so, her name would have been Alice O. Haggerty, (AOH) perhaps qualifying her to be a Charter Member of the Ancient Order of Hibernians! (Just joking.)

Not only was Alice adept at solving medical and mechanical problems, she was no slouch at solving mathematical problems. She not only could change the oil in her car, she could fix most any mechanical device that malfunctioned. Alice also was the person the kids went to with algebraic problems; not their father.

AS IF CARING FOR A GROWING FAMILY WASN'T OF SUFFICIENT CONCERN...

On a Friday in April 1975, while Alice was pregnant with our fifth child, she received some unsettling news from her primary care physician, Doctor William Hennessey. Dr. Hennessey detected an abnormal growth in Alice's thyroid, which he believed to be cancerous. Consequently, he scheduled an immediate thyroidectomy at the Providence Hospital.

We spent the weekend in complete disarray. Alice's parents were concerned, as were mine. My parents stopped for a visit on Sunday afternoon, and unexpectedly, received the troubling news. The prospect of such a serious medical issue was disturbing, and no one seemed to know how to cope with the dire news. As my parents commiserated with Alice in our family room, I paced aimlessly around our yard, in pensive silence.

Ultimately, when I did come in, my mother said, "Don't worry Danny, Alice just assured us not to worry because God is too good to leave Dan with four kids." I guess my faith wasn't as strong as Alice's because although her rationale made sense, I couldn't disregard the pessimistic concern Dr. Hennessey expressed.

On Tuesday, Alice and I took our customary route to Providence Hospital in Holyoke; the same route we had taken four times in the past five years to welcome the birth of our four children. This time, the car-ride was much more subdued. There was no joyful expectation. Instead, there was ominous silence.

As I brought Alice to the operating room, she assured me, "Don't worry Babe, I will be fine." I assured her that I would be praying. As soon as I left her, with a nurse by her side, I was off to the fifth-floor chapel at Providence Hospital, the same fifth floor chapel where I spent so much time awaiting the births of Katie, Patti, Anne Marie, and Danny.

At some point, I interrupted my time in the chapel and went downstairs for a cup of coffee. After a brief reprieve with a cup of coffee, I boarded the elevator for a return trip to the chapel when the elevator stopped at the 3rd Floor. The back door of the elevator opened, and a nurse wheeled in a gurney with a patient. I looked down and the patient said, "Hi" and I replied, "Hi." The nurse looked startled and queried if we knew each other, to which the patient said; "Yes, that's my husband." Calmly, while still in the elevator, with no outward appearance of emotion or demonstrative elation and in a matter-of-fact manner, as if there was never a doubt, Alice looked at me and said, "Dr. Hennessey told me I'm going to be fine, it's benign."

As the nurse took Alice to her room, I went to find Dr. Hennessey to verify that Alice wasn't under the influence of anesthesia. Thankfully, Dr. Hennessey affirmed what Alice told me!

My next stop was to the same telephone booth, where I previously placed telephone calls to Alice's parents and my parents after each of the kids were born. This time however the message was not "it's a girl" or "it's a boy." This time the message was, "it's BENIGN!" Deo Gratias!

Later I learned Alice's challenges did not end with the surgical procedure. While transferring Alice from the gurney to her hospital bed, the orderlies dropped Alice on the floor! Fortunately, she was only bruised and not injured. Thankful for the surgical results and thankful she wasn't injured when she fell, she didn't express any consternation or displeasure with the hospital staff. Her gratitude to God was consuming her every thought!

A few weeks later, another safety concern confronted Alice. Our backyard, which abutted the City of Springfield's Water Department's pipeline that transits water from Provin Mountain in Southwick to the City of Springfield, was another cause of alarm. As Alice was walking in the proximity of the pipeline, she heard a strange noise emanating from the ground; when she looked down, she saw a snake beginning to coil—a rattlesnake! Within a millisecond, she was practically in flight as she ran back to our house! After that encounter, we were much more cautious in allowing our kids to roam near the City of Springfield Water Department's pipeline.

AQUATIC ALICE

On an exceptionally hot Fourth of July, our Falley Drive neighbors Don and Jan Carrignan invited a seven-months-pregnant Alice and me to their home for a pool party. The Carrignans, parents of two young aquatic sons, recently installed a custom-made swimming pool with a depth at the diving board end of twelve-feet so their boys could perfect their diving skills.

Although I was not a swimmer, I recognized my issue with swimming: I couldn't get into a prone position! When I was in a prone position I could, in a sense, swim, thus the issue was being in a prone position. I theorized, by diving with the intent to land horizontally, I would be in a prone position, enabling me to swim the length of the pool. In theory, that seemed like a valid plan. In actuality, the plan was flawed!

Tentatively, I walked toward the end of the diving board, at which point I decided to flex my knees in order to determine the elasticity of the diving board, seemingly an intelligent tactic. Unfortunately, my anticipated euphoric entry into the beautiful blue water of the Carrignan's pool culminated in drastic vertical descent!

Within an instant of flexing my knees, the diving-board gave way under my weight as if it were a trapped door. In my attempt to test the flexibility of the board, it dipped and plummeted feet-first into, what I knew to be, twelve feet of water. As I rapidly descended, I was momentarily perplexed with the optical illusion of pool water rising. I quickly realized it was a critical situation, so I said a quick Hail Mary as I hurtled to the bottom of the twelve-foot pool.

The partygoers chuckled as they jocularly said, "Look, Dan is pretending he's drowning!" Immediately, Aquatic Alice, eight months pregnant, jumped from her lounge chair and ran toward the pool. As she prepared to dive in, she shouted, "he can't swim." At that point Don Carrignan restrained Alice and he and his two sons jumped in and rescued Dimwit Dan!

Alice's willingness to jump into the Carrignan's pool was, in a sense, redemptive. No longer could I good-naturedly needle her for her failed ploy in the waters of Doctor's Cove in Jamaica in 1968. She redeemed herself at the Carrignan pool in 1975.

DIVERSION FOR AN EXPECTANT MOTHER

In the middle of a July 1975 heat wave, I was fortunate to secure tickets at Fenway Park to a Boston Red Sox-New York Yankee baseball game. It seemed like old times, prior to the game, Alice and I dined at Jimmy's Harborside. Games against the Yankees were in high demand, so our seats were not as desirable as in previous years. We were in proximity to the Red Sox dugout, in section 14, but the seats were not as close to the field as in the past; they were in the last row!

Not only did expectant Alice have to walk up 25 or 30 steps to the last row of seats, the oppressive heat lodged between the roof and the last few rows. In the 2nd or 3rd inning, there was a violent thunderstorm, necessitating a rain delay. The storm seemed to intensify the humidity, yet Alice didn't complain; she sat in silence. In spite of the intense heat, she didn't want to spoil my day by prematurely leaving a Red Sox-Yankee game.

The night was reminiscent of Murphy's Law: anything that can go wrong will go wrong. When the rain abated and the game resumed, Yankee first baseman Joe Pepitone hit a grand-slam home run. Horror of horrors: first, climbing up numerous steps; second, sitting close to the roof, which trapped the oppressive heat; then the rain; and when the game resumed, the Sox were trailing 4-0, and it was just the 3rd inning!

Poor Alice, she must have thought I was some sort of sadist. Six years ago, I took a seven-months-pregnant woman to suffer through a brutal heat wave in the state of Maine, and now I brought an eight-months-pregnant woman to Boston, compelling her to climb an enormous number of steps just to endure hot and humid Fenway Park.

After Pepitone's 3rd inning home run, Alice didn't put up much resistance when, once again, I suggested we depart Fenway Park and head back to Westfield in our air-conditioned car.

A few weeks later, on August 16, 1975, Alice gave birth to our second son. At this point, I had abandoned my interest in naming a boy Kevin Michael. Alice and I agreed beforehand that if the baby was a boy, we would name him after my deceased brother John (Jackie) Kennedy, who died at nine months of age. Alice liked the name Francis, so our new born became John Francis Kennedy. The more I pondered, the more I realized that the name "Joseph" was the middle name of Alice's father and her parental grandfather, and it was the middle name of my father and paternal grandfather. Consequently, our newborn received two middle names: Francis and Joseph. When Alice brought John Francis Joseph Kennedy—a.k.a. Jackie—to Penacook Street for the first time, with tears in his eyes, my father said, "Thank you Alice for giving us back our "Jackie."

On September 8, 1975, at St. Mary's Church in Westfield, Father Francis M. Kennedy baptized our new baby boy, John Francis Joseph Kennedy, as witnessed by godparents Jeff Harlow and Lisa Golden. Five children, the oldest six years, the youngest a newborn baby, was aa foreboding challenge for a young mother. But multi-gifted Alice was more than equal to the task. In every respect, she epitomized what a mother is created to be. She was simply, THE BEST!

After the birth of every baby, while Alice and the new baby were becoming acquainted in Providence Hospital, I brought her a Waterford Crystal Glass to commemorate the birth of the new baby. Alice was almost as delighted with her fifth Lismore Waterford Crystal Glass as she was with Jackie, the fifth player on the Kennedy Family Basketball Team—a.k.a. the Kennedy Family Caboose!

As usual, Patti was an indispensable asset for Alice, she was constantly at Alice's side, rendering constant care for Baby Jackie, just as she so capably helped in caring for newborn Baby Danny. For the first few months of the fall, Alice's sisters and her Shaker Farms golfing friend, Mary Touhey, were available to help.

When Alice recovered her strength, Mary Touhey would pick her up on weekends for a round of golf on Sundays at Shaker Farms. One Sunday, Anne Marie, who was three or four years old at the time, wasn't particularly pleased when she saw Mary arrive to take her mother away. Anne Marie did not conceal her redheaded spirit. Emphatically, she said, "You can't come in this house. I don't want you to take my mother to play golf; I want her to stay here with me!" Attempting to placate her distraught daughter,

Alice responded, "It's all right Anne Marie, I will be back soon. Don't worry, Daddy will stay here with you." Anne Marie was temporarily appeased, but it was a long day as Anne Marie endlessly lamented, "I want my Mommy."

On another golfing occasion, in order to alleviate Anne Marie's concern, Alice said, "Daddy loves to play golf too. I met Daddy playing golf." At that point, pensive Anne Marie said, "Were you wearing your Wedding Gown when you met Daddy?" I'm certain Alice compassionately clarified that misconception, but realizing the mischievousness of Anne Marie's mother, she may well have considered saying, "Along with the rest of my prized possessions—jumper cables, engine oil, and a foreign car toolbox—my wedding gown was always secure in the trunk of my car."

FENWAY PARK; ALWAYS AN INTEGRAL PART OF THE KENNEDY WORLD

In October 1975, the Boston Red Sox won the American League Pennant for the first time since 1967 and were going to play the Cincinnati Reds. I was still remorseful about failing to produce World Series tickets in 1967; eight years later I felt obligated to redeem myself. Fortunately, I was able to obtain two tickets to the 1975 World Series between the Boston Red Sox and the Cincinnati Reds.

Alice was thrilled as she planned our excursion to Boston and the 1975 World Series. Unfortunately, once again, an intervening force thwarted our plans. Alice came down with pneumonia and was bedridden for several days. Although she seemed to be on the road to recovery on Sunday—the day of the game—she conceded she was not strong enough to attend the game. Alice seemed to accept the fact that she was unable to attend, but I was deeply disappointed—my attempted redemption was thwarted. My father was Alice's substitute!

Once Alice recuperated from pneumonia, she was back in her full-speed-ahead mode; devoting considerable time to Saint Mary's Parent Teacher Association, managing the Monthly Raffle, and preparing for Thanksgiving Liturgy.

IMAGINATIVE AND COMPASSIONATE

For the first time in my recollection, Alice expressed interest in a Christmas Present—a present for both of us. Alice persuaded me to purchase two large, three-feet-high Waterford Crystal Lamps for our living room end tables. The underlying motive of her request was not so much of herself in mind as it was the kids; they were always first and foremost in her mind.

Alice knew of a woman in Northampton, Helen Woods, who personalized custom-made lampshades and would embroider green shamrocks and the names of all five Kennedy Kids on lampshades. Though years have faded the artistic work of Helen Woods, the lamps are treasured by our children.

GOOD, BUT NOT QUITE PERFECT

While it is absolutely true that Alice manifested kindness and goodness, let the record read loud and clear: She wasn't perfect! Her goodness and her love for other people was obvious, but her proclivity to misappropriate napkins, towels or shawls—not as obvious.

Whenever we visited a restaurant, the hostess counting napkins at the end of the evening would likely find that there was a shortage. Somehow the missing napkins always seemed to find their way into Alice's pocketbook! Whatever hotel we may have visited, a towel from that hotel would subsequently appear in our bathroom!

When we entertained guests for dinner, there was a plethora of napkins to choose from. For Christmas dinners, she displayed red linen napkins;

Easter Sunday dinners, purple linen napkins; Saint Patrick's Day dinners, green linen napkins; and in the summer, nautical blue linen napkins. Although Alice was perfect in so many respects—first and foremost she was a human being, and she was...let's say susceptible to...misappropriating linen napkins!

A few months after Alice's entry into Eternal Life, on the thirteenth of January 2016, as I was going through some of Alice's personal belongings, I came across an old pocketbook of hers. Much to my surprise (I should not have been surprised) amongst her cosmetic items I discovered several rolled-up linen napkins; they were, obviously, larcenous acquisitions procured from an unsuspecting restaurateur!

Once again, in the fall of 1976, Alice and I were entertaining Scots. The General Attorney of the General Accident Board in Perth, Scotland, Angus MacDonald, visited us for the weekend. We arranged accommodations for Mr. MacDonald to stay at the Bay State Marriott Hotel in Springfield during his weekend in western Massachusetts.

On Saturday, Alice remained home with the kids, while I escorted Mr. MacDonald on a tour of the Berkshire Hills. I thought he would enjoy viewing typical New England College towns, so Amherst and Williamstown were on the agenda. The renowned Williams College Museum was of particular interest to Mr. MacDonald.

On Sunday, Gram, Pop, and Judy took the kids, and as we did with all our Scottish visitors, Alice and I drove Mr. MacDonald to see Plymouth Rock, Mayflower II, and then to Cape Cod to see the Cranberry bogs. Probably not a "politically correct" venue for someone from the Britain, but Mr. MacDonald was—as were all the Scotsmen—a truly wonderful guest; he accepted our sight-seeing tour as not only historical and educational, but he also thought it particularly appropriate during America's Bicentennial year.

When we returned home from our trip to the Cape, we, as they would say in the U.K., "gathered-up the young ones," and "regal" Mr. MacDonald played with kids on our living room floor. He seemed totally relaxed and quite at home, as change dropped out of his pants pockets while he was doing hand-stands on Alice's Kazvin rug. On Monday morning, I drove Mr. MacDonald to the Acadia Golf Club in Passaic, New Jersey for a luncheon with agents in the state of New Jersey.

EPITOME OF SECURITY: THE WHIP CITY

Alice and I, as well as our children, were comfortably settled in Westfield. If, however, the Springfield branch office continued to grow and prosper, the possibility of a transfer was undoubtedly a distinct possibility. A transfer would be remuneratively rewarding, an upward trajectory, however our permanency in Westfield would be compromised. Alice and I were well aware that ownership of an independent insurance agency would accomplish both objectives. Although I was pleased with career path opportunities with General Accident, I was not unaware of the potential earning power in owning an insurance agency.

Coincidently, two of the independent agencies—one in the West Springfield and the other in Westfield—asked me to consider acquiring their businesses. Phil Haley, of the Haley Agency in West Springfield, and Ray Bartlett, of the Bartlett Agency in Westfield, discussed the prospects of buying their businesses. With a young family, the prospect of owning a thriving insurance business in own community was certainly enticing.

Initially, Alice, with her business acumen, believed climbing the corporate ladder would provide more long-term opportunities than acquiring an agency. After much soul searching, we decided to pass on an agency acquisition opportunity and remain on the company side of the insurance Industry ledger. Perhaps, with Alice's Scottish heritage, she was fascinated with entertaining "Highlanders" with future expectations of an all-expense paid trip to Loch Loman Land. *Work willingly at whatever you do. (Colossians 3:23)*

In Alice's mind, owing a home precipitated preventive maintenance! Alice was so observant she anticipated every imaginable need. As for me? I was oblivious. Alice? she had an uncanny ability to identify any and all potential problems.

Alice was tactful in bringing these matters to my attention. She never phrased her observations with mandates. She merely pointed out that a certain situation needed attention. At various times, she would mention, "The hatchway needs painting. The toilet isn't flushing properly. The light socket in the lamp is loose, or the front door needs to be planed." My indifferent reaction was an indication of my unfamiliarity and insensitivity to, what were to Alice, significant issues. Oftentimes, I replied; "You didn't marry a painter," or "you didn't marry a plumber," or "you didn't marry an electrician," or "you didn't marry a carpenter."

Eventually, in a tone of exasperation in response to my noncompliant responses, she said, "Whom did I marry?"

I recanted, "You married a good-for-nothing, know nothing, mechanically illiterate husband."

Not to be deterred, Alice responded, "First of all, that may be true, but that's going to change, and second of all, there's nothing you can't do if you put your mind to it!"

My father was correct when he said, "Alice will be good for you." He must have included my mechanical malaise in that assessment.

It wasn't long before Alice handed me her monthly copy of Handy Andy Magazine, as she pointed to an article on painting houses, saying; "If you can read, you can paint; the house needs to be painted."

I replied, "You are probably right, the house "might" need painting but, I don't do painting, I detest painting!"

Surprise, surprise. A week later, I was on the top rung of an extension ladder, painting our house!

When the painting project was finally completed, Alice was delighted! She commended me on my efforts, "Great job Dan, I knew you could do it; you exceeded my expectations. Aren't you proud of yourself?"

I replied, "Relieved would be a more descriptive term."

Without stopping to draw a breath, she proceeded to say, "I really think a porch in the back of house would be great; it would enable all of us to gather in a cool breezy environment during the hot summer months." I certainly detected the underlying message; Alice's inferential intonation was unmistakable; she was about to declare another "Project Dan."

No question, Alice anticipated my less-than-ecstatic expression, as might be expected she was armed with supporting documentation—Handy Andy Magazine!

Pointing to an article entitled, "Constructing a Sun porch in Seven Easy Lessons," she said, "We have already established you know how to read." My mouth literally dropped at the concept of building a sun-porch.

She added, "This project will be a piece of cake for someone who reads as well as you!"

My rhetorical retort, "Why don't you cancel that subscription?" fell on deaf ears.

Before I knew what hit me, I was at the B.D. Nims Lumber Yard in West Springfield purchasing material in order to attach a 14' x 20' gabled roof to the rear of our gabled garage roof. One month later, the sun-porch project was complete and, most importantly, Alice was pleased with my *reading ability.*

To personalize the Kennedy Family sun-porch, I cemented a 1964 John F. Kennedy half-dollar into the center of the sun porch floor. As a skillful manager, Alice encouraged me to take pride in my accomplishments with the resultant effect that I would be more enthusiastic when presented with future household projects. Yes, I was proud of the workmanship and more compliant when Alice proposed future projects.

After our subsequent relocation to an older home in Needham, Assertive Alice and her adjunct professor, Handy Andy, discovered many more "projects" for me.

DECISIONS, DECISIONS, DECISIONS

In 1979 there was light at the end of the tunnel for Alice. She finally had a few hours of well-deserved free time. Katie, Patti, Anne Marie and Danny were enrolled at Saint Mary's School and Jackie was attending a pre-kindergarten program. What did she do with her free time? What would she do with her unlimited energy? She became an active member in the Saint Mary's School Parent Teacher Association so, in a sense, she too was "busy at school!"

Alice was thrilled when, in June, her sister Eleanor and brother-in-law Emil asked Alice and me to become godparents for their newborn daughter, Meghan Maureen Masi. Shortly after Meghan's birth on June 25th, I received an invitation to visit our General Accident home office in Philadelphia and meet with Jim Corcoran, the newly appointed chief executive officer.

At the meeting, Jim explained, "Serious consideration is being given to merging both Massachusetts branch offices (Boston and Springfield) into a *super-branch office,* which would be situated west of Boston and east of Springfield. It is also our hope you will amalgamate this merger in the capacity of regional vice-president. I was delighted that a prospective relocation would allow us to remain in the Commonwealth of Massachusetts and not require an out-of-state relocation. I couldn't wait to inform Alice of the possibility we would become Bostonians.

When I returned home and informed Alice, she too was thrilled with the prospect. As would be expected, she was like an unleashed bloodhound;

she immediately went in search of a town that would be a good fit for our five school-age children.

I too went on a fact-finding mission to determine the most advantageous and accessible location for the super-branch office. It wasn't long before reconnaissance revealed that, with the majority of our agency force domiciled in eastern Massachusetts, Framingham would be the preferential location. Jim concurred.

On the next reconnaissance mission, Alice accompanied me as we perused homes in the Wellesley, Needham, and Sherborn areas. Both of us agreed that a home on Amherst Road in Wellesley would be a suitable location; unfortunately, it was not meant to be.

CELEBRATING A GOLDEN ANNIVERSARY

In the summer of 1979, George Pumphret, the retired Boston branch manager, a Massachusetts insurance legend, and his wife Mildred, celebrated their 50th Wedding Anniversary at the elegant Statler Hotel on Park Square in Boston. Alice and I were among the invited guests, as were Jim and Rosemary Corcoran, Frank and Eleanor Tierney, and Bill and Helen Toner, all close friends of the Pumphrets.

At the anniversary reception, Alice mentioned to Jim that we were excited about the prospects of amalgamating the two Massachusetts Branch offices and relocating our family to eastern Massachusetts. Jim's response was surprising and somewhat disconcerting. "Yes, it would be an ambitious undertaking, "if it ever happens."

Alice was perplexed by Jim's remark, and when she informed me of his remark, I too was mystified. My suspicion was that the executives in Perth (Scotland) perceived the proposal to be too costly; after all, Scottish executives were Scottish! Two weeks later, I received a phone call from Jim Corcoran informing me that the super-branch proposal was temporarily suspended. Alice and I were definitely disappointed, yet in a sense relieved—relieved in that we wouldn't derail our family's comfort zone.

CHAPTER 4

"THE BELLS OF SAINT MARY'S"

A faithful friend is a sturdy shelter; he who finds
one finds a treasure. (Sirach 6:14-17)

While I am not absolutely certain of the time frame, at some point, Alice became aware that the husband of an elderly Saint Mary's parishioner, Mary Quirk, passed away and was without a means of transportation. Alice introduced herself to Mrs. Quirk, gave her our telephone number, and suggested whenever she needed a ride, she should call Alice.

Mrs. Quirk did call Alice, and for several years Alice transported Mary Quirk to Sunday Mass, the supermarket, and doctor's appointments. Mary was grateful for Alice's friendship, and Alice was always delighted whenever Mary called for a ride. It was a win-win for both Mary and Alice.

Alice also befriended Rita (Burke) Pearce, an elderly widow, also in need of transportation. Coincidentally, Rita was my mother's first cousin, so, in this instance, Alice's Good Samaritan kindnesses could be depicted as "All in the Family." In befriending others, Alice transmitted to her children, the importance of dispersing kindness and solicitousness.

As both mother and friend, Alice continually demonstrated that goodness conveys kindness, kindness precipitates smiles, smiles reflect gratitude, and gratitude connotes love. Love that is a divine gift is infectious when shared with others.

"TIME FOR YOU TO BECOME MORE ACTIVE AT SAINT MARY'S, DAN"

Alice's voice reverberated over and over until she finally convinced me to allow her to place my name on the ballot for a seat on the Saint Mary's Parish Council. Although I was not well known in such a parochial parish, at the June meeting I was, shockingly, nominated and subsequently elected chairman of the Saint Mary's Parish Council for a two-year term. The parish council recessed during the summer months, so my duties wouldn't commence until the fall.

In September, Saint Mary's longtime pastor, Msgr. George Shea, passed away unexpectedly and was replaced by Father Anthony (Tony) Creane. Alice explained to me that as Chairman of the Parish Council, it was my obligation to invite the new pastor, Father Creane, to our home for dinner. It was typical of Alice; she was always cognizant of helping others.

Father Tony not only visited us for an introductory dinner, in a short period he became an extremely close friend. He loved sports, especially golf; as soon as spring arrived the two of us were often seen on the links of the Springfield Country Club. Father Tony became a frequent visitor to our home on Falley Drive. Number 296 Falley Drive became Father Tony's home away from home. Whenever parish responsibilities seemed to be all encompassing, Father Tony would appear at our door unannounced. He felt comfortable relaxing with Alice and me, and we became lifelong friends.

Our kids grew up knowing the Pastor of Saint Mary's Church was a friend of their mother and father, and by virtue of that friendship, a friend of theirs. I feel certain Father Tony's love for the priesthood, his obvious love for people, as well as his intense interest in sports played a role in

Danny's youthful impressions of a priest. When Father Tony and I were in the backyard practicing chip shots, five-year old Danny's nose was eagerly pressed against the window. Twenty-eight years later, Father Tony Creane was delighted to attend the First Mass of Thanksgiving in Needham, Mass. celebrated by that, once-upon-a-time, five-year-old boy from Falley Drive in Westfield—Father Daniel J. Kennedy.

It was always a Christmas delight to attend Saint Mary's Annual Christmas Pageant! The festive evening always concluded with the entire student body and audience standing while singing, "The Bells of Saint Mary's, we hear they are calling...."

Saint Patrick's Day celebrations at Saint Mary's were also special occasions. The Parochial Vicars were the highlights. Father David Joyce sang the traditional Irish favorite "Danny Boy" and Father Francis Reilly sang and played his guitar. Father Reilly urged Alice to allow our kids to sing "Hello Patsy Fagan."

Initially, Alice was apprehensive because our kids hadn't displayed any musical talent and they were more pugilistic than artistic, with the exception of Katie singing Black Velvet Band. Thankfully, Father Reilly's perspective prevailed, and the five Kennedy Kids' premiere performance was a huge success. The thrill of a lifetime for Alice!

The frosting on the cake was Jackie strumming a kid's guitar as the five Kennedy Kids belted out the melody! The following morning, on the front page of the Westfield Advertiser was a prominently displayed picture of Jackie Kennedy playing a guitar at Saint Mary's Annual Saint Patrick's Day Celebration!

"Alice's face beamed with joy as she watched, proudly, while Katie, Patti, Anne Marie, Danny, and Jackie sang at the Saint Mary's School's Saint Patrick's Day celebration," recalled John Hooben, the first of my friends to meet Alice Marie Haggerty.

Christmas pageants were exciting occasions at Saint Mary's School in Westfield. Each year there were various pageant parts to play for every child: angels, shepherds, wise men, and innkeepers. Alice was intimately involved assisting the teachers as they prepared students for this happy occasion.

As soon as the Christmas season concluded and classes re-convened, it was time for Alice to shift gears. Alice was the principal organizer of Saint Mary's Annual Super Bowl fundraiser, selling grinders (submarine sandwiches) for Super Bowl Sunday. Alice's Super Bowl team was comprised of a determined parental sales force, spear-headed by the mothers and delivered by a strong paternal delivery team—a family enterprise that raised considerable capital for school projects.

Although there were no inside tracks to success, the student with the most grinder sales, and one who inherited her sales ability from her mother, was Grinder Queen of the Year, Katie Kennedy!

WET THEIR APPETITE (A DOSE OF COERCION MAY NOT HURT)

"They shall rise up and tell the story to their children." (Psalm 77)

Every Friday during Lent, Alice brought all five kids to the Lenten Devotions—Stations of the Cross. This family tradition was established and implemented by Alice; first at Saint Mary's in Westfield and it continued later at Saint Joseph's Parish in Needham. Alice was determined; all five of her children would grow to recognize the Way of The Cross, which is synonymous with Lenten Devotions. As she said, "I'm not preparing them to get into Harvard; I'm preparing them to get into Heaven."

In addition to the Stations of the Cross, after receiving First Holy Communion, Alice introduced each of them to First Friday Devotions. Christ promised to those who make nine consecutive First Friday Devotions, "My Sacred Heart will be their refuge in their final hour."

Thanks to Alice, on Fridays during Lent, the Kennedy Kids knew better than think of alternative plans; they were committed to the Stations of the Cross. Any other extra-curricular activity was secondary, and that applied to hockey or basketball practices and even homework assignments!

Deep is the wisdom of a mother's maternal heart!

"YOU BETTER NOT SHOUT, YOU BETTER NOT CRY..."

Alice was always thinking ahead, especially when it came to Christmas preparations. It wasn't unusual to hear her parental behavioral techniques during a moment of juvenile devilment. She often said, "Remember, Christmas is coming." She was also continually on the lookout for innovative Christmas decorations and, during our trips to the Cape she spent a good deal of time at The Christmas Tree Shop in Yarmouthport.

Part and parcel with her early interest in Christmas was the need for the kids to pose for our annual Christmas card picture. In order to assure the pictures would be developed well in advance of December, Alice wanted the kids to pose in late August or early September necessitating donning winter clothes in the heat of the summer. Wreaths, scarfs, and winter coats were mandatory to authenticate a "Christmas picture" setting.

While I manned the camera, Alice coerced the fighting Kennedy Five to "smile," which was not an easy task under the best of circumstances. But in winter clothes on a hot summer day, it was foreboding. Although there were moments of snarling and non-compliance with Alice's patience and perseverance, the kids endured the process and Christmas cards with pictures of the kids were printed.

In August, Patti, Jackie, Anne Marie, Danny and Katie are dressed
for winter as they pose for our annual Christmas card picture.

MOST WOMEN ARE BORN TO COOK; ALICE WASN'T ONE OF THEM

Alice was not the typical, "... out of my kitchen, I'm cooking..." homemaker.
She didn't begin her marital life with extensive cooking expertise. As was
typical of Alice, she was a quick learner and in short order she became a
good cook. Truth be known, she would prefer changing oil on a car than
frying eggs in the kitchen. Despite the fact that cooking was not her favorite
form of enjoyment, her homemade lasagna was fantastic and, of course, her
Christmas Eve Lobster Newburg was *delicious!*

When a cousin of mine and his bride from Annascaul County Kerry,
Ireland stopped to visit us in Westfield, Alice wanted them to experience
a flavor of "American" cuisine; she baked them a pan of lasagna! The Irish
Lad and Lassie were thrilled (at least they expressed excitement) as they
devoured Neapolitan cuisine in the home of Irish-American Yanks! (Alice

didn't think Italian food was on the bill of fare in Irish cottages on the west coast of Ireland.)

Katie, unlike her mother, loved to bake, and often asked for authorization to use the stove. Oftentimes, Alice would respond, "No baking today; *kitchen's closed.*" Katie responded, "Some women like to bake, and some women don't." Occasionally, Alice would relent and allow Katie to use the, heretofore, *closed kitchen.* Katie's admonition provided a long-lasting opportunity for family fun at the expense of Alice's aversion to culinarian obligations.

In 2014 at an Irish concert in West Roxbury, Mass., I was shocked, but pleased, to hear Katie's good friend Deirdre Reilly, a renown Irish singer, recall her memory of Alice. "When I was young, I always looked forward to visiting your home because Mrs. Kennedy always baked the most delicious butterscotch cookies," she said. At long last, when Alice was in the throes of a long-term illness, Deirdre dispelled Katie's damning declaration that Alice was among those women *who did not like to bake.*

Alice's unfortunate reputation of *not wanting to bake* was also repudiated as time went on, most significantly when Mr. Haggerty's health deteriorated. Every weekend, she baked a pan of bread-pudding for him, which included a generous portion of cinnamon and a taste of custard. Mr. Haggerty was delighted that his "machine-oriented" daughter became his "domesticated daughter."

ALICE'S RESTAURANT

In 1967, a twenty-year-old young man, Arlo Guthrie, wrote a song in recognition of his friend, Alice Black, who operated Alice's Restaurant in Stockbridge, Mass. The song became an over-night sensation and popularized the small-town restaurant adjacent to the studio of the famous Saturday Evening Post artist, Norman Rockwell. With Westfield only 40 miles from

Stockbridge, it wasn't long before an ALICE'S RESTAURANT ANNEX sign mysteriously appeared on the wall of our Falley Drive kitchen!

Although Alice would not rival Julia Childs, she was certainly adept at a few special menus of her own. In addition to her signature dish of lasagna, chicken casserole with provolone cheese was another of her specialties.

One of the more memorable dining experiences with General Accident executives dining on Falley Drive occurred in the fall of 1980, when Charlie L. Niles, President of General Accident, and his wife Mary (Murphy) Niles, were en route from Philadelphia, Pennsylvania to Burlington, Vermont to visit their daughter on Parents Weekend at Saint Michael's College. Alice prepared a delicious chicken casserole for our guests, who were invited to dine with the Rambunctious Kennedy Five. When Mr. Niles reached for his third helping of Alice's chicken casserole, Patti, devoid of Philadelphia High Society savoir-faire, reprimanded Mr. Niles for exceeding the family limit of one piece per person.

Charlie was not deterred. He anxiously filled his plate for the third time, and he commended Patti on her perspicacity and courage in publicly chastising him. Charlie was never known to be inhibited; he was noted for speaking his mind—a quality he admired in Patti.

BABYSITTERS: DIFFICULT TO FIND BUT AN ABSOLUTE NECESSITY

Since Katie was born on August 22, 1969, Alice's entire life revolved around her five children. There was absolutely nothing she wouldn't do for Katie, Patti, Anne Marie, Danny and Jackie. However, a break from the daily routine was therapeutic.

At arm's reach was Alice's ever-ready list of neighborhood babysitters, which included Theresa Nasser, Sally Glesner, Susan Andreski, the Johnson

Sisters and Sue Drummey. With five spirited Kennedy Kids, babysitting at the Kennedy house was not a walk on the beach.

Babysitting for the Kennedy Kids was succinctly summarized by Sue Drummey who, when asked how she liked babysitting for them, replied, "It's not babysitting, it's taming lions!" Sue didn't necessarily mean the kids were undisciplined; she meant handling five spirited, energetic kids within six years of each other was challenging.

CHRISTMAS EXCITEMENT

On Christmas Eve (day) 1980, Alice called me at the office to inform me Bishop Maguire called and invited our entire family to a televised Kid's Christmas Eve Mass at St. Michael's Cathedral. Before I could respond, she added, "I felt badly when I told him we wouldn't be available because we host a Family Christmas Eve gathering!" I was shocked Alice declined the Bishops invitation. "Your family is welcome to arrive as scheduled and we will be home shortly thereafter. How often does the Bishop of Springfield call and personally invite a family to Christmas Eve Mass? At my behest, Alice did call the bishop back and accepted his invitation."

As we were leaving for Christmas Eve Mass, Alice notified her sisters of our plans and, asked them to check on the Lobster Newburg, which she left simmering on the stove. The kids were excited to be at the Mass, especially since they would be on TV.

Bishop Maguire invited all kids present at the Mass to join him on the altar. Our kids were ready, willing and able, so they were the first to bounce up to the altar and proceeded to sit on the floor in the Sanctuary next to Bishop Maguire. Not only were the kids live on Channel 22, the following morning, Christmas Day, a picture of Bishop Maguire and the Kennedy Kids was on the front page of the Springfield Union!

The Kennedy Kids join Bishop Joseph F. Maguire at Saint
Michael's Cathedral for Christmas Eve Mass.

When we arrived home, most everyone was patiently waiting for our
arrival, unfortunately, just as Alice surmised, her mother was not a happy
camper. Mrs. Haggerty thought we should have rejected Bishop Maguire's
invitation and been home to welcome her relatives to Alice's annual Christmas
Eve celebration. Eventually, Mrs. Haggerty's consternation dissipated as

everyone reveled in the Christmas spirit; kids were gulping down pizza and excitedly ripping open Christmas presents. Joy, a.k.a. *bedlam* prevailed!

Unfortunately, the joyous atmosphere was short-lived when it was time for Alice to serve her Christmas Eve specialty; the Lobster Newburg had soured! Alice was heart-broken; she knew everyone would be disappointed, especially her mother. Betsy and Eleanor and their husbands understood there was no malice aforethought. The spoilage was an unintended consequence of the cooking process, and not in any way attributable to our presence at Bishop Maguire's Christmas Eve Mass. Mrs. Haggerty vehemently dissented.

She kept berating Alice, repeating over and over; "The Newburg spoiled because you went to the Christmas Eve Mass." I was not pleased to hear Mrs. Haggerty castigation of Alice, particularly when it was my idea to attend the Mass, not Alice's.

Mrs. Haggerty (center) with her three daughters Alice (left), Betsy (bottom center) and Eleanor (right) prior to learning the Lobster Newburg had spoiled on Christmas Eve, 1980.

As I stood near the kitchen stove, I was the one steaming, not the sour Lobster Newburg. Mrs. Haggerty's vitriolic castigation of Alice brought me to a boiling point, which only began to simmer after I heard Betsy's husband Lowell's reassuring voice. "Overlook it Dan, take it in stride, don't get upset," he said. Occasionally people are gifted with the ability to provide a calming influence in the midst of a chaotic moment. Thankfully, Lowell was one of those gifted recipients; he dispelled my discontent.

A month later, in North Adams, Massachusetts, as he was preparing for a typical day in the world of corporate sales, Lowell died of a sudden heart attack at age 42. The single most significant memory I have of Lowell Harlow was the common-sense advice he gave me on Christmas Eve, 1980.

WINTER RECREATION; FAMILY FUN

Confining five spirited kids within four walls during long and cold winters in the City of Westfield was becoming catastrophic and claustrophobic. In spite of the presence of several large trees in our Falley Drive backyard, I recouped our garden hose from winter hibernation and froze the backyard, hoping the kids would be enticed to develop an interest in winter sports, namely ice skating.

In spite of the abundance of tall trees scattered across our backyard, eventually we had an ice-covered terrain. Katie adapted quickly to the basic rudiments of ice skating and asked, "Can I take ice skating lessons? I want to be a figure skater like Dorothy Hamill." In short order, Katie was enrolled in a figure skating class at the Olympia Rink in West Springfield. After she acquired a few skating badges, Patti and Anne Marie expressed an interest in taking skating lessons and soon all three were practicing their Olympia Rink skating routines in our tree laden backyard. With his sisters as prime examples, Danny also donned skates—hockey skates and yes, Jackie was soon to follow.

Every day after school and every night after supper, especially if the snow was falling, Alice turned on the spotlight and all seven of us skated around the backyard rink amid falling snowflakes. There was, of course, the chance snowflakes would obscure the kids' vision as they skated slip-sliding through the sequoias, and come perilously close to colliding with the tall timbers.

Under the best of conditions, teaching young kids to skate is not without risk. Falling on the ice and, in our backyard, crashing into trees, was a probability. To provide balance, we equipped each of them with a hockey stick or a small wooden chair to develop basic skating techniques and skills to avoid the hazardous trees. Should Alice and I have been concerned they may have considered hockey sticks to be weapons? Yes! Fortunately, the sergeant-at-arms (Alice) ran a tight ship; no Kennedy blood was shed on our backyard rink!

Without the benefit of helmets, Alice instructed Anne Marie, Patti, Katie, Danny and Jackie in the basic rudiments of obstacle avoidance on our primitive backyard skating rink.

BUSINESS OBLIGATIONS AND FAMILY RESPONSIBILITIES

Regional General Accident meetings were most often held in Philadelphia, the New Jersey Shore or the Pocono Mountains in Pennsylvania — all within reasonable driving distance of Westfield, Mass. Rather than take a flight to the situs on a Sunday afternoon and fraternize with other attendees, I preferred to drive to the meeting on Monday mornings.

In my mind it was a win-win: it would lessen the number of evenings Alice would be alone with the kids' and I wouldn't have to spend time fraternizing with branch managers from other parts of the country on a Sunday afternoon. Did I really care about sipping cocktails and discussing insurance issues with Mike from Missoula, Montana or Ed from El Paso, Texas? Definitely NOT!

As would be expected, Alice, put my interest before her interest; she urged me to leave on Sunday like the other managers. She assured me, "We will be all right, and once you get there you will mingle and have a good time. Don't worry, I can handle the kids, go and have fun—FORCE YOURSELF!" I appreciated her willingness to wing it alone. So often and in so many ways, Alice's everlasting encouragement was my rock—she was simply THE BEST!

When Jim Corcoran was appointed CEO of General Accident Insurance Company in 1976, he was determined to apply his own imprint on the company, which was obvious when the annual managers meetings were held at more elegant resorts. He broadened the location from the customary stogy northeast resorts to Hilton Head, South Carolina, Sea Island, Georgia, Sawgrass Golf Club in Ponte Verdra, Florida, Indian Wells, California, El Conquistador Golf Club in Tucson, Arizona, and the Kapalua Golf Club in Maui, Hawaii.

Most importantly, wives would become fixtures at all future manager meetings...right up...Alice's Alley! In 1981, there would be an unusual treat: The Annual General Accident (GA) Manager's Meeting would be held out of the country at the Hamilton Princess Hotel in Bermuda. This would be Alice's first opportunity to associate with General Accident managers and their wives.

Before Alice and I departed for Philadelphia to rendezvous with other branch managers and home office executives, Alice engaged the services of two Sisters of Saint Joseph from Saint Mary's School to babysit our spirited progeny with the thought in mind the kids would be less apt to create a disturbance. Alice calculated that nuns from Saint Mary's would put the fear of God into the kids and they would less likely be a cause for concern.

When Jim Corcoran's wife Rosemary, the mother of seven children, learned Alice contracted with nuns to babysit, she thought Alice's ingenuity was absolutely BRILLIANT! In all the years Rosemary, the mother of seven kids, was in need of a babysitter she never thought of engaging the services of nuns. "Alice, you are absolutely amazing! You must have been vaccinated with a *resourcefulness needle*," said Rosemary. In short order, most of the guests at the arrival dinner learned quickly of Alice's innovative ability.

The bagpiper at the Hamilton Princess Hotel greets General Accident Insurance Company managers and wives; Jack O'Connor, Alice (Dan Kennedy's wife), Duffy O'Connor (Jack O'Connor's wife), Charles L. Niles, President of General Accident Insurance, Ralph Foster and his wife Clare.

Everyone enjoyed our stay in Bermuda, especially Alice. Formerly, when she was a member of Edgewood Country Club, she went on the club-sponsored winter golfing junket to Bermuda. Consequently, unlike most General Accident people, she knew her way around the island.

Alice was excited to go deep sea fishing but most of all, she was thrilled to ride Bermuda mopeds! She convinced me, and others, who were reticent about riding mopeds that we would enjoy the *moped experience*. "If you can ride a bicycle, you can ride a moped. You will be fine as long as you stay on the side of the road and lean into turns, and don't worry, I will be right there to help you." Easy for Alice to say. Nonetheless, she was convincing in her proposal thus was borne the General Accident Moped Brigade and, thankfully, safety standards were implemented and there were no accidents—General or specific!

Alice and her General Accident Moped Brigade, consisting of Duffy O'Connor, Marge and Tom McGill, Manager of the Cieveland branch office, as the "gang-of-4" prepare to attack the narrow roads of Bermuda.

Wherever GA Manager's Meetings were held, Daredevil Alice was first in line to sign-up for thrilling experiences, whether it be in Bermuda, Hawaii or the Holy Land. In Hamilton, Bermuda she led the GA Moped Brigade and, when the GA entourage was in Hawaii, she was the only member of the group to take a hellacious helicopter ride descending rapidly between the mountain peaks of Maui. During a subsequent pilgrimage to the Holy Land, Alice was the only one in our group with sufficient courage to vault onto the back of a fly-covered camel and trot through the ancient streets of Petra, Jordan! She was a tour director's delight, a daredevil's daredevil—ALICE KENNEDY!

As my father said shortly after meeting Alice, "She isn't afraid of anything—walking, diving, swimming or crawling." Truer words were never spoken!

DECISIONS, DECISIONS

In August, for an undisclosed reason, I was invited to Philadelphia to meet with Jim Corcoran. Prior to my appointment with Jim, I stopped to visit with various friends, one of whom was Claims Department Senior Vice-President Bob Schwemler. While seated in Bob's office, I was shocked that he was listening to a radio during business hours! In all my visits to the home office, never did I observe any executive listening to a radio when pressing decisions were under consideration.

As we spoke, I couldn't help but note a familiar tune was playing, so I asked Bob, a religious man, if he recognized the song; he did not. I explained, "That tune is a recently released religious hymn, 'Be Not Afraid,' composed by Father Robert Dufford, SJ."

Between the shock of a radio playing in an executive's office and the oft-time repetition of the phrase "Be Not Afraid," I construed the incident to be a message directed at me. Whatever the purpose of my visit to the home office, I did not know; what I did discern was; I should *Be Not Afraid*.

As soon as I sat down with Jim Corcoran, he informed me the initial plan of uniting both branch offices into one large office was no longer under consideration. He went on to explain, "Both the Boston branch and the Springfield branch will remain in their current locations. We are however proposing that you become Regional Vice-President (RVP), with the responsibility of overseeing our New England operation. We do expect the RVP will be in residence in the proximity of the Boston branch, which will necessitate relocating your family to eastern Massachusetts." My immediate reaction was the location of the Boston branch—it was not in Boston proper—it was situated northwest of Boston in the city of Peabody. Consequently, I was concerned residing in an area in proximity to the branch would make the trek to Cape Cod burdensome; we would have to travel through the Boston to access the South Shore.

As was the case when previous career opportunities were presented in the past, I informed Jim I would like to discuss his proposal with Alice. As might be expected, Alice was analytical. "The kids will change schools, lose friends, have less exposure to their grandparents and forsake the benefits of the Colony Club. No longer will they participate in Easter Egg Hunts or Santa Claus visits in the Club atmosphere." Then she added the positive aspects, "The kids will grow up in a Metropolitan area with a plethora of opportunities: museums, top of the line schools, professional sports teams and, if needed, the best hospitals in the country."

Alice, an adventurist at heart, didn't know the meaning of fear. Apprehension wasn't in her vocabulary. In her mind, the decision was a "no-brainer." She rationalized that the kids would be enriched growing up in an area with so opportunities and said "start packing Danny Boy. We're Bostonians now." Although re-location would be challenging, in Alice's mind, the greater the challenge, the greater the satisfaction, and re-locating five young kids would certainly be a challenge!

Alice not only endorsed the proposal, she was euphoric and intent on masterminding the move. She relished the prospects of masterminding the move, coordinating on-site issues as well as integrating her views with the home office relocation team. With Alice's unequivocal support, the decision was made. I accepted the proposal.

When I called Jim to accept the position, he informed me there was a compelling need for me to assume responsibilities immediately. I was concerned if I agreed to an immediate emergence in the Boston Branch, Alice would be alone with the kids for what would be a prolonged relocation process. I conditioned my acceptance with the understanding I would commute on a daily basis from Westfield to Peabody with an occasional evening spent in a local motel. Jim concurred. For the next five months, I was at the Westfield entrance of the Mass Turnpike at 5am and returned home in time to hear "school stories" and help put the kids to bed. Once I became acclimated to a daily routine, the trip wasn't foreboding.

As preparations for relocation progressed, Alice was in the forefront of everything. She negotiated the fine print in the financial aspects of the relocation package with our home office in Philadelphia, scoured newspapers for possible residential locations, and discussed selling our Westfield home with real estate brokers. Thanks to Alice, I was freed from these concerns and could concentrate on management matters in the Boston branch.

It was a financial challenge to move from a relatively inexpensive locality in western Massachusetts to the considerably more-expensive eastern Mass area. In view of that, GA's relocation department offered us an enticing package to facilitate the transfer. In addition to absorbing all costs, the company offered some creative financial concepts in order to assist us in the acquisition of a home in eastern Mass.

In Alice's spare time (?), she scrutinized the eastern Massachusetts real estate market, eventually zeroing in on homes in Needham where, most importantly, there was a highly regarded parochial school. Within a few days of identifying Needham as a desirable location, she engaged the services of the A. Clinton Brooks Real Estate office and began to become acquainted with a broker in firm named Mary Dunn. Soon Alice received a call from Mary informing her that a single-family home on Woodlawn Ave was going on the market the following morning and, if she was interested, Alice would have to move fast. *Alice was always moving fast;* quickly she called my parents to babysit, called her mother (Nana) to accompany her, and the two of them set-sail for Needham.

Alice listed two criteria first; the living room must accommodate her prized Kazvin living room rug. Second, there must be a sun-porch similar to the porch Carpenter Dan constructed in Westfield.

At that time there were no cell phones, so Alice couldn't contact me in Peabody until after she viewed the home. When she returned to the broker's office, she called to inform me she had just looked at the Woodlawn Ave home and it fulfilled her criteria. Excitedly, and in rapid-fire fashion, she continued, "It's a white Colonial with a living room large enough to accommodate our rug and, it has a screened-in-porch in the back just like the sun-porch you built in Westfield! I am however reluctant to make an offer until you see the house." What was left unsaid at the time was that it was "an older house," which would have conveyed there would be many opportunities for upgrade projects. In other words, don't cancel the *Handy Andy Magazine* subscription.

I responded, "Sounds good Alice, but I'm in the middle of several issues and I can't possibly go to Needham at this time. If you think the house would be good for us, then make whatever offer you deem appropriate."

Two hours later she called back and told me the seller accepted the offer just as she structured the offer. Alice stipulated that the seller, Thomas and Margaret Lovett, take back a second mortgage, at 0% interest, payable in 10 years.

The next move was to integrate GA's financial contribution into the deal Alice structured. GA was agreeable to bridge the gap between our equity in Falley Drive and the second mortgage from the Lovett's and upfront the difference as joint owners.

Their proposal seemed reasonable to me, but it was not reasonable to Alice. She said, "No way are we going to accept that proposal. If GA has a legal interest in our house, they too will benefit from the appreciation. We're going to make a counter proposal to GA, stipulating their loan will be a fixed sum of money, at 0% interest, independent of the purchase and sale agreement."

GA's home office concurred with Alice's counter proposal and loaned us $20,000, interest free. Thus, for the first 10 years on Woodlawn Ave, we paid monthly mortgage bills to GA and to the Lovetts. GA's Home Office Personnel and Relocation Departments met their match in negotiating with Alice. I couldn't have found a more effective agent to represent me than Alice. There is no doubt in my mind she could have out negotiated many seasoned attorneys, including highly regarded Major League Baseball player agent Scott Boras.

Before we met, unbeknown to either of us, both Alice and I passed the Massachusetts Real Estate Broker Examination and were licensed brokers. However, neither of us used our real estate licenses; we did, however, have similar intents. If we ever needed another source of income, we would have the broker's license as a supplemental means of remuneration. The difference between the two of us was that Alice remembered what she learned; I did not.

Alice certainly was a master negotiator and her effectiveness was never as apparent as was in evidence with the purchase and sale agreement for 45 Woodlawn Ave, yet her negotiating prowess was not limited to real estate transactions.

Alice's business acumen applied not only to abrasives and real estate, her skills in negotiating oriental rug acquisitions is well documented. When Alice was considering the purchase of oriental rugs, she fortified her extensive knowledge with her Persian Bible, the ever-ready oriental rug handbook book, *Oriental Rugs,* authored by Charles W. Jacobsen, an internationally renowned oriental rug expert from Syracuse, New York in 1962.

The following weekend, Alice and I drove to Needham and I viewed the house for the first time. I was pleased with the house, especially since it met all of Alice's criteria: a living room, an excellent neighborhood, within walking distances of schools, church, downtown shops, and easy access to two commuter rail station stops. It was another one of Alice's brilliant moves! The home at 45 Woodlawn Ave in Needham proved to be an ideal location for our entire family, which of course includes our West Highland Terrier, Shannon.

When I viewed the house for the first time, I met the real estate broker, Mary Dunn. In the course of our conversation, Mary asked me for whom I worked. When I told her General Accident Insurance, she shockingly said, "My husband used to work for General Accident." I said, "Paul Dunn? I know Paul, he's a friend of George Pumphret!" Yes, the wife of a General Accident friend of mine was the real estate broker representing the seller of 45 Woodlawn Ave. An amazingly small world! I met Paul Dunn, a proud alumnus off the College of the Holy Cross in 1965, when Bill Toner and I were visiting the Boston branch when it was located at Ten Post Office Square in downtown Boston.

Although Alice's primary concern was to enroll the kids in Saint Joseph's Parish School in Needham, she did research the Needham Public School System and discovered both public and parochial were held in high regard. As soon as the purchase-and-sale agreement was signed, Alice telephoned Sister Miriam Clare, SC, principal of St. Joseph's School, and scheduled an appointment to discuss enrollment. The Sisters of Charity of Nova Scotia staffed Saint Joseph's School. Alice scheduled an appointment to discuss enrollment. Although Sister Miriam welcomed Alice warmly, regretfully, she said, "At this time Saint Joseph's can only accommodate three of your children; two will have to enroll in the Needham Public School System."

Poor Sister Miriam, she did not know with whom she was dealing. In a matter of a millisecond, she would learn otherwise. "Perhaps, Sister Miriam, I wasn't sufficiently explicit during our telephone conversation. We have five school age children and we would like all five to attend St. Joseph's School. This is not a proposal for three individuals. This is a package deal—it's five Kennedy Kids or none!"

'Nough said. The next day Sister Miriam called Alice and assured her Saint Joseph's School will be pleased to accommodate *all five Kennedy Kids!*

A BEAUTIFUL DAY IN THE NEIGHBORHOOD

If a family opts to relocate in New England during the winter months, it is inevitable that at some point they will contend with snow. The first night of our 45 Woodlawn Ave occupancy, a winter snowstorm deposited several inches of snow in Needham and the wintery winds blew a substantial pile between our house and the garage.

During the night, as considerable heat escaped from a poorly insulated cellar, snow melted and frigid water cascaded through the foundation wall into our cellar. Several un-packed cardboard cartons, stacked on the cellar floor by the movers, were quickly saturated with unwelcomed winter water.

When Alice detected the deluge at 3 a.m. she swung into action, directing me to shovel the snow away from the foundation and divert the water flow away from the foundation and down the driveway. In the meantime, she was busy elevating cardboard boxes off the saturated cellar floor.

A few weeks later, thankfully, without a similar foundation-packed meltdown, another storm deposited snow on the town of Needham. During that snowstorm, Alice suggested that we enjoy the snow and take advantage of our proximity to the center of town. Ali and I did what we could not have done in similar snow conditions on Falley Drive in Westfield; we took a leisurely walk through blinding snow to the center of town.

As we sauntered down Great Plain Ave, we reminisced of the times we sat by the sliding glass window in Falley Drive, watching the kids, with snow swirling around them, skating on our backyard rink. There is something soothing in watching snowflakes filter to the ground and in Needham. We could stroll to the downtown area amongst those softly falling flakes. As Alice and I slowly proceeded through the accumulating snow, we stopped in Gino's Restaurant on Chapel Street for warming cups of hot chocolate.

Among the first neighbors we met in Needham was our next-door neighbor, Mrs. Theresa Lemaire, Mrs. Dorothy Kelly and Mrs. (Anne) Kinsley, both of who lived directly across the street, and Mrs. (Sally) Dempsey, who resided closer to the Powers Street intersection. Immediately Alice felt right at home. Mrs. Kelly was an elderly widow who lived alone—right up Alice's alley; she loved to fawn over needy people.

The name Lemaire was intriguing to me. In my undergraduate days at Saint Michael's College, I mentioned to Theresa that my freshman-year science instructor was Dr. Henry Lemaire. Immediately, Theresa said, "That was my deceased husband, Henry. He taught science and physics at St. Mike's!" Another coincidence, the family of my former college professor in northern Vermont, was our next-door neighbor in Needham. In just a matter of a few weeks, we met Mary Dunn whose husband Paul was a friend of mine and now our next-door neighbor, Theresa Lemaire, was the wife of my freshman-year science professor. We were obviously in a compatible community.

Thanks to Alice, our relocation didn't pose any perceived adjustment issues for the kids. The kids at Saint Joseph's were welcoming; in a short period of time new found friends were streaming in our door. Alice was quick to involve herself in the Saint Joseph Parent Teacher Association and she too was developing new friends. Even our aged West Highland Terrier, Shannon, acclimated well to our new environment.

Although Alice located a dog groomer for Shannon, between groomer appointments she continued to trim Shannon's nails. I could always tell when Alice clipped Shannon's nails, as there were bloody paw prints on the floor. Often in her exuberance to get the job done as quickly as possible, she tended to cut Shannon's nails too close to the nail plate, thus the poor dog paraded around the house leaving blood spots on the floor! Alice had the best of intentions in clipping Shannon's nails. She was truly sorry she drew blood. However, I couldn't resist saying, "In the event I ever become incapacitated, remember, I would prefer that someone other than you clip my nails. I know you wouldn't be happy to see my bloody fingerprints on your linen tablecloth!"

Years later, when Alice became ill and needed a manicurist, she was extremely apprehensive about having someone trim her nails. Alice, literally as tough as nails, became extremely frightened when someone trimmed her nails. Thankfully, Katie was skillful and kind in clipping Alice's nails, and she did not infringe on the nail plate.

Another of the many things that Alice handled in our relocation from Westfield to Needham was to secure a primary care physician. After securing a recommendation from a few Needham residents, she contacted Needham Family Practice and scheduled a meeting with the two doctors. Dr. Gerald Corcoran was on a winter vacation, so Alice met with Dr. Leonard Finn. Actually, *met with* is an inappropriate description; interrogation would be more descriptive.

After meeting Dr. Finn, Alice she told me, "I asked Dr. Finn where he went to medical school and to cite his perspective as a physician on abortion. When he assured me the doctors in his office were committed to the protection of unborn babies, I informed him that was the answer I waiting to hear, I then told him that Needham Family Practice has seven new patients!"

Since that initial meeting with Dr. Finn, Alice and he developed a mutual respect for each other. Whenever Alice scheduled an appointment with Dr. Finn, she came prepared to discuss current medical issues. Anytime she read about medical issues, she documented questions, and presented them to Dr. Finn for his professional assessment.

Looking back, I can only marvel at her abilities. Can you imagine the sheer logistical challenge of daily duties such as laundry, hygiene, dressing and feeding five children for every imaginable event, in season and out of season? Alice also chauffeured them to doctor and dentist appointments, sports practices, soccer games, hockey games and music lessons. Yes, Alice pulled it off with boundless energy and never a complaint. Aside from working for a living, I had one crucial task: *follow her orders!* At Alice's direction, I took my place in the rotation—driving, tutoring or coaching. Frankly, it wasn't until I assumed housekeeping chores in recent years that it began to register how hard she worked to keep our home a welcoming place for friends, family, and an endless stream of visitors.

In addition to her organizational skills, Alice possessed the gift of understanding both of which were evident in the many inherent similarities she shared with Danny. Whether it was, medical, academics, athletics, or spirituality, Danny was a reflection of his mother. Without a doubt Alice was, unquestionably, *The Heart of Our Home!*

A TRIP BACK IN TIME

After we transitioned to Needham, Alice maintained her long-time interest in hockey, but her allegiance shifted from the Springfield Indians to the Boston Bruins! Every time the Bruins played, she was attentively in front of the TV. Perhaps this was an ancillary reason for her enthusiastic support for our relocation to the Boston area!

From the time we were married, all night, every night, Alice listened to the radio. In Westfield it was station WTIC in Hartford with Father Nadolny at Midnight and the Bob Steele Program at 5 a.m. One night, during Father Nadolny's program, even though I was three quarters asleep, I thought I detected the sound of a familiar voice on the radio; a friend of mine from St. Mike's, Tim Dailey.

Tim was the younger brother of three Dailey boys, all of whom were extremely bright. Tim was a former Society of St. Edmund Seminarian at St. Mike's and certainly not a "pushover caller" on Theological matters. Much to my satisfaction, Tim acquitted himself well as he queried Father Nadolny on apologetics.

Unfortunately, the lack of radio reception in Boston prevented Alice from listening to WTIC in Hartford. No longer could she hear Father Nadolny during the night and Bob Steele in the morning. As soon as we arrived in Needham, she discovered a plethora of late-night radio stations. Alice was thrilled with the number of radio stations she could listen to, and listen she did, all night long.

Occasionally, in the middle of the night, Alice would wake/shake me to inform me of *Breaking News!* While in the depth of deep sleep, I would hear a faint voice saying, "Dan, are you awake? Are you awake?" Although the voice became progressively louder, the message was the same, "Dan, are you awake? Dan, are you awake?" at which point the strident voice became more assertive; "Dan, you have to wake up; wake up Dan."

The urgency in her voice was reminiscent of the nights I was awoken to hear that her nine months of pregnancy were coming to a conclusion. Obviously, whenever she woke me with *Breaking News* I was startled. Still half asleep, I murmured, "What happened?"

Excitedly, Alice would reply, "Betty Grable died."

Still thinking this was some sort of a dream I repeated, "What?"

She reiterated, "Betty Grable...she died!" At this point I was wide-awake and, not particularly thrilled to be wide-awake to hear such *breaking news* at 2 a.m.

These "Breaking News" flashes were not infrequent; I was among the first to be informed that Henry Fonda died, Grace Kelly died, or an airliner crashed, etc. Tragic though these incidents were, I couldn't imagine why Alice thought it was so important to share that information with me in the wee hours of the morning. I would succinctly, but perhaps not too pleasantly respond, "Go back to sleep Alice. Please provide the details in the morning."

To say I was well informed would be an understatement. I was kept up to speed on world events whether I was interested or not. In 1968, a few months after we were married, I must have been among the first people on the east coast to learn; "Bobby Kennedy was assassinated in the Ambassador Hotel in Los Angeles, California."

Alice's nightly comfort zone didn't change appreciably after relocating to Needham. In Westfield, it was WTIC and Bob Steele and Father Nadolny and, in Needham, it was WBZ and Larry Glick, a.k.a. The Commander. Now, in Needham, midnight news flashes were conveyed with the authenticity of "The Commander said..."

Several years later, Larry Glick's wife opened Glick's Hairdresser Shop in Needham and Larry spent mornings at the same bagel shop I frequented. The jovial radio personality was just as entertaining off-the-air as he was on-the-air; there was nothing pretentious about him. He roared with laughter when I told him about my early-morning death notifications!

Subsequently, Alice purchased an innovative radio, which improved reception and included earplugs!

Marital life is replete with opportunities for sacrifice; after 25 years of spousal sacrifice, no longer was my sleep disturbed. Without malice aforethought, modern technology deprived me of being among the first to hear daily death notices and no longer was I apprised of Alaskan and Baja Peninsula weather forecasts!

GENERAL ACCIDENT MANAGERS MEETING: A NEW VENUE

Yes, another GA manager's meeting and now that precedence had been established: wives would accompany their husbands to DISNEYWORLD in Orlando, Florida. Once again, Alice was thinking outside the box when she exclaimed, "Let's bring the kids!" I tried to curtail her enthusiasm when I alluded to the fact this would be a business environment not conducive for young children. To which she replied, "Let me give that some thought."

Within a few days, Alice's plan was revealed, "If Sister Miriam will approve of us taking the kids out of school for three days, then they could fly to Orlando and meet us at the conclusion of the conference." The only impediment Alice could foresee in the plan was, with school in session, babysitting nuns would be unavailable.

It wasn't long before resourceful Alice overcame that obstacle; she contracted with our neighbor, Natalie Andersen's daughter, Andrea, to babysit the kids. At that point, with great alacrity, Ali, party planner par excellence, swung into action and arranged a flight for the kids to Orlando. When Katie came home from school, Alice proudly informed her, "I just spent three hours on the phone with Delta Airlines and it was the best hours I experienced in a long time; I saved almost $300 on flight arrangements to Disney World for all five of you!"

The arrangements (a.k.a. deal...a.k.a. scheme) as concocted by Alice on the unsuspecting Delta airline ticket agent was to have Katie and Patti, age intentionally not disclosed (11 and 10 years old at the time) fly as "adults." Alice's proposal, ultimately accepted by Delta, reduced ticket costs for Anne Marie, Danny, and Jackie who would be accompanied by two "adults." Alice's Scottish grandmother would be delighted that frugality factored into her thought process!

Alice and I flew to Orlando for General Accident's managers meeting as our neighbor, Andrea Andersen assumed babysitting responsibilities previously entrusted to the Faculty of St. Joseph Parish School, the Sisters of Charity of Halifax, Nova Scotia.

In addition to hosting wives of the branch managers and home office executives, for the first time, Chief General Attorney Sir David Blakey of the Worldwide General Accident Plc Ltd. (Corp) in Pitheavlis Perthshire, Scotland, added a regal presence to the meeting.

The final conference of the managers meeting was proceeding positively when suddenly, without provocation, Jim Corcoran, CEO, became incensed.

Apparently, in his mind, he perceived an aura of indifference or apathetic response, which prompted him to verbally lacerate the entire group! Without exception, every manager and home office executive was shocked and appalled at Jim's unwarranted outburst. Perhaps he was attempting to impress Worldwide Chief Executive Sir David Blakey, a guest at the meeting, with his "tough taskmaster" persona; if so, it was a miscalculation. Even Sir David was at a loss for words, and he purposely avoided mingling with GA managers.

By nature, Mr. Corcoran was an easy going, low-keyed, well-composed person always displaying a pleasant disposition and a genuine interest in people; his behavior on that day was an aberration of the chief executive we knew. His public castigation of the entire corporate sales force was not only without cause, it was deeply disturbing and mystifying to everyone. Production results in the United States not only exceeded expectations, the United States 'Branch' of the General Accident also surpassed worldwide results; neither Australia nor any European operation attained the results we achieved. Resultantly, we were honored with Sir David Blakey's presence.

The dampening pall was not restricted to those in attendance at the conference. Word of the debacle spread quickly; wives who were not present at the Conference were also in a quandary. Tension permeated the entire atmosphere; everyone was notably uncomfortable as they filed into the banquet hall for the wrap-up dinner. Was Jim attempting to impress the worldwide chief executive with his militaristic demeanor? No one knew. Unfortunately, his outburst injected incalculable negativity.

There was little socializing at the wrap-up dinner; managers and their wives sat in stunned silence, intentionally avoiding Jim and Rosemary Corcoran who, like two lost souls, sat glumly at their table. No one knew whether or not Jim, whose reddened face radiated fury, was on the verge of another eruption and they did not intend to be in the vicinity if there was an explosion. As the band played softly, the entire corporate body dined silently, no one was on the dance floor, there wasn't a single person within the proximity of what appeared to be ground zero of a possible volcanic eruption.

By nature, Alice seem to recognize and empathize with the downcast, the dejected, and the troubled. She was extraordinarily gifted with a sixth sense in identifying need, and more importantly, she had the courage to act on her sympathetic inclinations. As Jim's disheartened facial expression continued to depict explosiveness, Alice sensed he might be suppressing remorse and asked, "Do you think I should invite Jim to dance?" I, uncertain as to whether she should embroil herself in a catastrophic corporate crisis, said, "Do what you think is appropriate."

Immediately, Alice left our table, crossed the barren dance floor, and walked directly to the pariah's table. After a minute or two of casual conversation, Alice and Jim were on the dance floor. Shortly thereafter, a few other couples ventured onto the dance floor. Tension diffused. Harmony was restored!

It was classic Alice; with more than 100 people at the managers' conference, she was the only person with sufficient courage to be a peacemaker. True to form, by extending her hand to the brooding chief executive, resentments were resolved and peace prevailed.

The following day, as participants prepared to depart Disney World for their return trip home, Rosemary Corcoran gave Alice a hug and succinctly said, "Thank you, Alice." Jim and Rosemary Corcoran were also, FOA—Friends of Alice!

Everyone, including Alice and me, were en route to the Orlando International Airport. However, we were not destined for the departure section; we were headed to the arrival section to meet the kids' flight from Boston.

As Meticulous Alice planned, on the day the GA annual meeting concluded, Andrea drove the kids to Logan International Airport where they boarded a Delta flight to Hartsfield Airport in Atlanta, Georgia, at which point they were to board a connecting flight to Orlando International Airport in Florida.

At Hartsfield Airport in Atlanta, as they were about to board the flight to Orlando, the Stewardess discovered that not only were there no adults accompanying three children, the two purported adults did not have airline tickets. Evidently, Andrea neglected to give Katie and Patti their airline tickets, thus Delta Airlines was confronted with a significant problem.

With the prospect of an internal investigation looming and five young children miles from their ultimate destination, Delta Airline decided to disregard the absence of adult tickets and allow the five Kennedy Kids to board the flight to Orlando International Airport.

Two Delta agents, both of whom possessed strong southern accents, personally escorted the five Kennedys through the Hartsfield Airline Terminal. The attendants marched the five kids in single file. As Katie recalled, "It was reminiscent of *Make Way for Ducklings*. I was the oldest, so I was placed first in line, and Jackie, the youngest, brought up the rear." One Delta agent was in front of Katie and another in the rear behind Jackie. As the five Kennedys marched through Hartsfield Terminal, the Delta agents loudly proclaimed, in strong southern accents reverberating throughout the terminal, "'Y'all stay together, Y'all' hear me? Y'all stay in line."

Thankfully, the two *Kennedy adults* and three *Kennedy kids* arrived safely in Orlando and were greatly relieved to see Mom and Dad waiting for them. They were excited to spend a few days in Disney World. I don't think they missed a single ride or any opportunity to pose for a picture with Mickey Mouse. Once again, Alice was right; the Disney World trip was a huge success, a memory to be treasured, and all accolades go to the Kennedy Family Planner!

Alice also possessed considerable managerial know-how; she knew where every dime was spent. She. like her parents, "threw money around as if it were manhole covers." In essence, Alice was the *personification of frugality!*

I too, as a youngster, in the eyes of my parents, was tight-fisted with a dollar. When I received money, I didn't spend it, I banked it. My father used to say to my sister and I, "Judy will always have money because she is generous, she gives her money away. But you, Danny, you horde your money, so finances will always be an issue for you."

Over the years, my penuriousness moderated, and I adopted a "need-based" perspective. To Alice's credit, moderation of monetary restrictions was occasionally in evidence. Frugality continued to reign; bargain hunting was essential.

Amassing an abundance of discount coupons was a daily endeavor. It was amazing to see Alice negotiate an acquisition. It wasn't a fair fight. She never lost her determination to find the lowest price, whether she was purchasing Persian rugs, an automobile or a residence, the seller had to contend with Master Negotiator Alice.

RAINY DAY FEVER

Like many people, Alice looked ahead, but not necessarily with rose-colored glasses; she looked preventatively toward the future. Although she loved to sit at the beach on sunny days, she knew every day wouldn't be sunny. So, she frequently cautioned the kids, "Save your money; the sun will set and rainy days will follow, so save your money." In Alice's mind, *tomorrow* was always a *daily* concern.

"A time will come when we are going to need this, so don't throw it away" was her theme song. She didn't believe in throwing anything away! I don't think it would be accurate to portray her as a pack-rat because she didn't save items simply for the sake of saving. She truly believed that there would come a day when we would need such-and-such and invariably, she was right.

If anyone was looking for a certain size bolt, nut, or washer (she just loved washers and plumbing gadgets), her response would be, "I think I have one of those." Alice would inevitably produce the appropriate item, and then with a beaming grin, she would hand me the item and say, "This would have cost you $30.00 or more at a hardware store—from me it's as free as the Grace of God." It was a win-win for Alice; first, she made use of an old item and second, it was cost effective!

Anytime we traded-in a car, she repossessed the spare tire from the trunk and stored it in the garage. In the event any of us needed to purchase a tire, the walls of our garage were lined with tires of various sizes, waiting for the day someone would need a tire. It never happened. Through the years, the quality of tires improved considerably, so the older tires were of little value. Still, they remained stacked in our garage, which became known as a Michelin Warehouse on Woodlawn!

One day, when she was about to stash another tire in the garage, in an effort to persuade Alice to stop accumulating tires and clear out the garage, I said, "If we bring the old tires to the Needham Dump (a.k.a. Transfer/Recycling Station), we will have room to put both cars in the garage; the fee is only $3.00 a tire." A major mistake! Alice's frugality took center stage: "I'm not paying $3.00 per tire to the Town of Needham. Those tires stay in our garage!" The toilet tanks in our house were filled with bricks in order to limit the amount of water used in flushing toilets. Obviously, a cost-saving technique she learned from faithfully reading Handy Andy Magazine.

INQUISITIVENESS PERSONIFIED

Alice was extremely inquisitive, always seeking to know how things worked. She was determined to learn how every mechanical device functioned.

Personally, I didn't care what made a clock tick or a toaster toast, but Alice certainly cared. Even though she delighted in solving mathematical problems, when it came to mechanical challenges, she was like a kid on Christmas morning. When a mechanical appliance malfunctioned, within minutes, screwdriver in hand, she dismantled the device to identify the source of the problem.

Alice was never completely comfortable with any gadget or mechanical device until she personally disassembled the brand-new item to see how it was constructed. I could care less, but Alice wanted absolute knowledge of the product so that, in the event that it broke, she could fix it herself! She didn't believe in spending money on something she could fix herself.

Alice's favorite companion, her toolbox, was never far away, nor was her favorite lubricant, WD-40. In the days before Google, Alice was probably in a small percentage of the population who knew the derivation of the brand name WD-40. Alice's inquisitiveness and resourcefulness fortified her with relatively little-known information that the 'W' indicates water, the 'D' indicates disbursement, and it took the chemists 40 attempts before they could find a solution that would disburse water. Thus, the name WD-40!

Alice was multi-talented; if there was a mechanical malfunction, she knew what needed to be lubricated. She could identify the malfunction, and invariably she could fix the problem. Alice never wanted to give-up when trying to solve a problem; she would feel like a failure if she had to call a plumber, a carpenter or a mechanic.

Alice was well informed on almost any topic, be it mechanical, mathematical, medical or financial. Occasionally, when Alice and I were out at a social gathering, someone would inevitably pose a question to me regarding insurance. Intuitively, I would suggest they direct their inquiry to Alice; she read the small print on insurance policies and she was familiar with coverages, exclusions and deductibles. Years ago, when I was in the underwriting department, I would have been abreast of coverages but without direct daily involvement I was at best, rusty. Rust was a dirty word to Alice; she lubricated mechanical parts so they wouldn't rust, and she read our insurance policies so my rust wouldn't negatively impact our coverage.

When the morning paper was delivered, I read the Sports section first and then the Obituaries (the Irish Funny Page) and finally, the Business section. The first section Alice read was Business, zeroing in on the Dow Jones Industrial Average. Her knowledge of the stock market and mutual funds was extensive. It was a joy to watch near-sighted Alice as she read the morning paper; she would whip off her eyeglasses and scrutinize the miniscule printed Dow Jones Industrial Average without visual assistance.

A PROGNOSTICATION?

With a myriad of responsibilities, Alice was always in perpetual motion. When the kids were young, rarely did she stop for lunch; she ate on the run. She did sit down for our family dinner. But as far as lunch? Forget about it! She was content with an energy drink in an aluminum can and perhaps a peanut butter cracker. At some point I read an article hypothesizing the results of a medical study indicating that drinking from aluminum cans may predispose people to dementia. I mentioned the article to Alice and suggested she consider abandoning the use of aluminum cans. She was skeptical of the study results and was not persuaded to abandon her affinity for aluminum cans. Did her persistence in energy drinks in cans contribute to her health issues? Probably not, but on the other hand, who knows?

ALICE BEING ALICE

Blessed are the merciful, for they will be shown mercy. (Matthew 5:7)

In what would become an oft-time occurrence, we received the first of many suppertime telephone calls; this call was from Dr. Tom Connolly, a prominent Needham pediatrician. Dr. Connolly called to thank Alice for giving his elderly mother, who he said was becoming forgetful, a ride to her home.

As Alice was driving home during the afternoon, she noticed what she perceived to be a confused woman walking near the town square. She stopped and offered the woman a ride home. In the course of the ride to the woman's home, she identified herself as Dr. Connolly's mother. Alice seemed to have a sixth sense; she was always aware of people in need. This occurrence may have been one of the first opportunities Alice assisted someone experiencing cognitive issues.

It was not unusual for Alice to offer rides to elderly people. On another occasion, Ali noticed a senior citizen walking hesitatingly on Great Plain Ave; per usual, she stopped the car and offered the woman a ride to her home. The woman, Mrs. Mitchell, spoke with a brogue and informed Alice that she and her husband were from Carndonagh County Donegal and lived on Hawthorn Ave, a few streets east of Woodlawn Ave. As was her custom, Alice gave Mrs. Mitchell her telephone number and told her to file her number under the letter A for Alice and dial A anytime she needed a ride.

Alice was thrilled to relate the story to me because not only did she learn that Mrs. Mitchell was from Ireland but, more importantly, she was thrilled when she learned Mrs. Mitchell was from the same townland in Ireland as a friend of Alice's from Saint Joseph's PTA, Carndonagh-born Frances Gallagher.

As Alice was relating the story to me, her exuberance was obvious, and I knew what she was thinking. Alice was going to arrange a gathering so the two Carndonagh natives could meet.

NOTHING TROUBLED ALICE UNTIL...

"I had just returned from grocery shopping when Alice called to invite me over for tea and crumpets, so I put my coat back on and went to Woodlawn Ave for a mid-day libation," said Frances Gallagher. "Surprisingly, Alice introduced me to an elderly woman, seated in her living room sipping tea and munching on a crumpet." Frances continued, "Alice was so pleased to inform me that the woman seated in her living room was from Carndonagh, County Donegal.

With a twinkle in her eye, Alice expected euphoria to rein but it did not. Unbeknown to Alice, elderly Mrs. Mitchell was an Irish Protestant who harbored deep seeded wounds from the days of *The Troubles*. Consequently, the tea cooled, the crumpets crumbled, and Mrs. Mitchell departed.

Alice was disappointed that her attempt to reunite two Irish-born women from the same townland did not bear fruit. First-hand, Alice witnessed lasting scars generated from centuries of hostilities extended into the 21st century, which continued to exist in Needham, Massachusetts.

MARCHING MUSIC

As a mother of five children, like steps on a staircase, it was mandatory that Captain Al develop a game plan; develop a game plan she did. Each of the five had a responsibility: set the table, clear the table, wash the dishes, etc. "Alice meted out assignments to her children replicating Maria von Trapp in the Sound of Music," said Mary Burns, a PTA friend of Alice.

Although Patti was far and away the most effective member of the Kennedy Gang of Five in assisting Alice, on occasion she would fail to execute the prepared game-plan, prompting Alice to query, "Are you an Amadan?" None of the kids, nor did I, know the etymology of that term;

apparently it was an old Irish term of chastisement Alice's parents used when she was a kid.

One day, while in Middle school, Patti didn't follow directions and the exasperated teacher, Sister Margaret McKeon asked, "Are you an Amadan? Patti responded, "My mother asks that same question." From that simple reference to the word Amadan, Patti and Sister Margaret became great friends.

Amadan is a myth in Irish Folklore describing a person who lives on the edge of oblivion. Not a particularly flattering observation, yet having heard it applied so often at home, in a sense, in Patti's mind, Sister Margaret was an extension of Alice; Patti and Sister Margaret's became long-term friends. Yes, in Patti's mind, Sister Margaret spoke Alice's language and Alice spoke Sister Margaret's language. Voilà.

SILENT SPIRITUALITY

Every Sunday, all seven of us attended Mass at St. Joseph's in Needham. Five of us were tacitly present at Mass, but two seemed to be more intimately associated with the Liturgy—Alice and Danny. When most people in the congregation were folding their hands in prayer, Alice opened her hands and her arms as if she were welcoming Christ. That gesture was not necessarily unique as other people worshiped the same way, but Alice was the only one in our family to open her arms in that manner. At the conclusion of Mass, Danny maintained the Saint Mary's Parish tradition; he knelt after the final blessing and prayed silently as the priest processed down the center aisle.

Alice didn't outwardly demonstrate the depth of her spirituality—she didn't walk around carrying a bible or passing out prayer cards—she loved Christ and, she lived the Gospel. She was always seeking opportunities to help other people; creating joy in others was her goal. Danny, like his mother, loved to make people laugh, and he too, developed a personal relationship Christ—virtues he acquired from his mother.

When Alice's mother began to show her age, her three daughters suggested she alternate living at each of their homes. This arrangement worked well. Mrs. Haggerty was delighted to live in the same home as her five Needham grandchildren and they were thrilled to dote on "Nana Haggerty." When Christmas arrived, the traditional Christmas Eve celebration was still hosted by Alice, the only difference is that it was a challenging drive from western Mass.

PART TWO

HAPPY
DAYS

CHAPTER 5

"BY THE SEA, BY THE SEA, BY THE BEAUTIFUL..."

Whenever Alice thought of an old-time song, she would pull me out of the chair, and the two of us would start singing and swaying around the kitchen. As you might suspect, the kids thought we were weird to impersonate vaudevillians. This may have been the prelude for later years, when after Alice's illness commenced, the two of us would sing and dance to light-hearted old-time songs, rejuvenating former moments of joy.

One night at dinner, as we continued to acclimate to our Needham home and shortly before school closed, Alice pulled me off the kitchen chair and started to sing and dance around the kitchen. Initially, I thought she was trying to prompt a reaction from the kids, which was partially true, but as I learned later, she had an ulterior motive.

As we started to dance, she began to sing, "By the Sea, By the Sea, By the Beautiful Sea, You and Me, You and Me, oh how Happy we'll be By the Beautiful Sea..." Yes, Alice was musically informing me and the kids that school vacation would be spent on the Cape! An ancillary benefit of residing in Needham was that the travel time to Cape Cod was much less than from Westfield. "During the workweek you can even take a ride to Dennisport in the evening," said the family salesperson.

As soon as school concluded in June, Alice and the kids were off to Dennisport. Their first summer at the Cape was a huge success. The Kennedy Kids were laborers in the morning and Sea Street Beach Bums in the afternoon. Laborers, a loosely coined expression, defined Alice's objective in conveying the necessity of earning spending money, so she secured jobs for each of them hawking newspapers for the Boston Globe at strategic street corners in Dennisport.

Initially, she bribed them with pastries from Wolfie's Bakery and gift cards to the Sundae School Ice Cream Shoppe. She even found a job for me as a weekend reader at Holy Trinity Church in West Harwich. Most importantly, the kids found summertime friends at the Sea Street Beach— the Reardon family.

The Reardon family lived around the corner from Ferncliff on Fenway. Age-wise, they were ideally suited for our kids, and the two mothers, Louise and Alice, had much in common and they too became close friends. When the kids weren't working, it was customary for the two families to spend their free time at Sea Street Beach. On the Fourth of July, it was a toss-up to see who was the most excited—not between the Kennedy Kids and the Reardon Kids—between Alice and her kids!

Alice was enthralled with Fourth of July celebrations. Wherever there were fireworks, she herded the kids into our station wagon and we were off to see fireworks over Nantucket Sound. Watching fireworks from the Sea Street Beach, Barnstable Harbor, the West Dennis Beach or the Fourth of July parades in Chatham and Orleans became family traditions. Alice could watch fireworks for hours, mesmerized by the multi-colored bursts in the sky as "oohs and aahs" were emitted from gasping observers.

Part and parcel of summer tradition was spending time frolicking on Sea Street Beach in Dennisport and attending weekend Mass, either at the Our Lady of the Annunciation in Dennisport or Holy Trinity in Harwichport. One particularly hot and humid summer afternoon, after a steaming hot day at Sea Street Beach, Alice and the kids joined me at the 4 p.m. Saturday afternoon Mass at Holy Trinity Church in West Harwich. I was scheduled to read at the Mass, so Alice and the five kids sat dutifully in the 3rd or 4th pew while I was seated in the Sanctuary. As I was proclaiming the Liturgical reading, I happened to glance in their direction, and much to my consternation, two of the kids were asleep!

Of course, I was furious; if there is such a thing as an evil eye, I did my best to display *an evil eye*. Did they awaken? No, they did not awaken, their somnambulance continued. Consequently, I re-directed my glare to Alice, in hopes my rapidly reddening face would communicate *a wake-up call* was in order. However, it is difficult to describe the degree of my consternation because when I looked at Alice, she too was fast asleep! I was tempted to abandon the designated reading and proclaim: *"You couldn't stay awake one hour with me?"(Matthew 26:40)*

A BREAK FROM SUN AND FUN CAN BE EXHILARATING

Although our family's first summer at the Cape was a huge success, we decided to curtail beach-time enjoyment and return to Needham in August to begin back-to-school preparations and take advantage of Needham's proximity to Fenway Park. We wanted the kids to experience a Major League Baseball game, particularly since Carl Yastrzemski (Number #8) was in the waning days of his illustrious baseball career. Another huge success!

Alice was especially interested in Carl Yastrzemski because they shared a common birth date; Yaz and Alice were both born on the same day—August 22, 1939! As a matter of fact, Al was incensed when she would hear Howard Cosell, Major League Baseball's National TV announcer, regaling the listening audience with the exploits of elderly Carl Yastrzemski.

In describing a Red Sox game, Howard, in his mellifluous voice, would often say, "Can you imagine, a man of his advanced years, running around the outfield catching baseballs and throwing them from that distance? He's a freak of nature!"

Alice retorted; "Cosell has nerve extoling Yaz with platitude after platitude lauding his geriatric exploits when, at the exact same age, I'm having difficulty walking up and down stairs!" At the time, Ali's comments were offered tongue-in-cheek, though ultimately, they did prove to be prophetic.

A year later, October 2, 1983, we were able to secure tickets for Yaz's swan-song game and Alice was thrilled! She and her guest, Anne Marie, were excited to sit in the premier "sky-view" seats at Fenway Park and watch #8, her *birth-date Buddy*, play his final Major League Baseball game!

The following year, the kids expanded their summertime employment opportunities. Anne Marie and Danny retired from the newspaper business and accepted full-time positions at Thompson's Clam Bar in Harwich Port; Katie and Patti commenced full-time employment at the Sundae School Ice Cream Shoppe in Dennisport; and Jackie was our sole surviving newspaper boy.

Alice, always a proud mother, was particularly pleased when her children were gainfully employed. Busy-ness was an essential component in Alice's nature and now that her children were ensconced with summertime employment, her desire to return to the workforce environment was rejuvenated; did someone say, "a long-term plan?"

Although Alice's promising business aspirations at Carborundum Corporation were usurped by motherhood, her ears perked-up whenever she heard of a business transaction or the invention of a new mechanical device. She was fascinated by the new world of computers, cell-phones, electronic inventions, and digitalization. If it was mechanical or business oriented, Alice was intrigued.

In addition to her avid reader interest in the Business section of the newspaper, she eagerly awaited the day when the Boston Globe published Peter Hotten's "Helpful Handyman Tips." She loved, absolutely loved, devouring Peter's tips on economizing and solving household problems. Al even went to an exhibit—it may have been at a fair—where Peter Hotten was conducting a demonstration just to personally pepper him with questions. Alice even told Peter the derivation of the name for lubricant WD-40!

In 1985, when all of the kids were gainfully employed during the summer months, Alice realized the same summertime employment logic should also apply to her. Unfortunately for Alice, there weren't many manufacturing opportunities at the Cape, so she casually mentioned to friends that she was interested in a part-time summer position, regardless of whether it was in manufacturing or not.

It wasn't long before an opportunity presented itself. Alice was asked to consider a full-time employment position, which would entail managing and maintaining an internationally recognized resort complex on the shores of Nantucket Sound.

"I knew of Alice's many contributions at Saint Mary's School in Westfield, so when a managerial opportunity presented itself at Dennis Seashores (DSS), Alice was the first person that came to mind," said Mary O'Neil, Chairperson of the Dennis Seashores Board of Directors in reflecting on Alice's affiliation with Dennis Seashores.

"When I mentioned to Alice that Dennis Seashores was in need of a full-time summer property manager, she was reluctant to commit to full-time employment," said Mary. "She had been away from the employment market for several years and, combined with her continuing maternal responsibilities, would prefer a part-time position. I suggested she spend an hour or two observing the current property manager in order to assess the extent of the occupational responsibilities. Alice agreed to spend a few hours of on-site observation in our Windmill (designed) Dennis Seashores office."

Unexpectedly, a family emergency occurred necessitating an immediate departure of the property manager. What was to have been *on-site observation* became *on-the-job-training*. Without benefit of an instructor or a training manual, Alice was faced with a Baptism of Fire." Mary continued, "Shortly after the Property Manager's sudden departure, I went to the Dennis Seashore office to assist Alice in coping with the emergency situation. As I entered the office door, I witnessed a disgruntled and agitated guest vociferously denouncing Dennis Seashore accommodations as she ferociously waved a dirty tablecloth in Alice's face demanding an unsoiled replacement. With compassionate concern, Alice held up the dirty tablecloth, and with an empathizing expression she ever so slowly turned the tablecloth over and re-assuredly said to the enraged guest, "The other side is fine. Why not put the clean side up until we replace it for you?'"

After Mary witnessed a *skillful Alice* pacify an *aggravated guest,* Mary said, "Alice, name your price, I'm going to recommend the board of directors hire you as our new Property Manager! The fact that Alice was not at all intimidated by a challenging encounter with a disgruntled guest assured me she was imminently qualified to manage Dennis Seashores," related Mary.

Apparently, Mary O'Neill's enthusiastic recommendation was sufficiently persuasive; Dennis Seashores Board of Directors offered Alice the full-time position of property manager. Obviously, Alice demonstrated not only a sense of calm under stressful conditions, she exhibited composed persuasiveness—a microcosm of Alice's abundant abilities. Alice was never a person to back down from an unsettling situation; in her mind, confrontations were not to be feared. They were to be viewed as opportunities— opportunities to change hearts and minds. Alice accepted the position.

As the board of directors would soon learn, Alice had no discernible limitations—multi-tasking was her forte. She was capable of doing most anything and, doing it exceptionally well. Alice was back in the work-a-day-world, and she was thrilled!

FIRST ORDER OF BUSINESS; UNITY

Shortly after commencing employment, Al learned, much to her chagrin, that the 35 individually owned cottages were not always united with Dennis Seashores' objectives. With Alice's innate business acumen, it was obvious to her that disjointed relationships must be repaired and commonality of interests be promoted. Alice recognized that a unified body of owners would be indispensable to the success of Dennis Seashores. She detected a divisiveness between owners of cottages on the ocean side of Chase Ave and owners on the inland side. In a quest of unity, she formed sub-committees with membership of owners on both sides of Chase Ave. Subsequently, post-haste self-interests became secondary to mutual interests.

Additionally, many of the individually owned cottages in the complex were in dire need of upgrading, and oft-times, owners were reluctant to expend the necessary resources to enhance the functionality of their cottage. When Alice factored in the apparent low level of the service staff's morale, it was not surprising that property betterment and human resources were at the top of Alice's list of priorities.

SECOND ORDER OF BUSINESS: REBUILD THE RESORT

Alice possessed many multi-tasking abilities, which were readily adaptable to her new responsibilities. She was skilled in evaluating, training, and motivating personnel, implementing accounting procedures, assessing and correcting mechanical issues, and most importantly, her people skills were extraordinary. She was proficient in placating perturbed people, be it an obstreperous guest or an owner. Ali recognized that Dennis Seashores was basically a service enterprise, and with her God-given helpful nature, she was a natural to develop a first-class summer resort.

Ali realized of all issues that may adversely affect Dennis Seashores' summertime sojourners must be identified and remedied. Alice's business acumen, combined with her magnetic personality, resonated with guests and owners alike, resulting in an immediate improvement in summertime joy for the guests and it was remuneratively rewarding for ownership.

Whenever an issue, or a problem, of any complexity occurred, the first principal Alice sought to apply was that the guest is always right. If, however, in her mind, contentiousness was without merit, she skillfully assuaged the complainant and persuasively dispelled the initial source of irritation.

At one point in time, after Alice resolved a particularly difficult issue, a sign mysteriously appeared on The Windmill Door synthesizing Alice's multiple talents that read... "GO ASK ALICE!" So appropriate! Everyone— owners, guests, and employees—knew Alice would have the solution to almost any problem. Not only was she prepared with a metal detector if someone lost a precious item on the beach, but she also had her yellow bag of family medications in case a guest had developed a rash, was allergic to seawater, or was in need of sunscreen. Alice was johnnie-on-the-spot. In the event someone's boat developed a battery issue, they were within arm's length of Alice's trusty jumper cables secured in the trunk of her car. Alice was prepared for any eventuality. She could have espoused the Boy Scout pre-amble: "Always Prepared" and, given her proclivity to assist people in need, she was always "The Good Samaritan!"

If, upon occasion, an individual cottage owner was in disagreement with the board of directors' policies, Alice was able to pacify the disen- chanted owner. Oftentimes, because of the rapport she enjoyed with owners and guests alike, Alice was able to convincingly communicate DSS policy decisions and bring harmony to volatile situations.

Alice radiated genuine sincerity and truly empathized with those prof- fering dissenting points of view, and after gaining their confidence she was able to assuage both sides. If there is, and I don't know that there is, such a thing as the Gift of Getting Along with Others, Alice was the prime example of that virtue!

Spectacular service was of course an essential element in promoting a favorable impression on guests; consequently, one of Alice's first orders of business was to establish a program of absolute cleanliness and spontaneous response to any perceived problem. Cottages were cleaned and impeccably scoured and ready for occupancy precisely at 2 p.m. on weekend afternoons. Alice excelled, as a matter of fact Alice thrived, in the fast-paced world of Dennis Seashore weekends! The greater the urgency, the greater the satisfaction for Alice. After solving a perplexing problem, Alice often requited, a happy guest will become a returning guest. *She opens her mouth in wisdom, and on her tongue is kindly counsel. (Proverbs 31:26)*

In addition to her academic proficiency, Alice was also capable of performing plumbing and carpentry repair projects, which not only upgraded Dennis Seashores cottages but expenditures for outsourcing was minimal.

Alice, as the old adage states, could think on her feet. She was quick to assess a situation and even quicker to offer a plausible solution. In addition to her effervescent personality, Al was imaginative, enterprising, but more importantly she was resourceful, all of which contributed to her infectious personality.

Most importantly, Alice recognized the importance of establishing a loyal and dedicated staff, which would be critical enhancing a family aura at Dennis Seashores. Alice knew the mission of a service industry; it was to radiate a genuine interest in guests. With that in mind, her goal was to develop not only competent staff but a pleasant, personable staff loyal to Dennis Seashores and, above all, one that was sensitive to the concerns of the guests.

Alice, who always wanted to help others, viewed the recruitment process through the prism of compassion. She not only sought to hire a competent staff, she sought to improve the lives of people she hired and, in some cases, to elevate their self-esteem. Alice's goal was to employ a staff that would not only be efficient and faithful to Dennis Seashores mission, but one that would also radiate kindness and reflect an upbeat persona to Dennis Seashores guests.

The first step she took in the recruitment process was to sit down with her good friend, Louise Reardon. Alice thought Louise epitomized the kind, caring, competent person who would be an asset on her "Dennis Seashores Team." Although Louise wasn't the extrovert Alice was—she was more reserved, more laid-back—she was a good mother to her six children and she knew Alice's goodness and competence would be a valuable commodity in assisting Dennis Seashores guests. Additionally, she thought Louise would benefit in getting out of the house and into a work environment. Louise, after listening to Persuasive Alice say, "Why not give it a try Louise? Just give it a try and see what happens." After 30 years, Louise is still "giving it a try." Another FOA—Friend of Alice.

Alice and Louise Reardon celebrating another a
successful Dennis Seashores summer.

The next prospect was another friend, Jim Crawford. Jim, an electrician by trade, was still grieving the loss of his wife of many years. Consequently, Alice thought an opportunity for him to, "get out of the house" might be beneficial during this difficult time in his life. Alice proposed that, with Jim's electrical background, he consider joining the staff as a weekend handyman. Jim, a man of few words said, "I'll give it a try." Now, 30 years later, he too is still, "giving it a try."

In the course of a lifetime, opportunities to help other people present themselves to everyone. However, with Alice, she didn't wait for a "presentation." She went in search of those opportunities; she seemed to be pre-programmed in identifying people in need. Often, her involvement entailed only small, insignificant, kind-hearted gestures, which may have had lasting effects.

"On a hot summer day as I was walking down Depot Street in Dennisport praying I would be able to find a job when, surprisingly, a car stopped and a woman I did not know, offered me a ride home; gratefully I accepted her kind offer," said Margaret Dunlap. "On the way to my home, the woman, who identified herself as Alice Kennedy, asked where I worked, to which I replied, 'I am unemployed.' Without hesitation, the kind woman exclaimed, 'You have a job now Margaret. I want you to work with me at Dennis Seashores. What a Godsend that was for me,'" Margaret exclaimed.

"I worked for Alice Kennedy at Dennis Seashores for many years and she helped me in a variety of ways. She purchased curtains, put screws in the wall and hung the curtains on all my windows. That wasn't all, she cleaned my apartment, bought me food, negotiated lower rates on my electric and telephone bills, arranged for me to obtain a place in Harwich Senior Living, and she moved my furniture. I will always call Alice, *My Angel*; she was sent to me directly from God," declared an obviously appreciative Margaret Dunlap. At this point I sound like a broken record; after 30 years Margaret too is still "giving it a try."

It was joy for Alice to help the helpless. She considered opportunities to help the Margaret Dunlap's and the Jeannie McGraths of the world to be grace-filled opportunities. There was not a self-serving bone in Alice's body; she loved to see people smile. Frequently, Alice would say, "It's good to see people smile; people in need are generally gifted with beautiful smiles!" Alice was also gifted a beautiful smile—God's goodness personified! ...*love each other as I have loved you...*" (John 15:12-15)

GOODNESS AND KINDNESS BEGET FRIENDSHIP

After Alice and Margaret became better acquainted, Alice realized Margaret possessed immense intellectual abilities but most important to Alice, Margaret was an active parishioner at Holy Trinity Church in West Harwich. Margaret also spoke several languages, including Russian.

In the later part of the 20th Century, many Russians began to immigrate to the United States, and a number of immigrants settled on Cape Cod. With Margaret's fluency in Russian, she was the first-person Cape Cod Police Departments called when they needed a translator.

At some point, Ali met a young Russian girl, Yulia Ivanova, a recent Russian immigrant in quest of employment. After a brief interview, Alice offered her a position at DSS. To assimilate into American culture, Yulia informed Alice she was changing her name Julia Johnson. An ancillary benefit for "Julia" was working with Margaret, who was fluent in Russian.

As might be expected, Alice took a personal interest in helping a young girl like Julia who was so far from home; she found a suitable accommodation for her and she assisted Julia in applying for a green-card application. Julia's mother, residing in Russia, was so grateful she sent Alice a long letter and a present to show her appreciation for helping her daughter. Another FOA—Friend of Alice.

In due course, Margaret shared with Alice that, at some point, she incurred an emotional challenge' she wasn't as cerebrally proficient as in the past. From that day forward, Alice assumed the job of an, unofficial, quasi-conservator for Margaret. Fortunately, Margaret obtained a Health-Care Aide position to augment her income when Dennis Seashores closed for the winter.

Alice pleaded Margaret's case with a variety of organizations, petitioning for benefits and price reductions; most importantly, she placed Margaret's name on the Senior Housing Listing in Harwich. Thankfully,

Margaret was awarded an apartment in the Town of Harwich Senior Housing Development on Bank Street.

In addition to Louise, Margaret, Jim, and Julia, Alice reached out to the Brazilian Community in Hyannis and employed several hard-working Brazilians. Alice believed people would be grateful for an employment opportunity, thus they would become loyal and proficient representatives of DSS.

Within a short period of time, Alice assimilated a competent and personable staff, all of whom were appreciative of the employment opportunity and soon became indispensable employees, emblematic of Dennis Seashores portrayal of a family atmosphere.

On another occasion, Alice was having lunch with a friend and noticed a woman sitting alone in the restaurant, so Alice approached her and suggested she join them. Julie Loomis was most grateful for the invitation; Julie and Alice became good friends. Julie was a senior citizen, who was well-educated and lived in El Paso, Texas during the winter and came to the Cape for then summers. Julie was not in need of summer employment, so she was not a member of the Dennis Seashores team.

Alice's benevolence was apparent to both Margaret and Julie, both devout Catholics, so it wasn't long before Margaret and Julie became close friends, both actively participating in Holy Trinity Church ministries.

Alice was continually promoting a family-friendly atmosphere at DSS—games for the kids, and parental involvement in organizing the games. She also invited kids to help with various DSS chores, providing them with a sense of ownership. A few Sundae School Ice Cream gift cards didn't hurt either. Newfound friends were the by-word of Dennis Seashores—both kids and their parents made lifelong friendships. The camaraderie was infectious. Most guests were anxious to register for the same weeks the following year so their kids could spend summer after summer, year after year, with the same DSS friends. Dennis Seashores' reputation was growing, and many recognized that it truly was a wonderful family environment for summertime seashore fun.

Alice believed it to be important to create continual opportunities for children to become engaged in various aspects of the Dennis Seashores operation. On a daily basis, Alice assigned one of the kids to be in charge of raising and lowering the American Flag, helping in the distribution of towels, picking-up discarded litter, and more. Alice mandated the American Flag should never be flown during inclement weather, nor should it be flown after sundown. All the Dennis Seashore Kids who assisted in daily DSS chores were compensated with gift cards to the Sundae School Homemade Ice Cream Shoppe!

A PROPERTY MANAGER'S DAY IS NEVER DONE

Ali's innumerable skills were not restricted to Dennis Seashores. Her aptitude for mathematics and mechanics enabled her to assist the kids with their summer reading assignments and algebraic projects and the Ferncliff neighbors with medical and mechanical issues.

Alice was never far from her trusty toolbox or her ancient yellow bag with medications for any illness that afflicted the five kids. She willingly administered appropriate medications, many whose shelf life expired years ago, for any cut or bruise, sustained during summer fun at DSS or on Ferncliff Road. Alice was ready, willing and able to help.

One of the Reardon kids, Kara, once came frantically running and barged into our house hysterically crying. Between gasping for breath and sobbing uncontrollably, Kara said, "Mrs. Kennedy, you need to come as fast as you can and please bring your yellow bag. Sean (her brother) just cut his finger with the hedge-clipper."

When Alice saw Sean's dangling finger, she realized it was far beyond the medications contained in her yellow bag. Immediately, she shoved Sean into her car and they sped off to the emergency room at Cape Cod Hospital. As soon as the emergency room doctors examined Sean, they realized they were ill-equipped to handle an injury as severe as a detached finger. Alice was advised to transport Sean to the Jordan Hospital in Plymouth immediately.

Thankfully, doctors at the Jordan Hospital were able to re-attach Sean's finger, but subsequent follow-up medical procedures were mandated. Consequently, Alice and Sean Reardon made numerous trips back and forth from Dennisport to Plymouth for follow-up examinations. After a few weeks, the doctors were confident Sean's finger would remain attached. Day to day family living in the Kennedy household in Dennisport or Needham was anything but uneventful, yet it was nonetheless stimulating.

CHAPTER 6

YOU HAVE FRIENDS; I'M YOUR MOTHER

...reject not your mother's teaching. (Proverbs 6:20)

With dexterity and with love, Alice was always able to balance a magnum of tasks. Specifically, she was capable of integrating love for her family and love for Dennis Seashores into her 24/7 life. Alice loved every aspect of life—she loved God, she loved God's people, and, in a special maternal manner, she loved the children that God gave her. She possessed a unique ability to benevolently correlate virtues of love, courage, and compassion into her everyday life. Whenever the kids would quarrel, which was often, Alice would say, "I'm not a referee; work it out. Make it work."

INSTILLING RESPECT

The transition from western Mass to eastern Mass coincided with our daughters' entry into every young girl's utopia—babysitting!

As our young family continued to adapt to Needham living during the school year and Cape Cod living during the summer, Katie, Patti, and Anne Marie became enthralled with seeking babysitting opportunities. One day, our three daughters, in unison, told our family matriarch, "Sally just asked us to babysit for her children next Saturday."

At her maternal best, Alice responded, "Sally? Who is Sally?" to which the response was, "Sally Dempsey."

Without hesitation, our matriarch emphatically said, "Do you mean, 'Mrs. Dempsey'?" They replied in unison, "She told 'us' to call her 'Sally.'"

Ali retorted, "I don't care what 'Mrs. Dempsey' told you to call her; you are to address her as 'Mrs. Dempsey.'" Alice pounded into all of our kids, "You are to look adults directly in the eye and address them as 'Mr.' or 'Mrs.'"

John Hooben recounted to me that at the conclusion of Alice's Funeral Mass, Jackie said, "Thank you Mr. Hooben for attending my mother's Funeral Mass." To which he responded, "Please, call me 'John.'" Jackie replied, "You were always 'Mr. Hooben' to me and I shall continue to call you, 'Mr. Hooben.'" *"Do not forsake your mother's teaching." (Proverbs 1:8-9)*

Alice was a perfect blend of compassion and fortitude. In effect, she was seemingly a paradox: compassionate and yet tough—tough as nails. Although she would be the first to help her kids, and upon restoration and recovery, she would voice the following: From now on, remember that you are responsible for taking care of yourself. Nobody's going to do it for you." When things didn't go well for the kids there was no pity party. "Be tough and suck it up," was Alice's by-word. She was from the school of hard-knocks, espousing tough-love and, she would regularly remind the kids to work it out and solve their own problems.

Like all mothers, Alice helped her children whenever they did need assistance, especially with difficult homework assignments. If they seemed befuddled, mesmerized or confounded, she would intervene, sit with them, explain the process, and then they completed their homework assignments.

REALISM and PERSISTENCE

Perplexing situations were right in Alice's wheelhouse; she loved solving problems! Mechanical, mathematical, scientific, or spiritual, Alice was always available with "the correct answer." She was solution oriented! Whether it was providing insight into the earth's orbit, algebraic equations, or the importance of the Stations of the Cross—Alice was ready, willing, and certainly able to help!

Intuitively, Alice knew when and where to "pat the kids on the back." At times "the pat" may have been on the upper back and, on other occasions, "the pat" was much lower than anticipated. Alice was a tough-love mother. She was simply *the best mother!*

If anyone rendered a compliment about one of her children—your daughter was so kind and helpful to other kids, or your daughter has such beautiful hair, or your son scored in the 97th percentile in an exam—Alice's response was always the same: "Thank you but, he or she, is just normal."

The message Ali attempted to instill in her children was; they were not special in any way shape or form. In her words, "They are just normal." Life's lesson of "normalcy" lovingly dispensed from their mother's heart of hearts inured to their lifelong benefit. Their loving mother pointed her children toward the Path of Humility.

Another lesson that Alice imbued to her five children pertained to unconditional love. Alice would frequently remark, "If a doll, a blanket, a baseball glove, a book, a hockey stick, or a dress is important to Katie, Patti, Anne Marie, Danny, or Jackie, then it was also important to us because—it's important to them."

It was Alice's hope and prayer that, as they grew into adulthood, the converse would apply—what was important to their mother and father would be important to them. On a daily basis, Ally reflected love, compassion, guidance, and humor; all of which were, in her words *"free as the Grace of God."* Deep is the wisdom of the maternal heart.

ALWAYS, BATTLE READY ALICE

Although Alice was never trained as an educator, whether it be a grammatical, algebraic or scientific issue, she was ready, willing and able to help the kids with their homework assignments. In addition, during the adolescent years, she was also an occasional visitor to their schools—sometimes as a voluntary visitor and on other occasions, an involuntary visitor.

Toughness, courage, and compassion were woven in the depths of Alice's being—woe to the person who may harm any of her five children. At one point, in Needham High School, a student stole one of Patti's jackets. Alice instructed Patti, who was more than capable of going toe to toe in any adversarial situation, to handle the situation herself. The next day Patti came home and said that she informed her homeroom teacher about the incident. Alice was less than sympathetic. "Work it out with the school administration," she said. "And let that be a lesson to you; secure your locker."

Although Alice realized it was the student's obligation to secure their lockers, she was disappointed that the school administration didn't seem concerned about recovering Patti's jacket. The following morning, Alice was at Needham High School taking matters into her own hands. At Needham High School, after Patti pointed out the "person of interest" who was wearing her stolen jacket, Alice was in the principal's office in a nano-second.

Apparently, Patti's homeroom teacher alerted the principal's secretary that a disgruntled parent was en route to the main office, because when Alice arrived, the principal's secretary informed Alice, "Dr. Fredey is extremely busy and will not be available for consultation with parents today."

"Busy or not, Dr. Fredey will see me." With her face flushed and fury raging, Alice barged into Dr. Fredey's office with an unceremonious greeting.

"Forget your paperwork, Dr. Fredey and come with me; I intend to show you the student wearing my daughter's stolen jacket."

A compliant and acquiescent Dr. Fredey deferentially followed apoplectic Alice as she proceeded to locate the student-suspect who was brazenly seated on the front steps of the school wearing Patti's jacket. She turned to Dr. Fredey and pointed to the indelible mark she permanently affixed to the pocket of Patti's jacket. Case closed; stolen jacket repossessed.

Not to be forgotten was a telephone call Alice received from the principal of Saint Joseph School, Sister Nancy Cavanaugh, CSJ. "Alice you have to come down to the school immediately, Jackie's behavior is unacceptable." Alice dropped what she was doing and with the speed of a jet plane, Alice was in the bedraggled principal's office as son John sat dutifully on the principal's bench.

Sister Nancy, obviously agitated, said, "Alice, John's homeroom teacher is disturbed and wants to expel John from St. Joseph's School. He came to school this morning with a Neo-Nazi haircut, which is in violation of school regulations and completely unacceptable. At the very least, he will have to be suspended from school for one week." Alice did not perceive anything offensive about Jackie's haircut and concluded that the teacher was pre-programmed to over-react at Jackie's motivation, due to previous misgivings about Jackie's proclivity to speak his mind in the classroom and to frequently ask the teacher for documentation.

Without batting an eye Alice said, "Don't worry any longer Sister Nancy. Relax. This situation will be remedied immediately. Jackie will accompany me when I leave but he will not be going home. I will take him directly to the barbershop. I'm certain the barber will trim his hair to be compliant with school coiffure regulations. Jackie is anxious to turn-in his homework assignment so he will be back in the classroom for this afternoon's session."

"Thank you for being so understanding Alice. We look forward to seeing John later today," said the beleaguered principal.

Alice's life was inexorably integrated with the lives of her children. She was pleased when her children achieved their academic goals. She was also delighted with their sports aptitude. From homework challenges to employment opportunities to athletic endeavors, Alice was the omni-present mother.

PROUD TO BE THE MOTHER OF A RENOWN SOFTBALL PLAYER

During Anne Marie's senior year at Needham High School, she was a starting pitcher on the softball team. Toward the end of the season, she was paired against Lisa Moore, a widely acclaimed strikeout pitcher for Wellesley High School. It was a game of significant local interest as Lisa was within reach of her 1000th strikeout and a large contingent of fans from Wellesley and Needham were in attendance. The entire Needham team was fearful they might bear the ignominy of becoming Lisa's 1000th strikeout victim. After Lisa's 999 strikeout, television cameras were trained on each Needham player as she came to bat.

When Anne Marie came to bat, her strawberry blonde hair was fluffing out from under her Needham softball cap as she determinedly stood in the batter's box. She was confident she would not strikeout. After sharply fouling off two pitches, once again she swung. She did not hit the pitch; strike three! Anne Marie Kennedy became Lisa Moore's 1000 strikeout victim!

After the game, the TV camera's continued to roll as sportscaster Bob Lobel of WBZ-TV (Channel 4) Channel 4 interviewed both the hero and the ignominious victim. At the time, in the life of a high school student it was a highly embarrassing moment but as Alice said in consoling Anne Marie, "As time passes, eventually you will be pleased that your name is in the Massachusetts high school record rook." Anne Marie received as much recognition for being the 1000th strikeout as did Lisa Moore, who accomplished the task.

With Alice's lifelong passion for hockey, she was thrilled when Danny and Jackie acquired a love for her favorite sport. It was a thrill for her to attend Danny and Jackie's hockey games, especially weekend hockey tournaments. One of her favorite winter weekends was our annual trek to Lake Placid, New York, where the Needham Youth Hockey teams participated in an International Hockey Tournament at the Olympic Ice Arena. Not only was she interested in the hockey games, she was excited to rent a ski-mobile and speed around Mirror Lake with her daredevil companion Danny, who was holding on to his mother's waist for dear life!

When the boys were older and Jackie was a graduate student at the University of Notre Dame, Alice enjoyed our annual trek out to South Bend, Indiana on football weekends. Often Danny would join the two of us and we would attend the traditional Notre Dame Pep Rally the night before the game, and of course, the camaraderie of the game-day tailgate parties at Notre Dame Stadium. Although her exuberance for "The Fighting Irish" was obvious during the game at Notre Dame Stadium, her greatest thrill was visiting the Lourdes look-alike, Grotto, which was serenely nestled behind the epicenter of the nationally recognized campus, in the shadow of the Golden Dome overlooking St. Mary's lake.

Dan, Jackie, Danny and Alice tailgating at a University
of Notre Dame football game, November 1999.

COMBAT CONDITIONS ON CAPE COD

Another unique opportunity to display maternal love transpired on a hot,
summer day in 1990. Danny just received his Massachusetts driver's license
and was beginning his first venture operating a car without an instructor.
This occurred in Dennisport. Big brother offered to chauffer his younger
brother Jackie on a short ride. Alice cautioned them not to go any further
than Dennis Seashores (a short distance), and then to drive straight home.

When the boys returned home from their abbreviated ride, they were
embroiled in a fistfight—viciously punching each other in the front seat
of the car. Alice authoritatively commanded, "Stop fighting and get out of
the car, now!" Ignoring Alice's directive, they persisted in pounding each
other with pugilistic punches.

Alice—no shrinking violet, never met a challenge she didn't conquer.
Her modus operandi was fight fire with fire. Apparently, the boys didn't

realize the depth of a mother's love. With fire in her eyes, irascible Alice, armed with her ever-ready hammer, swung into action and smashed the windshield of the car!

As shards of splintered glass flew through the front seat of the car, both boys—in utter shock and trembling with fear at their mother's peculiar demonstration of love—ceased hostilities and exited the car. Armistice achieved! As much as she loved her car, she sacrificed the windshield in order to seize the opportunity to underscore a maternal teaching moment.

The Iron-Duke of Dennis dispersed discipline and dispersed it justly. Without batting an eye, Danny's driver's permit was confiscated and Jackie's name removed from the Driver's-Ed Training Course. When necessary, *The Heart of Our Home* effectively displayed a vivid impression of Hard-Hearted Hannah! *A time to break down and a time to build up. (Ecclesiastes 3:1-8)*

"Mrs. Kennedy was a no-nonsense woman," exclaimed Doctor Diane Dermarderosian, a pediatrician and a close friend of Katie's. Obviously, this incident is testamentary evidence of Doctor Diane's assessment of Katie's mother. Everyone who experienced Animated Alice in action, particularly Dennis Seashore owners and summer guests, would attest to her love of people. But most of all they were well aware of her intrinsic ability to competently resolve complex issues.

Alice was all business all the time, especially when it came to her five kids. She epitomized filial love, but when the situation warranted remedial action, she was ready, willing, and quite able to administer a healthy dose of tough-love. The fact that all five of our children developed into fine up-standing adults is attributable to the grace of God, augmented, by the gift of fortitude bestowed on their mother when, as a young girl, she received the Sacrament of Confirmation!

DEEP IS THE WISDOM OF A MATERNAL HEART

Katie recalled another one of our memorable motherly moments on Cape Cod. Alice's maternal love was on display during lunch at one of her favorite Cape Cod restaurants, The Impudent Oyster in Chatham, when Katie broke the news, "I want to move to New Zealand." Unfazed, Alice asked, "What would you do there Katie?" Katie, our often shy and reticent firstborn, replied, "I really don't know what I would do, I just think it would be an amazing experience."

Accordingly, in her typical inquisitive fashion, Alice peppered Katie with an abundance of practical aspects of her venture—sustenance, habitation, health insurance, etc. To assure her mother this was a well-thought-through proposition. Katie replied, "I intend to find a job and a place to live, but I never considered health insurance." Without blinking an eye, Alice said, "I will pay for your health insurance premium and an up-front spending money stipend." It was classic Alice—always available for others!

Adolescent years are trying times for youngsters as well as parents. Alice was always empathetic to the difficulties confronting her children, and as she said on more than one occasion, "I know what they are going to do before they know what they are going to do." At one point, when our No. 2 son was struggling with adolescent years, she said, "Don't worry Jackie, we'll get you through this difficult time in your life."

During Danny's senior year at Catholic Memorial High School, he spent a considerable amount of time completing college applications. Fortunately, he had impeccable credentials—academic, athletic, spiritual, and in community service activities. His Catholic Memorial guidance counselors encouraged him to apply to the University of Notre Dame.

After months of intense preparation, Danny proudly presented a copy of the essay that he intended to submit to The University of Notre Dame to Alice. After reading the essay, his mother remarked, "You better be prepared to apply to another college because you will never be accepted at the University of Notre Dame when the admissions director reads this essay!" Danny was perplexed with his mother's caustic remark, "Why are you so negative Mom?" he asked. She responded, "No one, especially, a female admissions director, wants to read that you were tormented by your older sisters; you made a major mistake in selecting that topic for your essay. I can't understand how you garnered the guidance counselor's approval."

Everyone at Catholic Memorial High School, including Father Jim Haddad, Pastor of Saint Joseph's, assumed with Danny's credentials his acceptance would be a slam-dunk; they were wrong; Alice was right. The University of Notre Dame Admissions Department rejected Danny's application and he was absolutely devastated! *Deep is the wisdom of a maternal heart.*

BUSY IS BETTER

Alice's maternal instincts extended beyond her immediate family. In a sense, Dennis Seashores was the sixth child that she never gave birth to; in the winter months she seemed lost without her Chase Ave "baby."

Each year Alice's commitment, and her love for Dennis Seashores seemed to increase exponentially. In the fall, she was consumed with plans to shut-down for the winter months, yet she regretted closing the Wind Mill and down-shifting for the winter months. After closing Dennis Seashores for the winter months of ice and snow, combined with the diminishment of daylight, Alice's effervescent personality seemed unduly dampened. I concluded she needed a spark.

Even though she was busy 24/7 with five kids, I thought a diversionary interest would be stimulating for her. So, unbeknown to her, I contacted a close friend of hers from Saint Joseph's, Janet Corrigan. My thought was to find another focus for Alice during the short days and long nights, so she would have something other than the kids and her beloved flaming fireplace to occupy her time.

Janet concurred and said, "I know Alice, she is 'busy with the kids,' but she needs another type of 'busyness' to divert her focus." Janet was most supportive and said she would be in contact with Alice and suggest that she serve on a few parish committees.

"Alice is such a joy-filled person, whenever we are together, she always has me laughing hysterically," said Janet. "Don't worry, I will see that she gets involved with more groups."

It wasn't long before Alice was actively involved with magazine sales, fund raising, and other various school projects. In addition, there was a need for someone to help tabulate the weekend offertory collections at the parish, so Alice volunteered to help there as well. When Alice started to help out with the counting team, she expanded a new circle of friends, who included Ann Cosgrove, Sandy Mangini, Jean Cleary, Regina Woods and Mary Corcoran. The small group of counters was chaired by Pat McNamara, who resided in East Dennis on Cape Cod Bay during summer months and often would meet Alice at Cold Storage Beach in East Dennis. Pat, a summer friend at the beach, soon became a winter friend at the counting desk.

With Alice's exposure to a business environment and office experience, in short time she became of significant member of the counting team. As much as Alice's sharp mathematical mind was a good fit, her keen sense of humor introduced an element of informality to the Monday morning sessions. Alice's innate intelligence and gleeful demeanor was also a good fit.

"I will always remember Alice; she was seated at the calculator, checking and cross-checking contributions, and if the totals were out of balance, she was always able to locate and correct the discrepancy," said Mary Corcoran, new to the Counting Club. Between parish committees and the Counting

Club, Alice's pent-up energy was expended on church-related activities and she thoroughly enjoyed the participation.

As might be expected, it wasn't long before Alice formed enduring friendships with the counting team, one of whom, Regina Woods, sent Alice a meaningful note at a time when sadness entered her life. Regina wrote: "Dear Alice, when days seem long and the crowds are gone, if the thought crosses your mind to 'rage at the Heavens,' I will be here; you can rage at me—you're my friend."

Regina continued, "When I leave that mind-numbing weekly counting task, because of your kindness and your comedy, I am more light-hearted than when I arrived. You inspire all of us Alice, but most important, you are so darn smart."

"Many people caution me to be careful crossing the street, especially when there is ice and snow, but you without uttering a word, hold my hand and guide me. When your days are sad and lonely, Alice, please, let me hold your hand," wrote Regina.

"Alice was such a happy person, I was delighted when she decided to join us on the Saint Joseph's Counting Team," said Ann Cosgrove. "Beside her efficiency in tabulating currency, if any of us ever needed to prepare for a family gathering and intended on serving fruit punch, we always called Alice—her fruit punch recipe was superb. "When Alice left for the summer, we really missed her; she was so efficient, and, most important, she was so comical," said Sandy Mangini.

Whenever Saint Joseph's was blessed to have a newly ordained priest offer his First Mass of Thanksgiving, Alice volunteered to supply the punch at the Parish reception! Per usual, she had a system—first was the preparation process, then several bowls of punch were produced, and third, one of the bowls was placed on a bed of ice on table with a long white tablecloth in the center of the hall. Each daughter took shifts in ladling out the punch and last, but certainly not least, she concealed the two additional bowls of punch under the table, strategically placed in a large pan of ice. When the initial bowl was depleted, she accessed the concealed punch bowls under the table; never did a First Mass of Thanksgiving reception run out of Alice's delicious punch!

It was another 20 years before another First Mass was celebrated at Saint Joseph's and that Parish reception was at her son Danny's First Mass of Thanksgiving. Strange as it seems, Alice only vaguely remembered the times she was in charge of the punch table at First Mass Receptions. Unbeknownst to any of us, that slight lapse of memory might have been one of the first indications of the onset of an insidious illness.

WINTER TIME EXCITEMENT; PARTY PLANNER AT WORK

I have experienced much joy and encouragement from your love. (Philemon 1:7)

As we approached the third week in February 1983, Organizational Ali said, "In order to properly celebrate this sometimes-exasperating marital challenge, we're going on a surprise trip for our 15th Anniversary." She wouldn't divulge the destination, so yes, I was mystified. Shortly before we were to depart, my GA car needed repairs, so in recognition of the mystery trip, I decided to splurge and lease a Cadillac while my car was in for repairs. The fancy car of course added an aura of import to Alice's plan.

As I drove an over-sized Cadillac Eldorado, Ali proceeded to give me mile-by-mile directions. She had a ball directing me on the mystery trip; she coached me on a roundabout route from Falley Drive to the entrance of the Mass Turnpike. Then as she directed me east on the Mass Pike. Ali hesitatingly suggested that we might want to consider getting off the Pike at the next exit then, as we approached that exit, she would change her mind and suggest perhaps there would be less traffic if we took the next exit.

The further east we traveled, the more I speculated that we were going into Downtown Boston; I was wrong. That thought was expunged when we reached the Weston exit; we went south on Route 128. Eventually I concluded the destination must be to our Cape house, but I was surprised when she did not direct me to take Exit 9, the Dennisport exit. We continued east until we exited at Chatham/Orleans. After passing the exclusive Chatham Bars Inn, I presumed we were in route to Orleans or Provincetown when, suddenly, as a last-minute thought, Ali suggested we turn around and go back to Chatham Bars Inn for an anniversary cocktail.

As we proceeded to sip our cocktails, My Little Alice Blue Gown said, "Happy Anniversary Babe, this is our destination, we are booked at the Chatham Bars Inn for the weekend." She was thrilled that her impeccably designed ploy was so efficiently executed; I was completely fooled! It never entered my mind that we would be staying at such a lavish resort.

Al-Marie Haggerty Kennedy organized our honeymoon in Jamaica and now, on our 15th anniversary, she was once again, Organizational Al! Bill Saint Lawrence said their maternal grandmother Elizabeth Cameron McCarthy had it right when she said, "Little Ali's tiny but she can do anything; she's strong and she's a smarty." I was thrilled and Alice was delighted at the Chatham Bars Inn. Her well-conceived plan worked to perfection!

As we sipped our cocktails, in a sort of melancholy mood, I said, "We've had some good times in the past 15 years haven't we, Ali?" After a moment of silence, with the most serious of expressions, she replied, "When?" I burst out laughing, and every time I think of that remark, I continue to laugh. It was truly the laugh that never stops laughing. Although, as I write this today, I am laughing through misty eyes. Ali's comment was a completely extemporaneous remark to a genuinely serious question. Thus, Ali's straight-faced retort delivered with such authenticity made it so comical and so memorable.

Actually, with Alice's frugal mind, she took advantage of a Chatham Bars Inn Weekend Special. As beneficiaries of the weekend special, we received one night free, 50% discounts on all weekend expenses, plus a discounted two-day stay the following year! I don't know whether Alice was happier because she surprised me or because she took advantage of such a desirable bargain! Truly—it was a win-win.

The following year, during school vacation, Danny and Jackie were the recipients of the discounted two-day stay. That was also a success because the weather during that week in February week was unseasonably warm, thus Ali and her sons were able to access the Chatham Bars Golf Course. They only putted around the practice green, but most importantly, Alice had introduced them to the game of golf. As time went on, both boys credited their mother as the person who taught them how to play golf, so I commenced, tongue-in-cheek, to refer to Alice as The Instructor.

Four years later in 1987, when Jackie was 12 years old, he won the Knights of Columbus Massachusetts State Championship at the Crumpin-Fox Golf Club in Bernardston, Mass. At the conclusion of the tournament, reporters from several newspapers, including the Cape Cod Times and the Springfield Daily News, interviewed young Jack. During the interview, reporters asked him if his father taught him to play golf and he said, "No, my mother taught me to play golf; my father refers to her as The Instructor."

The following morning, I began to receive telephone calls from friends in Western Mass, chastising me for abdicating my paternal responsibilities. As I quickly learned, in an interview with a reporter from the Springfield Union, Jackie gave full faith and credit to his mother for his golf proficiency. Although bloodied but unbowed from the chastisements, I was pleased to have Affable Alice accept the accolades!

As much as Alice came to love the hustle and bustle of parish activities, she was always anxious to begin a new season at Dennis Seashores. Every year, especially after a severe winter, there seemed to be a unique set of issues that required problem solving. The stairs to the ocean were washed away in a winter Nor'easter. The flagpole was floating in Nantucket Sound.

T sails on Dennis Seashores landmark Windmill were casualties of the winter weather. Alice thrived on solving problems and she seemed to have an unlimited number of Dennis Seashores stories to recount during the dark days of blustery blizzards.

Year after year, story after story, in season and out of season—a day in the life of the Dennis Seashores property manager was anything but dull! All winter long, sitting in front of her raging fireplace, watching ominous weather forecasts and lamenting the potential damage a wild winter storm would inflict on the cottages on the shores of Nantucket Sound, Alice would often reminisce her favorite Dennis Seashores folklore stories.

A BEACHFRONT COTTAGE RULES THE DAY

Alice was always on the lookout for opportunities to persuade owners to upgrade the Dennis Seashores cottages. One of the more recalcitrant owners, a member of the board of directors and owner of one to the premier beachfront cottages, resisted replacing deteriorated window shades.

Astute Alice noticed that one of the summer guests on the reservation list for this prominent cottage was a family was named Bayer. Within a nanosecond, Alice was on the telephone speaking with the owner, suggesting he reconsider his recalcitrance.

Alice proceeded to inform the owner that the surname of a family on his reservation list was Bayer. In her typical whimsical way, Alice said, "I think you may agree, no one associated with Dennis Seashores, especially a member of the board of directors, would want to expose Dennis Seashores to an embarrassing incident. "Bayer people without window shades?" Case closed; owner concurred, and agreement was reached to install replacement window shades.

ENGAGEMENT RING CRISIS
...have something to share with one in need... (Ephesians 4:28)

Alice not only solved problems, but she also had the faculty to anticipate problems.

As Alice once related the story to me; a guest came charging into the Windmill hysterically crying. Between sobs, she struggled to say, "I lost my engagement ring in the sand and it must have been washed into the water!"

Alice endeavored to console her, but she was inconsolable! Eventually, Alice was able to convince the distraught woman that she too would join in the search. In a matter of minutes, Alice produced a metal detector that she stored in the Windmill for just such an emergency. Grasping the metal detector with one hand and the woman's hand with the other, Alice proceeded, with her habitual rapid gait, to the site on the beach where the ring was last seen. As waves were crashing ferociously against the shore, Alice scoured the beach. She did so with metal detector in hand and the distressed damsel's hands clasped in prayer. Within 10 minutes, Alice, the Savior of the Moment, found the lost engagement ring! The newly engaged woman jumped for joy and hugged Alice so hard she could have broken her back!

"Alice possessed innumerable qualities. She was a quick thinker, resourceful, and with spontaneity, she successfully solved difficult problems. I was impressed with her ability resolve complicated issues," said Paul Kelleher, a member of the Dennis Seashores Board of Directors. "More importantly, she was always prepared; she gifted with an ability to anticipate almost any eventuality."

WORLD SERIES IN REVIEW

One afternoon Alice came home and told me one of the guests had an emergency dental issue and she brought Mr. Gionfriddo to a dentist in South Dennis who was able to relieve the intense dental pressure he was enduring. I asked Alice to repeat the guest's name, to which she replied, "Does the name 'Gionfriddo' ring a bell with you?"

"Perhaps," I responded. "W here do they live?"

Alice said, "Cheshire, Connecticut. Why all the questions?"

"Your guest possesses an uncommon surname; when you check on his dental condition ask him if he is related to Al," I explained. "During the 1947 World Series, while playing left-field at Yankee Stadium, Brooklyn Dodgers left-fielder Al Gionfriddo made a spectacular catch of Joe DiMaggio's bid for a three-run game tying home run."

The following afternoon, Alice told me that "Mr. Gionfriddo confirmed his brother's name was Al, who played left-field for the Brooklyn Dodgers.

In appreciation for Alice's intervention with the dental issue, and the recollection of his brother, Mr. Gionfriddo gave me an autographed picture of his brother making the memorial catch in Yankee Stadium.

PIPING PLOVERS

On another occasion, a guest from the Midwest poured her heart out to Alice; she was distressed that people appeared indifferent to saving the whales and preserving the habitat of piping plovers nesting on the beaches of Cape Cod. After commiserating with the validity of the guest's concerns, she said, "There is considerable concern for piping plovers and whales, birds and mammals, but there is little mention about the millions of unborn babies who are aborted." Alice continued, "As important to our ecology as birds and mammals are, isn't a human life more important?"

The guest replied; "You have a good point Alice. I never associated abortion in that context. I will have to reconsider my views." Alice was not only confident enough to exercise the courage of her conviction, she possessed a command of the English language that enabled her to persuasively present her point of view.

A COSMETIC IMPACT

On another occasion when Alice came home from DSS, I thought that something looked different about her, but I didn't immediately detect what was different. She was never into wearing much make-up, so it wasn't the absence of color, but something about her face looked different. Before I could mentally compute what was different, she blurted out, "I had a problem today. The flame from a gas floor-heater blew back in my face!" Then I realized why she looked different; Alice didn't have any eyebrows or eyelashes!

The guest in one of the cottages knew exactly what to do when the pilot light on the gas-floor-heater went out, they asked Alice. Immediately, Alice, with her trusty toolbox in hand, went to the cottage, crawled under the house and attempted to restart the pilot light. Unfortunately, too much gas had escaped, so when she went to light the pilot, the gas ignited and a flame blew-back into her face. Thankfully her face was not burned! Undeterred by the frightening incident, she quickly recovered from the near catastrophe and, succeeded in re-lighting the pilot!

HURRICANE BOB

On Monday, August 18 in 1991, without much, if any, notice, Hurricane Bob, a category 3 storm suddenly struck Cape Cod with mind-boggling fury. Trees were down everywhere, as twisters seemed to be spawned by the winds of the hurricane. Dennis Seashores was without power for an entire week.

In the event of a power outage, there are extensive ancillary issues that don't immediately come to mind and, they are not insignificant issues—refrigeration, gasoline, heat, air conditioning, television and of course WiFi. Alice swung into action and was able to secure generators, fire wood, and identified gas stations that were functioning because of a supplemental source of electricity. The crisis was so acute that Alice was compelled to enlist emergency personnel—her children! Alice delegated Katie, Patti, and Anne Marie to deal with cottage damage and Danny and Jackie were assigned to heavy lifting tasks, such as fallen trees and extraordinary large amounts of seaweed, which they buried deep in the sands of the Dennis Seashore Beach. Team Kennedy was in action!

Subsequently, in the event of another emergency, Alice integrated our daughters into the weekend turn-over team and Danny and Jackie were the ground team (i.e., repairing damaged cottages and burying excessive amount of seaweed deep in the sands of the beach). Katie, Patti, and Anne Marie returned lawn furniture and toys to the cottage owners. In a matter of days, Dennis Seashores was restored to its pristine status, thanks to My Little Alice Blue Gown. As usual, she was resourcefulness personified. Team Kennedy was a melody in motion: well prepared, well oiled, well trained and capable of any unanticipated meteoric surprise.

As soon as the recovery operation from the effects of Hurricane Bob was completed, Alice found a Cape Cod entity that would print custom-made T-shirts that read on the front: "I SURVIVED HURRICANE BOB (August 18, 1991)." Alice ordered a sufficient supply for everyone who pitched in and helped with the recovery operation, and then distributed them to all the DSS guests with an understanding that early registration for the following year rental would ensure a discounted rental rate.

In Alice's mind, Dennis Seashores was truly her extended family. Although it is a trite expression, nonetheless, the following was affirmed with Alice and Dennis Seashores: "If you like what you do, you will be good at it." Alice not only liked working at Dennis Seashores, she loved everything about Dennis Seashores—once again, it was the sixth child she never delivered. It was truly her extended FAMILY which to her could be interpreted as *F. A. M. I. L. Y—Forget about Me, I Love You!*

WINNING FRIENDS AND INFLUENCING PEOPLE

"When my wife and I first met Alice, her multiple abilities were readily apparent," said Bill Early of Branford, Connecticut. "We have many fond memories of her, especially in her ability to administer a large complex of cottages. She was like a Fortune 500 CEO, implementing her well-planned agenda." Bill Early went on to say, "We were also impressed with her innovative Dennis Seashores "Chalk Board," which depicted "Estimated Time of Arrival," "Cottage Residency," and "Time and Date of Departure." Years in advance of informational technology, her organizational skills were well documented. Alice was efficiency personified with, most importantly, a winning personality."

According to Justine Early, "Alice possessed an absolutely unique ability to effectively interact with a myriad of personalities. If a guest was disgruntled, and if she believed the grievance to be warranted, Alice would apply "the guest is always right principal." But if, in her judgment, the guest was not right, she was verbally adept in convincingly explaining corporate

policy. Even if the guest was not completely placated, Alice presented a plausible explanation in a commiserating manner so the guest could appreciate the merits of Dennis Seashores' policy.

Bill and Justine Early's observation was astute; Alice personified multi-tasking. She would go to extremes to assure guests of a comfortable stay on the shores of Nantucket Sound. Her concerns for guests applied not only to their stay at DSS, she also empathized with the exasperating endurance summer guests experienced dealing with the notorious nightmare of

Cape Cod traffic. Nonetheless, her weekend responsibilities did not preclude her from attending 4 p.m. Saturday Mass. She did, however, leave instructions for guests who did not arrive at the prescribed 2 p.m. check-in time.

To accommodate weekend guests who incurred traffic delays, she inaugurated informative notes assuring late arrivals they could register the following morning. Every Saturday and Sunday night, she, or a designated family member, would trek down to DSS and, "check on late arrivals!" In season and out of season, this repetitive phrase became a Kennedy family household phrase; frequently injected in general family conversation...and primarily to elicit universal smiles from Alice and her kids. I doubt the "Earlys" from Branford were ever in the "late arrival" category.

Alice and a summer employee from Ireland, Seamus McCarthy, prepare for a typical day of summertime activities at Dennis Seashores.

ALL WORK AND NO PLAY... a NO-NO IN THE WONDERFUL WORLD OF ALICE

Alice loved everything about the Cape; she loved Dennis Seashores and she loved that her children were gainfully employed in booming Cape Cod businesses. But most of all, she loved *playtime!* Alice never met a boat that didn't delight her, a beach she didn't love, or a lobster she didn't devour.

On her day off, true to form, she was busy. She enjoyed going on a whale watching cruise from Sesuit Harbor in East Dennis, taking the Ferry from Woods Hole with her daughters to Martha's Vineyard or Nantucket. On her August days off, she looked forward to taking a tour of Nantucket Sound on Jon Stott's boat. When Alice decided to stay on terra-firma, the two of us went golfing.

When she returned home from her exciting nautical excursion, she and I would often go to one of her favorite seafood restaurants—the Impudent Oyster in Chatham, where she always ordered a scallop roll or, on occasion, a lobster roll!

Most often when Alice went for lunch, she would order a lobster roll, but she was extremely particular at which restaurants she would order it. A restaurant had to pass her personal test. Whenever there was more than a slight semblance of celery and/or lettuce in the lobster roll, she was disappointed. She expected a preponderance of lobster meat, otherwise she was not a happy camper! Her favorite spots for lobster rolls was Barnacle Billy's in Ogunquit, Maine, the Flying Bridge in Falmouth, and Sesuit Café in East Dennis.

When Ali saw a bright red boiled lobster or a colossal red king crab, her beautiful blue eyes lit-up, and quickly she grabbed a double-jaw lobster cracker and savagely attacked the unfortunate sea creature. With seemingly pent-up vengeance and malice aforethought, she tore off the tail, twisted off the claws, and menacingly broke the back of the shell with her steel-plated double-jaw lobster cracker, *delicately depositing the enticing red lobster meat* into a dish of melted butter!

Excited Alice, *livin' the dream,* as she prepares
for a typical Cape Cod clambake.

ALWAYS-AVAILABLE ALICE

"You shall love your neighbor as yourself." (Matthew 22:39)

Tim Clifford, a neighbor of ours on Ferncliff Road, passed away around the time of the millennium, leaving his widow, Lee, the sole occupant of their Ferncliff Ave home. Strange as it may seem in today's world, Lee did not drive a car, but she, like Alice, was resourceful. Lee loved to walk; she walked all the time but, on occasion, she would welcome transportation from friends. Alice and Lee's next-door summer neighbors, Bob and Jean Moran, qualified as "friends of Lee Clifford." The Morans were regulars in transporting Lee to Saturday afternoon Mass, grocery shopping, and, of course, to her hairdresser (Alice was her neighborhood back-up).

Whenever Lee, in her late 80s, needed something done around the house, she always assigned the project to her husband Timmy, but since he died, Lee would call on Alice because as she said, "Alice could fix anything— within minutes of my call for help, she would be strutting down the street carrying her trusty tool-box."

"The first time I met Alice was at Lee Clifford's house," related Bridie Burke, a neighbor from Fenway Road in Dennisport. Alice was on Lee's bathroom floor with her head in the toilet bowl! No, she wasn't sick; Lee's toilet was clogged and Alice was snaking out the blockage."

Another neighbor, Lorraine Salois, recalled that, "Every year on August 15th, I would receive a telephone call from Alice informing me "This is the Assumption of the Blessed Mother; a Holy Day of Obligation." Emotionally, Lorraine added, "I guess she wanted to keep me on the straight and narrow."

It was always with a great deal of sadness when Columbus Day arrived because it signified it was time to close the Windmill on Chase Ave and drain the plumbing on Ferncliff. Multi-tasking Alice did not look forward to the slow pace of life during the long winters on Woodlawn Ave in Needham.

CHRISTMAS-TIME in NEEDHAM

As usual, when the off-season commenced, Ali began to focus on Christmas shopping. Alice was not the conventional "shop until you drop" woman, but when it came to her five children, Alice became a Christmas shopper. She did put a great deal of thought into the presents she purchased, which she viewed through the *prism of practicality*. In her mind, Christmas presents should be useful. Most often her gifts were flashlights, first-aid kits, flares, etc. In Danny's case, she knew he, like herself, was interested in tools, so she shopped for him at Brookstone's in the South Shore Mall in Braintree, where she always found the latest in tools.

Like all mothers, Alice was intent on doing everything possible to make Christmas a joyful experience for our kids. Alice decorated the house, did all the shopping and, she prepared the Christmas Eve and Christmas Day menus. Alice wanted every Christmas to be memorable. My contribution was to put-up the Christmas tree, write Christmas cards, and wrap presents.

The exhilarating expression on Al's face when she opened Christmas cards was thrilling to witness. I always deferred to her when it came time to open Christmas cards; her excitement was beyond description. She couldn't rip open the envelope fast enough.

As the official despatcher of the Kennedy family Christmas cards I kept a log of the cards we received to update our card listing for future years. If, when receiving a care, anyone was thoughtful enough to write a personal message—the card was preserved. Every year in addressing cards, I reviewed the previously preserved cards. If I thought a past comment would momentarily perplex a pensive Alice, I went to the post office in the vicinity of the sender and re-mailed the old card to our Needham address.

A few years after we moved to Needham, our neighbors who resided directly across the street, Bill and Anne Kinsley, relocated to Dover, Mass. They were wonderful neighbors, who treasured two large Boxer dogs: Schooner and Champion. Not infrequently and, certainly much to the chagrin of their owners, Schooner and/or Champion would inevitably break free and roam the neighborhood. Within short-order, Woodlawn Ave neighbors were assisting in the pursuit of the two cavorting canines.

The first year Bill and Anne resided in Dover we received a Christmas card with a personal message assuaging any fear we may have had with the residential relocation of Schooner and Champions. "Schooner and Champion love their new neighborhood; they have made many new friends, several of whom come to play doggie games in our backyard," a message scripted on the Christmas card.

Fast forward, 10 to 12 years later, as I was writing our Christmas cards I decided to re-mail the Christmas card we received from Bill and Anne shortly after they relocated to Dover. I placed the old card in an envelope and in disguised handwriting, I addressed the envelope to Mr. and Mrs. Daniel J. Kennedy. I proceeded to drive to the Dover Post Office, and mailed it to 45 Woodlawn Ave. When the postman delivered the mail, I feigned indifference and pretended not to be overly interested as Alice opened the Christmas cards. I revealed an element of interest when I heard Alice exclaim, "Dover?" In disbelief she said, "Do we know anyone in Dover?" I remained, purportedly indifferent, yet waited clandestinely for a reaction.

As Alice ripped open the envelope, she slowly read the personal message aloud, "Schooner and Champion love their new neighbors...?"

Perplexedly, she said, "Bill and Anne?"

I attempted to display indifference with a nonchalant expression. As I leaned over pretending to fain minimal interest in the card, I innocently opined, "You're right Al, that is a bizarre note."

Alice responded, "Could this be from the Kinsleys? They moved to Dover, but we haven't heard from them in years."

I responded, "I think you're right Al. It must be from the Kinsleys." Still perplexed Alice said, "If it is from them, they must have been drinking when they wrote this ridiculous message."

At that point, I couldn't conceal my cover much longer. Al duly noted my attempt to suppress a gratifying smile and said, "Did you send this card?"

I didn't have to respond. My expression was a dead-give-away; both of us laughed heartily. I always loved to see Alice laugh. If Alice was happy, I was happy, and Alice was definitely HAPPY with the Christmas card from Dover! I would often do any stupid thing just to see her laugh! As Paul Harvey, the well-known radio commentator, used to say, "Now, for the rest of the story..."

A week later, on New Year's Eve Day, Alice took the commuter train from Needham to Boston to exchange some Christmas presents. While she was waiting on the platform at Back Bay Station for the Needham train, she heard a man on the platform singing, "Merry Christmas, Merry Christmas, Merry Christmas." Al thought it unusual that on New Year's Eve Day someone was singing Christmas carols, so she looked to see who was belatedly celebrating Christmas. Much to her shock, the musical interlude on the Back Bay Station platform was rendered by our former neighbor Bill Kinsley! Alice was so excited, exuberance exhilarating from every sinew of her body. Expeditiously, she ran toward the tipsy troubadour exclaiming; "Bill, Bill Kinsley? It's Alice Kennedy from Needham. Bill, equally surprised, excitedly said, "Alice Kennedy? I haven't seen you in years." Al's reflex response was, "Thank you for the Christmas card, Bill!"

Alice immediately regretted her tongue was in gear before she engaged her cranium. Bill too was in shock because he couldn't recall sending us a Christmas card. I don't recall how Alice said she handled the embarrassing situation, but I'm certain, she skillfully evaded a detailed explanation. Fortunately, with her sense of humor, she saw the comedic aspects of the Back Bay Station sequel to the *Christmas card that kept on giving!*

FUN and FROLIC in FLORIDA

In February, in order to break-up winter monotony in Needham, Alice's sister, Eleanor, and her husband Emil always stepped up to the plate and invited Alice and me to spend a few weeks with them at their condo in Naples, Florida. Alice was thrilled; she could leave the cold snowy streets in Needham behind and she could spend day after the day in the tropical sun at the 15th Street Beach in Naples. A joy to behold—Alice, Eleanor, and her suntanned husband Emil!

Eleanor and Emil were the epitome of the conscript "Beach Bums." They loved the sun and they loved the beach. Every morning Eleanor prepared a tote bag with delicacies., Emil packed the car and, with Al in tow, they left early enough to find a prime-parking place alongside their well-tanned friends. Occasionally, if they could tear themselves away from the Pelicans on the beach, Alice and Emil, who had much in common, would go for a boat ride or take in a local motor car exhibit.

Alice and Dan with Eleanor and Emil Masi at the Turtle Club, Naples, Fla.

Rather than join the sun-worshipers, I would opt to attend morning Mass at St. Peter's Church in East Naples, and then treat myself to a bagel and a cup of coffee at the local establishment and peruse the morning paper. Unfortunately, the paper only provided limited news on Boston Sports; consequently, I would relocate to the Naples Public Library and avail myself to a computer. Needless to say, an ancillary benefit was the avoidance of the tropical sun!

On days that were especially hot, I would leave the library earlier, drive to the 15th Street Beach, layer up with sunscreen, don a wide-brimmed hat, and venture onto the sandy shores of the Gulf of Mexico. The primary reason I put in a momentary appearance was to suggest that Alice might like a reprieve from the intense solar rays. Occasionally, she would concur and accompany me back to the condo.

Alice and I certainly affirmed the old adage, "opposites attract." Ali loved the sun, the ocean, boats, and sports cars, while my goal was to avoid all four. Al was also gregarious and ultra-friendly, always seeking to converse with strangers and intent on making new friends. Me? I preferred solitude.

On the rare occasion when I would venture onto the 15th Street Beach, Emil, who always had a comedic flare, would greet me with a tongue-in-cheek remark and ask, "Why don't you spend more time on the beach with Alice, Dan?" My response was always the same, "Separation keeps us together."

Our annual trips to Naples clearly illustrate the unique relationship Alice and I enjoyed; she, the proverbial "live-wire" and I the proverbial "dead-head." Alice accepted my idiosyncrasies, and thankfully, Eleanor and Emil endured them as well. With a huge smile, Alice would say, "That's just Dan being Dan!"

One year while we were visiting Eleanor and Emil, I acquired tickets before we left Needham so the four of us could attend a Red Sox Spring Training Game in Fort Myers. The timing was perfect. Emil was thrilled. John Henry, owner of the Boston Red Sox, displayed Model 'T' cars at the entrance to Edison Road Park, so Alice and Emil were double winners: a spring training game and a motor-car show.

On one particularly hot day, when I convinced Alice to take a reprieve from the blistering and brutal hot sun, we experienced an interesting incident on the ride back to the condo. While we were stopped at a traffic light on 7ᵗʰ Street, Alice pointed to a pedestrian and said, "That woman crossing the street looks like Anne Kinsley, doesn't she?"

I immediately thought, typical Alice. She was always hoping to establish familiarity with total strangers. I opined in customary fashion, "Not to me." What in the world possessed her to think a woman crossing the street in Naples was the wife of the New Year's Eve Troubadour? Preposterous; I saw no resemblance, but Alice was not to be dissuaded. She rolled the window down and shouted; "Anne? Anne Kinsley?" The woman abruptly stopped walking, turned, and with a face radiating shock, looked directly at Alice and said, "Yes!" When Alice introduced herself, a broad smile came across Anne's face. Once again, Alice prompted a pleasing reaction from a total stranger!

First, in a most unlikely of circumstance, Alice noticed Bill Kinsley on the Back Bay Train Station platform in Boston. And now, years later, in Naples, she recognized Anne Kinsley crossing 7ᵗʰ Street in Naples.

Anne Kinsley was thrilled that Alice recognized her and explained that she and Bill sold their home in Dover and became permanent residents of Naples in 1995. Anne insisted that Alice and I come to their home for a visit. I was especially excited at the prospect of listening to an encore of Bill's Christmas carols, the New Year's Eve rendition. Alice and I had an enjoyable evening renewing old acquaintances with Anne and Bill and, yes, I did mention the Saga of the Christmas card, and no, Bill did not offer to sing Christmas carols.

CHAPTER 7

TIME TO SMELL THE PEAT

...an offering by fire is soothing aroma to the Lord.... (Numbers 15:14)

E very year our good friends Frank and Eleanor Tierney traveled to Ireland, and in 1985 they persuaded Alice and me to accompany them and their friends, Larry and Mae Good, on the trip. The annual Tierney family treks fortified Frank with an in-depth knowledge of all aspects of Irish culture, so we were most fortunate to have him as our "Ireland Tour Director."

As our Aer Lingus flight descended over the west coast of Ireland, the sun was rising above the blue sea, Irish Music was softly playing, and the green hills and valleys were radiant in their fabled 40 shades of green. It was a magnificent view to behold—forever etched in our minds. I can still recall Alice grinning from ear-to-ear with unbridled joy as the plane touched down on the Shannon Airport Runway in County Clare. Alice, who always seemed to operate on high-octane fuel, an always on-the-move gal, was unusually serene and relaxed as we traveled the beautiful Irish Countryside en route to our accommodations in Killarney Town.

Immediately upon arrival at Shannon Airport, we rented a large van. Larry Good was our designated driver and he drove directly to County Kerry and the Great Southern Hotel in Killarney. Once we were settled in the Great Southern, the first thing Frank did was locate Eddie Sheehy, the owner of the John B. Shea Funeral Home in Holyoke who spent the entire summer at the Great Southern Hotel in Killarney. We had a wonderful time listening to Eddie Sheehy, a funeral business associate of Alice's father, regale us with stories about Ireland. The next day it was on to Dingle Peninsula and, a much-anticipated visit with my Irish relations.

Although Frank Tierney's knowledge of Ireland was extensive, neither he, nor the rest of us knew the geographic origin of their forebears. Consequently, our tour director purposely designed our itinerary to commence where my relatives emigrated, County Kerry.

COUNTY KERRY and KENNEDY RELATIVES!

Alice and I were excited to learn Frank Tierney's Trip-Tic Travel Planner's primary focus was locating my relatives in Annascaul, County Kerry. I was, of course, anxious to meet my father's first cousin, Margherita [Rita] Kennedy and her husband Michael Fitzgerald, who resided in a typical Irish cottage just beyond the hairpin bend, on the main road from Tralee to Dingle Town. The sharp turn is truly comparable to a hair-pin; within the space of 100 feet, the highway suddenly develops a dramatic U-turn, circumventing an obstacle too burdensome to relocate.

Many years ago, in Annascaul, two young Irish lassies, Kathleen (Kate) Barrett and her sister Mary Barrett married Kennedy boys—not Kennedy brothers. Mary (Barrett) Kennedy became my father's mother and Kate (Barrett) Kennedy was Rita's mother. Thus, Rita Fitzgerald was my father first cousin.

As we proceeded toward Dingle, we stopped for directions in the small village of Lispole, which was sandwiched between Annascaul and Dingle— the birthplace of my paternal grandfather, Patrick Joseph Kennedy. Unusual occurrences and coincidences seem to occur when visiting Ireland; the following is no exception!

Larry Good parked our rental van at a small convenience market so I could inquire as to the location of the Fitzgerald home. The convenience market was located directly across the street from the rustic remains of an old Catholic Church where, presumably, my great grandparents, Maurice Kennedy and Mary Hanifin, were married.

As I entered the store a tall, young man was exiting. Assuming in a small community people may know the domicile of most inhabitants, I imposed upon his good nature and asked, "Would you be kind enough to direct me to the home of Rita Fitzgerald?" The stranger responded, "I would be pleased to direct you to Rita and Michael's home, but it will do you no good. They are visiting their daughter in Dublin and will not return until months' end."

I expressed my disappointment and said; "You certainly do have extensive information on neighborhood people." He replied, "Why wouldn't I be well informed? I always know when my parents are on holiday." I was shocked to have randomly met the son of my father's first cousin—my second cousin! I did know from my aunt Helen Kennedy that Rita and Michael were parents of a daughter, Anne, and a son, John Kennedy Fitzgerald. Bumping into him in a tiny Lispole convenience market was mind-boggling.

Alice, May, and Larry Good, and especially Francis Xavier Tierney (FXT) were deeply disappointed that we missed visiting family connections where they anticipated an hour or two of Irish craic with my Kennedy family relatives.

Resultantly, we had no recourse but to shift to Plan B, which was Father John McLaughlin's admonition that I visit O'Cinnede Pub in Annascaul and introduce myself to proprietor Mrs. Mary Hartnett, one of his relatives.

Mrs. Hartnett was indeed home, and as all Irish people are, she was extremely hospitable. She was a typical gregarious Irishwoman—hardworking, and genuinely glad to meet us. As soon as we were in the pub she said, "Our best is none too good for a Kennedy. Come into the parlor and sit yourselves down."

As the six of us sat at Mrs. Hartnett's parlor table, she toasted the Kennedys of Annascaul and Father John McLaughlin and proudly proclaimed she was a "Double Kennedy." Both her mother and father's surnames were Kennedy.

Alice was never reticent about participating in conversation. "Truculence" was her bye-word and "intestinal fortitude" her modus operandi. But on rare occasions, she deferred to me for input—and such a demurrer transpired in Mrs. Hartnett's parlor. Unobtrusively, Alice whispered to me, "Ask Mrs. Hartnett if there are any Haggertys in this area." With the first lull in the conversation, I injected, "Mrs. Hartnett, could you tell us if there are there any Haggertys in this area?" With a thick west-coast-of-Ireland brogue, which could certainly be construed as disdain, Mrs. Hartnett emphatically responded, "There are NO HEGARTYS here!!"

It's doubtful Mrs. Hartnett intended to convey contempt, yet her intonation clearly denoted there were no Haggertys on the Dingle Peninsula. Mrs. Hartnett's remark did however provide Alice with the opportunity to play the role of an aggrieved relative, concluding Mrs. Hartnett's reference to be disparaging to her Irish ancestors.

As soon as we returned to our rental van and began to drive away, Alice's consternation was vociferously expressed. "Who does that no-good-double-Kennedy think she is, belittling Haggertys!" she said. The laughter at Alice's consternation was a foretaste of the many laughs and pleasant moments we would experience on our first trip to Ireland in the fall of 1985.

As we departed the Dingle Peninsula, we passed through the tiny town of Inch, where the movie "Ryan's Daughter" was filmed with the beautiful water of Dingle Bay so prevalent. From Inch, we toured the Ring of Kerry and Cahersiveen, where Daniel O'Connell, The Great Emancipator, was born—another highlight for me.

It was exciting to ride the roads and environs of Annascaul and Lispole, places where my paternal ancestors emigrated, culminating on the Ring of Kerry, where my maternal great grandmother, Elizabeth O'Connell, was born. My maternal grandfather, John Francis Burke, often said, "We are direct decedents of the Great Emancipator, Daniel O'Connell."

All six of us had a fantastic time touring Ireland. Larry Good exhibited professional skill in negotiating the narrow and tortuous roads and Frank tripled as travel agent, navigators, and tour directors, as he programmed a litany of surprises that made for a most interesting trip. Frank never let on where our next destination would be, so the Goods and the Kennedys were in constant suspense as we anxiously awaited the ultimate daily surprise. After years of traveling with Frank, his wife Eleanor had a general idea of what surprises were in store for us.

We circumvented the Republic of Ireland, north (Donegal), south, east, and west and we stayed in the finest of hotels; in the Tierney World no reservations were to be made in bed and breakfasts! From the Great Southern Hotel in Killarney to the Burlington Hotel in Dublin, our City of Holyoke Yank and Tour Director Extraordinaire Frank meticulously mapped a most memorable excursion through a country of immense greenery. One of the more impressive sites was our view of Glandore Harbor from the Marine Hotel. With the exception of Frank, it is unlikely many Yanks would have known of this hidden jewel. The quiet, sleepy little town in West Cork not only consisted of a beautiful harbor, there was a plethora of watercraft of every imaginable variety all neatly nestled in the tranquil waters of Glandore Bay. For Alice, the quaint town of Glandore was the best of both worlds: a water view and the sweet smell of a peat-fire. Alice always loved a water view and now she acquired an equal admiration for the aroma of a peat fire.

Glandore, not far from Kinsale and Skibbereen, is a summer home to the aristocracy of Europe, including several of the United Kingdom's members of Parliament, several of whom own lavish summer homes in

Glandore overlooking the beautiful waters of Glandore Bay. As we departed Glandore on the Kinsale Road, we stopped at the Ballinspittle Grotto in West Cork, where it was reported, in July (1985), a roadside statue of the Blessed Mother was reported to be, at times, moving spontaneously. There were a number of people praying in front of the statue on the side of a hill but, as far as we could see, the statue did not move. Frank didn't miss a beat; we stopped at all the well-known Irish landmarks: Irish poet William Butler Yeats' famous Ben Bulben Forest, the Blarney Stone and the Cliffs of Moher. As our trip was nearing its final days, Frank revealed his ultimate surprise—an overnight stay in the elegant Ashford Castle in Cong! On his visit to Ireland in 1984, President Ronald Reagan was a guest at the Ashford Castle, and it was in Cong where *The Quiet Man* was filmed.

Our tour-guide, Frank Tierney, is pleased to point
out the Cliffs of Moher to admiring Alice.

The climax of our trip was to the village of Knock, County Mayo on August 21, 1879, where an apparition appeared at the south gable end of the small parish church. The Blessed Mother, Saint Joseph, Saint John the Evangelist, angels, and Jesus, the Lamb of God were seen by 15 people whose ages ranged from five years to seventy-five and included men, women, teenagers, and young children.

A full 20 years prior to our visit, in thanksgiving for a personal blessing, Frank made a vow that he would visit Our Lady of Knock Shrine annually, and he never missed a year of that commitment. In 1985, Alice and I were privileged to accompany Frank and Eleanor in completing their annual commitment.

Since Alice's initial insult when Mrs. Hartnett infamously said, "There are no Haggertys here," uninformed as we were, none of us realized the name "Haggerty" was an Anglicized version of the Irish name "Hegarty." We spent our entire trip, unsuccessfully, seeking "Haggertys."

Fortuitously, on one of our final days in Ireland, at Our Lady of Knock Shine, in County Mayo, Alice in her customary convivial manner, struck-up a conversation with a nun whose surname was, surprisingly, HAGGERTY! As Alice learned, she was not from Ireland, but she was Sister Anne Haggerty, a Sister of Charity from Nova Scotia, who knew several of the Sisters of Charity who taught at St. Joseph's School in Needham! Indeed, another FOA—Friend of Alice.

Alice (Haggerty) Kennedy unexpectedly meets Sister Anne Haggerty SC during a visit to Our Lady of Knock Shrine in County Mayo, Ireland.

NO LONGER A GUIDED TOUR

On subsequent trips to Ireland, when Alice and I were on our own, we followed the Frank Tierney template, always beginning our visit with a stop in County Kerry. On our first trip without Frank and Eleanor, we arranged beforehand to visit with Rita and Michael Fitzgerald. After our visit concluded, we motored across the short bridge on the Dingle/Milltown line and began to drive up the hill toward Fahn when Alice noticed a young girl hitchhiking. As I nonchalantly proceeded past the hitchhiking young girl, Alice suggested we stop and offer her a ride.

We did stop and the young girl was most grateful. She was exasperated, as she had been waiting several hours for a ride. Unlike the large rental van we enjoyed with the Tierneys, this vehicle was small and stuffed with bags and packages. In spite of our luggage cramped in the back seat, the young lassie was able to squeeze in amidst the packages and suitcases.

Lucie Zacharova, an attractive young blonde from the Czech Republic, had no particular destination in mind; she was spending her holiday hitchhiking through Ireland. Alice suggested Lucie might like to accompany us on our trip to the Blasket Island Museum and view the ocean as we traveled around the Slea Head Loop. Lucie would not only receive a historical and geographical education, she would have an opportunity to meet Irish-speaking people on the West Coast of Ireland, albeit with inept tour directors from Needham.

Lucie accompanied Alice and me to the Blasket Island Museum in Dunquin and also accompanied us for a visit with Eibhlin (Eileen) O'Shea. Eileen resides in Dunquin, the western-most point in Europe, thus the closest European location to the United States of America. Eileen, as did all Irish in the Slea Head area, spoke in the native Irish language, Gaelic. After centuries of English oppression, with the exception of the West Coast of Ireland, the Irish language has been deprecated, thus meeting Eileen, fluent in the Gaelic language, was a thrill for Alice and me. It was of course an added bonus for Alice's new friend, the Belle of the Baltics.

After an enjoyable dinner at the Half-Door Restaurant in Dingle Town, Alice and I drove Lucie to Killarney so she could rendezvous with her friends and continue her Irish holiday adventure. We shared addresses with Lucie and for many years we corresponded. Lucie Zacharova, Czech Republic, another...FOA—Friend of Alice!

As Alice and I continued our Ireland excursion, much to our delight we discovered the Old Ground Hotel, in Ennis, with of course a famous pub called the Poet's Corner. Alice was thrilled. Even though there was no water view, there was a peat-fire burning brightly in the fireplace and Alice loved it! Yes, once again, as Alice was enjoying the warmth and aroma of the peat, she noticed an elderly woman, sitting alone and sipping her afternoon tea in the Poet's Corner Bar. As I've mentioned, it was not unusual for Alice to befriend a stranger; she always viewed people who were alone through a crucible of concern.

When I returned from my tour of the Old Ground Hotel, Alice and the elderly widow Mary O'Riordan from Kilrush in West Clare were already fast friends as both sat and enjoyed the atmosphere and the craic. Alice and Mrs. O'Riordan continued to chat as she waited for the evening bus to bring her back home to Kilrush.

Alice and I were vaguely familiar with West Clare as we recently read a book written by two New York City journalists—Niall Williams and his wife, Christine Breen, a husband and wife author team that relocated from New York City to a farm they purchased town in West Clare, Kiltumper. When they weren't farming, they wrote a series of books about rural Ireland, one of which Alice read prior to our trip to Ireland. It was called *The Pipes are Calling.*

Even though Mary O'Riordan lived in an adjacent township in West Clare, she did not know of Niall Williams and Christine Breen until Alice mentioned them. She was thrilled that a Yank informed her about her American neighbors. Obviously, communications in the United States were more informative than communications in rural Ireland. *A Prophet is not without honor except in his native place. (Matthew 13:57)*

Until Mary passed away in 2000, she and Alice corresponded with each other with the undying hope we would take one more excursion to the Old Ground Hotel in Ennis, County Clare. When Mary passed away, her son sent Alice a beautiful note thanking her for befriending his mother on a cold afternoon in Ennis, West Clare. FOA—Friend of Alice.

YES, THERE ARE HEGARTY'S HERE!

Prior to our departure from the Olde Sod, we stopped in the Killarney Library to research Hegarty family genealogy. The Librarian in the Killarney Library immediately called Frank Hegarty on the telephone and insisted that I speak with his father, Mick Hegarty, an acknowledged Killarney town historian. Frank informed me that his father was currently in the Tralee Hospital recuperating from heart surgery; nonetheless, he insisted that we visit him. For several reasons, I was reluctant. First, as a total stranger, we didn't want to disturb a man in a weakened condition and, secondly, we just left Tralee Town and a trip to the Tralee Hospital would necessitate backtracking.

Frank was not at all ambivalent as he emphatically said, "My 90-year-old father would be deeply distressed to learn a relative from America was dispassionate on a visit to Killarney and did not visit him during his recuperation." Against my better judgment, so as not to offend Alice's relative, we did in fact, backtrack to Tralee Town.

I thought back to another member of the Hegarty clan—Alice's father, Charlie Haggerty, who was unable to attend our wedding because he too was confined to a hospital with a "heart issue." Just as Mr. Haggerty appeared to be the picture of health in Mercy Hospital in Springfield, so too did Mick Hegarty look to be the picture of health in the Tralee Hospital in County Kerry; both were alert and spirited, definitely displaying a healthy demeanor.

Mick Hegarty informed us that the Hegartys were originally from County Donegal. They came south to fight the Battle of Kinsale in 1601 and eventually settled in Glenflesk, a small townland on the road from Killarney to Cork. When I asked Mick who won the Battle of Kinsale, he said, "The British." With a straight face I responded, "Would you consider the Hegarty's to be losers?" He quickly retorted, "Hegarty's are not losers, we have people in high positions in Ireland; my cousin's son, Eamon O'Casey, is the Bishop of Galway."

Alice and Dan during their search for Hegarty
relatives in Glenflesk, County Kerry, Ireland.

As we were concluding our most recent trip to the Land of the Leprechauns in 1993, I was comfortably seated in the Aer Lingus Departure Lounge of Shannon Airport when Alice excitedly came running up to me and said, "I just spoke with the ticket agent and asked if there is any chance our flight might be over-booked, and she said that was a slight possibility. I told her if that materializes, we would be interested in relinquishing our seats; let's hope they are over-booked."

An hour later, over the loudspeaker we heard, "Alice Kennedy please come to the ticket agent." The flight was over-booked by two seats and Alice's offer to surrender our tickets was accepted. Once again, she returned with a bounce in her step and said, "You haven't heard the rest of the story, we can fly, round-trip, and do so anytime, anywhere and...this is the best part...on any airline!"

Yes, Alice the Family Trip Planner was in her glory; she was wheeling and dealing! Alice never met a bargain that she didn't like, and she certainly recognized this as a big-time bargain. Even though we waited six hours in Shannon International Airport, Alice was thrilled to sit and contemplate our free, future round-trip!

Upon arrival at Logan Airport, Alice went directly to the baggage carousel to recover our luggage while I went looking for a luggage rack to accommodate our bags. Shortly, Alice came running up to me excitedly exclaiming, "I just saw Father Jerry Whyte (an Irish priest from the Congregation of the Sacred Hearts of Jesus and Mary) at the baggage carousel and I told him we would drive him down to the Cape tonight." I replied, "If we drive to the Cape tonight, it will be close to midnight Ireland time, so why not stay in Needham as we planned and drive down in the morning?" Alice retorted, "Father Jerry has to say Mass at Holy Trinity tomorrow morning, so we have to drive him down tonight."

Other than by sight, neither of us knew Father Jerry; we only knew he was a summer visitor on Cape Cod and he celebrated Mass at Holy Trinity

Church in Harwich. I did remember a Homily he gave advocating a realistic appraisal of self when he said, "Six of the most important words in the dictionary—'I admit I made a mistake.'" Once again, Alice's sixth sense and awareness came into play as she identified someone in need of assistance.

Father Jerry rode with Alice and me back to Needham to drop off our luggage and pick-up things for the Cape. While we were in the house, a close friend who was disheveled stopped to visit with Alice. Immediately, the poor woman burst into tears as she described the dilemma of dealing with her teenage son.

As Alice did her best to console her distraught friend, she introduced her to Father Jerry, who had been in an adjoining room. Father Jerry proceeded to assure her that the Lord was with her during this difficult time and gave her his blessing. That spiritual moment would not have occurred had Alice not spoken to Fr. Jerry at the baggage area at Logan International Airport. FOA—Friends of Alice.

REAPING THE BENEFITS OF SEAT-SURRENDER:

The following year we reaped the rewards of Alice's airline ingenuity; we boarded a plane of British Airways at Logan International Airport and, we were *In the Air Again* headed to Heathrow International Airport in London. Once again, the arrangements were impeccable. Alice selected a wonderful tour company, Frames-Richards Coach Tours of London, which ran tour-buses from the City of London to the Southwest coast of Great Britain and north to Scotland, the land of her grandmother's birth.

Although Alice didn't encounter anyone in need of her compassionate concern on the high roads, the low roads or on the bonny, bonny banks of Loch Lomond, in the land of her grandmother Elizabeth Cameron McCarthy's (Nana) she was obviously filled with nostalgia.

In a melancholic moment, before our Scotland trip, Alice confided to Katie, "My grandmother 'Nana' was the most religious woman I ever knew." Wasn't that a wonderful recollection to convey to 'Nana's' great-granddaughter Katie? In so many ways, passing along that recollection was reflective of the depth of Alice's most endearing qualities: respect for her family, honored by her heritage and, most of all she wanted to acquaint her own daughter with knowledge of her great-grandmother's religiosity.

Elizabeth Cameron McCarthy was born in Dumfries, Scotland in 1878 and died on January 14, 1952 in Holyoke, Mass. Dumfries, in the Southern Uplands, was also the birthplace of Blessed Dun Scotus, considered to be one of the three most important philosopher-theologians in the High Middle Ages. On January 13, 2016, one day shy of the 64th Anniversary of Nana McCarthy's death, her wee-little granddaughter, Alice (Haggerty) Kennedy died in Needham, Mass and, at Alice's funeral, her cousin, Bill St. Lawrence recalled Alice's propensity for mischievousness as he related their Nana's reaction to Alice's youthful antics: "I'm going to skelp yer wee behind, Ali."

Nostalgia became more evident as our tour bus crossed the North Sea at the Firth of the Fourth and we exited the tour-bus in Center City Edinburgh, Scotland. Edinburgh is truly a beautiful city filled with centuries of history but for Alice, she contemplated what life must have been for her Cameron ancestors growing up in the tiny town of Dumfries and, on special occasions, visiting the beautiful City of Edinburgh. It was also a delight for Alice and I to view the memorial dedicated to Robert Louis Stevenson, a Scottish novelist and author of *Treasure Island* in Center City, Edinburgh.

After touring Robert Louis Stevenson Memorial Park and Edinburgh Castle, our Tour of Edinburgh was about to conclude when we stopped at Holyrood Palace, which was constructed for Mary, Queen of Scots in the 16th Century, and for many centuries was the residence for many Scottish Monarchs. The "rood" in Holyrood is Scottish for "Cross." The tour guide at Holyrood Palace explained that centuries ago, when a young Prince, three or four years old, was playing on the castle grounds, a bull came charging toward the young boy with the obvious intent to gore the little Prince. As the queen viewed the impending disaster, she said a quick prayer to God, pleading with Him to spare the Prince. Just as the bull was about to gore the boy, a rood (cross) appeared above the bull's horns, and abruptly the bull halted his charge and meekly returned to his habitat. As a consequence of that miraculous incident, the Palace became known as Holyrood.

Alice frequently said the following to me as our tour group sang Harry Lauder's famous song, *Roamin in the Gloamin:* "Just think Dan, THIS HAS BEEN a FREE-BEE!" Yes, wee-little Alice (Miss Frugality) did justice to Elizabeth Cameron McCarthy and her Scottish Heritage!

DOG DAYS in HYANNIS

On a Friday night, exasperated after enduring a typical summer time traffic jam, I arrived in Dennisport to be greeted by five kids and a wife begging me to, "Get back in the car dad, we want you to drive us to Hyannis to see a cute little Westie puppy." Just what I wanted, another ride in the car.

I was so glad to see the six of them happy, I said, "Ok, let's go!" All of us jumped into Alice's station wagon and off we went to the Cape Cod Mall in Hyannis. The kids and Alice couldn't run into the mall fast enough. They wanted to see the cute little Westie puppy. When I sauntered into the pet shop, the kids yelled to the attendant, "We told you we would bring our dad; here he is!" With excitement ruling the day, the attendant enthusiastically reached into the cage and handed me the puppy and said, "He's such a cute little puppy; you can hold him!" I said, "Hold him? I only came here to see him, not to hold him." Then I left the pet shop and went out to the mall corridor and sat on a bench reading the newspaper.

One by one all of them kept coming out pleading with me to come back in and see the cute little puppy. I wasn't the least bit interested in a pet shopping—we already had a dog. I was at my obstinate best. "We do not need a puppy roaming around the house," I said. "One dog was sufficient." In rapid fire succession, one by one, they came out of the pet shop. Finally, Alice pleaded, "I just talked to the attendant and he said they'll drop the price 60%. We can't pass up this bargain, Dan."

Then she hit me with her closing argument. "You do know Dan, Shannon is sixteen years old and he won't be with us much longer. He should meet his replacement." With tears flowing, in between sobs, in unison, the kids said, "Mom is right, Shannon needs a friend." People looked as they were passing by. Five crying kids stood there while a determined mother lectured a beleaguered man sitting on a bench looking for peace and quiet in the sports page of a newspaper.

As a last resort, I turned to Alice and rhetorically said, "Shannon needs to meet his replacement? How would you feel if I brought another woman into the house and said, 'I think it would be a good idea Alice if you, met your replacement?'" The slightest semblance of a smile seemed to emerge as she realized the fallacious logic to her argument. I always loved to see Alice smile, and I think that slight smile won the case for her.

Yes, I caved. We bought the cute little Westie puppy. Have I previously mentioned Alice was a Master Negotiator of indomitable determination, possessing an inestimable power of persuasion?

Everyone was so ecstatic to show their appreciation, as we drove away with Alice cradling the little puppy, the kids said, in unison, "Thank you Dad, you can name the puppy." The car radio was tuned to Irish music as I navigated the massive traffic jam on Route 28. The song playing was, *The Wild Colonial Boy, Jack Duggan Was His Name.* I accepted their good faith offer and said, "His name shall be, 'Duggan.'"

Shannon didn't have much time to get to know his replacement. He met his maker in November at the Stoughton Animal Hospital. In hindsight (yes, pun intended), as always, Alice was right!

ALICE THE ADVENTURER

In the fall of 1995, everything was relatively tranquil with the Kennedy Clan. Katie was on a three month stay in Katmandu in Nepal. Patti was in Washington DC working at the Brown, Cutter and Platt law firm. Anne Marie was employed at the Commonwealth of Massachusetts Division of Insurance. Danny was immersed in the everyday fabric of Providence College, while studious Jackie found time to captain the College of the Holy Cross golf team. With considerable time on her hands, Alice was confronted with a dilemma: what to do to occupy her time. She did not intend to succumb to the old adage: "Idle hands are the devil's workshop." *They get into the habit of being idle. (1 Timothy 5:13)*

A NEW EXPERIENCE; THE ANCIENT WORLD

It wasn't long before The Family Planner established a course of action. We don't live far from Plymouth, Mass, so why not become Pilgrims? Once again, our esteemed Family Trip Advisor swung into action; before I knew what hit me, the two of us were signed up to be pilgrims. No, not Plymouth Pilgrims—Holy Land Pilgrims!

Alice learned that Father Bob Howes, a priest who celebrated Mass at Our Lady of the Assumption Chapel in Dennisport during the summer, was organizing an October pilgrimage to the Holy Land. The pilgrimage departure coincided with the conclusion of Alice's Dennis Seashores seasonal responsibilities, and she knew I would love to visit the Holy Land. Typical of Adventurous Alice, she loved surprises, excelled in organization, and most importantly, she was always thinking of others.

Father Howes, a priest from the Diocese of Worcester and a graduate of Massachusetts Institute of Technology (MIT), was on lend-lease to other United States Dioceses, assisting them in diocesan planning projects. Father

Bob spent summers in Dennisport and celebrated Mass at Our Lady of the Assumption Chapel in Dennisport. During his Homilies, Father Bob frequently referenced the Saint of the Day, which resonated with Alice. She was impressed when Father Bob would frequently state, "Everyone is an apprentice saint." Alice was convinced we would be recipients of many blessings if we joined Father Bob Howe's Holy Land pilgrimage.

As always, Alice was right. We were blessed to walk in the footsteps of Jesus as well as experience a brief voyage on the Sea of Galilee. We met many wonderful pilgrims as we experienced the trip of a lifetime in the Holy Land and in Jordan.

The pilgrimage departed from JFK International Airport in New York, where we rendezvoused with pilgrims from the Diocese of Arlington, Va. and flew to Queen Alia Airport in Amman, Jordan. Upon arrival in Amman, we boarded a Jordanian bus and proceeded through the city to the General (British) Edmund Allenby Memorial Bridge. We were shocked to see soldiers on the roof-tops of buildings in Amman equipped with rifles in their hands! We crossed the Jordan River via the Allenby Bridge and entered the West Bank Territory. It wasn't long before Alice, as might be expected, formed friendships with pilgrims from the Diocese of Alexandria in Virginia. Catherine Quigley and two sisters, Nona and Aurora Garcia, were Alice's constant companions. As might be expected, visiting the Holy Land was a spectacular experience. We visited many Holy sites—Jericho, Bethany, Nazareth (hill country), Tiberius, Sea of Galilee, Mount Tabor, Mount of Olives and ultimately, Bethlehem and Jerusalem.

Alice, Father Bob Howes (Spiritual Director) and Nona
Garcia on the shore of the Sea of Galilee.

We were fortunate to have Michael Walbech, who was born in the
Town of Bethlehem, as our Catholic tour guide. Michael informed us that
the majority of Holy Land tour guides are not Catholic. Consequently,
we considered ourselves to be especially privileged. Our pilgrimage also
included visits to Capernaum and the Mount of the Beatitudes—Mount
Tabor, which at the summit of the exceptionally steep mountain, was the
site of The Transfiguration! *He led them up a high mountain...he was trans-
figured before them. (Matthew 17:1-13)*

As we proceeded to enter the Church of the Transfiguration, the security
guard refused to allow Alice admittance, alleging that her Bermuda shorts
were too short. During our 10-day visit to the Holy Land, never did any
security guard at any Holy Site question Alice or, for that matter, question
anyone else on our pilgrimage; only Alice was questioned and only at the
Church of the Transfiguration.

Alice was of course extremely embarrassed, and in the opinion of everyone on the Pilgrimage, this event was unwarranted. Our Catholic tour guide Michael took exception to the accusation and eventually negotiated a wraparound shawl for Alice. Problem resolved. Alice was allowed admittance to the Church of the Transfiguration. Ever since that day, anytime I read or hear of The Transfiguration, the *Alice incident* always comes to my mind.

As we continued our trip up to Jerusalem, we stopped in Bethany, only a short distance from Jerusalem and visited the place where Lazarus was raised from the dead. Although it was necessary to descend a steep set of stairs to view the burial area, we could imagine hearing Jesus as he said, *"Lazarus, come out! Untie him and let him go." (John 11:43-44)*

It's only a short distance from Bethany to the Mount of Olives, so within minutes we disembarked from our tour bus and gazed across the Kidron Valley at the City of Jerusalem and the prominent dome of the Temple Mount.

At that spot on the Mount of Olives, Bedouin Caravans were offering rides on camels. Only one member of our pilgrimage had the courage to accept a ride on a fly-infested camel. Guess which member of our pilgrimage accepted the offer to ride a camel? Correct! Daredevil Alice gleefully glided away on the back of a camel while the rest of us marveled at her courageousness! We were happy for two reasons: 1) Alice was thrilled to saunter off on the back of a camel; and 2) Thousands of flies feasting on the odiferous skin of the camel were also off on the camel ride!

As we descended the Mount of Olives, we stopped at the Garden of Gethsemane in the Kidron Valley and meditated on the enormity of the tree trunks in the garden, some of which may have been in existence at the time of the Crucifixion. From the Kidron Valley, we proceeded up a steep hill to Old Jerusalem, where we walked the "Way of the Cross" to the Church of the Holy Sepulcher. Unfortunately, we were unable to enter the Sepulcher itself as the line was extremely long and our tour guide wanted us to view the Church of the Nativity in Bethlehem.

The birthplace of our Lord was not only a spiritual experience, it was a window on life. Several religious factions jealously maintain control of their agreed upon area in the Church of the Nativity. Thankfully, the birth-place of the Lord was accessible to everyone.

Alice and Dan on the Way of the Cross as they walk through streets of Old Jerusalem en route to the Church of the Holy Sepulcher.

The following day we were, once again, at the Allenby Bridge and we re-entered the State of Jordan for our final pilgrimage stop: Petra, the Rose City. Petra is a famous archeological site in the southwestern desert of Jordan with temples, edifices, and amphitheaters carved into strikingly pink sandstone cliffs (circa 300 BC). Why was I not surprised when our family daredevil mounted a horse in Petra and galloped off into the Jordanian desert?

BACK HOME IN THE BAY STATE

Upon returning to picturesque Cape Cod, the Holy Land Pilgrims agreed to meet periodically to relive our Holy Land experience. Marge and Lincoln Lynch from Harwich graciously hosted monthly reunions at their South Dennis home.

Father Bob Howes was not only a regular at the monthly meetings at the Lynch house, he became a frequent visitor to the Windmill on Chase Ave. With regularity, on his way back to his Dennisport cottage, Father Bob stopped in for coffee and conversation with his Pilgrim friend Alice.

According to Alice's good friend Kathleen Flynn, originally a neighbor of hers in Chicopee and currently a resident of East Dennis, said, "Alice was always such a thoughtful and caring person. When she realized Father Bob Howes was badly in need of casual clothes, she confiscated several of Danny and Jackie's shirts and sweaters and gifted them to Father Bob."

GOOD OLD DAYS: NEVER TO BE FORGOTTEN

Although Alice was busy with end-of-the-season responsibilities, she was never too busy to keep her eyes peeled on a Mercedes. And surprise, surprise, in October she spotted a pre-owned 1994 C- 220 Mercedes with 31,300 miles at a dealership in Hyannis! Without hesitation, she deemed finding the car to be as fortuitous as mileage. The 31,300-mile odometer reading was similar to my father's lucky number 313. His birthday was March 13th, so she deemed the mileage to be a reinforcement of her desire to own a Mercedes. Alice's undying love for Mercedes preceding her years as the Kennedy Family Matriarch was all too evident in her eyes. I concurred. She should be the owner and operator of a C-class Mercedes!

After an absence of 25 years, once again, Alice owned a car she really, really loved. Like a kid on Christmas morning, she was beyond excited!

Since 1970, she sacrificed her love for a Mercedes and never exhibited any rancor, remorse or desire to acquire another Mercedes. Any personal interests and desires she may have had were secondary to her five children. Whether it came to clothes, cars, or recreation, she never thought of herself; the kids were her 24/7 focus, not clothing, not jewelry, not golf, not even...a Mercedes!

"Alice was never ostentatious, nor was she overtly pretentious, but she thoroughly loved her little green C-Class Mercedes. She always gave me a 'toot' when she drove by," related Janet Corrigan. "Alice was such a joy-filled person, she kept me in stitches with her wonderful sense of humor, and she was so smart. I always knew who to call for an answer to a tough question," said Janet.

"Ali always seemed to be mechanically inclined; as a young girl, she purchased 'fix-me-up cars' and she knew where to have them 'fixed-up.' Although modest in size, she also managed the Haggerty Family mutual fund portfolio," said cousin Bill St. Lawrence, adding that "she knew the real estate market like the back of her hand."

Yes, Alice always managed money wisely. To her, frugality should be an essential component in everyone's constitution. Alice was extremely cognizant of where and why money was spent. If any mechanical mechanism malfunctioned, the first thing she did was analyze the problem, take out her toolbox, and attempt to make necessary repairs. If her attempt to make a repair was unsuccessful, she would go to her stash of saved items, which were preserved for years for any possible eventuality. She abhorred purchasing replacement products.

"It was not unusual to see Alice's head under the hood of a car as she quickly removed her glasses, which were unnecessary for near vision, and took a close-up view of the carburetor or checked the dip-stick to make certain there was adequate oil in the crankcase," said longtime friend and wife of cousin Bill, June St. Lawrence. "Alice was one was one of the first people who realized the potential of a new product, Mobil One Synthetic Oil. She saw the merits of the product and told Bill and me to buy Exxon Mobil stock because of their new product."

She also extoled the benefits of Mobil One to me, but her explanation of its merits was wasted; I wouldn't know one type of oil from another, nor would I know a dip-stick from a walking stick or a crankcase from a suitcase."

If a mechanical item malfunctioned, she was determined to fix the broken item herself. To call an artisan would be admitting failure and she was a winner. Alice wouldn't give-up until she found the solution, and then when she did figure out how to fix the broken item, boy was she was happy! With a smile of satisfaction on her beaming face, she proudly proclaimed, "Problem solved!" If you purchased a replacement from Harvey's Hardware it would cost over $100." *"Ask and it shall be given to you; seek and you shall find; knock and it shall be opened for you." (Mathew 7:7)*

Another pet project of Alice's was the ornamental trim mounted on the hood of Mercedes-Benz automobiles. "These distinctive Mercedes ornaments are an attractive nuisance for kids and prone to vandalism; there must be replacement parts available," said the Master Mechanic. With Alice's ingenuity, she was fully prepared to meet that problem head-on; she located a wholesale supply house in Michigan that marketed Mercedes-Benz hood ornaments and she purchased a carton of hood ornaments at a wholesale price. Once Alice established the connection with that wholesaler, she purchased other replacement items—windshield wiper blades, taillight bulbs, etc. She had her own auto-parts supply depot in our cellar.

Alice advised other Mercedes owners in town, that if their cars were ever vandalized or if they needed any other minor replacement parts, to call her before calling a Mercedes dealer. It was not unusual to see a delighted Alice leave with her toolbox in one hand and a replacement ornament in the other. After replacing the missing ornament, she would say to her friend, "It's as free as the Grace of God."

RECOGNIZABLE IN SO MANY WAYS

Janet Corrigan put it so well when she said, "It was easy to recognize Alice, if not as she buzzed around town in her green C-Class Mercedes, but with ever-present baseball caps or, on Sundays, with her go-to-Mass hats." One evening on a hot stifling summer evening in August, she was recognized by another attribute.

Holy Trinity Church in West Harwich was presenting an evening Parish Mission, which Alice attended. As darkness was setting in and Alice was standing in line proceeding into the church, as might be expected, she was conversing with the person next to her in line. Suddenly, a man several people in front of her said, "Is that Alice Kennedy I hear?"

When the man turned around, much to Alice's surprise, it was the Bishop of Springfield, Joseph F. Maguire! Since we relocated to Needham, we seldom encountered Bishop Maguire but, apparently, Alice's voice had a mellifluousness, which was indelibly imprinted in the bishop's cranium. Everyone knew Bishop Maguire was gifted with an uncanny ability to recognize and remember people, we did not know he had an auditory ability as well. Bishop Maguire was pleased to see Alice and she was delighted to see him—doubly impressed in that she was identified by voice recognition.

When I first met Alice, I thought she had a unique intonation, but over time like so many other accidental attributes, her voice seemed to blend into the fabric of her being. Evidently, the unique quality of Alice's voice, although no longer apparent to me, retained its distinctiveness to Bishop Maguire.

"ON THE ROAD AGAIN, JUST CAN'T WAIT TO BE...."

In 1998, while Jackie was spending a year of volunteer work in New Orleans, La. and Danny was on corporate assignment at Duke Energy in Charlotte, N.C., our innovative Family Trip Planner sprang into action.

In February, Alice suggested delaying our annual Anniversary celebration until springtime. I was mystified as to what scheme she might be contriving, but she relieved me of my suspense when she said, "I've made March airline reservations to visit Jackie in New Orleans; that will be this year's Anniversary Surprise!"

We loved New Orleans and we enjoyed meeting Jackie's students and faculty members of Brother Martin High School, situated on Elysian Blvd in the heart of New Orleans. Jackie introduced us to the Brothers of the Sacred Heart, who administered the school. A few of them joined us for brunch at the famous Pat O'Brien's Restaurant in the Old French Quarter of New Orleans.

As we concluded our visit with Jackie, Alice's AAA TripTiK travel planner directed us to rent an auto and head north through the state of Mississippi to visit Danny, on assignment from Andersen Consulting Corp, at Duke Energy Corp. in Charlotte, N.C.

Alice's bottomless bag of surprises continued; she knew I enjoyed watching the Eternal Word Television Network (EWTN) and its founder, Mother Mary Angelica, PCPA, a show that originates from Irondale, Alabama. On the way to Charlotte, she suggested we stop in Irondale, Alabama to attend Mass at the EWTN Chapel.

Thankfully, we arrived in time to attend Mother Angelica's Wednesday evening telecast, "Mother Angelica Live." At the conclusion of the telecast, she personally greeted everyone in the audience. As Mother Angelica mingled with the guests, Alice said, "My husband watches you so much I think you might be his girlfriend." Mother laughed and pleasantly posed for a picture with Alice and me. Subsequently, Alice mailed the print to Mother Angelica and requested she autograph the picture; thankfully she did autograph the picture. If the Catholic Church were to canonize Mother Angelica, that picture would become a 3rd-class relic.

Dan and Alice with Mother Mary Angelica, PCPA, on
Saint Patrick's Day, 1998, in Irondale, Alabama.

As our journey resumed, we headed east from Birmingham, Ala. to Atlanta, Ga., which brought to mind the devastation General Sherman wreaked on this beautiful country-side 140 years before on his infamous *march to sea* during the Civil War.

SETTING FOOT IN THE TAR HEEL STATE

Danny was thrilled to welcome Alice and me to his, albeit temporary, home-away-from-home in Charlotte, N. C. He was pleased to show us around

Charlotte, but he wasn't overly thrilled to be so far away from Boston. Alice, with her inherent maternal instinct, hypothesized that Danny's tenure with Andersen Consulting was not going to be permanent.

After spending a couple of days with Danny, we headed due east to Pinehurst, N.C. to visit with our good friends Tom and Marge McGill. Before we left Needham, Alice called Tom McGill to forewarn them we would be in North Carolina and, if time permitted, we intended to drive to Pinehurst for a short visit. Thankfully, the McGills were home and we spent a few days with them.

It was always so much fun with the McGills. When they visited us at the Cape, we spent day after day laughing and singing and it was no different in Pinehurst, North Carolina.

CROSS COUNTRY

In the summer of 1999, my employer, the Automobile Insurers Bureau (AIB) of Massachusetts, offered an early retirement for eligible employees; I qualified and accepted.

Alice seized the moment and convinced me to spend a portion of the severance package and purchase as a Mercedes. Really? Me? As I've mentioned, Alice loved the Mercedes brand her entire adult life, and ever since she acquired a 1963 Mercedes 190SL she wanted me to experience the same enjoyment.

Not only was she a Master Planner; she was a Master Negotiator. She was always well-fortified with pertinent information; she did her home-work, extensively researched the subject matter, and knew precisely how to converse with a variety of persona.

After an extensive discussion with Clair Mercedes's sales woman in Dedham, Mass., Alice, extracted an attractive offer, which she appeared to favor. Then, in a subtle and unanticipated about face, Alice declined the offer. Out of earshot of the salesperson, Alice whispered to me that the offer was attractive, but she thought we could do even better.

After Alice turned down the offer, she presented a counter-offer with a "take it or leave it" proposition. After consulting with the sales manager, the salesperson informed us that the dealership would accept Alice's proposal. It was always a delight to see Alice negotiate with people; it was never a fair fight—between her brains and upbeat personality, Alice inevitably prevailed. The opposing party, in this case, the dealership, was at a decided disadvantage. Thanks to Alice, I became t the owner of a 1999 maroon Mercedes E-320 Sedan.

Alice rationalized that as long as I no longer had any employment responsibilities, Jackie was a student at the University of Notre Dame and Katie working in San Francisco, why not go for an extended ride—a coast-to-coast, cross-country ride!

It is not inconceivable that this was Alice's plan from the moment she knew the AIB offered an early retirement package. First, she had to convince her husband to accept the offer. Second, she had to convince a Mercedes ignoramus to spend a portion of the retirement package and purchase a Mercedes, and third, she had to persuade me to drive the Mercedes to the west coast. What are the chances this proposition was well-orchestrated and skillfully implemented by the Master Family Planner?

As much as Alice LOVED a Mercedes, she did not exhibit an insatiable interest in driving our new E-320 Mercedes. Truly, in the goodness of her heart, Alice wanted me to share the joy she experienced when she drove a Mercedes and she did not intend to usurp my driving time. It was another classic demonstration of Alice putting the other person first.

In every imaginable way, Alice was one of God's finest creations!

"CALIFORNIA...HERE WE COME...."

On Monday, the eighteenth day of October 1999, we left our home at 45 Woodlawn Ave in Needham, pointed the E-320 toward the Mass Turnpike (Interstate Rte. 90) and headed due west to Seattle, Wash. with various stops along the way. The first destination was South Bend, Indiana, where we stopped for a brief visit to Jackie, who at that time, was studying at the University of Notre Dame Law School. Alice and I assured Jack our return trip from the west coast would coincide with the Notre Dame-Boston College football game. He was pleased.

As we traveled further west through Iowa and South Dakota, Route 90 was reduced to a harrowing two lanes with deep ruts imbedded by numerous tractor-trailer trucks. Considering the narrowness of the roadway, the speed of passing two-wheelers, and the deeply rutted pavement, the drive was at best, challenging. The deep grooves in the road made it difficult, for me, in attempting to pass other private passenger autos as we dodged tumbling tumble weeds.

During one of those harrowing days on Route 90, two huge CBS Tractor-Trailer-Trucks roared past us at a speed approximating 90-95 mph. We theorized they were en route to Seattle, Wash. to televise a Monday Night Football Game.

A brief respite in Spearfish, South Dakota gave us an opportunity to relax and observe some serious looking cowboys, replete with spurs on their boots while devouring meals that could have fed a cadre of men. After our brief respite, we resumed our coast-to-coast cruise. As we were about to exit the rest stop area, Alice offered to drive, which I thought was a great idea; less stress for me, and I could relax and read the newspaper.

Did I say, relax? With Alice at the wheel, it was far from a relaxing ride. Skillfully, she negotiated her way into high-speed truck traffic and, like an experienced truck driver, she immediately aligned the treads of our tires within the imbedded tracks of the road. Once she was safely secured in the rutted road, she floored the accelerator—instantaneous speed!

As my head snapped backward and tumble-weeds tumbled across the shiny maroon hood ornament, Alice excitedly exclaimed, "This 'Benz has real power; now...we're going to catch those CBS trucks!" My initial shock turned to raucous laughter; hopefully, she was kidding! Alice had a wonderful sense of humor. We always enjoyed laughing at each other's comedic attempts.

With winter winds and blinding snowstorms in the offing, Yellowstone National Park closed in October, so we were unable to spend time in that renowned memorial. We did see elks sauntering, buffalo grazing, geyser's erupting but, thankfully, we did not see grizzly bears guzzling.

From this point on it was a straight shot to the Space Needle in Seattle, where we viewed beautiful Puget Sound. After a few days in Seattle, we arrived in San Francisco and spent a few days sightseeing with Katie. She guided us through the City of San Francisco and the Napa Valley. After departing San Francisco, Alice took the shore route and stopped at the internationally renowned Pebble Beach Golf Course on the Monterey Peninsula.

From that point our junket took us to Las Vegas, the Hoover Dam, and ultimately to Saint Louis, Missouri, where we visited the famous St. Louis Cathedral, noted for its magnificent mosaics. One of the mosaics depicts Father Francis McGann, a wonderful parish priest who served at St. Joseph's in Needham for many years. When Father McGann was a newly ordained priest, a person from his parish in Quincy contracted to construct mosaics in Saint Louis Cathedral and asked young Father McGann to pose for one of the mosaics.

Another unanticipated bonus was the revelation that directly across the Mississippi River from St. Louis, Mo. is Belleview, Ill.—home of the beautiful Shrine of Our Lady of the Snows. Without question, the Shrine was an attraction; regardless if our return to South Bend, Ind. was delayed, we could not pass on the opportunity to spend time at such a beautiful shrine.

Our Lady of the Snows, staffed by the Oblates of Mary Immaculate, refers to the Basilica of Saint Mary Major in Rome where legend says snow fell in the midst of the summertime heat. The Shrine had various devotional sites—a Grotto comparable to Lourdes, a devotional area to Our Lady of Guadalupe, and a natural amphitheater depicting the Stations of the Cross. Additionally, we viewed an area dedicated to Doctor Tom Dooley, a native of St. Louis and alumnus of the University of Notre Dame who devoted his life to humanitarian work in Southeast Asia.

Time was of the essence and we were racing against the clock to attend the Boston College-Notre Dame football game with Jackie. We did cut it close, but we did make it back to South Bend in time for the game.

After Sunday Mass at the Basilica of the Sacred Heart on the campus of the University of Notre Dame campus, Alice and I pointed our E-320 due east toward Woodlawn Ave. in Needham. We had a wonderful time on our cross-country trip, and thankfully, we arrived home from our 10,000-mile excursion just in time for Thanksgiving. We certainly did succeed in breaking-in our new 1999 Mercedes E-320!

Alice, Jack and his Aunt Judy prepare to attend
a Notre Dame Football game in 1999.

IF THANKSGIVING COMES, CAN CHRISTMAS BE FAR BEHIND?

As usual, our family congregated around our Woodlawn Ave. dinner table to devour Alice's scrumptious turkey from Owen's Turkey Farm, a local favorite poultry farm in Needham. It was a great day. Danny invited a seminarian from Louisiana to spend Turkey Day with northerners; he seemed to adapt well. At the end of the day, the family focus turned to Christmas preparations.

As had been our custom years, we displayed our Advent Wreath shortly after Thanksgiving. No longer were the kids around to light the candles, so Alice and I assumed that responsibility! Another custom we maintained was our annual Christmas Season Luncheon at the Ritz-Carlton Hotel, which at the time was directly across from the Boston Common. Once a year, at Christmas time, Alice and I felt justified to treat ourselves to the ambiance and festive atmosphere of the Ritz-Carlton, dining with the "upper-crust." This year, in particular, it was an opportunity to thank God for the innumerable gifts of the past year, and to ask for a grace-filled millennium!

It was, however, a disturbing time for Alice, as she had recently learned of a breach in her generational family. Alice constantly preached the importance of family harmony, which necessitates overlooking offenses and focusing on our precious consanguinity relationships. She always stressed there is a caveat in the "Our Father" prayer, "... forgive us *as we* forgive others." In effect, the forgiveness extended to us, is contingent on the forgiveness we extend to others.

From that point on, Alice continued to look for opportunities to bring peace in her family; she was continually trying to find a formula to restore the ruptured generational relationship. Unfortunately, for several years, her efforts were in vain, but she never stopped praying for, and trying to find, a harmonious resolution.

With the onset of a new and younger generation traveling a long distance from western Massachusetts to Needham, for our Christmas Eve celebration the number of attendees was reduced to the seven of us and a few neighbors. Alice was in love with everything Christmas: Carols, presents, Lobster Newburg, egg nog, and Midnight Mass. She was so anxious to give presents she wanted to commence exchanging gifts on Christmas Eve. The primary reason she wanted the seven of us to exchange at least one present on Christmas Eve was to experience the Joy of Giving as she watched the kids open their presents.

With one exception, six of us agreed to open at least one present on Christmas Eve. Seldom, if ever, did the lone dissenter disagree with his mother, but in this case Danny disagreed. He was a traditionalist; Jesus was born on Christmas Day; therefore, Christmas presents should be opened on the day of Christ's birth—December 25th—CHRISTMAS DAY. Danny truly loved Christmas as much as, if not more than, most people. In spite of the fact opening his present on Christmas Eve would be pleasing to his mother, Danny was determined to adhere to tradition; Christmas presents are opened on Christmas Day!

As 1999 drew to a close and January 1st loomed on the horizon, the entire country, the entire world, was anxiously anticipating the new millennium! My cousin, Patty Stott and her husband Jon, invited Alice and me, my 91-year-old mother, my sister, and a multitude of Stott Family friends to a Gala Millennium gathering at their home in Osterville, Mass. It was wonderful to see my mother celebrate, not only a new century, but also a new millennium—the year 2000!

ONCE AGAIN, EXCURSION TIME

Prior to the new millennium, Danny accepted a position with Cabot Corporation. Unlike Andersen Consulting, which required extensive on-site presence, visits to worldwide Cabot facilities were for limited periods of time. In the course of his employment with Cabot Corporation, he traveled to Europe, Asia and South America but never longer than a week at a time. When Alice learned Danny's travels included Paris, her ears perked-up and, soon she accompanied Danny on a trip to Paris.

They treasured the time they spent at the Eiffel Tower, The Louvre, and Versailles, but their favorite sites were Notre Dame Cathedral and viewing the incorrupt body of Saint Margaret Mary Alacoque, domiciled above the Altar of the Apparition at the Monastery of Visitation.

Alice and Danny were inseparable, they were alike in so many ways—both possessed effervescent personalities, a keen sense of humor, and a deep spirituality that was securely nestled in the silent confines of their hearts. Mother and son considered their relationship with the Lord to be imminently personal, but the Joy in their demeanor demonstrably displayed and continually radiated the Love of Christ.

For whatever reason, upon her return from France, Alice seemed fixated on dogs. Evidently while touring Paris, she was enraptured with the sizable number of people walking dogs, which renewed nostalgic memories of her beloved West Highland Terrier, Duggan. Almost immediately upon her return, she began to lament the loss of Duggan and commenced to lobby for a replacement dog. After assessing the depth of her loneliness, I concurred; it was time to acquire a replacement for Duggan. Unbeknown to me, but not surprising, Alice had already identified a breeder, and within minutes we were on the road to a dog kennel on Washington Street in Norwood. We acquired a cute little Westie puppy and both Alice and Danny were thrilled with Westie #3!

As we transported the recently born pup to his Needham home, Alice was cooing and cuddling as the puppy was whimpering and shaking; he was so frightened that he cried all the way home. Alice named the little rascal, Riley! Our premier Westie, Shannon, lived 17 years and, if Riley reflected similar longevity, Alice and I agreed he would outlive both of us. And if our new Westie possessed similar life expectancy, Alice and I agreed that Riley would bury both of us.

Alice was so proud of her new puppy she couldn't wait to take a trip to Chicopee to introduce Riley to her mother-in-law Eileen (Gram) Kennedy.

A NEW YEAR, A NEW DECADE, A NEW MILLENNIUM

From our perspective, the new millennium was certainly off to a good start, a trip to Paris, a new dog, and, most importantly, Alice and I were the recipients of a surprising announcement in the summer of 2001. While Danny dined with Alice and me at Clancy's Restaurant in South Dennis, he informed us that, in spite of the fact he enjoyed his employment at Cabot Corporation, he was taking a leave of absence to enter Saint John's Seminary in Brighton, Mass!

Neither Alice nor I anticipated this news, but we were delighted with Danny's decision to discern whether or not he was called to be a priest. As thrilled as Alice was, she cautioned him, "I am delighted to hear this news Danny, but you do know, at times, the volatility of your personality has been an issue, so bear in mind there is no place for pugnacity in the priesthood."

The aspiring seminarian responded, "Mom you do know that I love to play hockey; my combativeness is rink-oriented. Don't worry, I'll be fine."

My 90-year-old mother, not a party-person, was so thrilled with Danny's news she organized a party to celebrate Danny's entry into Saint John's Seminary because "I won't be around when Danny is ordained, so I want to celebrate now." It was a small gathering at Judy's house at the Cape, and although it was somewhat embarrassing for Danny, he catered to her wishes because "Gram" wanted to have the get-together.

Danny seemed to hit his stride as a seminarian; he did well academically and he loved his parish pastoral assignments. In Brockton and Scituate, he met so many wonderful people, many of whom would become life-long friends. He was particularly pleased to meet many enthusiastic young Catholics at both locations, which gave him great hope for the future of the church.

WHAT? NO PARTY?

When 2003 rolled around and our 35th Wedding Anniversary was on the horizon, my expectation was that The Family Planner would dig into her bag of anniversary surprises. But I was wrong. Either Alice anticipated an anniversary surprise from me (not a chance) or she was just sick and tired of improvising. At any rate, there were no 35th Anniversary plans. In retrospect, could this change in modus operandi have been an early sign of cranial sluggishness?

Ultimately, we decided a replication of our traditional Christmas Luncheon at the Ritz-Carlton would be appropriate, so at the last minute, I called the Ritz and reserved a table for two overlooking Boston Commons.

In retrospect, it was fortuitous that Alice didn't orchestrate her usual impeccably planned anniversary scheme. When our 2003 Anniversary Day arrived, it was obvious we did not need to make reservations at the Ritz;

Boston was in the throes of the heaviest February snowstorm in meteorological history. Alice and I were undeterred; we walked from Woodlawn Ave to the MBTA Commuter Rail Station in Needham Center, with wintery winds whipping sheets of snow at our faces.

Upon arrival at South Station, we gleefully strutted through the downtown area proceeding to Boston Common, while wintery winds whirled and snow pelted out faces. Neither Alice nor I had a care in the world, we had a wonderful time plodding through piles of plowed snow in quest of an exquisite anniversary lunch at what was to be, a desolate Ritz-Carlton dining room!

Perhaps we were overly enthralled with the intensity of the snowstorm or perhaps I have selective memory; at any rate, I don't recall that we experienced any snowstorm remorse. In a sense, it was an opportunity for the two of us to recall snowstorms of the past; days of wintery winds, and resounding joy.

Weather conditions were somewhat reminiscent of previous memorable moments. On February 18, 1968, as we left Saint Thomas Church in West Springfield, we were greeted by a raging snow-squall and, in Westfield, with the spotlight focused on our backyard skating rink and a fire raging in our family room fireplace, we would sit by the sliding glass door and watch snowflakes rapidly descend onto our backyard skating rink. When we first moved to Needham, during blinding blizzards, the two of us would walk down Great Plain Ave. to enjoy a leisurely lunch at Gino's Restaurant in Needham Square.

Memories, memories, the gift of memories! By the time the February 17, 2003 snowstorm finally abated, there was a record 27.6 inches of snow on the streets of Boston.

TRIUMPH AND TRAGEDY

After another, extremely successful, joy-filled Dennis Seashores summer season in 2003, Alice's exuberance was channeled in another direction; her beloved Boston Red Sox were playing the 7th and deciding game of the American League Championship Series against their bitter arch-rivals, the New York Yankees.

Both Alice and I were nervously optimistic as we sat in front of our Cape Cod TV on the night of October 16, 2003 to watch the 7th game from Yankee Stadium in the Bronx, New York. Our optimism was attributable to the Red Sox starting pitcher, Pedro Martinez, the most dominating pitcher in the Major Leagues. The game was evolving as we hoped. Pedro was pitching well, and the Red Sox were leading the vaunted, pennant winning, evil empire by a score of 5-2.

When the Yankees came to bat in the last half of the 8th inning, I said, "Good night Al, I'm going to bed."

Alice, the eternal optimist, replied, "You're kidding! It's the 8th inning, the Sox have a three-run lead, Pedro's pitching well and you're going to bed?"

I responded, "Absolutely."

Not to be deterred by my reticence, she commanded, "Sit back down in that chair and watch them win this game!"

I retorted, "Why should I aggravate myself? I've seen far too many Yankee comebacks. I'm not putting myself through that agony again. I'm going to bed."

"Stick around; they're three runs ahead," urged Alice. "No way, I'll read about it in the paper tomorrow morning; good-night."

Two hours later, in the wee hours of the morning of the 17th of October, I was awakened from a sound sleep, as a dejected Red Sox fan came into our bedroom glumly announcing, "They lost." The tone of her voice was all too obvious, what lifelong Red Sox fan wouldn't be disappointed? Alice, a forever-faithful fan was understandably crushed. Although it took a while, eventually her disappointment dissipated as she switched her allegiance to the New England Patriots.

In 2004, after 10 years of service, Shirley Petrocelli, the reservation manager and a close friend of Alice, retired from Dennis Seashores. During the winter, the board of directors hired a new person for the role, Barbara Myers. Barbara, with several years of hotel management experience in upstate New York, recently relocated to Harwich with her husband, Bill.

Dennis Seashores did not provide on-site office space for reservation managers; they were expected to be accessible seven days a week so they worked from a home-office environment. Barbara Myers' DSS home office was located at her residential address, Cottonwood Drive in Harwich. Barbara's husband Bill was involved, but to a limited degree. He curried pertinent reservation information between the off-site "Cottonwood Drive home-office" in Harwich and The Windmill in Dennisport. Alice and Barbara's responsibilities interacted, so Alice trained Barbara and familiarized her with the DSS accounting system.

Alice was impressed with Barbara's ability; they interacted well with each other, but Bill was a different story. From the beginning of Barbara and Bill's affiliation with Dennis Seashores, Alice had misgivings about Bill. For whatever reason, she didn't think he demonstrated sufficient intellectual depth to be involved with resort reservations. She was particularly perplexed in that he never called her by name. His greeting, which she abhorred, was, "Hello Doll."

Bill and Barbara were beyond ultra-private; they were recluses. They never allowed any Dennis Seashore person into their "Dennis Seashores home-office" in Harwich. Alice thought their hermitage-prone characteristics might be attributable to their rural residency in the woods of upstate New York; solitude was their by-word. Occasionally, Barbara would visit The Windmill at DSS to meet with Alice, but generally their business was transacted on the telephone. Barbara and Bill's insatiable quest for solitude did however provide me with fodder.

As I sat down to address our annual Christmas cards, I discovered a package of cards that said, "MERRY CHRISTMAS from OUR HOUSE to YOUR HOUSE," with a slot to insert a picture of the sender's house. Bingo, a lamp was lit; Alice will be smiling at Christmas.

Unbeknown to Alice, I drove from Needham to the site of "Dennis Seashores home-office" on Cottonwood Drive in Harwich and snapped a picture of Barbara and Bill's house. Subsequently, I inserted the picture of their home into the Christmas card along with a personal message, purportedly from Barbara, inviting Alice to visit their Cottonwood home when "the snow melts." In order to authenticate the postmark, I mailed to Mr. and Mrs. Daniel J. Kennedy from the Harwich post office.

When the card arrived at our house, Alice noted the postmark and, almost inaudibly, said, "A Christmas card from Harwichport?" I pretended to be pre-occupied with other items, when suddenly she said, "Dan, look at this card, it's from Barbara Myers and she wants me to visit her when the snow melts! That's a hot one; she won't let me or anyone else near her damn house and now she's inviting me for a visit after the snow melts?"

With a straight face, I responded, "Be more understanding Alice, Barbara was thoughtful in sending you a Christmas card; she really has the Christmas spirit." Then Alice noticed, what must have been a revealing look on my face, as she said, "Did you send this card?" It wasn't necessary for me to verbally acknowledge culpability; facial expressions do convey messages. Alice was not only duped for a moment or two; she smiled and was happy to be duped. Both of us enjoyed teasing each other.

It is paradoxical that Alice, who was so smart, so discerning, yet so credulous in opening Christmas Cards. In retrospect, perhaps she was just playing along with my stupid little tricks; maybe the joke was on me? Could I have been the one who was fooled?

At the onset of a subsequent Dennis Seashores summer season, a distraught Barbara Myers called Alice and confided with her that Bill had just been diagnosed with advanced Alzheimer's and she didn't know what to do. Alice seemed intuitively to know how to guide a distraught Barbara. After commiserating with Barbara, she assured her that she would contact various local geriatric support organizations for guidance. Within a day or two, Alice lined up several organizations in the Harwich area and passed the information on to Barbara.

Alice's previous misgivings about Bill, his ineptitude and never calling her by name were now understandable; his short-term memory was deficient. Realizing Barbara and Bill were from the rural area of New York, Alice asked Barbara if there were any guns in her house. When Barbara replied in the affirmative, Alice emphatically told Barbara to immediately dispose of the weapons. A few weeks later, when Barbara didn't answer Alice's telephone calls to the Cottonwood Office, Alice called the Harwich Police Department and requested a wellness check at Barbara's home.

After conducting the wellness check, Harwich Police informed Alice that the two occupants at the Cottonwood address were deceased—a double homicide. After an investigation, the Harwich Police Department concluded Bill shot Barbara and then himself. Could this tragedy have been averted if it were diagnosed sooner or if it were diagnosed? Why didn't Barbara seek help long before she confided in Alice? Did this incident alert Alice in the recognition of cognitive impairments?

In absence of a replacement for Barbara Myers, Alice assumed Reservation Manager responsibilities *pro-tem;* unfortunately, *pro-tem* extended into the following season.

Fortunately, in the winter season, Dennis Seashores hired Jack Keith and his wife Barbara to replace Barbara and Bill, thus Alice gladly relinquished the reservation responsibilities. Dennis Seashores' Board of Directors did a good job in securing the services of John Keith; within a short period of time he was fully integrated into the Dennis Seashores family, and his competence was greatly appreciated by Alice. It was interesting in that 40 years earlier, John Keith and I played on the same softball team in western Mass.

TOO YOUNG TO RETIRE

Fear not, I am with you. (Isaiah 41:10)

At the Annual Dennis Seashores Wrap-up Meeting in October of 2006, surprisingly Alice tendered her resignation as Dennis Seashores' Property Manager, to be effective when DSS opened in the summer of 2007. She explained, "I will need to spend considerable time planning for Danny's forthcoming Ordination, which will preclude me from devoting sufficient time in preparing for the 2007 season." The board of governors was in shock, and pleaded with her to reconsider, suggesting a six-month leave of absence with a considerable increase in salary upon her return. She was grateful, but undeterred.

Given Alice's penchant for planning, I assumed she would have shared with me that she was considering retirement; she did not. Apparently, privacy pre-empted disseminating personal information. It was only a week before DSS' October annual meeting when she revealed her decision to me. Generally, Alice would discuss with me any prospective DSS changes she was contemplating; to inform me after the fact was unusual behavior. This decision must have been so unnerving and traumatic for her that she kept it in the deep recesses of her heart. What appeared to be an abrupt decision must have been preceded by agonizing weeks of introspection.

At the time, I thought perhaps a sabbatical would be invigorating, speculating she might have become worn down by the day-in, day-out grind, and that she didn't want to admit that to anyone, including me. Subsequently, in analyzing the rationale of her decision, she must have sensed health concerns; if so, she certainly concealed those concerns.

Alice was by nature an extrovert of immense proportions. She absolutely loved people and couldn't contain expressing that love. In spite of her gregarious nature, Alice was a deeply private person, zealously guarding her innermost thoughts and woe to anyone who dared to intrude on her privacy. Her son Danny inherited that privacy trait from his mother.

EQUILIBRIUM CONCERNS

After Dennis Seashores closed for the season and Alice and I were back home in Needham, she screamed from kitchen, "Dan, come quickly, did you hear me Dan? Hurry, I need your help!" The urgency in her voice was obvious; I ran from the den to the kitchen and found her slumped against the counter, informing me she was dizzy and couldn't walk. Everything seemed to be spinning and she was afraid she might fall. She spoke coherently, but the fact that Alice, who was never afraid of anything, was frightened, alarmed me.

When the problem didn't abate, I helped her to the car and drove to the emergency room at Beth-Israel Deaconess Hospital (BIDH) in Needham. The hospital staff diagnosed the episode as vertigo. Fortunately, a few hours later, Alice regained her balance, with no apparent lingering effects.

TIME TO PREPARE FOR FUTURE FESTIVITIES

That year, Alice was in top form organizing our traditional Thanksgiving and Christmas celebrations, with an eye on January 2007 when Danny would ordain to the Transitional Diaconate for the Archdiocese of Boston. On January 27, 2007, Cardinal Sean P. O'Malley ordained seven men from Saint John's Seminary to the sacrament of Holy Orders, Transitional Deacons.

After the Diaconate Ordination to the Holy Priesthood in May, Father Brian Manning graciously offered Deacon Dan the opportunity to assist at the Holy Sacrifice of the Mass at Saint Mary of the Nativity Church and, for the first time, Alice's son proclaimed the Gospel of the Lord.

On January 27, 2007, Cardinal Sean O'Malley, OFM Cap, Archbishop of Boston, ordained Alice's son Danny a Transitional Deacon at the Cathedral of the Holy Cross in Boston. Deacon Dan and his teary-eyed mother share the joy of the occasion.

As weeks passed, we celebrated birthdays, Saint Patrick's Day, Easter Sunday, and Mother's Day, yet at each family event the topic of conversation was the rapidly approaching Rite of Ordination in May. It was common to see seminary classmates at our house discussing ordination preparations with Danny, determining who will be the Homilist, the Master of Ceremonies, the Altar Servers, etc.

Mother's Day 2007–Anne Marie, Katie, Dad, Jackie, Deacon Dan, Patti and Ashley celebrate with the Queen of the Kennedy Family; Alice Marie.

A KENNEDY FAMILYPRIEST

You have brought them abundant joy and great rejoicing. (Isaiah 9:2)

The summit of our family blessings occurred on May 26, 2007, when our son Danny was ordained to the Holy Priesthood of Jesus Christ at the Cathedral of the Holy Cross in Boston.

Family and friends of the seven ordinandi crowded into the beautiful cathedral, where the stained-glass windows were radiant with streaming sunlight. The entire congregation rose and eagerly broke into song as the Cathedral choir began to sing "This is the Feast of Victory for Our God." A seemingly endless line of priests and bishops, followed by the seven ordinandi and Cardinal Sean O'Malley, processed down the center aisle of the Cathedral as the cacophony of the choir reached a glorious crescendo.

Tears of Joy were glistening on Alice's cheeks, dropping gently on her azure blue dress as she witnessed her red-headed son become "a Priest

Forever, according to the Order of Melchizedek." At the conclusion of the Rite of Ordination, prior to receding from the Cathedral, Cardinal O'Malley knelt before each newly ordained priest to receive the first priestly blessing.

As the procession proceeded up the center aisle of the iconic Cathedral of the Holy Cross, the seven newly ordained priests beamed with gratitude and the congregation applauded with joy as tears silently trickled from Alice's eyes. There was always a strong bond between Alice and Danny, and now mother and her priest-son were forever linked in perpetuity. DEO GRATIAS!

Cardinal Sean Patrick O'Malley, Archbishop of Boston, Laying on of Hands during The Rite of Ordination of Deacon Daniel J. Kennedy.

FIRST MASS OF THANKSGIVING

The following day, May 27, 2007, Pentecost Sunday, Father Daniel Joseph Kennedy offered his First Mass of Thanksgiving at 2:00 p.m. in the Church of

St. Joseph in Needham. Father Dan celebrated Mass at the same altar where, in 1982, he received his First Holy Communion, where he served Mass while a student at St. Joseph's School and as a student at Catholic Memorial High School and, where he received the sacrament of Confirmation.

As we entered St. Joseph's Church 30 minutes before Mass, Alice turned to me and said, "Dan, look at the size of the crowd. I'm shocked to see so many people!" In her exuberance, Al Marie must have lamented that her mother and father weren't alive, but she was delighted to see so many relatives, parishioners, and friends who came to witness Father Danny's First Mass. She was especially thrilled to see Danny's elderly friend from his childhood days, Mrs. Clayton Lester, a surprise attendee. As soon as Alice saw Mrs. Lester, seated in her customary front row seat, Alice went directly into the Sacristy where Father Dan was vesting and imparted her motherly advice. "Mrs. Lester is here," she said. Immediately, Danny responded to his mother's maternal message and rushed out of the Sacristy to greet his longtime friend with an ear-to-ear smile and an affectionate hug.

Mrs. Lester told him, "I have been praying for this day since I first witnessed you serving Mass when you were a young boy." Mrs. Lester's daughter read the notification of Father Kennedy's First Mass in the Parish Bulletin, and she requested authorization from Briarwood Healthcare Center to bring her mother to Father Kennedy's First Mass of Thanksgiving. Mrs. Lester was filled with gratitude as she witnessed her little altar boy celebrate his First Mass of Thanksgiving at the same altar where he served Mass years ago.

Father Dan greets his longtime friend, Mrs. Clayton
Lester, prior to celebrating his First Mass of Thanksgiving
at the Church of Saint Joseph on May 27, 2007.

During the First Mass of Thanksgiving Alice (Haggerty) Kennedy was proud to present her son, now "Father Danny," with a Chalice appropriately inscribed:

> *In Memory of the Haggerty and Kennedy Families*
> *Reverend Daniel Joseph Kennedy*
> *Ordained to the Priesthood of Jesus Christ*
> *May 26, 2007*
> *Love, Mom and Dad*

Father Dan designed his Chalice with Catholic Memorial High School in mind: a silver Chalice encircled with red trim, representing the school's colors and its motto, "Vince in Bono Mallum" (Good Conquers Evil).

Alice was delighted to see several of her Cape Cod friends in attendance at Danny's First Mass of Thanksgiving. But I'm certain, in the deep recesses of her heart, she was no doubt thinking of how proud her parents would have been to see their grandson celebrate the Holy Sacrifice of the Mass. She also must have thought of her Carborundum Corp. colleague Jeanie McGrath, a deeply religious woman whom Alice cared for during the later years of her life.

When Kathleen Flynn, a longtime friend, asked Alice to describe her emotion at Danny's Ordination, she was inspired by her response.

"Obviously, the Ordination was a special occasion Kathleen," Alice said. "But, for me, the highlight of the weekend was Danny's First Mass; for it was the first time he consecrated bread and wine into the Body and Blood of Jesus."

Kathleen added, "There was something unique about Alice and Danny. They were so much alike in many ways; they loved people, they loved to laugh, and both exhibited such deep faith in God and now they seemed to become inexplicably entwined."

Father Dan's Ordination Reception was held at the Weston Golf Club, where Dan and Alice celebrated with Father Tony Creane, Pastor of Saint Mary's Church during the time we resided in Westfield.

In October, another Kennedy Family event occurred; Jackie married Elizabeth Leonard at Saint Michael's Cathedral in Springfield, Mass. Alice was doubly proud. She was not only the mother of the groom; she was also the mother the celebrant. She looked lovely in her light blue calico dress (Alice Blue Gown). Father Dan was his usual engaging spiritual self as he officiated at the wedding of his brother in the sanctuary of Saint Michael's Cathedral, where the celebrant and the groom's father and uncle, John Barrett Kennedy, were baptized.

Shortly after the wedding, another unexpected episode of vertigo struck Alice. She became extremely dizzy during the wedding reception and, once again the room seemed to spin. Alice was unable to regain her balance, necessitating an immediate return to our hotel room. As we approached our room on the eighth floor, she acknowledged she couldn't look down at the atrium without exacerbating her dizziness. This particular incident exhibited not only dizziness and instability in walking; she also became physically ill. Thankfully, as was her experience during the previous incident, the effects of vertigo abated after several hours.

When we returned to our Needham home, Katie suggested administering a candle-wax therapy treatment designed to draw wax out of the inner ear and lessen the probability of future occurrences. Thankfully, the candle-wax therapy was effective, and Alice never encountered another episode of vertigo. I often wondered whether the Vertigo issue might have been a precursor of forthcoming cranial issues.

During the fall of 2007 and the winter months of 2008, the board of directors at DSS continued to plead with Alice to reconsider her retirement and return to Cape Cod. Attempts to entice her were relentless, but she was adamant and persistently declined many remunerative proposals. It was a given that the board would have difficulty replacing Alice; she was exceedingly capable and interacted extremely well with guests and owners alike. Most importantly, she absolutely loved her job!

In my mind, it was therapeutic for Alice to be in the center of the daily Dennis Seashores' hustle and bustle, so I encouraged her to reconsider retirement. Eventually, she confided that, regardless of the enticements, she was not recanting retirement because "I'm just not as sharp as I used to be."

I thought to myself, "Enough said. Don't ever mention it again." In retrospect, with that insight, the Lord must have been preparing Alice to bear burdens yet to be revealed.

In November, a close friend of our family, Peg Reilly, passed away and Danny con-celebrated the Funeral Mass at Saint Mary's Church in Longmeadow with Peg's son, Father Francis E. Reilly, a longtime friend of Danny. The Reilly Family and the Kennedy Family were next-door neighbors on Hungry Hill in Springfield.

When Danny was employed by Cabot Corporation and traveled to Paris, he used to take the train to Louvain, Belgium to visit with Father

Fran Reilly who, at the time, was on the faculty of the American College of the Immaculate Conception. It was certainly an integral component in Danny's priesthood discernment.

After the interment at Saint Mary's Cemetery in Westfield, Alice and I were delighted to attend a Reilly Family get-together, where family and friends gathered to celebrate the lives of our former Hungry Hill neighbors, Midge and Peg Reilly.

Alice, Father Dan, Judy, and Father Dan's Dad attend a Reilly Family reception.

On December 24, 2007, at Saint John the Evangelist Church in Winthrop, Alice and I experienced the thrill of a lifetime. Father Daniel J. Kennedy, resplendent in a Gothic Golden Chasuble, celebrated Christmas Eve Mass. In a memorable Homily, he spoke of his employment on the USS Nimitz, and discussed the relationship between the brilliance of the stars over the Pacific Ocean to the Star of Bethlehem.

"We have come a long way from the time we were criticized for bringing our kids to Christmas Eve Mass celebrated by Bishop Maguire," remarked Alice. "Now one of those young kids is celebrating Christmas Eve Mass."

Christmas 2007, with Dan, Alice, Ashley, and Jack rejoicing with the newly ordained – son, brother and uncle Father Daniel J. Kennedy.

UNFULFILLED EXPECTATIONS

Fear not I am with you, I will strengthen you and I will help you.
(Isaiah 41:10)

With great expectations for the new year, Alice and I toasted 2008 at our Woodlawn Ave home, looking forward to January birthdays, our 40th wedding anniversary in February, Father Danny celebrating his first Easter Triduum in March, and summertime on Cape Cod.

Was the Kennedy Family Planner plotting another surprise 2008 excursion? Perhaps another trip to Ireland or, our first trip to the Vatican? Expectations, expectations....

Alice was looking forward to a happy year, which would commence with Anne Marie's birthday on January 13th and Danny's birthday on January 16th. Comparable to his reluctance to open Christmas presents prior to the 25th of December, Danny never wanted to make a "big deal" out of his birthday. Consequently, he informed me he would be too busy to stop by our house on his birthday.

I pointed out: "Always remember Danny, birthdays are more important to mothers than to their children. Always make certain you find time to share birthday cake with your mother on January 16th."

Alice was delighted when Danny adjusted his schedule and joined us for birthday cake on January 16th. Much to his relief, it was a low-keyed gathering. Only a few members of our musically challenged family were present and, he didn't object to our off-key rendition of "Happy Birthday, Danny." With Alice and Danny in the same room, we couldn't help but laugh and have fun; he was happy he came for the family party.

The last family picture of Father Dan as Ashley, Katie, Mom and Dad celebrate his 34th birthday.

Unfortunately, 11 days after Danny's birthday, our new year expectations disintegrated. There would be no surprise anniversary trip. No holiday in

Ireland. No maiden visit to the Vatican. Nor would Father Dan be celebrating the Easter Triduum.

On January 27th, a late-night telephone call informed me that on his return trip home from Baptizing Kelly Elizabeth Blute at Saint Thomas Aquinas Church in Fairfield, Conn., Danny sustained a cardiac arrest and he was in critical condition is Saint Francis Hospital in Hartford, Conn. Immediately, I bounded upstairs to wake Alice and convey the devastating news. The look of dismay and unbelief on her face as she woke from a sound sleep is permanently etched in my mind. It was as if she was attempting to determine if this was a bad dream. Unfortunately, it wasn't a dream. With a stunned expression still on her face, within minutes we were en route to Hartford.

We were in the process of breaking the Mass Turnpike speed limit when Jackie called and informed us the doctors were unable to resuscitate Danny. Upon hearing such devastating news, we pulled into a service stop in Charlton to gather out thoughts and cry our eyes out. Alice suggested we abort our trip to Hartford and return to Woodlawn Ave and comfort our daughters.

This was not only a shock for our family, it was also a shock for the Archdiocese of Boston. Danny's extensive network of priest friends were devastated. This unimaginable news impacted so many people, especially the presbyterate of the Archdiocese of Boston who looked forward to Danny's priestly ministry. If anyone seemed to be indestructible it was Danny; he was a marathon runner, a conditioned athlete and, by United States Navy standards, physically fit for duty.

When we arrived back in Needham, our daughters were being consoled by neighbors, parishioners and many of Danny's priest friends. Thankfully, most remained with us until long after midnight as all of us sought, in vain, to understand the Will of God. We did, unquestionably agree, though incomprehensible to us, this was indeed God's Will undoubtedly designed to be of benefit in ways unknown to us. Father Dan, who was anxious to commence his new assignment at the Altar of Saint Brigid/Gate of Heaven Churches in South Boston, would instead be lying in a coffin at the foot of the altar at Saint Joseph's Church in Needham.

Around 4:00 a.m. on the morning of the 28th day of January, after our friends departed, Alice and I closed the front door, stood in the front hallway, and hugged each other as we cried uncontrollably. Then, as if a spark ignited a flame, Danny's heart-broken mother said, in a confident tone while no longer trembling, "Just think, just think; Danny's with the Blessed Mother."

The tears that formerly flowed down her flushed face abated, her reddened eyes no longer depicted sadness, and with over-powering assertiveness and joy radiating from her beaming face, she emphatically repeated, "He—is with the Blessed Mother!" Alice was obviously comforted as she contemplated her priest-son in the presence of the Blessed Mother. *Holy Mary, Mother of God, pray for us, sinners, now and at the hour of our death!*

Among all the comforting words exchanged during that long evening, I don't recall anyone mentioning the Blessed Mother. Evidently, God granted Alice the Grace to empathize with Mary as she too lost a son at a comparable age. *Deep is the wisdom of the maternal heart.*

Alice and I believed, Danny was *twice-called* by God; first, he was called to the priesthood and secondly, he was called to his Eternal Home! Deo Gratias!

Alice's deep faith was a source of ongoing support for our entire family. Sad though she was, her devotion to the Blessed Mother was apparent. Her composure and courage were so important to me, and it was of tremendous import to our entire family and her vast circle of friends, all of whom marveled at her strength during such a traumatic time. Katie later related to me that, amidst her unfathomable grief, Alice revealed to her, "There is no one I would rather endure this ordeal with than your father; he is so strong."

Alice was indefatigable in her belief that "God brings good out of difficult situations," and, as she said, "this will be no exception." Alice, ever the peacemaker, had great expectations that Danny's death would bear fruit. After years of prayer and numerous attempts to bring a resolution to an ongoing extended family dispute, she said, "Hopefully, by the Grace of God, the sorrow of Danny's death will pave the path to peace between the Masis and the Harlows."

Indeed, it did! Deo Gratias! *Blessed are the peacemakers, for they will be called children of God. (Matthew 5:9)*

WHEN THE GOING GETS TOUGH, IT'S TIME TO TOUGHEN-UP

During the week-long bereavement from the Sunday January 27th until the day of his Funeral Mass on February 1st, there was a steady stream of priests, relatives, friends, even strangers commiserating with us on Woodlawn Ave. Their presence promoted an aura of the traditional "Irish wake," featuring intense sadness, mitigated by moments of joy and laughter. Alice and I were grateful when one of our good friends, Elaine Parks, stopped in and offered to coordinate the development of Father Dan's Funeral program, which evolved into a wonderful depiction of his 247-day ministry as a priest of the Archdiocese of Boston.

On Thursday, the day of Danny's wake, Alice woke up with an extremely high fever. She could barely speak. Under normal circumstances, she would have taken one of her self-prescribed medications and spent the day in bed. But certainly, this would not be *a normal day.*

Alice was so sick I urged her to forego attending Danny's wake in hopes that an additional day of rest would enable her to attend the Funeral Mass on Friday. Not unexpectedly, Alice did not concur. She was determined to attend the wake. She did, however, agree to return home after a brief amount of time at the wake.

In spite of what was an obviously debilitated Alice, she not only refused to take a break, she stood and greeted every person in the endless line of grief-stricken consolers. Never did she leave her post; never did she sit down! Devoid of her customary energy, the sick and weaken mother of her deceased priest-son, grief-stricken as she was, somehow manifested super human strength. Alice did as she always instructed our kids: "When the going gets tough, it's time to toughen-up."

I will never understand how she summonsed sufficient strength to stand over eight consecutive hours of emotional and physical strain. Typical of Alice, in spite of such personal trial and tribulation, she rose to the occasion and stood statuesque aside the casket of the apple of her eye, her priest-son.

The following morning, February 1, 2008, the day of Danny's Funeral Mass, Alice's health was completely restored; surprisingly, her debilitating illness disappeared! Hopefully, it symbolized a shared period of trial and, God willing, Danny too was free of disablements and in the Presence of the Lord!

Deep is the wisdom of the maternal heart.

FUNERAL WEEK AND RELATED "COINCIDENCES"

February 1, 2008 was the Feast Day of Saint Brigid, and the Patron Saint of the South Boston Parish where Father Dan was to have commenced his new presbyterial assignment. February 1st was also the birth date of Father Dan's maternal grandmother, Alice Helen (McCarthy) Haggerty. Long ago, when Danny was a young boy and few recognized a possible vocation, she said, "Danny's going to be a priest, isn't he?"

Many of our Western Mass friends who were unable to attend Danny's wake or funeral in Needham were in attendance at Saint Mary's Cemetery in Westfield on the day of interment, February 2, 2008. Danny's good friend, Bishop Joseph F. Maguire, Bishop Emeritus of Springfield, along with Timothy A. McDonnell, Bishop of Diocese of Springfield and Father Brian F. Manning, officiated at the Committal Rites.

After the Committal Service, many joined us at a reception at Storrowton Tavern's Carriage House in West Springfield. Alice did her best to disguise the fact that she was deeply wounded, but most of her longtime western Mass friends could detect she was concealing deep and painful grief.

In a sense, it was fortuitous that the site of Danny's after-burial reception was in the Carriage House that was the site of our wedding reception 40 years ago. On February 17, 1968, could anyone have imagined the next time Alice and I would be in that location would be after the burial of our priest-son on February 2th 2008? Within two weeks, February 17, 2008 would hold emotional significance: our 40th Wedding Anniversary and the 34th anniversary of Danny's Baptism. Within a 30-day period, three significant dates pertaining to Danny occurred: the 16th of January, his birth-date; the 27th of January, the date of his death; and the 17th of February, the date of his Baptism.

With sadness in our hearts, on February 17, 2008, Alice and I tried our best to commemorate those joyful times; our anniversary and Danny's Baptism. In spite of the fact that we believed Danny died in God's good Graces, our anniversary discourse fluctuated between lamenting Danny's death and what might have been in his priestly ministry while, at the same time, recalling the joy he exhibited as a priest.

Once we discarded our melancholic lamentations, Alice held her cherished Lismore Waterford Crystal glass of Zinfandel as I held my glass of Single Malt Scotch, and we toasted the multitude of blessings we shared. Then, as we nostalgically sipped our cocktails, Alice voiced an anniversary observation. "In 40 years, whenever one of us was upset with the other, somehow, the person in disfavor was able to bring a smile to the other and diffuse differences; we have been blessed."

I assured Alice, "I have been blessed in so many ways, but to have been married to the best of wives, with you, I have enjoyed the best gift life can convey." What I did not realize was the best was yet to come.

PART THREE

THE
LONGEST
DAY

CHAPTER 8

PREY FOR PROMOTIONS

A woman who fears the Lord shall be
praised. (Proverbs 31:30)

As Saint Patrick's Day approached, wintery winds diminished, tulips and crocus emerged, I had great expectations our January ordeal would become more manageable. In a way, we did focus on the Good News of Easter and the annual optimism of Opening Day at Fenway Park, but memories were not expunged.

The 2008 summer season was also on the horizon and hopefully, it would serve as a doldrums diversion. In the world of Alice, May flowers signified that it was time to be off to Cape Cod with the happy environment she loved. Before we departed for our traditional Cape Cod summer, Alice and I thought it would be nice to invite Father Matt Westcott to join us for dinner as he was still reeling from the shock of January 27th. Matt concurred and agreed to swing by our home prior to dining at a local Needham restaurant.

Matt, who was never late, for the first time arrived just a few minutes late. Alice glanced at her watch and abruptly said, "Matt's late! I'm going to bed." Although I would generally construe a similar remark from Alice as evidence of her keen sense of humor, somehow, I knew she was not joking. Before I could react to her remark, the doorbell rang while she was on her way upstairs to bed. I was dumbfounded, a totally inadequate word to express my perplexity; no phraseology could possibly describe my level of shock.

As I was attempting to digest Alice's sudden departure, I offered Matt a beverage, and discreetly went upstairs to convince Alice to come down. After extensive attempts at persuasion, she finally agreed to come downstairs and say hello to Matt. A few minutes later, she appeared in the living room, in her pajamas. Turning to Matt, she said, "I won't be joining you for dinner Matt. Enjoy yourself; good night."

Although I couldn't understand Alice's irrational behavior, this must have been an indication that she was experiencing some deep-seated difficulties in dealing with Danny's death. In some way, Danny's close friend, Father Matt, must have been a reminder of what Alice was attempting to suppress.

Subsequent to Danny's death, several people recommended Alice and I attend a bereavement meeting but neither of us believed we needed consoling. We truly believed Danny died doing the work of the Lord, so we were comfortable with the belief the Lord would take care of His priest-friend from Needham. Our human hearts need not worry; he died a friend of Christ.

Although it was unrecognizable at the time, this incident must be amongst the first indications Alice was in the process of anesthetizing remembrances of Danny. It was several years later before I linked the absence of Alice's interest in any discussion about Danny with self-induced repression.

A FIRST OPINION OPINES FOR A SECOND OPINION

Before we left for the Cape, I scheduled an appointment for my annual physical with our primary care physician, Dr. Leonard Finn. I took the opportunity to discuss behavioral changes in Alice since Danny died. In essence, I explained, "She isn't her customary effervescent out-going self. Contrary to her persona, she defers to me when she is carrying on conversations with her friends." I also acquainted Dr. Finn with her propensity for silence as well as vague recollections of recent events. Often during periods of silence, she would incessantly tap her fingers.

Dr. Finn assured me these behavioral changes may be attributable to the aging process so I should not be unnecessarily alarmed. He did suggest I continue to monitor her behavior and he would conduct an examination at Alice's next appointment.

SUMMERTIME DIVERSION, CAPE COD

When we arrived at the Cape, I was hopeful Alice's customary enthusiasm would be rejuvenated; I was wrong. Outwardly, especially to others, she appeared to be her former self, but to me, her demeanor was different. She was not as ebullient, certainly less feisty, and in a way devoid of her customary animation. In my mind, I attributed personality changes to the retirement syndrome; an absence of the fast-paced life at Dennis Seashores. I also factored in that Alice was approaching her septuagenarian years. I hoped, after announcing her retirement, she would immerse herself in household projects, which did not happen, Alice was no longer summertime busy.

In the past, Benjamin Franklin's words of wisdom, "if you want something done, give it to a 'busy person,'" was an apt description of Alice's modus operandi. But unfortunately, Ben Franklin's famous quotation no longer applied to Alice. Her innate multi-tasking ability enabled Alice to simultaneously handle a multitude of projects and handle them extraordinarily well. Unfortunately, after retirement, she was the polar opposite; she was listless.

After a relatively sedentary summer in 2008, we returned to Needham in October. I was still under the misguided impression that Alice's lethargy could be remedied if she were busy. Consequently, I suggested that she consider volunteer work at Beth-Israel Deaconess Hospital (BIDH) or at the Needham Senior Center. Surprising to me, she exhibited absolutely no interest in volunteer work and dismissively said, "I'm busy enough with the St. Joseph's 'Counting Team.'"

I knew she enjoyed the group of women who helped count weekend collections on Monday mornings, but I didn't think one day a week was sufficient to keep her mind churning. Concomitantly, apart from her friends on the Counting Team, I began to detect a reluctance to speak with close friends. Could it have been that, in her mind, a church-related project provided a secure and comforting environment?

I was wholeheartedly in support of her interest in maintaining a presence on the Counting Team. However, I felt it would be good for Alice to augment counting money with more *busyness*. In my mind, I thought it would be beneficial if she could become more intellectually active, so I contacted another friend of Alice's, Edie Kelly, who was involved with the (BIDH) Volunteers. My thought was, if a friend invited her to volunteer, she would be more receptive to an invitation, particularly one not coming from me. Edie concurred and called Alice, inviting her to join the hospital volunteers; regrettably, Alice declined Edie's invitation.

Unlike her customary "up and at-em" early-riser years, our on-the-go Alice was now taking full advantage of sleeping late in the morning. In the past, when I came home from early morning Mass, Alice would be gone. But now, when I returned home, she was not only home, she was still in bed. It was most unusual! In order to motivate her, I suggested going out for breakfast. Alice responded, "Great idea!"

In Needham, we typically went to Fresco's for breakfast. When we were on the Cape, it would typically be Dino's in Harwichport, the Breakfast Room in West Dennis, or our most frequented spot because it had Alice's favorite water-view location—the Sesuit Harbor Café in East Dennis. At

Sesuit Harbor Café, Alice was in her glory. She enjoyed sitting at a picnic table, under protective umbrellas, within 20 feet of the Sesuit Harbor inlet, watching boats come in and go out of the harbor. Alice simply loved a water view, especially with a continual flow of boats.

For her, an added bonus was that, in a picnic table environment, she always seemed to find a stranger with whom to converse. Although she had become uncomfortable speaking with close friends, she was still her former extroverted-self when speaking with strangers. I am convinced, in her heart of hearts, Alice realized she was unable to converse with friends in her customary manner, but strangers did not know the formerly Gregarious Alice, so they were not as "threatening" to her.

Traditionally, after our Cape Cod evening meals Alice and I would take a ride, ultimately ending at an ice cream shop. When at the Cape, prior to stopping for ice cream, a drive past Dennis Seashores was obligatory. Retirement did not alter the importance of Alice's primary interests: love of God, love of family, and love of Dennis Seashores. After retirement, our trips past DSS increased exponentially—every time we left the house, she insisted driving past Dennis Seashores!

As we drove past Dennis Seashores, she insisted that I drive slowly so she could assess the bustling activity. Although she insisted I drive slowly, under no circumstance would she sanction stopping the car!

With regularity I would suggest parking the car so we could walk around the grounds and visit with guests who would be delighted to see her. "ABSOLUTELY NOT," she vehemently instructed. "DO NOT stop this car; keep driving."

It wasn't until Alice's illness became evident that I began to under-stand her rationale. In refusing to visit with the Dennis Seashore guests whom she loved so much, Alice was denying herself the joy of visiting with friends because she knew she wasn't her former self. Those must have been particularly painful moments for Alice; she, the personification of a "people person," was unable to converse with people whom she genuinely loved.

Regularly, after driving past DSS after dinner, our nightly excursion would include stops at the Sundae School in Dennisport for Paul Endres' famous Hot Fudge Sundae with freshly whipped cream or Dairy Queen in West Harwich for a Blizzard. On hot humid summer nights, our next stop would be to Corporation Beach in East Dennis, to slowly consume our ice cream. But more importantly, as Patti Page used to sing, "to watch the sun go down on Cape Cod Bay." Although it wasn't the same as "watching the sun go down on Galway Bay," it was a close second.

If the weather was not conducive to watching the sunset, Alice was content if we found a choice parking spot close to the Sundae School take-out window. For Alice, an alternative to a water view on a summer evening was watching the hustle and bustle of summertime family life—kids munching ice cream cones!

When Katie, Patti and Jackie were young and worked at Sundae School in the 1980s, Alice used to love to find a parking place in front to the Sundae School window so she could watch her kids scurrying from customer to customer who waited anxiously at take-out windows.

MANDATORY CAR-RIDES

Alice's repetitive requests to go for a ride became increasingly more noticeable during 2008 and 2009. I was still under the impression these constant demands were attributable to her early retirement from Dennis Seashores. Neither the possibility of dementia nor extensive grief over Danny's unexpected death factored into my assessment of Alice's change in behavior. As a matter of fact, I thought Alice was managing grief better than I. On occasion, mostly at Mass, I would suddenly, without any indication, become emotional and burst into tears; stoic Alice would lean over and touch my hand.

As time went by, Alice's requests for car-rides seemed to occur later in the evening when it was not practical to take a car-ride; she wouldn't be able to see anything—too dark! When Alice expressed late night requests, I would attempt to logically explain why it wasn't the appropriate time to go for a ride; too dark, gas stations closed, bad storm headed in our direction, etc. Often after what I was convinced I "made the sale," much to my surprise she would adorn herself with one of her favorite baseball caps and say, "I'll be in the car!" or "Give me the keys, I'll drive myself." Even though her facial expression appeared to reflect comprehension, it belied the fact my message was unintelligible to her. Obviously, the comfort of riding in the car, without any need for conversational exchange, was of over-riding significance.

Oftentimes, Cape Cod rides would lead to the Chatham Lighthouse, which overlooked the shores toward Nantucket. It was one of Alice's favorite Cape Cod water views. A prime parking spot positioned her precisely in view of para gliders serenely descending and ascending above the tranquil waters of Chatham's Lighthouse Beach. She was especially intrigued with the numerous seals languishing on the shore, just as she had been transfixed by the vast number of seals languishing on Fisherman's Wharf in San Francisco.

Alice absolutely loved to look at the rippling ocean waves. She was content to sit silently, for endless periods of time, gazing and gazing in serene silence. If a storm was in the offing, we would drive to Orleans to see the power of the Atlantic Ocean's violent waves crash ashore at Nauset Beach. Even if a storm was not in the forecast, the ferocity of the Nauset Beach waves alone was always thrilling for Alice.

After one of our usual respites at Chatham Lighthouse Beach, we were proceeding north on Route 28 toward Orleans when Alice spotted a tag sale in a parking lot on the Chatham/Orleans line. Alice never met a tag sale she didn't like. With a reflex reaction, she often blurted out, "Tag sale;

let's stop!" Alice was delighted when she discovered the tag sale that day displayed a few of her favorite Oriental rugs!

At the time, Alice's mind was functioning, albeit nowhere near as well as in the past, but when it came to Oriental rugs, she knew a bargain when she saw a bargain. Within a nanosecond, she zeroed in on a few bargains. With Alice's Oriental rug know-how, combined with her negotiating expertise, it wasn't a fair fight; the sales agent didn't stand a chance! Alice acquired several rugs at considerably less than a wholesale price. Without hesitation, she urged me to secure the rugs in the car and head off to our destination before the sales agent could recant the agreement. Actually, in spiritual circles, it may have been grounds for Confession!

As we continued on our trek that day, I said, "Alice you took unfair advantage of that unsuspecting salesperson!"

She retorted, "If they were ill-equipped to barter, that's unfortunate and certainly their lack of knowledge is not my fault; a bargain is a bargain!" The acquisition of Persian Rugs was always a thrilling experience for Alice, especially the negotiation process. For a fleet moment in time, the Alice of old was momentarily rejuvenated. She was...STILL ALICE!

REGRESSION, ALBEIT GRADUAL REGRESSION

As time progressed, Alice became increasingly less likely to spend any length of time at points of interest that formerly occupied 100% of her attention. In the past, she was anxious to see the ocean and often time she enjoyed getting out of the car to smell the salt air and view the water from close range. But now she resisted getting out of the car and, she didn't want to linger. I encouraged her to join me and take a short walk, but it was all for naught. She was unmotivated and unwilling to leave the car. Soon this became her modus operandi; the only time she would consent to leaving the car was if we were going to church. Soon it even became difficult convincing her to get out of the car in our own driveway.

As Alice's illness progressed, her interest in car-rides accelerated. Without question, she felt secure sitting in the front seat of a car. Given her lifelong affinity for cars, it was not surprising that they were her comfort zone. At this point in her life, in spite of diminishing cognitive prowess, in the deep recesses of her mind, she must have been able to recall recollections of her MG and her Mercedes 190-SL. In our 17,498 days, her love for cars never faltered; she provided rides for people without a car and now, the most secure place she wanted to be was in a car.

TIP OF THE CAP to THE CAP OF THE DAY

Another item that was always close to Alice's heart (in reality, close to her head) were baseball caps! Although Alice had forgotten most of the people she knew and loved, she never forgot her craving for baseball caps. Before she would go-for-a-ride, she always donned one of her many, many baseball caps. Whenever we went on vacation, whether it be to Ireland, Scotland, California, or Florida, she always came home with a souvenir baseball cap!

In the summer months, Alice wore baseball caps all day, every day. When we were at the Cape, she wore baseball caps to Mass. When we were in Needham and the weather was cooler, she wore an Irish cabeen, or as they term it in South Boston, Scally Cap. During the cold winter months, for Sunday Mass she would dress, as she termed it, "to the nines," which included stylish dress-up hats. Even when Alice's mind was at its customary perspicacious self, she was determined to live life in the Pre-Vatican II world when women wore hats to Mass. Alice was not the "Last of the Mohicans," but she certainly was among the last of the women to wear hats in church!

Among Alice's favorite's caps were a Catholic Memorial hockey cap, "The Dock" cap from Naples, Fla, and, of course, a Boston Bruins cap.

Alice was thrilled when her first grandson, John Barrett Kennedy, was baptized at the Church of Saint Joseph in January 2010. Unapparent was her forgetfulness and her lack of conversational interest. I was delighted Alice was...STILL ALICE! Thank you baby Jack!

MINOR MATTERS MATTER; MAJOR MATTERS MATTER MORE

On a spring afternoon in 2010, after a long and cold winter, Alice and I took a relaxing trip to the Cape to check on winter wear and tear on Alice's pride and joy, Dennis Seashores and our cottage on Ferncliff. During the inspection of our cottage on Ferncliff, as customary, I went across the street to check on our elderly neighbors, Gerry and Elaine La Mothe.

I was shocked to learn from a distraught Gerry that his wife Elaine, after dealing with dementia for several years, succumbed during the winter. Gerry, 93 years old, cared for his cognitively afflicted wife during her illness and now that she had passed away, his burden became heavier—lonesomeness.

Due to past personality issues, Gerry dueled with and became estranged from abutters. As a result, his neighborhood confidants were few. Alice and I however, remained in his good graces, so we always made it a point to verify on their well-being when we were in Dennisport.

Since the onset of Elaine's illness, oftentimes Gerry would share his caregiver frustrations with me. Possessing zero medical ability, all I could do was provide a sympathetic ear. Year after year, story after story, through tear after tear, I listened to his frustrations with Elaine's bizarre behavior. As I would come to learn, while listening to Geriatric Gerry's lamentations, God was preparing me for an insight into coming attractions.

One time during Elaine's illness, which may have commenced around 2006 to 2007, Alice noticed Gerry attempting to climb through a window to gain access to their house. Evidently, Elaine forgot Gerry wasn't home and locked the door. Alice to the rescue! Equipped with her every-ready, handy-dandy toolbox, she went across the street, pried open the living room window, and boosted Geriatric Gerry through the window and into his house!

Periodically, when Elaine would fall on the floor, Gerry would come over and ask me to pick her up and put her into bed. When these incidents occurred, I always informed their son Jay, who resided a short distance away in West Barnstable. After one of those episodes, Jay stopped at our house to thank Alice and me for keeping an eye on his parents and remarked, "These incidents wouldn't occur if my mother eliminated drinking." That was the first I heard liquor might have been a factor in Elaine's disorientation. Gerry never mentioned a similar concern.

It's possible that Jay was in denial about the severity of his mother's cognitive degeneration, hoping against hope that by limiting alcohol consumption his mother's memory deficiencies would dissolve. In retrospect, initially I too was of the opinion that wine may have been a contributing factor in Alice's cognitive challenges.

On this particular day in April, just a month or two after Elaine died, the gravity of Geriatric Gerry's grief was heart wrenching. In order to minimize his sorrow and subscribing to the "the misery likes company theory," I shared with him my concern. "I am fearful Gerry that Alice is also exhibiting signs of cognitive diminishment." As tears trickled down his face, Gerry put his arm on my shoulder and said, "Danny, if that's the case, I feel so sorry for *you*; it's a terrible disease. In life, Danny, we are confronted with many minor matters, but this is a major matter. It's so difficult."

For a man of advanced years, Gerry's mind was exceedingly sharp; he was amazingly bright and he was absolutely correct in his assessment—it is a terrible disease and it does rob a person of their mind. However, he didn't need to "feel sorry for me." Although, at the time, I didn't realize the ominous illness that was beginning to creep through Alice's cranium would become a blessing, but it did—a double blessing. First, it was a blessing for Alice in that she couldn't knowingly offend God, and secondly, it was a blessing for me in caring for Alice as she carried a challenging cross.

As Gerry and I continued to talk, Alice hollered from across the street, "I'm going to the Mason Jar (Harwichport restaurant) for sandwiches." I did not foresee any potential problem with Alice driving a short distance for sandwiches; my only concern was her propensity to repetitiously repeat stories and to demand car-rides.

Alice was a punctual person; never tardy. She was always where she was supposed to be, when she was supposed to be there. On that chilly spring afternoon in Dennisport, an hour elapsed and Alice had not returned from a relatively short-distance errand. As I paced up and down Ferncliff Road, contemplating my next move, I spotted her car at the end of the street. To say I was relieved would be an understatement! As soon as Alice parked her car in front of our house, I gave her a big hug.

In the past, my initial reaction would have been to say, "What took you so long?" My suspicion was disorientation and cognitive issues may have played a role in the inordinate delay. Thus, I did not mention the undue delay.

My decision to avoid any mention of the delay in her minor mission for sandwiches was affirmed when I noted a look of indescribable bewilderment on Alice's face. What had been a minor mission gave me insight to a major problem. I knew from her ashen white face and the vague look in her eyes that the issue was not physical, nor was it material. It was a cerebral issue. There was no body damage to her car. Obviously, this apparent cognitive lapse lent credence to the hypothesis I just espoused to Geriatric Gerry. Several months later, another incident of concern occurred.

On a warm summer evening on the Cape, Alice and I went to dinner at one of her favorite *bargain-night* restaurants—Villa Roma Restaurant in Harwich. In order to take advantage of a 20% discount on "Early Bird Specials," we had to be seated before 6:00 p.m.

Per usual, as we were exiting the restaurant after dinner, Alice would stop at a table of total strangers and ask if they had an Early Bird discount coupon. If they did not, then she would open her wallet, and as she produced a coupon with an ear-to-ear smile, she would say, "You have one now, enjoy your dinner." Alice horded coupons and gratuitously dispersed them to strangers who did not realize coupons were offered.

After we left the restaurant, Alice suggested she drive to the Glendon Road Beach to watch sailboats gliding across the tranquil waters of Nantucket Sound and see families frolicking on the shore. As she drove down Lower County Road, Alice passed Glendon Road without drawing attention to the fact she didn't turn on Glendon Road. I matter-of-factly suggested, "The next left will bring us to Glendon Road Beach." Not realizing she had passed Glendon Road, she assured me, "I'm going to turn down Glendon Road." It was inconceivable to me that Alice, who knew every street on the Cape like the back of her hand, didn't realize we just passed Glendon Road.

I saw no point in belaboring the issue, as there were several more opportunities to take left-hand turns. As Alice continued to pass several left-turn options as she looked for Glendon Road, I continued to maintain my silence.

After reaching the Dennisport/West Dennis line with no longer any opportunities for a left turn, Alice dejectedly pulled into the Swan River Fish Market parking lot. I proffered, "I think if we turn around Babe and look for a street on the right-side of the road, that might lead us to the beach." Without rancor, retort or rebuttal, she accepted my suggestion, and eventually we arrived at Glendon Road Beach. Alice and I enjoyed the aquatic activity of swimmers, boaters, kites, para-gliders and "old folks" strolling the beach.

When I mentioned to Alice's close friend, Kathleen Flynn, a former nurse practitioner at the Yale-New Haven Hospital, that I had reviewed my observations of Alice's short-term memory issues with Alice's primary care physician, Dr. Finn, she was pleased. Kathleen told me, "It's important for a patient to have a good relationship with their primary care physician and Alice certainly has that affiliation with Dr. Finn," she elaborated. "Several years ago, Alice told me when you and she were out for dinner, Dr. Finn went out of his way to bring his wife over to your table just to meet Alice, who he introduced as 'one of my favorite patients.'"

MEDICAL NEEDS ABOUND

In September of 2011, after attending 9:00 a.m. morning Mass at Holy Trinity Church in West Harwich, and after conversing with David Russell's mother, Sally, in the church parking lot, I began to sense an unusual numbness in my left leg, which I proceeded to disavow. The numbness in my leg persisted when I arrived at my favorite coffee shop, so I decided to dispense with my morning coffee ritual and drive directly back to Dennisport.

Upon my premature return home, Alice was momentarily perplexed, which followed immediately with a shocked expression as I said, "Alice, I need you to drive me to the Town of Dennis Fire Department for a physical evaluation." After a cursory examination, fire department personnel decided to send me, by ambulance, to the Cape Cod Hospital in Hyannis. The doctors suggested I sustained a minor stroke and needed to be hospitalized for three days.

When Patti brought Alice to the hospital to visit me, Al barely spoke; she just stared at me as I lay in the bed. The absolute blank look on Alice's face underscored to me the diminishment of her cognitive skills. It was obvious Alice could not process why I was where I was.

It was at that precise moment that we learned of Alice's newfound method of extricating herself from uncomfortable or confusing situations. She turned to Patti and commenced in rapid-fire repetition, what was to become her modus operandi in coping with uncomfortable situations, "Let's go, let's go, let's go, now!"

The vague expression on Alice's face as she looked at me will be permanently implanted in my mind. Her expression was not dissimilar to the look of bewilderment she displayed after her prolonged car-ride to pick-up sandwiches at the Mason Jar.

Upon discharge from the Cape Cod Hospital, I was determined to return to Needham as soon as possible. In the event of another stroke, I preferred to be in the proximity of Boston-area hospitals. In addition, I wanted a second opinion from our primary care physician, Dr. Finn. Even though I only sustained a few residual effects from the stroke, I knew I was incapable of driving back to Needham, so I asked Alice to drive; she refused!

When Alice disagreed with my request to drive back to Needham, I learned another aspect of her illness. Even though she might appear to act rationally, it did not necessarily indicate cognitive comprehension. Alice was programed to leave the Cape after Columbus Day, and regardless of any intervening cause, departure from the Cape prior Columbus Day was unacceptable.

"Alice dear, I need to visit your friend, Dr. Finn, and then we can return for Columbus Day." With the mention of Dr. Finn's name, combined with my fabricated assurance we were coming back within a few days, she recanted her objection. I thought to myself, "How many days will I spend in Purgatory for that little white lie?" Obviously, I was calculating that once we returned to Needham, she would forget the Dennis Seashores Columbus Day closing date. On that score, I was right.

Thankfully, Dr. Finn and a Massachusetts General Hospital neurologist rendered an encouraging diagnosis, and thanks to Alice's short-term memory deficiency, she never mentioned Dennis Seashores again. Deo Gratias!

THE FAMILIAR CONFINES OF THE TOWN OF NEEDHAM

In previous years, after returning to Needham from the Cape, Alice would resume cooking, but this time she did not. As had been our typical behavior at the Cape, on nights when we opted to eat at home, I was in the backyard grilling. After a long and stressful day at Dennis Seashores, it was not unusual for Alice to be inactive in the kitchen, so I was the chef de jour. In the past when we returned to Needham, Alice assumed cooking responsibilities. However, in what was a surprise to me, in 2011 when we came home Alice did not resort to her customary culinary contributions. Further, she exhibited no awareness for meal preparation.

I too was adjusting—adjusting to Alice's demeanor changes—which to an extent I still believed (i.e., hoped) were attributable to a combination of senioritis (if there is such an illness) and/or an elongated cocktail hour. I was hoping for a cause other than a cognitive deficiency.

Grocery shopping was no longer on Alice's agenda; she exhibited absolutely no interest in purchasing groceries. When I suggested that both of us go into the store, she would reply, "You go." Ever so gradually she began withdrawing from daily life. As a result, I shopped for groceries while Alice remained seated in the front seat of the car.

As the weather proceeded toward sub-freezing, I brought my backyard culinary "skills" indoors. Fortunately, Whole Foods opened a new location in Wellesley, offering an extensive selection of prepared foods. I took full advantage of this location. My strategy worked well for two reasons. First, I was able to select items I knew Alice would love. Second, within a microwave-minute, there was a nice warm meal on the table for Alice.

Traditionally, our family budget was predicated on providing Alice a bi-weekly stipend of $200, which we deemed to be "food money." It was also considered to be discretionary income, (i.e., *Alice's spending money*).

In essence, Alice's sound judgment dictated how she apportioned the $400 monthly stipend.

At times, Alice's visual appearance combined with presumable cognitive comprehension belied the fact that her thought process was not as perspicacious as in previous years. Even I, who observed her on a daily basis, continued to be influenced by her uncanny ability to rise to the occasion and display logical behavior. Still, certain things like food money just did not compute to her. Innumerable times I explained, in view of the fact I was purchasing the groceries from my own financial resources, we should adjust the formerly agreed upon bi-weekly food money allocation.

To say Alice was vehemently opposed to any monetary adjustment would be an understatement of grandiose proportions; she was accustomed to receiving $200 every two weeks and nothing less than $200 every two weeks was acceptable. At that point, I began to realize her disaffection with grocery shopping and her resistance to a food-money adjustment were not logic issues, they were dementia-oriented. Even though I was aware of the erosion of Alice's mental acumen, from an appearance perspective, I continued to see her through the lens of normalcy. She looked physically the same, so I continued to believe I could reason with her "logically." But I was wrong! Reasoning logically with an illogical person is, of itself, illogical.

In an attempt to convince Alice of the cost of groceries, I presented her with the sales receipts. I was under the assumption that if she saw, in print, the receipt, it would present irrefutable proof that the stipend should be reduced; once again Danny Boy, you were wrong. In Alice's mind, sales receipts be damned. "Show me the cash Danny Boy, show me the cash," was her view. Some things were slower to change. Case in point was Alice's interest in monetary matters.

At Alice's next scheduled appointment with Dr. Finn, I remained in the waiting room while Dr. Finn examined Alice. During the appointment, Dr. Finn left the examination room and came out and sat next to me in the waiting room. He solicited what I perceived to be changes in Alice's behavior. He took copious notes when I informed him, "In spite of a good night's sleep, often she falls asleep during the day, always looking for a spot "to flop" or lie down. Cantankerousness has become her by-word, vehemently refusing to do things she used to love, in addition she has become extremely obstinate. I also informed Dr. Finn she had become impulsive; she wants what she wants when she wants it!" In essence, I informed her physician that the word "repetitiveness" describes her daily demeanor. She will repeat the same request over and over ("let's go, let's go, let's go...now").

After our brief discussion, Dr. Finn asked me to join him in the examination room for the remainder of Alice's visit. Dr. Finn proceeded to ask Alice various questions pertaining to year, month, day, my birthday and her birthday. In addition, he asked her if she knew the headline in today's newspaper, etc. Even though she may not have known the correct answers to all his questions, her answers were generally within a ballpark range.

On all subsequent visits, Dr. Finn requested my presence in the examination room. At one these examinations, out of Alice's ear-shot, he said, "At this point, it is difficult to conclude whether or not it is age or dementia; she seems to answer most questions correctly." Although I was pleased with Dr. Finn's somewhat encouraging assessment, I remained skeptical. I was of the opinion that, in spite of memory deficiencies, Alice's keen intellect allowed her to reason to the correct conclusion, thus masking her illness.

On another occasion, after completing his customary litany of questions, Dr. Finn asked Alice if she had any questions for him. She responded immediately, "No Doctor, I don't have any questions for you; do you have any questions for me?" Both Dr. Finn and I smiled, impressed with the alacrity of Alice's response and how quickly she turned the tables on the doctor. Her response in itself was revealing; she didn't remember Dr. Finn had just concluded asking her questions. Nonetheless, I was so proud of her; she demonstrated that her mind was still functioning well enough to "toss the ball back into Dr. Finn's court." In my opinion, it was evidence of her sharp mind.

Alice was so bright; she always seemed to summon-up sufficient neutrons to fool and out-smart other people, including medical personnel. Whether it was Dr. Finn office visits or the subsequent visits to a neurologist, Alice was spot-on with correct responses.

Even though her responses to medical personnel were in direct contradiction to my input, whenever I heard Alice voice correct responses to a series of questions, I was so proud of her. I said to myself, "Good for you Alice, you outsmarted these doctors."

DOWNSIZING ON WOODLAWN AVENUE

One day David Coughlin, the son of Regina Coughlin who lived a few houses away from us on Woodlawn Ave, called to advise Alice that his mother intended to sell her home and wanted to offer Alice the opportunity to purchase the home. Apparently, at some point Alice had previously mentioned to his mother that she would be interested in possibly purchasing the home if his mom ever decided to sell. Proactive Alice said she might be interested in downsizing to another Woodlawn Ave home in the future.

When I conveyed this news to Alice, I was shocked with her reaction or lack thereof; she displayed no reaction whatsoever. She looked perplexed and made no comment. I was well aware of Alice's sporadic moments of vagueness, yet I remained hopeful those incidents of indifference were less frequent than they actually were. However, I was in spousal denial.

To most people, including our family, Alice looked and spoke like the wife, mother, and friend we knew so well and loved so much. But under her façade of "sameness" was an Alice that neither she, nor we, recognized or understood. Securely concealed in the confines of her inner most being was the Alice all of us were longing to see.

After a few days of Alice's apathy, I called David Coughlin. I thanked him for conveying his mother's remembrance of Alice's interest, but told him the timing wasn't right for us to consider relocating.

A ROAD, PREFERABLY, NOT TO BE TRAVELED
Even though I walk through a dark valley, I fear no harm. (Psalm 23: 4)

As days and weeks passed, it became patently obvious Alice was traveling down a road, and not a particularly desirable one. Unlike the challenge of driving on the left side of the road in Jamaica and Ireland, Alice was now experiencing a more challenging road, a road with tortuous turns with yet-to-be-revealed unknown experiences.

Gradually, one by one, activities Alice loved were becoming distant memories. She exhibited little interest in her cute little Westie, Riley. No longer was there an omni-present blaze in our fireplace. Her rabid allegiance to the Bruins abated. In place of her enthrallment with the Bruins, she developed a newfound admiration for the New England Patriots. Apparently, the flight of a football was easier to comprehend than the path of a puck.

Alice loved to be in attendance at a New England Patriots football game, but now her allegiance was manifested from a distance.

After a Patriots game, Alice and I continued to enjoy our nightly cocktail hour, which was always highlighted by a backrub for Alice's congenital bothersome back. Even as a young girl, her back muscles seemed to tighten during the course of the day and she needed a minute or two massage to loosen muscle tension. Although we went through the motions, it was obvious our traditional cocktail hour and nightly back-rub was no longer of any particular interest to her.

For me, the most important aspect of our cocktail hour was never the cocktail nor the shrimp; my delight was a toss-up between massaging Alice's back and serving Hors d'oeuvres! I just loved filling a small plate with a variety of Hors d'oeuvres; walking over to where Alice sat and serving her. She would always say, "You don't have to get up, Babe, I can get the cheese and crackers myself." I told her over and over, "I just love bringing Hors d' oeuvres to you; I love waiting on you." Unfortunately, those joyful days were now in the rearview mirror.

I was pleased with Alice's newfound obsession with Bill Belichick's Super Bowl-bound Patriots. The games were typically played on Sunday afternoons when both of us could watch without falling asleep. There was little chance we would stay awake for the evening Bruins games.

One Sunday afternoon, as we were watching the Patriots on TV, Alice went out to the kitchen. Soon I heard her speaking with someone on the telephone. The phone had not rung, so she obviously dialed a number. It was quite unusual to hear Alice talking on the telephone at this point in her life. I didn't want to be constantly looking over her shoulder, so I continued to watch the Pat's game and gave little thought to her telephone conversation. It wasn't until she opened the front door and said, "I'll be back," that I realized there must have been a purpose to the telephone conversation.

Fifteen minutes later, Alice was back. I asked, "Where did you go?"

She explained, "A friend of Ashley's left her medication on our kitchen table and I wanted to return the meds to her. I looked her name up in the telephone directory, called her mother, and brought the medications to her." Resourceful Alice. Helpful Alice. Yes...STILL ALICE!

That evening, the girl came back to our house to pick-up the medications she had forgotten. When she learned Alice delivered the meds to her mother's house, she burst into tears! Evidently, the girl and her mother were having some family issues and she was living with her father. In doing what she did her entire life, helping someone in distress, Alice inadvertently caused grief for the young girl. Evidently, "a good deed doesn't go unpunished."

A SPECIAL CHRISTMAS PRESENT

Shortly after Thanksgiving, in what was a role reversal for me, my curiosity was aroused when I saw a newspaper advertisement promoting a Kirby vacuum cleaner. The dealer was offering to vacuum a rug free of charge.

Unlike 43 years ago in Westfield, this time, I was the instigator in soliciting an in-house Kirby demonstration!

Alice's memory seemed to be revived when she saw the Kirby Van pull up and the salesman come to the front door. Alice was elated. The joy on her face was obvious. Just as was the case on that day many years ago, happiness radiated on her face. The difference this time was that I also radiated happiness in seeing the joy it brought to Alice. Throughout our married life, I would do any crazy or stupid thing I could think to do just to make Alice smile and laugh! I just loved to see her happy and now she was happy! This time I didn't have to do something crazy to make her smile; a simple demonstration of a Kirby vacuum cleaner did the trick.

Yes, at long last, after years of begrudging acquiescence, I came full circle. I was actually promoting the purchase a new Kirby vacuum. Alice did not offer any opposition when I suggested we trade in the old Kirby for a brand-new product. Yes, in 2011, we bought Kirby #2, 43 years after purchasing Kirby #1! If Alice was in her prime, she would have negotiated a much better deal, but I did my best to impersonate "Alice the Negotiator."

Just before the new year, Alice's niece Brenda Harlow stopped for a visit, and Alice excitedly said, "Bren, wait until I tell you what I received for Christmas...a brand-new Kirby vacuum cleaner!" Later while Brenda and Alice were driving over to Patti and Ashley's apartment, Alice repeated, "Bren', you're going to love this, I have something to tell you. My Christmas present was a brand-new Kirby vacuum cleaner!" For the second time, within an hour, Brenda received the same exciting news. Obviously, Alice short-term memory was revived; she couldn't tell people often enough how happy she was with her new Kirby vacuum!

What I didn't take into consideration was that Alice was no longer capable of comprehending operating instructions. For someone who could skillfully operate most any kind of mechanical equipment, turning the "on-switch" of a new Kirby was an insurmountable challenge for Alice.

At this point in her life, our *Master Mechanic* was, sadly, a marooned *Master Mechanic*.

As 2012 commenced, reality continued to elude Alice's thought process. Occasionally various people would mention to me they were sorry to learn that we were selling our home. Sally Dempsey, one of the first neighbors we met when we moved to Needham in 1982 came to our front door with tears in her eyes as she said, "I just learned you sold your house and you're moving."

I asked Sally, "What makes you think we are selling our home?"

She replied, "Alice bumped into Pat (her husband) at the grocery store and she shared the information. She said you are selling and moving to the Cape."

While I was attempting to dispel the erroneous information, Alice came into the front hallway and remonstratively rebuked what I was saying. "Don't listen to him Sally," she said. "We are moving and we received a wonderful offer: $875,000."

Alice spoke with such conviction and authenticity that Sally looked perplexed. She was in a quandary, as she attempted to ascertain which one of these contradictory statements was misguided. During this confused period of time, my mind-set was never to overtly contradict Alice; I did not want to inflict additional confusion, so I merely said, "At some point we will undoubtedly sell our home and relocate, but time and place is yet to be determined." Sally seemed to understand the current Kennedy Family dynamics.

Not only did Alice *believe* we were selling the house, but she commenced with preparations pursuant to packing household furnishings. First, she started to save old newspapers and cardboard boxes. Then she purchased excessive amounts of bubble-wrap plastic to cushion her precious Waterford Crystal.

Day after day our back porch accumulated piles of old newspapers, cardboard boxes, and reams of plastic bubble-wrap material; it was reminiscent of the cluttered back porch of Mrs. Morgan's house on the corner of Otis Street and Manning Street. Years ago, every time we drove past Mrs. Morgan's house, Alice would frequently comment on the clutter on Mrs. Morgan's back porch. Surprise, surprise, now that Alice had started to horde everything imaginable, Mrs. Morgan's back-porch had nothing on ours.

Alice's reluctance to speak with her friends seemed to be sporadic. Some days she was her former conversational self, other days she sought to avoid interpersonal conversations. When she did engage in conversation with friends, she was effective in disguising her cognitive issues. When she did opt for conversation, the content of her contribution was delivered with such conviction that the veracity of the message was irrefutable. As a result, the town of Needham was under the impression we were in the process of moving.

Sally Dempsey's visit wasn't an aberration; other neighbors and friends stopped by to express similar regrets. If Alice wasn't present, it would have been easy for me to explain the misunderstanding. But when Alice was privy to the conversation, she would blatantly contradict me and vigorously affirm, "Shhhh. Dan doesn't want people to know. Yes, we sold the house and we're moving to the Cape. We received a great price."

"I'm sorry to hear you and Alice are moving to the Cape, Dan. We'll miss you," said Father Michael Lawlor, Pastor of St. Joseph's Church in Needham. Before I could rebut his erroneous information, he added, "Saint Joseph's will miss the Kennedy Clan."

I inquired, "Where did you hear that Father?"

He replied, "Alice mentioned it to the Counting Team at the Rectory."

I pointed out, "Alice has always contemplated selling our Needham home and moving to the Cape. Now, to her, it has become reality. I would caution that eminent departure of the Kennedy family from Needham is, to say the least, premature." As rumors abounded, Alice forged ahead with plans to package personal property. If her lifelong determination was to retain the superfluous, now her predisposed disposition to save was carried to extremes.

Nothing, absolutely nothing, could be thrown away. Everything, and I mean everything, must be saved and packed, necessitating an abundance of bubble-wrap, cartons, etc. Our entire family was keenly aware of Alice's propensity to save for *a rainy day*. Now Alice had gone to extremes. She was like Noah preparing for a *gigantic flood;* she wanted to save two of everything. Yes, preservation of extraneous items became an Alice obsession.

Traditionally, Alice was always reluctant to throw things away. She believed that a need will arise for any given item, so she retained them at all costs. "This bolt (or whatever else) *might be* useful at a future date." The operative words *might be* were now replaced with the operative words became *"will be"* useful when we move. Alice was now, unquestionably, in Hoarding Heaven.

As a matter of course, if I deemed certain items to no longer be of use, I put them into trash bags pursuant to disposing of them at the Needham Transfer Station. Now that Alice was pre-occupied with "our move," she rummaged through the trash bags destined for the dump and retrieved various items I designated as dump material. One day I discarded a disgusting ratty-old sneaker, not at all concerned about its missing mate, which probably was deposited in the Needham dump years ago. While rummaging through the trash bag, Alice resurrected the ratty-old sneaker and told me she would keep it until she located its mate!

Whether it be in Needham or in Dennis, Alice had a field day at dumps. She always reclaimed a discarded item. She particularly interested in confiscating broken wicker chairs, which she repaired and prominently displayed on our back porch.

Based on previous discussions with Dr. Finn, he strongly urged me to allow Alice to do whatever she desired, as long as I deemed it not to be harmful. That admonition became my by-word. If I could possibly justify allowing her to do things where she may derive comfort, that was precisely what I did. If, on occasion, those leniencies resulted in negative after-affects, I was willing to deal with them at the time.

One of her loves at that time was surfing the internet, which I believed to be therapeutic for her. I did not voice any objections, although on occasion she did make some questionable acquisitions. When I diplomatically suggested she should exercise discretion when purchasing items, she felt I was infringing upon her PC privacy.

DISCERNMENT? NON-EXISTANT. GULLIBILE? ABSOLUTELY

Alice always enjoyed time on our computer, and I encouraged her to continue because it kept her mind working and provided a sense of self-esteem. Eventually, after becoming inundated with non-sensical items she purchased and numerous telephone calls from various organizations, I began to question whether I carried Dr. Finn's "keep her comfortable" advice too far.

With increasing regularity, I began to receive telephone calls from life insurance companies, construction companies, weight loss companies, teeth-whitening companies, etc. When the caller asked to speak with "Daniel," my antenna went up, as no one refers to me as Daniel. After inquiring as to where they obtained the name "Daniel," the caller informed me I responded to a survey or an online promotion. Years before, when we first purchased a computer, it was registered in the name of "Daniel." I soon realized that Alice must have clicked on a survey, and in the sophisticated world of electronics, the response was attributed to Daniel. Who would have "thunk" it? By nature, Alice was discernment personified, and now she was prey for promotions. *See that you are not deceived. (John 21:8)*

I received a call from a life insurance salesman who wished to visit with me to discuss selling me a policy for "Daniel." I responded with a most enthusiastic tone of voice. "Great idea, I would be most interested in scheduling an appointment with you; life insurance tops my bucket list! I have recently been treated for three Melanomas and two strokes, so please, before the clocks runs out on me, bring me a life insurance policy!" The salesman quickly slammed the phone down.

On another occasion, a teeth-whitening salesman called and asked for Daniel. I informed him, "Yes, you are speaking with Daniel and, yes I am interested in white teeth. However, I am currently on a 'do-it-yourself' whitening program; I merely go Harvey's Hardware, purchase a pumice stone and my teeth are white as the driven snow." (I did have my fun needling those sales people; Purgatory time?)

It is not unusual for senior citizens to be victimized by cleverly devised computer promotions, but it is much easier for a cognitive impaired person to be victimized. In order to prevent a major acquisition, I discretely inquired from Alice if she may have, inadvertently, clicked on any promos. Alice of course, in her mind, was completely truthful when she disavowed any culpability. I realized that by merely posing a question, even in a normal tone of voice, it was perceived by Alice to be accusatory. Thus, I attempted to develop a subtler surveillance approach; some might call it spying.

Whenever Alice was working at the computer, I peeked over her shoulder and the first thing I would do was commend her on whatever was on the monitor. If it was innocuous, I encouraged her to continue. If it was something I perceived to be detrimental, I suggested she click on another website. My approach, as I looked over her shoulder, if possible, was to always look for reasons to commend her on what she was doing and, if necessary, to suggest she use an alternate website.

In spite of my plan to dissuade her from certain sites, the UPS delivery truck continued to beat a path down Woodlawn Ave and deposit purchased items at our front door. One of Alice's computer acquisitions was purchasing preventive powder to deter bed-bug invasion. The Bed-Bug Defense Kit purportedly protected people from irritating itches resulting from bed bug infestation. In over 40 years, we never had any discernable issue of itching, so I couldn't understand why we could no longer survive without Bed-Bug Defense. However, Alice's persistence predominated her every thought. "We need bed-bug protection Dan, and that's final!" It was another example of how elderly, credulous people are prone to be prey for sophisticated marketing promotions.

Alice assumed the role of de-facto Commander-in-Chief of the Kennedy Family Bed-Bug Defense Department. As commander-in-chief, she took all the necessary (or unnecessary) steps to protect every bedroom and every couch with strategically embedded Bed-Bug Repellent devices. In my mind, I rationalized these nominally priced acquisitions as the "cost of doing business" items; that is, they come with the territory and, in this case, the territory was dementia.

In the interest of full disclosure, I don't believe these acquisitions were solely attributable to dementia; even in Alice's pre-dementia days, *a bargain was a bargain*! Alice was always anxious to listen to a sales promotion. I was not. I thought Alice was unduly credulous; she thought I was unduly skeptical. Somehow, even with disagreements, through the Grace of God we overlooked each other's idiosyncrasies.

One of Alice's more expensive acquisitions during this conflicting period of cognitive confusion and bargain hunting was the purchase a $400 floor heater for our living room on Woodlawn Ave. Formerly Frugal Alice was now intent on squandering money on superfluous items. For some reason, in Alice's mind, after 30 years of comfortable heating conditions in our living room, she was convinced heat was suddenly inadequate. In spite of the fact I didn't perceive there to be a problem, I acceded to her suggestion that we purchase a portable floor heater for our living room. When the unit arrived, Alice situated it adjacent to the fireplace. As soon as the unit was plugged in, fuses started to blow, so we called an electrician to install another circuit.

There certainly was no false advertising—the floor heater certainly provided heat—heat in abundance! Between the heat from the now occasionally used fireplace and the heat from the new floor heater, Alice and I were sweltering as we sat in sauna-saturated clothes. Eventually, Alice conceded the room was much too warm, so we turned off the unit. The heater was without a doubt functional; however, we did not lack heat, and a floor unit was an unnecessary expense.

In the latter part of the summer, the United Parcel Service (UPS) delivery truck stopped at 35 Ferncliff Road in Dennisport and the driver proceeded to unload a huge box. I asked what he was delivering, and he said a floor heater! Yes, my little Alice Blue Gown ordered another $400 floor heater. When Alice returned from an errand, I told her we received another floor heater. She explained, "Great, you know it can be really cold at the Cape in September and October. Now we will have additional heat."

When a plumber came to Dennisport on another matter, he commented on the heating unit. I explained that Alice was concerned about inadequate heat. He proceeded to tell me that a floor heater does provide heat, but it uses a tremendous amount of electricity and would double our electric bill! When I told Alice, she just rolled her eyes and said, "What does a plumber know about electricity?" Not the well-informed logical response Alice would customarily contribute to a home betterment conversation.

We weren't home from the Cape more than a week or two when another UPS truck pulled up in front of 45 Woodlawn Ave. I approached the delivery driver and inquired what he was about to deliver. He replied, "a portable floor heater." Floor heater number three was about to grace our humble abode! Without hesitation, I told the delivery driver, "Put the heater back in the truck and to mark it 'return to sender,' stating that the customer refused delivery!"

A few days later Alice asked, "Have you seen the UPS truck recently? I'm expecting a delivery."

"No Alice dear, I haven't seen the UPS truck in over a week," I replied. (More Purgatory time...pray for me.)

SUNDAY SAGA

From October through May, Alice and I attended the 11:00 o'clock Sunday Mass at St. Joseph's Church. After Alice's illness progressed, we still attended the 11:00 o'clock Mass, but now when we entered the church it was with a "flourish." By nature, Alice was outgoing and friendly, but never ostentatious or a show-off; now, upon entering the church, she was overtly friendly—waving, shouting, and speaking in a loud tone of voice to everyone. She was in an "unlike Alice" demeanor; she was unrestrained, brash and flamboyant.

In essence, before Mass began, she conducted herself as if she were in a football stadium or a raucous concert hall and not a consecrated House of God. One of her favorite people to befriend was Ashley's friend, Maddie Zwirello, who, along with her parents, was always seated a row or two in front of us. As we proceeded to our customary pew, Alice would yell, in a loud voice, "Hi Maddie! How's school Maddie? Do you have passing grades Maddie?"

Even to Affable Alice, the conspicuousness of such brash and ostentatious behavior would have been an embarrassment. Fortunately, people who knew Alice realized this aberrant behavior was an anomaly and that she was, at heart, "Still Alice."

NEUROLOGICAL ASSESSMENT

After a period of observation and evaluation, Dr. Finn felt Alice's condition warranted a neurological examination. Consequently, in October, Dr. Finn referred Alice to Dr. Marybeth Toran, a neurologist at Newton-Wellesley Hospital. After a preliminary examination, Dr. Toran recommended, as a first step, a battery of tests from a neuropsychologist.

As soon as Alice and I entered the neuropsychologist's office, I was puzzled at its Spartan appearance. The drab and dour decor did not reflect the conventional medical office atmosphere; there was no receptionist, the waiting room was dark and dreary, and the window shades were tightly drawn, with the sole source of illumination being a dim 20-watt lamp. There were no patients, no soothing music playing, and certainly no reading material. Presumably, my apprehension may have been attributable, at least in part, to the fact this was our first visit to a "shrink's" office!

Shortly after Alice and I were seated alone in the darkened, dingy waiting room, a door from an adjoining room opened, and silently, in slinked the shrink. He was not wearing customary medical attire; rather, he was dressed in a conventional business suit.

Bereft of personality, the shrink inaudibly directed Alice and me into the inner sanctum of another dark and dingy room. It may have been my pre-conceived conception, but to me, the room appeared to signify an atmosphere of doom and gloom.

In a somewhat somber tone, the shrink posed, in a matter-of-fact manner, a few general questions pertaining to Alice making notations as I responded. After completing the joint interview, he informed us that he would render a comprehensive assessment at the conclusion of three separate, one-on-one sessions with Alice.

Alice sat silently, with no apparent adverse reaction. As I reflect on docility, it seemed to be a harbinger of the placid reaction she would demonstrate in future medical evaluations. She never exhibited any apprehension in the company of doctors or nurses.

After Alice's third visit to the neuropsychologist, with both Alice and I seated in the darkened dungeon, he rendered his long-awaited diagnosis.

"Examination results indicate Alice does not have a problem, there are no discernible cognitive issues. For a woman of average intelligence, Alice is only slightly below the norm."

I was appalled!

Not only was it incorrect to suggest that Alice did not have a problem, it was also incorrect to infer inadequate intellect. I disagreed with his optimistic diagnosis and resented his conception that Alice was of average intelligence. Alice most certainly had a problem, otherwise we wouldn't be sitting in his office.

With a purposely non-expressive bland reaction, compliant with the austere aura of his office, and in a subdued tone of voice with uninformed intonation, I asked, "If you don't mind my inquisitiveness, on what basis did you determine Alice was of average intelligence?"

The shrink imperiously proclaimed, "Well, she only has a high school education."

I paused momentarily, and with a subdued self-deprecating tone I rhetorically responded, "Really?"

After a momentary pause, I added, "Would you like my medical opinion on your diagnosis?" With what appeared to me to be, a sardonic expression, the shrink indignantly responded, "Your, medical opinion?"

I replied; "Yes! In my medical opinion; your diagnosis is BULL SHIT!"

"Your reliance on 'only a high school education' as a determining factor for the level of Alice's acumen disregards her intellectual quotient. Throughout her life, Alice has been in the company of doctors, attorneys, engineers, educators, and Fortune 500 CEOs, none of whom struck her with a sense of awe. Alice would stand toe-to-toe with exceptionally bright people and intelligently engage them in conversation in their field of expertise. Consequently, predicated upon a false premise, your evaluation is flawed!" Alice is not of 'average intelligence,' she is of 'above average intelligence.'

Thus, her current condition represents a much more significant decline than your diagnosis indicates."

He retorted that when Alice comes for another visit a year from now, we will have this as a benchmark with which to measure any change.

I said, "Surely you jest; this has been a total waste of our time. Our feet will never cross this threshold again."

I believe in my heart of hearts, if Alice could have expressed herself, she would have said, "Thank you Babe, I couldn't have handled that any better." At Alice's next appointment with neurologist Dr. Toran at Newton-Wellesley Hospital, I discussed my opinion of the three sessions with the neuropsychologist. Assumedly, for insurance purposes, a neuropsychology examination is mandatory in diagnosing neurological issues. While we held Dr. Toran in high regard, in my opinion, the shrink's contribution, or lack thereof, was a non-productive component of our discovery of Alice's illness.

DINING OUT WITH ALICE

Dinner continued to be a special event for Alice, but unfortunately, her interest in fortifying herself with discount coupons for Early-Bird Specials had long been forgotten. Another indication of regression was her inability to order from the menu. Alice would ask me, "What do I like?" Although such a question was not all that unusual for a senior citizen, for Alice it was a major shift. Only just a few years ago, she was far from acting like a senior citizen. She was a young and vibrant woman hustling around as if she were 20 years younger than her age, but now she was a mere shadow of her former self. Even though the reality of her verbalization was sad for me to hear, in a peculiar sort of way I felt honored that she looked to me to fortify her memory. Often a waitress would say, in a pleasant tone of voice, "Sir, please let the lady order for herself." The waitresses thought that I must be one of those "controlling husbands," dictating decisions for a taciturn wife. Nothing could have been further from the truth!

At this stage of Alice's illness, her physical appearance belied her cognitive malfunction, so I completely understood the reaction of some waitresses. Had I not experienced first-hand the cognitive regression Alice was enduring, I too would have thought the same thing. At an opportune moment, I discretely explained why I ordered for Alice, and the waitresses were apologetic.

DINNER-TIME IN NEEDHAM

Occasionally, as the clock was approaching dinner-time, I would ask, "Would you like to go out for dinner sometime?" My expectation was that these words would prompt her to remember the difficulty I had in asking her for out on a date.

As I waited for a response, Alice's expression was staid and solemn and, on rare occasions, after pondering my query, she verbalized the reply I was hoping to hear, "that...would...be...nice."

I was absolutely jubilant to hear her response! I was so happy to hear her slowly enunciate those words. Immediately, my eyes began to well up as I noted a slight semblance of a smile on Alice's stoic face. I knew in my heart of hearts that she connected with my leading question, and I was absolutely ecstatic when I heard her appropriate response. In spite of her cognitive deficiency, Alice was able to recall our prolonged conversation from many years ago in the parking lot at Shaker Farms Country Club in Westfield!

Alice's remembrance of that memorable occasion was a Gift of God; a moment of lucidity amongst the dark days of dementia. Deo Gratias! Hallelujah!

THANK GOD FOR FRIDAYS: FISH FOR DINNER

Friday meals were always special treat for both of us. As the popular delectation T.G.I.F. (Thank God It's Friday) indicates, we too gave thanks to God it was Friday. Fridays were always special days, albeit for a counter-cultural reason. There was a spiritual aspect to our Friday culinary menu; they were meatless Fridays. Alice never, even when her mind was sharp, accepted the churches elimination of meatless Fridays. Even though the whole wide world of Catholicism was released from the meatless obligation on Fridays, in Alice's mind, abstinence from meat continued to apply to the Kennedy Family. Consequently, on Fridays, out menu included a variety of seafoods: stuffed clams, cooked shrimp, cocktail sauce and fresh swordfish from Captain Marden's Fish Market in Wellesley, Mass.

As was our family tradition, on December 13th (Patti's birthday), Alice and I began decorating our home for Christmas. Unfortunately, Alice exhibited limited interest in decorating the house. Through the years, Alice accumulated many special Christmas ornaments that she absolutely loved; she especially loved Byers Carolers, and she delighted in placing them in nooks and corners of our house.

In addition, Alice loved her prized Christmas Tree ornaments, many of which had significance since her days at home with her parents in West Springfield. Every year she would painstakingly place them strategically on our Christmas tree. Alice absolutely LOVED to admire our beautifully decorated Christmas tree.

Although she still decorated the tree and thought it looked beautiful, she didn't put as many ornaments on the tree as she did in previous years. Neither was she as fastidious in displaying her special Byers Carolers; she only opened a couple of the Byers Carolers' boxes. Even though they were still on display, they were fewer in number. Her interest in Christmas was still apparent, but based on the fewer number of ornaments on the tree and the fewer Byers Carolers on display, it was clear to me her interest had waned.

A few days before Christmas, Alice went to the Beth Israel Needham Hospital (BINH) for a colonoscopy, the results of which confirmed that her colon was in top-flight condition and she wouldn't need another colonoscopy in the foreseeable future.

As Christmas approached with festivities and decorations on everyone's mind, Alice seemed apathetic and exhibited little or no interest in the Christmas preparations. Since Alice's illness, by default I became the family chef (no Emeril Lagasse, I can assure you), but I did prepare the traditional Christmas Eve dinner Alice loved—Lobster Newburg with plenty of lobster meat! Frugality was a constant in Alice's modus operandi, evident even on Christmas Eve. With Alice's penurious nature, even though she loved lobster, the cost of lobster at Christmas was so high that she purchased a limited amount of lobster and supplemented the Newburg sauce with the more economical langostinos, which is neither a true lobster nor a prawn, but more closely related to hermit crabs.

Contrary to Alice's customary frugal nature, in 2012 I stocked the Newburg sauce with plenty of fresh lobster meat and dispensed with langostinos! Formerly, my only contribution to our annual Christmas Eve celebrations was to prepare Caesar salad and a bowl of egg nog flavored with nutmeg and served in a Waterford Crystal Bowl. To keep the Egg Nog cold, a pint of vanilla ice cream floated in the bowl. As my mother would have said, "By default, Danny, you have become the chief cook and bottle washer."

Alice seemed drained and more lackadaisical than a few days ago. She seemed drained and more lackadaisical than a few days ago. I was uncertain whether she was coming down with a cold or whether her lethargy might be attributable to a reaction from her recent colonoscopy. It was obvious to everyone that Alice was making a valiant effort to display the "Christmas Spirit," but unfortunately, her energy was certainly depleted.

Shortly after we sat down at the dining room table for our Christmas dinner, Alice disengaged herself from dinner-time conversation, left the table, went into the living room and laid down to watch TV. Evidently, she found it difficult to engage in, or follow, general conversation.

The first thing I did on the morning of December 26th was to take her directly to Dr. Finn's office. Alice was in such a weakened condition she kept slumping in the chair; Dr. Finn was alarmed and told me to take her directly to Newton-Wellesley Hospital (NWH). After a few hours of intensive examination, the staff at NWH concluded that Alice's extremely low blood pressure must be a residual reaction to the anesthesia administered during her recent colonoscopy.

Evidently, in some instances, it may take dementia patients a week or two for the body to completely process the effects of anesthesia. The emergency room doctors instructed me to give Alice as much liquid as possible in order for her body to disperse the after-effects of anesthesia. Thankfully, within a few days, Alice gradually began to regain a semblance of energy.

ENTERTAINMENT CENTRAL: THE LIVING ROOM COUCH

With Alice's loss of interest or lack of ability in using the computer, she became passively immersed in watching television. She was content to watch religious programs, Catholic TV, or EWTN. I think viewing priests or nuns revived familiarity in her mind. Even though she was content to watch religious programs, it didn't dilute her interest in going for a ride. I doubt Alice absorbed much if anything from watching TV, but it was obviously comforting for her. Before her illness took control of her life, Alice was never particularly interested in watching religious programs. As a matter of fact, when she came into the living room and I was watching EWTN, I would switch to another channel I knew she would prefer.

Prior to dementia days, when it was time for Ali to go upstairs to bed, she would take a book with her. But now she had no recollection of taking a book. She wanted me to put the religious program she was watching in living room on the bedroom TV. She became extremely displeased when I couldn't provide CTV or EWTN on our bedroom TV. I explained that we didn't have a cable connection on our bedroom TV. She refused to accept my explanation and demanded the remote so she could find her programs. The Button Pusher was at her 'button pushing best,' but without success. In another attempt to reason with her, I said, "The battery must be dead Ali, let me take the remote downstairs and replace the battery." She agreed. Thankfully, when I returned a few minutes later, she was asleep.

Night after night, this mechanically proficient woman, who could fix most anything or, at least determine the cause of malfunctions, could not comprehend why her programs were not available on the upstairs TV. The following day, I called Comcast to have a cable connection installed in our bedroom, but before their scheduled appointment, Alice forgot about our upstairs TV.

NO LONGER IN DOUBT

My ways are above your ways and my thoughts above your thoughts.
(Isaiah 55:9)

Thankfully, shortly after New Year's Day, remnants of Ali's reaction to anesthesia receded. On a follow-up visit with her neurologist, Dr. Toran scheduled a Magnetic Resonance Imaging (MRI) examination at Newton-Wellesley Hospital to determine the extent of Alice's cognitive problem. As I sat in the waiting room for the completion of the MRI, I was surprised when Alice returned in a matter of minutes from the examination. I had presumed the test would comprise the better part of an hour.

The time period was so short I was concerned the intense sound of the machinery may have frightened her, rendering the exam null and void. The staff assured me they obtained the necessary data. A few days later, Dr. Toran's office informed me that the results of the MRI scan were sent to Dr. Finn's office and he would review the results with me.

Within a few days, I sat down with Dr. Finn and he informed me the MRI revealed that Alice had incurred a few slight strokes, which contributed to pre-existing brain shrinkage. Specifically, Alice was diagnosed with frontal lobe dementia. As Dr. Finn continued to explain the intricate aspects of the diagnosis, he handed me a box of Kleenex and he started to cry! I didn't need Kleenex. The news of Alice's affliction was not a surprise to me. After witnessing Alice's steady decline the past few years, it was apparent Alice was experiencing a problem that was difficult to quantify. Dr. Finn informed me that at Alice's next appointment with Dr. Toran, she would provide further information as to the path forward.

Subsequently, Dr. Toran advised us there was no known medical remedy that could reverse frontal lobe dementia. She did, however, prescribe medication designed to lessen anxiety and slow the pace of the disease. Evidently, there are numerous types of dementia, most commonly categorized under the umbrella of Alzheimer's. From my perspective, the specific strain of dementia is irrelevant; the common denominator is that the illness is irreversible.

I first began to detect slight changes in Alice's demeanor shortly after her unanticipated retirement from Dennis Seashores which, coincidentally, occurred contemporaneously with Danny's unexpected death. Perhaps Alice was pre-disposed to this illness. However, the question remains: Was her struggle with Danny's death complicit in her accelerated cognitive decline?

As I continued to reflect on Dr. Finn's diagnosis, I couldn't help but recall the bewildered look on Alice's face when she returned from her inordinately elongated trip to the Mason Jar Restaurant in Harwichport. Undoubtedly, after that incident, she must have known her initial suspicions prompting her early retirement in 2007 were affirmed after her abortive attempt to locate the Mason Jar Restaurant in 2010.

As Dr. Finn and I continued to commiserate on Alice's diminished abilities, I voiced my opinion that it would serve no purpose to affirm what Alice must have already surmised. She knew more so than me that she was in a life and death battle; so why remind her now? Dr. Finn concurred and, to my knowledge, no one ever communicated the diagnosis to Alice.

As time went on and I became more aware of other unfortunate souls afflicted with cognitive illnesses, there seemed to be a preponderance of afflicted males and females who possessed a high level of intelligence.

COMFORT THE AFFLICTED

Dr. Finn frequently reiterated: The first order of business was to provide as much comfort as possible for Alice. The benchmark in providing care should always be, if in my mind, I didn't foresee harmful effects, allow Alice as much latitude as possible. Safety restrictions were of importance but dietary restrictions—not so much. "If it will make Alice feel better, go with it," was Dr. Finn's parting advice.

I concurred.

As a young girl, one of Alice's favorite morning rituals was to dunk donuts into her cup of coffee. Frequently, I would bring home a cruller donut that would be consumed along with her customary half-and-half cup of coffee. Frugal Ali didn't require top-of-the-line coffee. She was more than content with instant coffee, but she was, however, particular when it came to ingredients. She not only preferred milk in her coffee, she *demanded* milk in her coffee; under no circumstance would she tolerate cream.

Alice was not only comfortable riding in the car, she took great delight in comfort foods as well. Often on our daily rides, we stopped at Guarino's in Norwood for a few Italian cookies and biscotti—cookies she munched on in the car, and used the following morning with her coffee in a biscotti dunk-a-thon. Lunch and dinner menus generally consisted of a meatball grinder, or, on Alice's proscribed meatless Fridays, tuna-melts. On special occasions, we had a lobster roll. During the week, the dinner menu generally consisted of prepared foods: lasagna, steak strips, or roasted chicken. On Fridays, I would broil scrod or salmon, along with plenty of mashed potatoes. Over time, Alice's slight stature became considerably more...statuesque!

On Sunday afternoons, the two of us would often drive to Wilson Farm in Lexington, purposely parking the car so Alice could watch people pushing their packed carriages and loading them into their cars. On weekends, Wilson Farms has several complimentary kiosk's serving a variety of delicacies that I would bring out for Alice to munch on while sitting in the car as she watched customers scurrying to and fro. One of her favorite Wilson's treats was strawberry shortcake, as evidenced by often-repeated "De-licious!" Unfortunately, over a period of time she began to pile on more weight than desirable, but again, her happiness was my primary objective and, considering the circumstances, she was happy!

I also discovered that, among Wilson Farms' specialties was a custard-based, homemade bread pudding, long an Alice favorite. Whenever her father was sick, she frequently baked a pan of delicious bread pudding for him. Consequently, on our regular trips to Wilson's, it was customary to purchase a large bread pudding container which she devoured during the week.

Occasionally on our ride home from Wilson Farms, I would stop at the Weston Golf Club in hopes that Alice's would enjoy watching golfers swing their clubs. I tend to think she did enjoy watching the golfers as she sat quietly in the front seat of the car, but I really don't know; it was difficult to interpret her proclivity for silence. Even when I reminded her that it was at Weston Golf Club that Danny's friend Patrick Murphy arranged for him to celebrate his Ordination Dinner, her stony silence was unimpacted.

One night after bringing Alice upstairs, and saying a few Hail Mary's, I went downstairs to settle in for Monday Night Football. An hour later, I was shocked when Alice came back downstairs and, she was fully dressed! No longer was she in pajamas; she was adorned in her favorite azure blue dress replete with high heels and her *Sunday go-to-meeting hat!* First, I was shocked to see her come downstairs and, secondly, I was amazed she had the ability to dress herself and to look so well coordinated.

As she came into the living room, she said, "I'm ready...let's go."

I said, "You look beautiful Ali. Where are we going?"

She replied, "To Jack Moriarty's funeral of course."

I said, "You're right Alice, we are going to Jack's funeral, but the funeral is tomorrow. We're going to the funeral in the morning." (White lies certainly came in handy; Purgatory time is mounting!)

Seemingly, appeased by my explanation, she was cooperative as I led her back upstairs to bed.

Truth be told: Jack Moriarty, husband of Alice's cousin Betty Hicks, died several years before this 'momentary' remembrance of Alice. I have no idea what possessed Jack's name to enter her mind at this point; we hadn't discussed Jack in years. I do know she had great admiration for Jack and, at the time of his death, she was greatly disturbed and asked rhetorically, "Why wasn't there a Funeral Mass for Jack? He was a cradle Catholic; there should have been a Funeral Mass."

When Betty and Jack began to age, they relocated from their native home in Holyoke, Mass. to Madison, Conn. to be closer to their daughter Susan. A year or two after they relocated, Betty died and Jack moved into an assisted living facility in New Haven, Conn. Although we didn't visit Jack often, whenever we did, Alice insisted we stop at Rein's Delicatessen in Vernon, Conn., to pick up a corned beef sandwich because "Jack's Irish; he's from Holyoke and loves corned beef."

I suppose, in a sense, Alice's interest in attending Jack Moriarty's Funeral Mass paralleled her frequent queries pertaining to whether relatives and longtime friends had died, and if so, "Did we attend the Funeral Mass?"

It may be that Danny's death somehow factored into her increasing confusion with the concept of death. Other than the first few weeks after his death, she never mentioned Danny's name. Even if his name came up in conversation, she didn't display any visible interest. In posing questions as to whether other people died, she must have been, in her mind, wrestling with the concept of death, or looking for affirmation. Considering the multiple times she speculated on Funeral Masses for people long since dead, she never inquired if her son Danny had died, which seemed strange. I believe deep in the recess of her mind, she purposely inquired about older people whom, in all probability would have most certainly died, such as her parents and my parents.

CHAPTER 9

OPTICAL ILLUSIONS; OPTICAL SOLUTIONS

"If your body is full of light it will be as a lamp illuminating you with its brightness." (Luke 11:34)

Alice's misconception that our home was sold seemed to be a precursor of other cognitive illusions. In the *eyes of Alice's mind,* she was absolutely convinced certain preposterous events were occurring. Optical illusions became the norm. Alice saw certitude and reality in the context of hallucinatory experiences.

The most pronounced source of agitation pertained to an imaginary old man who was living in our shed. Frequently, she would demand I call the Needham Police and have him arrested or, at least, taken back to his house on Hawthorn Street. Even though I knew "logic" was beyond Alice's ability to understand, I continued to offer logical explanations.

When Joanne Curry, a friend of Danny's since his days at St. Mary of the Nativity in Scituate, accepted an early retirement from the Archdiocese of Boston, she gave her "retirement gift"—a rocking chair—to Alice and me. The beautiful black rocking chair bears the logo of the Archdiocese of Boston and is appropriately inscribed:

Rev. Daniel J. Kennedy
Ordained May 26, 2007
Loving son, priest, and friend

Since we were first gifted with the rocking chair, Alice placed it in front of our living room window. Day after day, Alice sat in the Archdiocese of Boston rocking chair and watched people walking up and down Woodlawn Ave. Her intensity in observing neighborhood activities alternated between looking out the window and staring penetratingly at me as I worked assiduously at the near-by computer in our den. It often was unnerving to realize Alice was continually staring at me, speaking only to inform me an animal was crawling up our sidewalk and I needed to "kick it out of our yard."

To appease Alice, I would go outside and, as she watched from the window, I pretended to "kick" the invisible object off the sidewalk. When I came back inside, she would ask, "Did you chase him away?"

I would always assure her, "He's gone now and won't be back."

"Good, keep him out of here," she would reply.

Other times she thought a bug was crawling down the drape near where she was seated or a man in a car was watching our house. To placate Alice, I would brush off the drape and go outside, approach the unoccupied car and pretend to carry-on a conversation with an imaginary operator.

Alice's belief that we sold our home, although untrue, was a tangible plausibility; hallucinations were intangible perceptions. Selling the house was good news, which she wanted to share. Hallucinations were not good; they were fearful, and she wanted them eliminated. Her most worrisome hallucination was the "old man" purportedly living in our shed! When she looked out the living room window facing the backyard, she became concerned and dispatched me to see if the "old man" was still in the shed.

To allay her fears, I tied a bright red bow on the one and only door of the shed, hoping that would convince her if the bright red bow was not disturbed, "the mystery man" couldn't possibly have gained access to the shed and retied the bow if he were in the shed. Again, any attempt to present a logical proposal to a person devoid of logic was absolutely foolish; I plead guilty to the crime of foolishness. The red bow proposal did not assuage her concerns.

Whenever anyone came to visit us, Alice would ask them to accompany her to the shed to see if the "old man" was still there. Obviously, she was not satisfied with my efforts to expunge him from our property. Alice must have considered me a complete failure and wanted to engage more competent personnel. To some degree, she did appear to be momentarily relieved when other people ascertained the "old man" was gone. However, in her mind, the old man would never be gone; he was there infinitum, indelibly etched in her world of misunderstanding.

Eventually, she did conclude the "old man," a.k.a. *shed-man,* resided in a home a short distance away; Hawthorn Avenue. From that point on, whenever we went for a ride, which was often, it was mandatory that we drive down Hawthorn Ave. so we could see if he was in his yard, but she could never identify his house. Over the course of years, many homes are torn down and replaced with new homes, which must have occurred to the home Alice believed to be the home of the *shed-man.*

During our Hawthorn Ave. espionage missions, on occasion, we would pass friends of Alice's who were out for a walk. When they waved, I would stop just to say "hello." Gradually, over a period of time, Alice became more and more agitated whenever I would speak to people; she wanted no part of any conversation, casual or otherwise. She was especially displeased if I stopped the car to speak briefly with friends of hers who lived in the proximity of Hawthorn Ave.

I believe she realized that she couldn't communicate as in the past and wanted immediate relief from what had become uncomfortable situations.

When the car was idling as I was speaking with her friends, Alice would quietly, and presumably out of earshot of her friends, repeatedly say, "Let's go, let's go, I want to go! Now!" I tried to be as discrete as possible so her friends wouldn't know she was anxious to leave, but she increased the decibels, so I spoke even louder to her friends to conceal Alice's front seat admonition to leave.

THE 'HAWTHORN AVENUE MAN'

At long last, my memory was rejuvenated; years ago, Alice gave a ride to Mrs. Mitchell, an elderly woman, who lived on Hawthorn Ave. I surmised that, in Alice's mind, the "old man" purportedly living in our shed might be Mrs. Mitchell's husband!

During one of our daily investigative espionage escapades up and down Hawthorn Ave., frustrated with her inability to identify the *shed-man's* home Alice demanded I take aggressive action. "I want you to go to the police station and have *him* arrested!" None of the diversionary tactics I employed seemed to appease her so, as we drove back to Woodlawn Ave, I said, "I have an idea; why don't you lie down on the living room couch while I go to the Needham Police Station and ask for his arrest?" Finally, there was concurrence with a plan of attack.

After she lay down on the living room couch, I left the house but, instead of going to the Needham Police Station, I went to the United States Post Office to mail a letter. When I returned expecting to see Alice sound asleep on couch with the *shed-man* a distant memory, she was sitting in the rocking chair looking out the window and waiting for my return. Short-term memory intact, as soon as she saw me, I was greeted with, "Is he going to be arrested?"

Once again, out of my bag of *dealing with dementia* techniques, I pulled out my favorite weapon: a little white lie. Disappointingly, I explained,

"Chief Thomas Leary informed me in order to have the *shed-man* arrested, we will need to obtain a Writ of Complaint, which will necessitate engaging an attorney at the cost $1,000."

Realizing Alice's penchant for frugality, I then asked, "Do you think we should spend a thousand dollars to have the "old man" arrested?" Alice's short-term memory wasn't the only dormant characteristic that was restored; frugality was also restored. She emphatically said; "No, we can't afford to spend that kind of money!" Problem resolved! (and more Purgatory time for me!)

Still tormented with fear of the *shed-man*, one morning while I was taking a shower, there was a sudden pounding on the shower-door and Alice was shouting, "Who's in there? Who's in there?" I calmly responded, "It's your husband," at which point she paused for a second or two then went back to bed. It was, to me, a bizarre moment; the shower located in our bedroom and only was used by Alice and me. How could she possibly believe someone else was in our shower? Did she think the person in our shower might have been the *shed-man*? If so, I commenced to be concerned; perhaps some night Alice, never "a shrinking violet," may think I was the *shed-man* and while asleep, she may hit me over the head with a lamp or with her favorite tool—a hammer.

In a millisecond, I reasoned that if God's plan permits Alice to hit me over the head, so be it. I will continue to take care of her to the best of my ability! Thankfully, God's plan did not permit an act of violence; never was there any threat of bodily injury. In addition to Alice's innumerable God-given gifts, she must also have been blessed with The Gift of Restraint!

The common denominator to these imaginary illusions was the element of fear. If Alice had been a timid and laid-back person, I could understand the onset of fear and trepidation. But Alice was never afraid of anything; she was absolutely fearless. Regardless of precarious situations, she had unimaginable courage. Her mindset was danger be damned, full steam ahead! She was a daredevil's daredevil.

Alice always considered risk to be inconsequential and danger to be irrelevant. With every sinew of her body, she adhered to Jesus's admonition, "Be not afraid." Alice was, absolutely, never afraid! Consequently, it was difficult to witness such a courageous woman, impervious to fear, become so frightened and so scared.

ALICE'S ANCHOR: SUNDAY MASS
"I am the bread of life." (John 6:35)

Until the final stages of her illness, Alice was determined to go to Sunday Mass. Often, she was prompted to go to Sunday Mass during the middle of the week when she would abruptly say, "Put your coat on, it's time for Mass." After several unsuccessful attempts to convince her it was not Sunday, in an effort to appease her, I drove her to Saint Joseph's, which only added to her confusion. She was shocked to discover that the doors to the upstairs church were locked.

On one of these mid-week visits to attend Sunday Mass, Father David Michael, Pastor of Saint Joseph's at the time, passed by and Alice asked him why the church was locked.

Father David replied, "We just finished the last Mass of the day Alice."

She replied, "Then we're off to Saint Bart's, they will have a Sunday Mass."

As we began our drive to Saint Bartholemew's Church on the other side of Needham, I suddenly recalled, "We need to pick-up a prescription at CVS (a fake story), so let's do that before we go to Saint Bart's." Thankfully, that was a sufficient distraction and her fixation on a weekday Sunday Mass abated. She was content to go-for-a-ride to CVS."

At this point, with Alice's interest in the church of paramount importance, she mentally remained in the Pre-Vatican II Catholic Church. Not only did she continue to wear hats to Sunday Mass, she fasted from midnight, considering herself unworthy to receive Holy Communion if she ate breakfast or consumed a cup of coffee after midnight. In her mind, she if had not complied with obsolete fasting regulations, she wouldn't receive Holy Communion. Week after week, I attempted to explain the Catholic Church revised those regulations and it was permissible to receive Holy Communion without fasting since midnight. Even when I explained that people over the age of 60 were exempt from any regulation, she remained unconvinced and adamantly refused to receive Holy Communion.

In spite of the fact that Alice became uncomfortable speaking with longtime friends, there was one glaring exception—the St. Joseph's Counting Team. Alice may have been totally confused day after day, but every Monday morning she was out the door, in her car, in attendance at the 9:00 o'clock Mass and then to St. Joseph's Rectory to help count weekend collections. Evidently, her mathematical and problem-solving skills were still sharp, strengthening her self-confidence in the company of her Counting Team friends! It was such a boost for Alice to spend Monday mornings counting collections with her friends at Saint Joe's! It was obvious to her Monday morning friends, she was...STILL ALICE.

I often asked the Counting Team if Alice was contributing in her customary manner and, without exception, they would assure me, "Everything is going well; the money is counted correctly. Father Lawlor is pleased and all of us have fun."

One day when I inquired from Alice how things were going on Monday mornings, she volunteered that her summertime Cold Storage Beach buddy, Pat McNamara, was, in Alice's estimation, "starting to become forgetful." If that isn't the pot calling the kettle black! Alice, rapidly proceeding down the path of forgetfulness, had the audacity to comment on senior moments confronting other Counting Team members. Note that as I type these recollections of Alice in 2019, Pat McNamara is still "counting" on Monday mornings after Mass at St. Joseph's.

CAR-RIDE COMMENTARIES

Sandwiched between Alice's relocation preparations and incarcerating the "shed-man," our daily diversionary drive to irrelevant destinations was of the utmost importance. Generally, daily rides consisted of trips through the western suburbs of Boston—Westwood, Dover, Medfield, Wellesley, Natick, Newton, or Weston and, on occasion, to West Roxbury, Brookline and Brighton.

- As we traveled along our customary routes, Alice would offer various commentaries. She was keenly observant and would voice pertinent remarks about certain landmarks. It wasn't for conversational purposes that she verbalized observations. I believed she was, in effect, re-assuring herself that she still possessed in-depth knowledge relative to churches, stores and neighborhoods.

- Even though Alice's commentaries reflected elements of accuracy, her rapid-fire repetition of the obvious was indicative of cognitive erosion. On a daily basis, Alice would function as our tour-guide, pointing out various and sundry landmarks. She disseminated extensive information, not so much as to edify me but to affirm her own recollective ability.

- If we drove down Otis Street, at the intersection of Manning Street, Alice would point to the house on the corner and say, "This is Mrs. Morgan's house. We haven't seen her recently, and I hope she's not sick. At least there are no cardboard boxes on her porch." (Mrs. Morgan had died within a few years of our arrival in Needham, 30 years before Alice became ill.)

- In driving down Great Plain Avenue, we passed #711, the house formerly owned by her good friend, Peg Lovett. As we passed, Alice would always wave. (Peg and her husband Tom, who sold us 45 Woodlawn Avenue, moved to Sun City, Fla in the 1990s and both were deceased, yet Alice she still waved.)

- On another occasion, an alarming remark from Alice revealed significant regression of her cognitive skills. As we approached Needham Center, Alice pointed to the building on the corner of Chapel Street and Great Plain Ave. and said, "What happened to The Crest? Is The Crest gone?" (The Crest, formerly a thriving greeting card/gift shop, closed at least 20 years prior to her observation.)

- If we happened to drive down Harris Avenue, Alice would point and correctly say, "That's where Mary McGillicuddy lives." Mary was ever vigilant in praying for Danny's vocation.

- When we drove past St. Joseph's Rectory on Highland Avenue, or for that matter, any other Rectory, she would also wave.

- In driving past Saint Patrick's Church in Natick, Alice would always say, "That's Father Dan's (Twomey) church."

- In Wellesley, when we drove down Amherst Road, Alice would say, "We were going to buy a house on this street" (She was correct, "if" in 1979, the consolidation of GA's two Massachusetts branch offices materialized, the Kennedy Clan would have resided at 43 Amherst Road.]

Daily car-rides were often incomplete unless we stopped at a Dover Horse Farm to see horses. As a young girl, Alice's boyfriend's family owned horses, so she was accustomed to horseback riding. I knew she would enjoy watching horses grazing. She watched intently as some horses grazed and while others galloped around the coral. She often murmured, "Big Horsies."

When the galloping horses came to graze near where our car was parked, Alice became scared; formerly Fearless Alice was quick to say, "Let's go, let's go."

Occasionally, we would stop at the Bubbling Brook ice cream shop on the Westwood/Walpole/Medfield line for an ice cream cone and, without fail, Alice would say, "I thought we might see the Reardon's here today." As we were driving on Route 109 in Westwood, Alice would say, "That's Kevin Reardon's store." (In fact, at the time it was roughly 25 years ago that Kevin had sold the convenience store and moved to the Cape.)

On other occasions, Alice would authoritatively give me instructions, often incorrect instructions, "Red light, GO. Green light, STOP." When traffic was heavy, she would say, "Now GO, Now GO, GO, GO." The emphasis and the urgency in the tone of her voice was, to such a commanding degree, it almost induced reflexed compliance.

Often when returning home, prior to approaching our customary left-hand turn onto Woodlawn Ave., Alice would say, "turn here, turn here," and then as we proceeded down Woodlawn Ave. as we approached #45, Alice would say, "turn here, turn here." [Although she spoke as if I needed instructions, she was so pleased that she was still aware of various locations; again, she was affirming to herself that she knew various landmarks.]

Alice's daily commentaries were, in a sense, self-assurances for herself, which, in my mind, was a good thing—a really good thing. It enabled her to feel good about herself. My mindset was always affirmation, affirmation; no matter how far afield she may be in her thought process, I did not correct her, and, if I could find a plausible reason to commend her, I commended her!

My goal was to acknowledge her helpfulness and to praise her at every opportunity, emphasizing her amazing recollections. I sensed the repetition of recollections was self-gratifying in that she was proving to herself she was still mentally proficient, which, in and of itself, revealed she suspected there may be a deficiency issue.

Daily car-rides often would take us to West Roxbury, past Catholic Memorial High School, or if we were in the Newton area, past St. John's Seminary. If time permitted, I would park on the premises in the hopes Alice's memory of Danny would be revived; unfortunately, it was not revived.

Traditionally, on weekend car-rides the radio was tuned to the Irish music program on WROL. Since the early days of our marriage, every Saturday Alice and I listened to Irish music. One Saturday as we were driving past Boston College in Newton, I decided to drive through the grounds of St. John's Seminary, and we parked in front of St. John's Hall. As we sat in silence, coincidentally, "Danny Boy" was playing on WROL as nostalgia gripped me. Alice sat in stony silence. In hopes that, between the lyrics of "Danny Boy" and the premises of St. John's Seminary, Alice's memory would be revived, I added, "This is where Danny came to become a priest, Alice." Even though at this time Alice was still able to talk, she remained unemotional and unaffected; she continued to sit in stony silence.

It was sad to observe the emotionless mother of a priest-son be unresponsive to the mere mention of his name; tears trickled down my face, but she continued to sit silently. Alice seldom cried, so I wasn't surprised there were no tears. I was, however, disappointed her facial expression didn't reflect any semblance of recollection. I have come to believe Alice's solemn silence was a Gift from God, insulating her from the recollection of unimaginable grief. In suppressing Danny's existence, Alice was, in essence, insulating herself from untold grief.

MEMORIES NOT FORGOTTEN!

In February, as was our annual custom, Alice and I met Dick and Janice Butcher at Leo's Ristorante in Worcester for our annual rendezvous and family updates. When Janice called our house to confirm the date, I answered the phone. The first thing Janice said to me was, "The best news

I've heard in a long time Dan is that you and Alice are going to be moving back to Westfield."

I, of course, was shocked and, even though I anticipated Janice's subsequent explanation I asked, "Where did you hear that Janice?"

She replied, "When I called Alice to coordinate the date for this get-together, I mentioned your old house on Falley Drive was for sale and Alice said you would like to put in an offer because you are planning on selling the Needham house and she would like to move back to Westfield." I cautioned Janice that to draw that conclusion might be premature. (Thankfully, on the night of the Butcher dinner, Alice rallied to the occasion. She was "on-top-of-her-game" and never mentioned an interest in moving back to Westfield.)

As Alice would often say, "It's always enjoyable to be with the Butchers." This was certainly no exception. We shared many, many laughs and Alice actively participated in the gaiety of the occasion that day. The only serious moment occurred when Janice, out of Dick's earshot, told me her blood pressure was astronomically high in the realm of 275/150. The numerical numbers were so high that I truly believed she did not recall the correct figures. With her obvious reluctance to discuss it in front of her husband, I expressed my shock at the numbers but did not pursue the discussion.

Unlike Alice's frequent reluctance to carry-on conversations with long-time friends, she was so comfortable with the Butchers it was so refreshing for me; Alice was her former conversational self; the life of the party. Obviously, some friendships from years past revitalized Alice and her engaging personality was a joy to all.

In remembrance of Abraham Lincoln, "You can fool some of the people all of the time and all of the people some of the time, but you can't fool all of the people all of the time." In this situation, Alice was able to fool the Butchers...during dinner time. She certainly rose to the occasion that night at Leo's Restaurant, and for one memorable evening she was...STILL ALICE!

A week later, in recognition of our 44th wedding anniversary, the kids gave us a gift certificate to the elegant Copley-Fairmont Hotel in Boston's upscale Copley Square. Although Alice was not the same vibrant Alice of years past, she was excited at the prospect of dining in style at the Oak Bar and Grille on our 44th!

The two of us had a wonderful experience at the Oak Bar and, as we relaxed and reminisced, Alice said, "In all the years we have been married, whenever we were 'out of sorts' with each other, somehow, one of us was always able to say or do something to deflate the issue and bring a smile to both of us; truly, we have BEEN BLESSED!" It was another memorable moment from a now more melancholy, Alice Blue Gown.

As the winter snow of 2012 began to gradually melt away and spring flowers began to bloom, there was considerable media publicity about a roving bear on Cape Cod. Evidently, a disoriented bear that came out of winter hibernation was cited roaming from town to town. Somehow, the wayward bear transited Cape Cod Canal and was easterly bound; heading toward Chatham. After a weeklong search, the elusive bear was eventually apprehended in Chatham and relocated to western Mass.

For the next year, or two, long after the roaming bear was no longer roaming, every time we passed a wooded area during on our daily car-rides, Alice would remark, "There must be bears in those woods." For whatever reason, Cape Cod's roaming bear was foremost in Alice's short-term-memory-afflicted mind.

THE COMFORT OF CHURCH

Shortly after Easter Sunday in 2012, while Alice still had a semblance of a rationale, one of our daily rides took us to downtown Boston, to Saint Anthony's Shrine on Arch Street for Confession. As God has done for us so often in the past, whenever we took a step toward Him, He would reach out to provide for us. That brisk spring day in the City of Boston was no exception.

On a day when a long walk would have been difficult for Alice, we approached Saint Anthony's Shrine and found a vacant parking space directly across from it! Alice would not have to walk more than a few feet and...there was sufficient time on the meter! *Seek, and you shall find: knock and it shall be opened to you." (Matthew 7:7)*

While we were waiting in the pew prior to going to Confession, we were surprised to see Deacon Bill McCarty. Several years ago, Deacon Bill, formerly a permanent deacon at Saint Joseph's in Needham, had relocated to New Hampshire. Alice and I were delighted to see Bill, but sorry to learn from that his lovely wife Madeleine died in September 2011. Alice was sorry to learn of Madeleine's fate as she and Alice worked on many St. Joseph's School projects together.

On our way home, Alice spoke of the irony of meeting Deacon Bill and cited memories of Deacon Bill when he was in Needham. But strangely, she didn't mention memories of Bill's deceased wife, Madeleine.

On that pleasant spring day, Saint Anthony's Shrine depicted Divine Providence in action! First, something prompted me to bring Alice to Saint Anthony's Shrine for Confession. Second, we found a prominent parking place and, lastly, after many years, we crossed paths with Deacon Bill, enabling him to share with us his bereavement in losing his saintly wife, Madeleine.

Imagine the Grace that God distributed that day: The Grace of the Sacrament of Reconciliation for Bill, Alice, and me; the Grace of Recall in remembrances of a saintly woman; and finally, the Grace of the Communion of Saints! Hallelujah!

CAPE COD RECOLLECTIONS

The year 2012 marked the fifth year since Alice retired from Dennis Seashores, and she was more adamant than ever in not visiting the seashore love of her life. Even though she was imminently interested in driving past Dennis Seashores since 2007, but absolutely did not want to be seen on that property; now she was indifferent about driving past the former "love of her life." She was also indifferent about the Cape and its restaurants and ice cream shops, but she was not indifferent about attending Mass at Our Lady of Annunciation Chapel in Dennisport.

Alice was clearly still affected by the familiarity of one of her favorite Cape Cod localities—Our Lady of Annunciation Chapel in Dennisport. As soon as the Entrance Hymn commenced, unlike in previous years, Alice turned toward the back of the church to see if one of her favorite priests was celebrating Mass. If it was a portly, retired former Navy Chaplain, Father Ryan, an ear-to-ear smile emerged on her pretty face. As soon as she realized Father Ryan would be the celebrant, she began to wave and shouted in a loud voice, "Hi Father...Hi Father!" It was much like as a little kid would express excitement. Father Ryan looked directly at Alice and a comparable smile would cross his face.

Neither Alice nor I knew Father Ryan, yet her exuberance was an outlandish display by an adult. I conjectured, it's possible Alice's demonstration of affection was attributable to Father Ryan's years as a military chaplain and she associated Father Ryan's Chaplaincy with Danny's deployment as a Chaplain on board the USS Nimitz. Interestingly, Alice never greeted any other celebrant on the Cape or off the Cape with such display of enthusiasm. It was just for Father Ryan.

In August, Betsy and Eleanor came from Maine to celebrate Alice's 73rd birthday, which for Alice, was an absolute delight. Those "three-sister" conclaves were always fun. Their father, Charles Joseph Haggerty, used to term them "Charlie's Angels."

A SUMMER SHOCKER; ANOTHER DEATH-DEALING DAY

".... you do not realize now but you will understand hereafter." (John 13:7)

Little did Alice and I know at the time of our annual February dinner with the Butchers at Leo's Restaurante in Worcester that, on June 12, 2012, Janice Butcher would die of a massive heart attack.

Since the onset of Alice's cognitive regression, she developed difficulty conceptualizing the concept of "death." Apparently, she was able to grasp the significance of Janice's death. Stoicism personified Alice's lifelong demeanor. She was never emotional. Seldom, if ever, did she cry. However, when she saw Janice lying in a casket at Firtion-Adams Funeral Home in Westfield, she cried. As became more and more apparent since the onset of her illness, death and the implications of death seemed to elude her intellectual comprehension. But it was not so when Janice died.

Alice grew up in a funeral home environment and, more than most people, was acutely aware of the finality of life as we know it on earth. She realized the enormity of bereavement.

So often since her illness was manifested with regularity, Alice would ask me perplexing questions. "Did your father die? Did your mother die? Did my mother, my father die? Did my aunts die? Frank Tierney? Bill Toner?" All of whom, if alive, would be well into their 100s. When I rendered a subdued and affirmative reply, she would ask, "Did we go to the funeral?" When I assured her that we did attend the funeral, she seemed relieved. From her father's funeral home days, Alice retained the format of a Catholic burial procedure: caskets, sorrow, wakes, funeral Masses, and, ultimately, interment.

When we were on the way to Danny's grave, upon occasion she would say, "Don't forget to buy a plant." She never said, "for him." It was just, "buy a plant." Assumedly, she knew the plant was for Danny's grave. On the other hand, she may only have realized when people visit cemeteries, they customarily bring plants.

I always invited her to walk to the grave, but she would simply say, "You go." As I walked to the grave, she watched me intently, but remained silent in the front seat of the car as the raucous sound of the F-15 Jet's from nearby Barnes Airport roared overhead. When I returned to the car, she seemed content as she sat in silence; never did she voice her pocket phrase, "Let's go, let's go." When I eventually turned on the ignition, she would say, "Let's go visit Janice, she's over there," gesturing to another section of the cemetery. She always waved as we passed by her grave. Alice verbalized Janice's name, but for some reason, never voiced Danny's name.

After we spent a few minutes at Janice Butcher's grave (Alice remained in the car), we exited the cemetery. I would routinely suggest, "Why don't we stop and visit Dick Butcher on Falley Drive?"

Instantly, Alice became enraged, she was absolutely furious. We're not going to Falley Drive!"

To allay her concerns, I would say, "We won't have to stop; we can just drive past the Butchers house and our old house."

"Absolutely not," she shouted, as her agitated voice reached a crescendo.

Every time we visited Saint Mary's Cemetery, I posed the same suggestion and, I received the same response when I suggested going to Falley Drive. On another visit, when I made a similar suggestion—surprise, surprise—Alice's expressed no objection.

As we drove down Falley Drive, Alice said, "There's a car parked in our driveway," adamantly instructing me to "pull in and throw them out of our house."

As I pulled the car into our driveway, she insisted that I go into the house and kick them out of *our house*. Bizarre as her perception may have been, I was pleased memories of years past were momentarily restored to her cognitively-depleted memory bank.

To pacify Alice, I went to the door, rang the bell, but unfortunately nobody answered the door. In a way, I was anxious to get a peek at the house myself. When I returned to the car and informed Alice no one was home, she seemed appeased, at which point I suggested, "Perhaps we should go next door and visit with Mr. Butcher?"

In a day of surprises, Alice agreed. Not only did she concur, as I parked the car in the Butcher family driveway, like a flash, Alice exuberantly jumped out of the car and rapidly advanced to the front door. When Dick Butcher answered the door and saw Alice, he was more than delighted.

As soon as we were in the house Alice asked, "Where's Janice? Where's Janice? I came to see Janice." Momentarily stunned, Dick subsequently replied, "She's gone shopping, Alice." Dick's explanation seemed to appease Alice, and after a short visit she turned to me and said, "Let's go, let's go." Soon we were en route to the Mass Turnpike for our trip home to Needham.

When October rolled around and the weather became colder, I suggested bringing in firewood so we could have a fire. But Alice said, "We don't need a fire." I was shocked. Alice, who absolutely *loved* to see a fire blazing in our fireplace, said that we don't need a fire? A few days later, once again, I suggested bringing in a few logs to start a fire, and once again, she repeated, "We don't need a fire." A fire was part of the fabric in Alice's frame; she loved to sit close to a crackling fireplace.

A fireplace was omnipresent in Alice's life since she was born. Many years previous to our first meeting, as a little girl in Chicopee Alice was accustomed to a fireplace. Her family was never without a raging fire during cold winter months. Could it be that after a lifetime of loving a fireplace, she was fearful of flames? In assessing Alice's loss of interest in so many things she loved, I recalled her past interest in—the Boston Bruins, all-night radio programs, wine before dinner, people contact, and now the fireplace—all now gone from her memory. Sad, so sad.

After her former interests evaporated, in their stead, human touch became important to her. When I helped her into her living room bed night after night, she wanted me to sit and hold her hand. It seemed that former interests had been supplanted with the human touch.

Throughout our married life, Alice and I were definitely not romantics. With five young kids, we didn't have time to focus on each other, and, unlike many married couples who do customarily hold hands, if we held any hands, they were typically the hands of the kids. At this point in Alice's life, holding hands became reassuring for her, so I held her hands to soothe her. After Alice was sound asleep, I typically went to the kitchen and brought back my portable supper, which I consumed as I sat in the chair next to her bed.

A VORACIOUS APPETITE....an INSATIABLE APPETITE

Alice's quest for frequent meals continued to accelerate. Most recently, her obsession for food seemed to begin and end with requests for a meatball grinder! In Westfield, the nomenclature was a meatball "grinder," but in Needham it was a meatball "sub." Alice's incessant request for a meatball grinder puzzled not only our own family, but also the clerks at Gianni's or Nicholas' pizza parlor in Needham.

One day, within minutes of consuming a huge meatball sub, Alice demanded that I call Gianni's for a meatball grinder as she pleadingly said, "I'm starving, I'm really, really, starving!" It had become common practice for Alice to continually demand a meatball grinder—for breakfast, lunch and dinner. But starving? Perhaps a third-party might believe she was famished, but truly she was not starving. I did accede to her meatball sub wishes, but not as often as she expected.

PATIENCE IS A VIRTUE AND, LACK THEREOF, A CHALLENGE:

When Alice first began to express undue contrariness, obstinacy, and objections, I cited previous incidents when her compliance was critical in accomplishing our goal. When that argument became less persuasive, I played the gratitude card. "Thank you, Alice, for understanding. Your willingness is so important to me, etc." When her incessant demands to go-for-a-ride commenced to be non-stop and overwhelming, I decided to employ a new strategy—a Litany.

When Alice would repeatedly say, "Let's go, let's go." I responded, "Pray for us, pray for us."

She persistently repeated, "Let's go" and I persistently responded, "Pray for us."

After several renditions of "Let's go" and "Pray for us," Alice began to repeat my line, "Pray for us."

So, in the same vein, I began to respond with her line, "Let's go!"

Although it wasn't my intent, I may have been unduly cruel to Ali. Anyone with or without any mental challenges could be confused by that charade.

If my little "Alice Blue Gown" was confused before, she must have been totally confused with my newfound strategy of employing a Litany as a diversionary tactic. Nonetheless, Alice didn't display any outward agitation. Her focus on a car-ride was of over-riding significance and, of course, to comply with her request, we did go on a car-ride. Thankfully, she was not overtly annoyed at my stupid little game after all; she tolerated years of my stupid humor so my babble must have had a ring of familiarity.

On other occasions, after numerous requests to "go-for-a-ride," I employed other diversionary tactics. I would concoct logical justification about why, at this particular time, it wasn't logical for us to go-for-a-ride.

Alice would sit, and listen attentively and presumably comprehend my meritorious explanation, and just when I was absolutely certain she agreed with my suggestion, suddenly she would reverse herself 180 degrees. Abruptly, she would stand up and with complete disregard for my, presumably convincing proposal, and cryptically say, "I'll be in the car!"

Soon thereafter, I learned that Alice occasionally began referring to me as "Dictator Dan," given my more-assertive role in caring for her while her cognitive abilities waned. When I learned of this new moniker, it made me smile. I was not offended by my new nickname. Rather, it provided a sense of normalcy to a tough situation for her, and I recognized that it was derived from her cognitive impairment. In her earlier years, Alice was an absolute "take charge" personality. A natural-born leader, she typically gave the orders and led. At this stage in her illness, hearing her new nickname for me served as a sign that her sense of humor was still intact. It also represented her perhaps lighthearted way of expressing an exacerbating reality—that she was now often following my direction, as opposed to providing it to me.

Alice continued to demonstrate atypical behavior. One time when I went to look for her, much to my chagrin, she was not in the kitchen, nor was she in the dining room. She was gone, and I was alarmed. Eventually, I looked out the window and discovered Alice was seated contentedly in the front seat of our car. She had not requested a car-ride. She was sending me a silent, yet visible, message: "She wanted to go for a ride." I took her hint; we went for a car-ride.

Numerous people advised me to be on-guard, as most dementia patients have a tendency to arbitrarily take a walk and not know the route back home. I really didn't have a fear that Alice would walk-off, as I could never convince her to take a short walk with me on Woodlawn Ave. I attributed her reluctance to walk as a concern she may encounter friends and not be able to converse with them, so she avoided that possibility and did not exhibit any interest in walking. In retrospect, my logic could have been wrong. Perhaps at a later stage, she would have forgotten her reluctance to speak to friends and walking-off could have been a problem. Thankfully, she never walked away.

Another motivating technique that proved to be effective was addressing her as ALICE! For our entire marriage, although I don't remember the rationale, Alice and I always referred to each other as "Babe." At some point, as her illness progressed, without any conscious intent on my part, and with no pre-conceived plan, I began to refer to her as "Alice" instead of "Babe." Unwittingly, the more I referred to her as Alice, the more responsive she became. Like many of her cognitive skills, the nebulous name "Babe" became a thing of the past.

The comforting car-rides would often conclude at a supermarket. With regularity, Alice demanded we park in the blue-marked section for handicapped or wheelchair accessible folks. I told her, "Without a Handicap placard, Ali, it's illegal to park in those spots." She was not happy with my explanation.

One day as a snow was accumulating, I opted to park on the street and not in Sudbury Farms' parking lot; I parked on Highland Avenue and left the motor running and an Irish CD playing. Alice would be warm and entertained while I was in the store. As I returned to the car, snow was swirling, wind was blowing, and I was lugging two bags of groceries and anxious to join Alice in the comfort of a warm car. This was not to be, as the car doors were locked! While I was in the store, inadvertently, Alice pushed the lock button.

Realizing Alice's inquisitorial nature, I should have anticipated she would experiment with buttons, but I did not. Previously, she had pushed a button necessitating a trip to the auto dealer to reset the alarm mechanism, but that was not during blizzard conditions. This time, the Button Pusher pushed again during a blustery snowstorm!

"Alice, please unlock the door" I pleaded and cajoled. But the Button Pusher just looked at me and smiled. She didn't have a clue as to what I was saying, as Dictator Dan continued to suggest that she push a button. Alice remained bemused with the look on my frantic face and she continued to smile. In the past, this type of incident would have all the earmarks of an Alice practical joke, but those days of joking around were long gone. Perplexed? Yes. Annoyed? Not in the least. I knew Alice was unable to comprehend the mechanism to unlock the door and viewed my attempts to resolve the predicament as comical!

After what seemed like an eternity, but it was probably only 10 or 15 minutes, the Button Pusher finally pushed the "unlock" button, and I quickly pulled the door handle and gained access. Whether it was the fact that Alice was smiling through the entire incident or whether it was a relief to be inside the car, I too began to laugh at the humorous incident.

On future car-rides, if I had an errand to do, I continued to leave the motor running so she could enjoy the warmth of the car. I did, however, purposely lower the driver's window a few inches. If Alice happened to lock me out again, I would be able to reach my arm in and manually unlock the door. I clearly wasn't bright enough to bring a spare key with me.

ADDITIONAL MEDICAL CHALLENGES

On Valentine's Day in 2013, three days prior to our anniversary, we decided to treat ourselves to lunch at the Blue on Highland restaurant in Needham Heights. It was truly a wonderful day, an absolutely fantastic day—a lucid day! Alice enjoyed a Cosmo before lunch, and most importantly, she was her former self—alert, conversational, comical and, purportedly cognitive. It was truly a great day, and it seemed just like the good old days! In hindsight, it was probably like Gaudete Sunday during Advent or Laetare Sunday during Lent—a day of Joy amidst a time of preparation and sadness!

I couldn't help but recall the theme song on Arthur Godfrey's (1950's) radio program, "Seems like old times...having you to talk with...Seems like old times, having you to walk with..." I will always remember our luncheon at Blue on Highland; it seemed like old times and it was an absolutely sensational afternoon! It would also prove to be the last time the two of us dined out together.

When she became forgetful, Alice would ask me, "What do I like?" She asked me that exact same question on February 14, 2013. Even though she asked, she didn't seem to be nearly as vague as in the past. What a thrill it was for me to see Alice so happy and so with it. In the interest of full disclosure, she was nowhere near as perceptive as in former years, but she was substantively sharper than her more recent self. I considered her role reversal to be a spectacular occurrence—another Gift from God!

When we came home after lunch, Alice decided to flop on the couch, so I decided to seize the opportunity and take the walk I hadn't been able to squeeze in for a few weeks. An hour later, after my walk, Alice was still flopped on the couch. As I inquired if she enjoyed a nice sleep, she responded, "There is a black spot in my eye." Initially I thought this may be another optical illusion like a bug crawling up the wall or an animal on our front lawn. But the more I thought, I became concerned she may be having a stroke, so I rushed her down to the Emergency Room (ER) at the Beth Israel-Deaconess Hospital (BIDH) in Needham.

After an extensive examination by a team of doctors in the ER, thankfully, they concluded Alice was not having a stroke; she sustained a detached retina, which would require an immediate transfer to the Mass Eye and Ear Infirmary (MEEI) in Boston.

As Alice lay in the ER at the BIDH waiting for the ambulance to take her to MEEI, her sense of humor was intact and she said, "I hope they don't bring that archaic ambulance parked at Hazel's Bakery!" Alice was still in the great form she demonstrated at Blue on Highland. She not only remembered the antiquated 1950-ish baked-goods delivery ambulance parked by the owner at Hazel's in Needham's Bird's Hill section, but she was able to present her recollection in a humorous vein. It was more evidence that Alice's day was with filled with unusual acuity.

Realistic yet unafraid to face the future, Alice, in her classic, deal-with-matters-promptly- and-definitively mode," stated, "I want to be taken to Doherty Funeral Home." I assured her "the MEEI would certainly be equipped to remedy her eye problem and she would be fine, so Doherty need not be optimistic and Eaton Funeral Home need not worry."

Alice was extremely fortunate to be treated at the MEEI by one of the foremost retina ophthalmologists in the world, Dr. Dean Eliott. After extensive examinations by several doctors at the teaching hospital, Dr. Eliott explained to us the delicate surgical procedure this type of retina tear necessitated. The surgical procedure would last approximately three hours and Dr. Eliott would insert a microscopic gas-filled balloon into Alice's left-eye, which if the recovery went as anticipated, would disburse and plug any microscopic tears and minimize the damage to her retina. Dr. Eliott assured me that he had performed thousands of similar surgeries and he was optimistic the surgical procedure would be effective.

On the day of the surgical procedure, I was apprehensive, but Alice portrayed no visible signs of concern; she walked into the surgical area completely unfazed. Whether it was her God-given courage, which she had in abundance, or whether she was oblivious to the seriousness of the surgery, I don't know. I do know she was always tough as nails, as was evidenced that morning at MEEI.

Realizing Alice was in the care of such an accomplished team of surgeons, I decided to take a short walk around the hospital campus. As I was walking on Cambridge Street looking for a coffee shop, my iPhone rang; it was the anesthesiologist calling from the operating room. He wanted my verbal authorization to administer a general anesthesia. Before I assented to his request, I explained that Alice experienced significant after-effects from the general anesthesia she received during a recent colonoscopy. When the anesthesiologist learned of Alice's past experience, he decided to use a local anesthesia and not general anesthesia.

OPTICAL SOLUTIONS

At the conclusion of the surgery, Dr. Eliott met with me and appeared more than pleased that an optical solution had been achieved. His elation was however, conditioned on Alice's adherence to the retina surgery recovery and recuperation program, which necessitated that she remains in a face-down position 24 hours a day for two months.

Consequently, we decided to place the TV on the floor in the living room enabling Alice to lie on the couch, in an acceptable MEEI sanctioned face-down position, watching TV, so the gas-filled balloon inserted in her eye could slowly disperse and plug any microscopic tears.

The doctors also prescribed four different eye-drops that were to be administered at various times of day and night. In spite of Alice's cognitive challenge, she did her best to maintain a face-down position and she sat completely still as I administered drops to her left eye, putting the eye-dropper as close to her eye as possible. In spite of her cognitive challenge, Alice was an excellent patient.

Dr. Eliott also informed me that a by-product of the retina surgery would be the accelerated growth of a cataract and, depending upon the size of the cataract, that may have to be surgically removed.

During the protracted MEEI recovery period, Alice wore a black patch covering her rehabilitating eye and, with one eye she looked forward to our daily rides to horse country in Dover and Medfield. Her eyesight did not seem to be impeded as she watched the "horsies," but impatience and fear continued to be dominant characteristics. When she wanted to "see horsies," she wanted to see "horsies *now*," but when we parked next to the horsies, she wanted to leave the horsies, *now!*

A REVOLTING DEVELOPMENT

For years, Alice personified patience and courage—two of her many virtues that now eluded her. At times, she seemed scared and frightened. In addition, she became extremely impatient. When she wanted something, she wanted it *immediately.* If I took an item out of the freezer for supper, she wanted it right away! She could not understand why I put it in the microwave for an "endless" amount of time (e.g., one or two minutes).

One day Anne Marie brought an uncooked dinner for Alice from Harrows Chicken Pies in Dedham and she wanted to eat immediately. Anne Marie informed me it would require 45 minutes to cook, so I persuaded Alice to go for a car-ride. With her interest in car-rides, it was not a difficult sell. Before we left the house, I turned the oven on to the required 400 degrees, let Riley out, and off we went for our 45-minute ride.

After riding around aimlessly for 45 minutes we were back in our drive-way as planned. Mission accomplished. As we opened the front door of the house Alice said, "I want to eat, *right now.*"

Assuredly, I said; "You're absolutely right Alice we are going to eat, *right now!*" As she sat down at the kitchen table, I proceeded to open the oven door and, in a moment of shock, I discovered the oven was stone cold and the pie was not cooked!

I knew immediately what must have happened; while I was letting Riley out, Alice noticed the red light on the stove signifying the oven was on, so she turned off the oven (have I mentioned she was frugal?).

In a reflex reaction, I blurted out, "Alice you turned off the damn oven."

Up to this point, everything had gone according to plan. Alice had a nice ride, we were in home for a hot chicken pie dinner precisely the time she wanted her dinner but, because she turned the oven off, she was not going to eat her hot chicken pie dinner on time. Instantly, she detected my frustration and said, "I'm sorry, I'm so sorry." Alice's genuine expression of contrition, the sorrowful look on her face, will be forever etched in my mind.

In today's world, adults seldom say they are sorry. If they do say they're sorry, sorrow may be superficial or they may not be truly sorry. But when kids say they are sorry, their contrition is obvious, they're sorrow is unquestionably real!

Alice expressed her sorrow as a little kid expresses sorrow; she was truly sorry. Her sincere response to my demeaning remark rightly made me feel like a first-class jerk! Whenever I recall that incident, I can still see the depth of sorrow on her face. I will never forget that true penitential look when she said, "I'm...sorry," with sadness emitting from every sinew of her body. She demonstrated a disconsolate expression. *Unless you become like little children you will not enter the kingdom of heaven. (Matthew 18:2)*

With tears in my eyes, I responded, "My poor little Alice, you never have to say you are sorry to me. I'm the one who is sorry; I'm so, so, sorry for what I said."

Fortunately, I had some chop suey in the freezer, which qualified as an acceptable, easy-to-prepare backup meal.

THE BARK OF SAINT PETER

On March 13, 2013, after our daily car-ride, I parked at Whole Foods in Wellesley. Fortunately, I found a spot near the front door, so Ali was delighted! Just as I was about to exit the car, the radio program was interrupted with a "Breaking News" announcement. Both Alice and I (although she didn't comprehend) listened intently as it was announced that "white smoke is emitting from the Sistine Chapel!" I decided not to go into Whole Foods and immediately drove home to watch the introduction of the new

Pope. There was speculation that an American Prelate, Cardinal Sean P. O'Malley of the Archdiocese of Boston or Cardinal Timothy Dolan of the Archdiocese of New York, may be under consideration.

Alice and I arrived home in time to see and hear the announcement Habemus Papa! A relatively unknown Jesuit Cardinal from Argentina, Jorge Cardinal Bergoglio, was introduced as Pope Francis, as he made his first appearance to thousands of cheering people in Vatican Square.

In April, after the stipulated two months of recuperation concluded, Dr. Eliott's anticipation of a cataract growth proved to be a correct prognosis. However, Dr. Eliott was unpleasantly surprised when he discovered the cataract grew so excessively large that it prevented him from evaluating the retina surgery. At the outset, there was a possibility subsequent cataract surgery; now it was mandatory.

Dr. Eliott referred Alice to a world-class ophthalmologist at MEEI who specialized in cataract surgery—Dr. Scot Greenstein. I watched intently as Dr. Greenstein examined Alice's eye and realized from his reaction that he was concerned. Abruptly, the doctor left the room and returned a few minutes later with several colleagues who also examined Alice's eye, after which all doctors left the examination room. Shortly afterward, Dr. Greenstein returned, examined Alice's eye once again, turned to me and said, "This is an unduly large cataract, but I've done over 10,000 of these, so I think I can do this one too." I knew from his actions, and his remark, this would not be a routine surgical procedure. I was relieved to learn of Dr. Greenstein's vast experience, and I had full confidence in his ability.

I wanted Dr. Greenstein to be aware that Alice previously had an adverse reaction to general anesthesia. He assured me he would inform the anesthesiologist of her past history and he would propose local anesthesia. The prospects of another optical solution were hopefully in store for my "Little Alice Blue Gown."

FOLLOWING HER EDICT: WHEN THE GOING GETS TOUGH, THE TOUGH GET GOING

To witness Alice confidently stroll into the operating room for both optical surgeries was inspiring. Fear, which had become a by-word during her illness, was submerged as she courageously walked through the doors of the operating room. She displayed absolutely no reticence whatsoever; it was as the old axiom says, "when the going gets tough, the tough get going."

At times like this, Alice's innate toughness seemed to rise to the occasion; perhaps it was a Gift from God that seemed to periodically occur during her illness. In pre-surgical and post-surgical examinations, she responded to medical queries assertively and intelligently. If I had not informed medical personnel that she was suffering from dementia, no one would have known she had cognitive deficiencies. Alice always seemed to be on top of her game whenever a doctor elicited her input. She managed to fool them with her proficiency. Just as she engaged her mind when responding to questions from Dr. Finn, somehow she managed to put her thinking-cap on as she correctly answered queries at MEEI.

UNINHIBITED ALICE

Discretion will watch over you, understanding will guard you.
(Proverbs 2:11)

As Dr. Eliott reacted after the retina procedure, so too did Dr. Greenstein react after Cataract procedure—he was ecstatic! He informed me that everything went extremely well and Alice should make a complete recovery. He cautioned it would require two months of follow-up appointments to make certain there were no additional cataract issues. Consequently, for a prolonged period of time there would be numerous follow-up visits with both Dr. Eliott and Dr. Greenstein.

At every follow-up examination with Dr. Eliott, there was an extensive wait. Dr. Eliott's patients came from all over the world and his waiting room was jammed packed. Realizing the undue delay, I always tried to schedule Alice's appointment for 1:00 p.m. in the afternoon so she would be among his first patients, avoiding a potentially long wait to be seen by Dr. Eliott.

At a teaching hospital like MEEI, a series of trainee physicians examine each patient prior to the primary doctor, so the traditional 20-minute exam is multiplied by additional examinations by aspiring ophthalmologists. A long wait, up to four hours, is unduly long for any patient, and especially for Alice who, since the onset of dementia, was impatience personified! Surprisingly, she never exhibited any impatience when waiting prolonged periods of time for Dr. Eliott and Dr. Greenstein. It was remarkable to witness the serenity and composure that Impatient Alice exhibited as she sat in silence with a group of strangers. Alice was *Impatient Alice* no longer!

Once a month, over a period of four months, Alice often endured those long visits in Dr. Eliott's waiting room. Dr. Eliott's congested waiting room consisted of numerous card-table-type folding-chairs placed against the perimeter walls, with two rows of chairs, back-to-back, in the center of the room. Consequently, the knees of the patients in the center rows were within two feet of the knees of the patients sitting directly across from them.

On one of our follow-up visits, in the midst of waiting room silence, Alice turned to me and in a loud voice said, "If you want to see a 'comb-over' get a look at the man sitting across from you." Not only could the man sitting across from me hear what Alice said, every person in the waiting room could hear what Alice said. I must have turned purple!

I couldn't help but sneak a peek at the man who was seated directly across from me. Alice was right. The gentleman sitting across from me must have let his hair grow to at least 10 or 12 inches long so he could flip the hair from one side of his head to the other side, completely covering his head. Talk about being embarrassed; I was mortified. Fortunately, the man pretended to be engrossed in the magazine he was allegedly reading.

On another occasion, as we waited for the bevy of doctors to evaluate Alice, there was another interesting incident. When the nurse for her called another patient, a rather portly woman walked past us for her appointment. Alice, completely uninhibited, shouted out loudly, amidst perhaps 20 to 30 patients, "Get a look at the arse on that woman." These out of the ordinary remarks may not be unusual in a neurologist office or a nursing home, but they certainly were uncommon in the MEEI.

It was difficult to imagine Alice, a kind, caring, and compassionate person, publicly insulting and humiliating people. Alice would never knowingly hurt anyone's feelings. But now, even though she was STILL ALICE, sadly at times the dementia dispossessed her caring nature.

WHEN SPRING DEPARTS CAN SUMMER BE FAR BEHIND?

At this point in Alice's recuperation program from MEEI, the month of May arrived in 2013, birds were singing, flowers were blooming, and Alice was programmed to go to The Cape! Day after day, the new battle-cry was, "Let's go to the Cape, Let's go...to.... THE CAPE!" I assured Alice that we would definitely go to the Cape as soon as we finished with the MEEI follow-up visits. Once again, I incorrectly assumed a logical explanation would allay her concerns; it did not!

As prescribed by the MEEI's face-down requirement, Alice was still sleeping on the couch in the living room. One night at 3:30 a.m. when I heard voices, I assumed I was dreaming—wrong! I quickly realized the voices were not in a dream, they were emanating from people in our house. I jumped out of bed, rushed downstairs, and much to my chagrin I encountered two Town of Needham police officers, two Town of Needham firefighters with apparatus strapped to their backs, and Alice, all standing in our front hall. Four of them looked perplexed and one, Alice, looked indifferent as if she was asking, "What's the big deal?"

As Officer Lamb explained, "At approximately 3:00 a.m., my partner and I observed a private passenger vehicle repeatedly circling Needham Town Square, precipitating our curiosity. As we were in pursuit, the vehicle proceeded up Great Plain and into your driveway. The operator was your wife." The officer continued, "Mrs. Kennedy informed us that she packed the car with her clothes, including her dog, and they were driving to Cape Cod. Obviously she was disoriented and couldn't access Route 95. Based on our assessment of Mrs. Kennedy, we contacted the EMTs."

Alice stood passively as I assured them, she was not under the influence of alcohol; she was dealing with a cognitive issue. The police were most sympathetic and recommended that I file a report with the Needham Police Department, so there would be a dossier available if another Alice event should occur. That was the last time Sport's Car Club Alice ever operated a motor vehicle; car keys were confiscated! I thought depriving her of the love of her life would be a significant loss, but thankfully, she seemed to accept the absence of operating a motor vehicle without any rancor.

Subsequent MEEI check-ups verified that both of Alice's surgical procedures were successful and, in June, she was honorably discharged from her program. Alice was more than pleased; now we were *off to the Cape*. Deo Gratias!

As the summer progressed, I thought Alice would visit Maine to rendezvous with Betsy and Eleanor for another "Sisters Reunion." All three were excited, especially Betsy, who loved to distribute the annual dividend derived from stock that Mrs. Haggerty willed to her three daughters. At every reunion, all three sisters (Charlie's Angels) rationalized, "Lobster rolls for the three of them was a gift from...mother."

Since the onset of Alice's illness, she seemed to have lost a mental filter that most of us, by nature, put into gear to prevent untoward remarks. At this point, Al no longer possessed that filter; she was prone to say or do whatever thought came into her mind. She was completely devoid of any inhibitions. What would be embarrassing to most people was now not be the least bit embarrassing to Alice. One such incident occurred at "The Sisters Annual Reunion" in August.

When Alice saw Betsy's longtime companion, Jim Callahan, a high school classmate of mine, she was shocked to see that Jim displayed a somewhat wider waistline than the last time she saw him. Aghast at Jim's obvious additional weight, Alice proclaimed, "It doesn't look like you've missed many meals Jim!"

Everyone, including Jim, burst into laughter. The honesty of the statement was evident to everyone and the unintended humor resulted in spontaneous laughter. Most people would have diplomatically concealed recognition of the self-evident; Alice did not! Alice loved to laugh, and she must have enjoyed the hilarity she unintentionally precipitated! *A time to laugh....and a time to cry.... (Ecclesiastes 3:4)*

Jim Callahan loved to sing, so Jim and the three Haggerty Sisters provided the entertainment at the annual Dividend Distribution Dinner. Although Alice was not in Jim's class, musically she acquitted herself well at the Reunion Songfest.

The joy Alice experienced with her singing-sisters breathed a new life into our nightly "old-time music" songfests on Woodlawn Ave. When the kids were young, they were embarrassed when Alice and I would waltz around the kitchen singing old-time songs, but now they were delighted to witness the renewal of our former song and dance routine. As happy as Alice was when the two of us danced in the kitchen years ago, she was even happier at this time in her life. She was thrilled that she could dance and sing; it was a momentary memory revival! Like a little kid, her face radiated happiness as she danced across our kitchen floor; she was so proud of herself! I think she wanted her kids to know that she remembered how to dance and sing. She was without a doubt...STILL ALICE!

CAPE COD: THANKS FOR THE MEMORIES, DISTANT THOUGH THEY MAY BE

Shortly after Katie returned Alice to the Cape after attending the Haggerty Sisters Annual Reunion in Maine, her beloved 2004 C-240 Benz began to develop mechanical issues. With Alice in the passenger seat, I drove the car to the Dennisport Mobil station so a mechanic friend of hers, Phil Griswold, could assess the perplexing noise. After checking the engine, Phil informed me that we needed to bring it to the dealer in Hyannis. "Maybe the dealer can repair the engine, I cannot," he said. Immediately, I headed for the Mercedes dealership in Hyannis.

As we were driving west on Route 28 through West Dennis and South Yarmouth, smoke started bellowing from under the hood, the car began to vibrate, and the power steering was gone. I thought it would be prudent to pull off the road and call a tow-truck, but I was fearful Alice would become unnecessarily agitated, so I opted to continue driving to the dealership. Thankfully, the car survived the trip and we reached our destination, Trans-Atlantic Mercedes-Benz.

After a cursory diagnosis, the service manager informed me it would cost approximately $8,000 to repair the car. I concluded it would make no financial sense to spend that amount of money on a car that, within a month would be 10 years old. I spoke with a salesman and asked him to show me the lowest-priced auto on the lot and, even though Alice's green 2004 Mercedes C-240 had only 14,000 miles, we traded it for a black 2007 C-280 Mercedes with 95,000 miles. Even though the mileage was somewhat of a concern, I was determined to keep Alice in a Mercedes and this was our most economical option.

Although Alice was adjusting to her restored vision, she could still see and could still reason that her pride and joy was disabled, and she did not want to accept its dissolution. She was not happy! She adamantly refused to get out of "my car" because she intended to drive "her car" back home. Eventually, between the sales manager and me, we convinced her that we would come back the next day and pick-up her repaired car (another white lie). Thankfully, the following morning, she had no recollection of "her car."

UNINTENDED OPTICAL CONSEQUENCES

As Alice's extended recuperative period from her optical procedures proceeded, she concluded those issues would prevent her from resuming her position on the St. Joseph's Counting Team. After the courageous way she responded to the surgical procedures at the MEEI, I thought her ability to participate with the Counting Team was still intact, but Alice was reluctant to return. Her decision was disappointing to me, as I deemed her association with the Counting Team to be of utmost importance in Alice's battle with memory issues. Alice loved the camaraderie and, as long as she wasn't a detriment, I wanted her to continue. She did not concur, attributing her "retirement" to optical issues.

Long after Alice retired from the Counting Team, whenever she saw Pat McNamara at 11:00 a.m. Sunday Mass, she would seek Pat out and say, "I'm sorry Pat, I won't be counting tomorrow." Pat, familiar with Alice's situation, pleasantly replied, "Don't worry Alice, we have enough Counters this week."

EAT TO LIVE OR LIVE TO EAT

During the median stage of her illness, she exuded an insatiable appetite—she lived to eat! Sadly, in the final stage of her illness she was unable swallow. Consequently, she couldn't eat to live.

When Alice was consuming non-stop comfort calories, Anne Marie was wonderful in providing Alice with her favorite foods. She used "Mom's Recipes" to prepare specialties Alice loved: homemade mac and cheese and, one of her all-time favorites, the bread pudding that Alice used to bake for her father when he was sick. Alice's response was always the same, "Thank you Anna, that was de-licious. I'll have more Anna. I'll have more!" It is not an exaggeration to say Alice developed an insatiable desire for food; she seemed to eat 24/7. Literally, she couldn't keep her hands off food. Many times, those hands of hers were grabbing food...from someone else's plate!

As Alice's patience continued to erode, whenever I went to the refrigerator or freezer, she pointed to her place setting and emphatically said, "Put it here, put it HERE!" As her voice began to rise, she continued, "I said, PUT IT HERE, PUT IT HERE... RIGHT NOW!" When Alice was more agile and I didn't respond as quickly as she demanded, like a flash she would jump out of her chair and attempt to take the frozen food out of my hand. Alternatively, if I was cooking, she would attempt to reach the hot frying pan. Although she was still vocally insistent, she was less likely to bound out of her chair and head to the stove.

As Alice continued to deteriorate, both her verbal skills as well as her mental acuity lessened. I thought it beneficial, especially at dinner time, to verbally remind her of what was formerly second nature to her. At every meal, she endured my steady chant of, "Chew, swallow, take a break, and take a drink." After Alice finished consuming, we would swing into our nightly sing-along sessions.

Alice's rapidly fading verbal skills were periodically revived during our renditions of "You are my sunshine, my only sunshine..." Amazingly, Alice was able to recall most of the lyrics and, on occasion, insert a word or two at the appropriate time and place. At the conclusion of the lyrics, "You are my Sunshine...please don't take my sunshine away..." Alice would lean forward, rub her nose against my nose, and in a barely audible voice, enunciate the last few words.

One night, when Al was having considerable difficulty speaking and eating, as usual I went through the nightly litany of, "Chew, swallow, take a drink, take a break, etc." I was determined to see if she comprehended my instructions, so I tried to elicit a sign of perception. "After all these years of *giving orders* to this entire family, Alice, how does it feel to be *taking orders* from the family dummy?" I was hoping for a reaction, any kind of reaction, some indication of awareness. Unfortunately, there was no reaction, just a blank stare.

However, I kept looking at her. After a minute or two of silence, with no facial expression, she said, in a barely audible tone, "It's...TOUGH!"

I couldn't contain myself from bursting out into laughter! Her vague look belied the wisdom of her remark. Somehow, she managed to grasp what I said and, more importantly, she constructed a perspicacious response.

In between my laughter and tears of joy, I said, "Thank you for saying that Alice! Your answer makes me so happy!" I may have been unduly optimistic, but I thought her eyes displayed a look of enjoyment at my elation.

However Alice managed to connect the wires I will never know. I do know she responded with the correct answer! If, years ago, anyone suggested to Alice that, some day, she would be taking orders from me, I know precisely what she would have said, "NEVER in a million years will that happen; NO WAY!"

I always interpreted these occasional moments of lucidity—and there were several—to be God's way of communicating encouragement to me.

Alice, currently with a challenged mind, was able to periodically communicate logical responses. In my mind, these were "attaboy" moments, a spiritual pat on the back, a "Laetare Sunday" during Lent, a "Gaudete Sunday" during Advent, and momentary joy during an extended period of trial.

FOOD IS OF THE ESSENCE

On our routine car-rides, I always carried a package of cookies, a bottle of cranberry juice or plum juice so Alice could dine in luxury as we took short drives through the Massachusetts countryside. Alice liked to stash her bottle of cranberry juice in the side compartment of the passenger door. Every so often she would help herself to a cold drink. She was happy, secure, and independent; she could quench her thirst by herself, on her own timetable.

Whenever we stopped at a store, Alice would spot an empty, blue-marked parking place near the main door and direct me to "take that spot." Unconvincingly, I explained, "that blue spot is reserved for handicapped people Alice, and we are not handicapped." She never accepted my explanation, and I know that in her heart of hearts she considered me to be disobedient when I didn't take the reserved handicapped spot. She just could not understand; if the parking place were unoccupied, why wouldn't I park there? As usual, I resorted to lying and said, "I think the space is too narrow for our car. A large truck might park next to us and his door might hit our car; I know you would not like your car to be damaged."

It never dawned on me that Alice might fit the description of being "handicapped," but it did occur to Katie, who persuaded me to ask Dr. Finn for his opinion on procuring a placard for the handicapped; Dr. Finn agreed with Katie's admonition and soon the Massachusetts Registry of Motor Vehicles (RMV) approved Alice's application and issued her a handicap placard.

When I saw Alice's picture on the placard, once again, I couldn't help but cry. The RMV affixed a picture of Alice on the placard, which was taken from an old Massachusetts automobile license when she was young and vibrant; now her illness robbed her of those qualities. Actually, in hindsight, we waited too long to obtain a placard. Alice had deteriorated to the point where she no longer expressed any preference as to where we parked the car.

The placard was a benefit; now that we could legally park in a blue designated parking space, Alice was closer to the main entrance where she could view the hustle and bustle of shoppers coming and going. Alice was definitely pleased to be up close and personal, as she observed every move made by animated customers.

In the oppressive heat and humidity of a brutally warm August in 2013, we were delighted to be in the somewhat cooler climate of the Cape. Although it was no longer visually discernable, I do think Alice enjoyed traveling around the Cape from beach to beach, watching the frolicking tourists jumping for joy on Nantucket Sound.

As dementia continued to erode Alice's brilliant mind, she was devoid of facial expression and her speech was basically non-existent. On the rarest of occasions, she would enunciate a "yes" or a "no." Unfortunately, substantive verbalizing was in the distant past. An exception to the Wordless World of Alice occurred one day as we drove past a used car lot on a main road in Hyannis. Alice shouted out, "There's an MG, there's an MG; it's just like mine!"

As we were passing the lot, I glanced out of the car window and saw a small green sports car and asked, "Was your car the same color, Alice?"

She responded instantly, "No, mine was black and mine was a 'T' series; that car is green and it is not a 'T' series."

Obviously, in a fleeting moment, as we drove past a used car lot, she not only spotted an MG, she identified the model, recalled explicit details, and verbally expressed comprehension. Taking into consideration the advancement of her cognitive deficiency, this was an absolutely AMAZING moment! In a matter of seconds, 50 years after trading in her MG, she noticed, identified, and categorized the smallest of details in a 60-year-old MG.

Even though it was oppressively hot and humid, Alice believed it was October and began to take steps to close down our Dennisport cottage. Since we purchased the cottage in 1972, every fall Alice drained the pipes, poured anti-freeze in the toilet bowls, turned off the water, disconnected the water meter, brought in all the yard furniture, and turned off the electric pane. That was her mindset in August of 2013!

Unlike September 2011, when she didn't want to close-up shop until Columbus Day, in the heat of the summer in 2013, she wanted to close-up in August. "It's time to leave, we have to go back to Needham," and she began lugging in lawn chairs, unplugging electrical appliances, disconnecting TVs and pouring anti-freeze into toilets.

I thought it prudent to go-for-a-ride; this time with a determined destination—Needham. Even though it was much warmer in Needham than at the Cape, when we arrived Alice was content. We were home and prepared for winter weather. And we were home for perpetuity; never again did Alice, nor did I, see our Ferncliff cottage.

HELP IS ON THE WAY

...the Lord watches over the way of the just.... (Psalm 1)

In the fall, at Anne Marie and Katie's instigation, they scheduled a meeting with an Alzheimer's Association representative. The initial meeting with Coach Carol was held in a private room at the Needham Public Library. The three of us met with Coach Carol on two different occasions, and she offered various caregiver techniques that would assist in caring for a cognitive-afflicted person.

Coach Carol's program provided an insight into caring for a person. I also maintained a belief that, as God gives parents enlightenment when caring for their children, so too, does he give enlightenment to a spouse in caring for an afflicted wife. I believed caring for Alice was God's gift to me, and I treasured that gift.

Coach Carol's strongly recommended purchasing a shower-chair, which would alleviate Alice's fears of a daily shower. Unfortunately, even with a shower-chair, Alice was extremely agitated and fearful of the water, so I abandoned the shower-chair until I reviewed her reaction with Dr. Finn. He reminded me that our "comfort at all costs" strategy takes precedence. He assured me, "If taking a shower is upsetting for Alice, forget about a shower; a sponge bath will suffice." Thank you, Dr. Finn.

OBSESSION WITH WESTFIELD

In vain, I tried a variety of strategies in an attempt to divert Alice's frequent demands to take her home to Westfield. In response to her conceptualizations, which included, "Our furniture is in Westfield; we have to go home to Westfield," I would respond, "Where do you live now?"

She would correctly answer, "Needham."

I would ask, "Whose rugs are these? Whose chairs are these?"

She would reply, "Mine."

So, I said, "if you live in Needham and your rugs and chairs are in Needham, then your home must be in Needham."

"No, my home is in Westfield," said Alice.

Often, after dinner, when she proposed "going home," I would go into great detail as to how traveling to Westfield would work better in the morning. I felt confident she accepted my explanation, but I was wrong. Within minutes of our conversation, Alice would suddenly be at the front door with her clothes packed in a paper bag, stating, "All set. I'm packed. Let's go, let's go. I'll be in the car."

The Alzheimer's Association denotes a tendency of dementia patients to develop behavioral problems in the evening, which is identified as a sundowning syndrome generally attributable to anxiety. Alice's repeated requests "to go home" did occur in the late afternoon, so from that perspective her symptoms seemed to synch up with known behavior, which was probably a manifestation of anxiety.

It's interesting to me that Alice seemed to exhibit a "selective" long-term memory in purposely recognizing Westfield as her home. Quite obviously, Westfield was a pleasant memory and she "selected" the pleasant experience of living in Westfield as a comforting concept.

THE GRACE OF NO RECALL

...Even should she forget, I will never forget her. (Isaiah 49:15)

It was interesting to note Alice recalled Westfield as her home but she didn't recall any memory of Danny. Perhaps she considered her time in Westfield as pleasant and memory of Danny's death was far from pleasant. Even when our daily car-rides took us through areas associated with Danny, she didn't display any recognition recall. In driving past Catholic Memorial High School, the Heartbreak Hill section of the Boston Marathon or St. John's Seminary, never did she express recollection of Danny.

Upon occasion, I would park the car at Catholic Memorial, St. John's Seminary or the Weston Golf Club, in hopes that might stimulate her memory. Occasionally, I would remind her, "This is where Danny went to high school. This is where Danny learned to become a priest; this is where Danny played golf and had his Ordination Dinner." Unfortunately, there was never a response. Solitary silence is deafening.

It wasn't often that Danny's name was mentioned, but whenever it was mentioned, Alice remained silent—it was so sad! It wasn't until she was well into the throes of dementia that I began to realize, Alice did not forget Danny, she suppressed the memories of Danny!

I also began to realize Alice's cognitive deterioration was, in a manner of speaking, a blessing for her. First, I came to believe, in her current condition, she was incapable of giving the full consent of her will to offending God! Secondly, as her cognition skills continued to dissipate, she suppressed any memory of Danny to eradicate a most painful occurrence in her life.

"I will never recover from this," Alice confided to Lorraine Salois, her Cape Cod neighbor, shortly after Danny's death. At Alice's wake, Lorraine, who also suffered from the loss a son, said, "I think Alice was right, she never did recover; that was the beginning of her downward spiral."

After Alice died, with privacy issues no longer a consideration, I asked Dr. Finn to review Alice's medical records with me. Dr. Finn's records indicated that, on several occasions, Alice confided to him, "I'm still grieving for Danny." I really don't know if Dr. Finn's assessment reflected Alice's voluntarily voiced sentiments or whether they were in response to leading questions proffered by Dr. Finn. At any rate, in Dr. Finn's professional assessment, he concluded that Alice was inwardly grieving before any of us were aware of her cognitive deterioration.

At the time of Danny's death, neither Alice nor I believed we needed to go to bereavement sessions. Both of us truly believed in our heart of hearts that Danny's sudden death was truly God's will, and for the better good of many. As difficult as it was from a human standpoint, Alice and I unequivocally accepted the Will of God.

I do know that for weeks, even months, after Danny died, upon occasion, and especially at the 11:00 o'clock Sunday Mass at St. Joseph's, I would burst into tears and Alice would reach over and squeeze my hand. Alice was the epitome of stoicism; she didn't overtly portray emotion, and she didn't visibly display grief. On the other hand, my moments of emotion were outlets.

Alice, in spite of her external effervescence, was an extremely private person; she never displayed emotion. She was strong-willed, and seldom did she cry. Consequently, I assumed her silence to be stoicism and that she was handling Danny's death much better than I was handling his death.

When we would embark on the hour-and-a-half ride to Saint Mary's Cemetery, even when Alice was conversational those trips were devoid of discussion. Infrequent though those trips were, Alice was content to remain silently seated in the car and alone with the stillness of her thoughts. Even when I dutifully positioned a plant and prayed in front of Danny's gravestone, she did not venture out of the car.

I can only imagine the pain a mother sustains with the loss of a child; unquestionably, it is a far more intense than the pain sustained by a father. A mother has the privilege of participating with God in the creation of human life; she nurtures that life for nine months and for every subsequent moment of the child's life.

Only God, the Creator, knows the depth of pain a mother sustains when confronted with the loss of a child. The magnitude of a mother's pain is incomprehensible to a father. "A Mother's Love is a Blessing." It is truly a mystical love!

THE WONDERFUL WORLD OF ALICE

In Him we live and move and have our being...for we too are His offspring.
(Acts 17:28)

One morning when Alice and I traveled to Connecticut to visit Jackie, young Jack, and Celia, we were mired in abominable summertime traffic on the Mass Turnpike. The delay was of course annoying to me, but Alice remained unfazed; car comfort continued to rule her day. Alice, who exhibited so many moments of impatience during her illness, suddenly became inordinately patient on a long and agonizing ride to Connecticut.

After an enjoyable lunch with Jackie and the kids Alice was anxious to get back in the car and "go-for-a-ride," this time to her home in Needham. As we proceeded north on Route 10 toward the Westfield entrance to the Mass Turnpike, I thought, as long as we were passing through Westfield, perhaps Alice would like to ride past our former Westfield home—the home she longs to see. "Would like to take a ride to Falley Drive Alice?" I asked. Shockingly, she replied, "No." Consequently, I continued directly to the Mass Turnpike.

The end of daylong driving was in sight; first in the heavy westerly-born traffic in the morning and now, heavy easterly born-traffic in the afternoon. Eventually, as darkness was beginning to descend, we pulled into our Woodlawn Ave driveway. As soon as I turned-off the ignition, Alice said, "I don't want to stop here, I want to go home." Adamantly, she refused to get out of the car. Like the rat-a-tat-tat of a machine-gun, she demanded, "Take me home; take me home; I want to go home; I want to go home."

Just a few hours before, she summarily rejected my suggestion to take a side-trip to Falley Drive, and now, a short time later, she insisted I take her home—home to Falley Drive. Sadly, *The Heart of Our Home* did not realize Woodlawn Ave in Needham had been her home for over 30 years.

None of my cajoling tactics were effective so, in order to pacify her and hopefully divert her attention, I consented to take her "home." This entailed a short-ride around Needham and Dedham. When we arrived back at Woodlawn Ave, I was hopeful, after an extended day in the car—morning to night—she would be anxious to go into the house and flop on her couch. Once again I was wrong; obstinacy was becoming a challenging issue.

Alice resolutely refused to exit the car and became extremely agitated at my suggestions. Every attempt I made to redirect her focus was rebuffed; she wasn't swayed by the short car-ride around Needham Dedham. and she had absolutely no interest in flopping on the couch (just for a few minutes). My customary bag of diversionary suggestions was ineffective, so I called Katie and Jackie and informed them of my dilemma. Out of Alice's earshot, I arranged a ploy with Jackie. I would pretend to call the Needham Police Department, and he would play the role of a policeman. Perhaps, we could convince Alice to vacate the car. Unfortunately, Jackie did not win an Academy Award for his performance of a Needham police officer; Alice was intransigent.

I was concerned that if I went in the house and left Alice in the car, I might fall asleep. So I just paced back and forth around the yard. Finally, at 10:30 p.m., I decided to call the Needham Police Department.

Soon Officer O'Leary arrived and immediately began to query Alice as she sat stone-faced in the front seat of the car. Looking directly at Alice, he said, "Has this man been mean to your mam?"

I thought to myself, "Oh no, she is not at all pleased with me; I might be charged with abusive behavior." Thankfully, my fears were unwarranted; Alice did not throw me under the bus. She replied, "No, he just won't take me home." Officer O'Leary was also unsuccessful in persuading Alice to leave the car. Fortunately, it wasn't long before Katie arrived from Westwood and she too failed to persuade Alice to vacate the vehicle. Obstinacy trumped persuasion.

As I paced back and forth behind the car, Katie had the thought to say, "Mom, dad has gone to bed, you will have to get out of the car and go in the house." Somehow, this seemed to spark a flicker of curiosity from Alice, so I continued to remain behind the car. Eventually, between Katie and Officer O'Leary, they played up the fact that I had gone upstairs to bed, which assuaged Alice's obstinacy, and, ultimately, she finally agreed to vacate the vehicle.

Once Alice entered the house and Katie and the Officer O'Leary were gone, I locked all doors and secured the keys. Alice's desire to go home to

Westfield was not extinguished; she tried every imaginable way to unlock the doors saying, "I'm going to drive myself home."

When all else fails, and all else certainly did fail, she still wasn't buying the fact we were not going back to Westfield. I assured Alice, "Yes, we will definitely go home to Westfield; the first thing in the morning we will go to Westfield. But now both of us should take a nap." Eventually, she did agree to flop on the couch but "only for a few minutes." Thankfully, those few minutes lasted all night and, in the morning going home to Westfield was forgotten!

CAREGIVER SUPPORT GROUPS ARE HELPFUL

As Alice's illness continued to accelerate, many friends and family members urged me to participate in Caregiver Support Groups, but I resisted. I listened to their concerns and their recommendations. I was certain support groups are beneficial. My feeling was that if and when I became exasperated, I would consider a support group. At this point, however, I didn't believe fatigue factored into the picture. Each situation is, of course, different, but I didn't believe I was at that point of need. More importantly, I was afraid Alice would unnecessarily worry if I wasn't in the house. I thought my presence and the house might, in her mind, be synonymous, so I was concerned my prolonged absence may cause unnecessary confusion.

I viewed my role in caring for Alice in a similar vein to caring for children. God entrusted them to both of us. I believe God grants Grace to parents, and so too does He protect patients and give Grace to caregivers. As Alice traveled this long and tortuous route, I had absolute confidence the Holy Spirit would point me in the right direction, provide me with appropriate words, and equip me with the courage and assurance my wife was...STILL ALICE!

There was no doubt Alice's obstinacy and incessant demands were challenging, particularly during the stage when she didn't buy into alternative suggestions. In my "tricks of the trade" portfolio, I attempted to redirect her mindset. Occasionally I was successful, and occasionally not.

In spite of Alice's reluctance to accept logic, I never deemed it advisable to point out questionable logic. I preferred to agree and then parry her contentious response. Ultimately, whether it was truthful or not, I would assure her we would certainly try to do as she suggested.

OUTSIDE INTERVENTION

Alice was still alternating between sleeping on the living room couch and sleeping in her second-floor bedroom. One morning, as Alice began descending the stairs, in a loud voice, I hollered up the stairs, "Who's coming?"

Without responding, she slowly descended. So, once again, raising my voice a decibel or two, I inquired, "Who's coming?" I was hopeful my query would elicit a response similar to Jackie's morning greeting of years ago, when Alice prompted him with a similar question. At the time, Jackie was a two-year-old descending the Falley Drive stairs. As Alice's youngest child tottered down the Falley Drive stairs, in response to Alice's query, Jackie would reply, "It's Sunshine! Here comes Sunshine." At which point, Jackie would begin singing, "I'm the Sunshine of Mommy's life and everything about me makes her happy."

Alice was of course thrilled when she heard that serenade. Actually, the entire family was thrilled when we heard that serenade and always equated Jackie singing *The Sunshine Song* to his mother.

I was so hopeful in coming down the stairs on Woodlawn Ave that Alice would recall those happy days and repeat what Jackie said. But I was wrong. There was no response from Alice. As she reached the bottom step, once again I asked who was coming. Alice looked directly at me and instead of saying, "It's Sunshine," she said..."it's your daughter!"

BINGO! That response was even better than what I hoped to hear; what a revelation! Alice thinks I'm her father, Charlie Haggerty! In the deep recesses of her mind, Alice, who idolized her father and was now currently enduring a most difficult and confusing period in her life, in some way was seeking her father's protection!

From that point on, I commenced to speak to Alice as a father speaks to a son or daughter—affirmatively. It became another arrow in my quiver of daily living tactics; no longer was obstinacy an inexhaustible issue. I saw this as another Gift from God!

After implementing this newfound father-daughter strategy, no longer did I have difficulty in motivating Alice; obstinacy was no longer an issue. In the past, when I would inform Alice in a jovial voice that it was, "time to get out of the car," it implied that Ali had a voice in the decision. Obstinacy had the upper hand. After this revolutionary revelation, I securely held Alice's hands, and with a *loving paternal voice*, I authoritatively said, "Now Alice, we're getting out of the car!" It worked like a charm! Some of my daughters would hear my tone of voice and ask, "Why are you speaking so dictatorial to Mom?" When I explained my rationale, and they saw her compliance, they understood. Good-bye persuasion; hello authority!

A month or so later, Alice, who was still alternately sleeping upstairs, reinforced the preeminence of her father in her mind. In the middle of the night, Alice woke me and insisted I take her to the hospital.

Fearing an emergency medical issue, I asked, "What's wrong Alice?"

She responded, "I'm having a baby, and I need to go to the hospital right now."

As I filtered what she said and pondered a response, she continued, "I know it is unusual for a 75-year-old woman to have a baby, but that's what happening, I'm having a baby. The baby's name is Charlie, so you will have to take me to the hospital right now!"

Calculating that it was not a pain in her abdomen, in which case I would be making a major mistake, I reassuringly responded, "Yes, I will definitely take you to Beth-Israel Hospital, but first we need to eat breakfast, then we will go to the hospital and you can have Baby Charlie." She seemed content with that explanation and soon she fell back to sleep. Thankfully, in the morning, she had no recollection of her midnight baby crisis.

The relevance of the two events is interesting. First, she informed me she was my daughter, and second, she named her unborn baby "Charlie." During the time of her baby perception, the concept of her father must have been a source of comfort, thus the name Charlie.

CHRISTMAS SHOPPING; NOT A FORGOTTEN MEMORY

With Christmas 2013 rapidly approaching, Alice and I went on our annual Christmas car-ride viewing—the beautiful, and enormous, blue-lighted elm tree in Needham Square, and the meticulously decorated homes in Needham. Formerly this was such a joyful time for Alice; she and her mother both loved driving around Needham viewing the many homes decorated for Christmas. But now Alice was seemingly indifferent.

Her indifference disappeared when she said, "Let's go to Talbots so I can buy Christmas presents for the girls." Not only did she have the thought to buy Christmas presents, she knew where she wanted to shop. In spite of her recalcitrance to leave the car, upon arrival at Talbots, she was out of the car in a flash. As was the case when Dr. Finn examined her or when the eye doctors at the MEEI examined her, Alice demonstrated a faculty to rise to the occasion.

Alice dutifully selected gifts for Katie, Patti, Anne Marie and Ashley. It was thrilling to watch her plod through racks of blouses and sweaters until she selected exactly the right gift for each girl.

The salesperson at Talbots, Ellie Devlin, whose mother was also challenged with dementia, said, "From the way Alice shopped, she knew precisely what she intended to purchase, right down to the color the girls would prefer. If I didn't know she was battling dementia, it wouldn't have occurred to me." The following week we were at Brookstone looking for presents for Jackie.

I learned later from Anne Marie, that Alice asked her to go Christmas shopping because, Alice had said, "I want to give Dad a pair of blue corduroy pants for Christmas." Despite her condition, she had the presence of mind to remember everyone.

THE WONDERFUL WORLD OF ALICE
Unless you become like little children you will not enter the kingdom of heaven. (Matthew 18:3)

When I was picking up one of Alice's prescriptions at CVS, I noticed a large Santa Claus manikin, seated in a chair, which was on sale! I recalled when Alice's mother was experiencing some senior moments, she thought a similar-sized Santa and Mrs. Claus in our front hallway was real people, and she conversed with them. With great expectations that Alice too may think a Santa Claus manikin sitting in a chair was real, I purchased the Sitting Santa. Thankfully, Alice, like her mother several years before, also thought manikins were real people!

Alice was so infatuated with Sitting Santa that we positioned him in front of the fireplace, for which she no longer displayed any interest, so she could admire Santa all winter. On cold winter nights, it was not uncommon to hear, "Are you warm enough Santa? Are you happy Santa? I love you

Santa!" Alice was in love with her new friend, Sitting Santa. He was a new FOA—Friend of Alice.

Anne Marie realized her mother's past love for horses, so for Christmas, she gave her a small furry toy horse, which she immediately named "Gracie." From that point on, Gracie, the toy horse, was Alice's constant companion. Whether Alice was sitting comfortably in the front seat of the car or lying on the couch in the living room watching TV, Alice and Gracie were inseparable. "Are you happy Gracie? Do you like this show Gracie? I love you Gracie," were common refrains, as Alice cuddled and talked to her toy horse. It was quite a role-reversal; as a young girl, Alice was never into playing with dolls. Her only interest was in bayonets and machine guns. Now, in her senior years, she was content playing with and talking to a toy horse.

EVENING ENTERTAINMENT

Since Alice's retina issue, she slept in the mandated facedown position on the living room couch, and she developed a habit of roaming around the house during the night. I viewed Alice's proclivity to wander around the house at night to be a good thing: an affirmation of independence! I didn't want *The Heart of Our Home* to be imprisoned in her living room. As precautionary controls, I disconnected the stove, hid keys to the house and to the car, and locked all the doors. As far as I was concerned, if Alice put silverware, dishes, or even trash in the freezer, it wasn't a critical issue. I believed freedom to walk around or sit at the dining room table reading her high school yearbook a justifiable trade-off, and of over-riding significance.

When I occasionally came downstairs to check on her during the night, I would sometimes find her sound asleep at the dining room table. While perusing her West Springfield High School yearbook, she would dose off with her face rested on her yearbook. I would awake her and suggest she may want to go back to bed, as it was still early in the morning. As soon as Alice's head hit the pillow, she was fast asleep. Alice derived so much enjoyment perusing her high school yearbook; minute after minute, hour after hour, thumbing through the yearbook was sheer delight. Locating it after many years was a godsend!

I also placed a couple of pads of paper and a few pens on the dining room table so she could doodle or write (scribble) notes; that too was a godsend! Initially, Alice's handwriting was legible, but as time progressed, her penmanship regressed. The words she wrote were readable, but they seemed to be isolated or incoherent. Night and day, from 2013 to 2016, she looked at that book incessantly.

Even though she was speaking sporadically, as we sat together looking at her yearbook, hoping she would have a verbal comment, I would say, "This is your picture, Alice." I continued, "Of all the girls in West Springfield High School, you were the prettiest." Disappointingly, there was no response at times. Infrequently, she would appear to comprehend with what I perceived to be a hint of a smile.

There were also other early morning surprises. Sometimes I would find the kitchen faucet running, or on occasion, I would find Alice was lying on the living room floor next to the couch. Thankfully, she was never in any kind of physical discomfort; she didn't fall, she slid onto the floor while getting off the couch.

Unable to comprehend directions that would have assisted me in boosting her back onto the couch, I dialed the Needham Fire Department. Within minutes, four muscular Needham Fire Fighters stood Alice up and walked her into the kitchen. After a glass of cranberry juice, she regained her bearings and I brought her back to her living room bed. Soon, she was fast asleep.

The general consensus was that this incident was evidence for the acquisition of a hospital bed or installation brackets aside the couch. I continued to disagree; sleeping at the dining room table, putting dishes in the freezer, or an occasional slide to the floor was secondary in my mind to Alice's independence. Freedom to roam over-ruled the confinement in a hospital bed; I just did not want her independence to be prematurely restricted.

TAX REBATES OF A DIFFERENT NATURE

Certainly, Alice and I were beneficiaries of Needham taxpayer dollars at work. As I mentioned previously, I once called the Needham Police when Alice refused to leave the car. On another occasion, the Needham Police escorted Alice back to Woodlawn Ave after she was seen circling Needham Town Square looking for a route to Cape Cod. And now the Needham Fire Department was available whenever I needed assistance in picking Alice up after she found herself on the living room floor. Another time, the Needham Police Department was the source of vital assistance, albeit unknown to them, when I explained (i.e., lied) to Alice that, "Chief Leary told me in order to arrest the shed-man we would need to engage the services of an attorney to file a court order for probable cause."

CHAPTER 10

"MY FOREVER FRIEND"

"I have called you friends." (John 15:15)

Recognizing their mother was socially oriented and thoroughly enjoyed interacting with people, the kids convinced me to consider enrolling Alice in a local adult day-care facility. I thought it to be a meritorious suggestion and, after extensive research, they enrolled Alice in the Julia-Ruth House on Canton Street in Westwood.

The Julia-Ruth House provided their guests with breakfast and lunch, and a variety of activities: singing, games, bingo and, most importantly, social interaction in a home-like setting. Guests of the Julia-Ruth House were treated to periodic celebrations: birthday parties, Fourth of July festivities, Christmas parties, etc., all replete with entertainment from local singing and musical ensembles. On the first Tuesday in the month of February 2014, Alice Marie Kennedy became a registered guest at this facility.

When Katie brought her mother to the Julia-Ruth House for the first time and Alice saw a considerable number of elderly guests, she turned to Katie and asked, "Is this a nursing home Katie?" Katie, in spite of the emotion of the moment, visualizing her mother amidst so many frail people, summonsed every ounce of enthusiasm she could muster, and responded, "No, Mom, this is not a nursing home. It is a fun place and you will love it. YOU will NEVER be going to a nursing home." Hooray for Katie!

As an attendant introduced Alice to the staff and other guests, it was obviously love at first sight; they loved Alice and Alice loved them—an instantaneous bond.

Katie remained for an hour to see how Alice acclimated to the daily routine. The first activity of the day was putting golf balls, a natural activity for Alice of Shaker Farms Country Club fame. Within a millisecond, she was on her feet, putter in hand, putting the golf ball directly into the cup. It wasn't long before Alice was instructing other guests on how they should grip a golf club and position their feet before hitting the ball!

Alice was in her glory—playing golf, helping others, and making new friends. It was the re-birth of the former Alice we knew and loved. And now, once again, she was...STILL ALICE! Hallelujah!

Spending a full day at Julia-Ruth's was a radical change for sedentary Alice—transiting from a couch potato in Needham to a social butterfly in Westwood warranted a period of adjustment. The first week or two, when she came home from a day at Julia-Ruth's, she was extremely fatigued. In fact, she was over-tired and unable to fall asleep! Resultantly, she was sleep deprived and became much more difficult to re-direct. It took several weeks before her system adjusted to the increase in daily activity.

On the February 17, 2014, there was a diversion from Alice's weekly routine at Julia-Ruth's. Katie and Anne Marie surprised Alice and I with a surprise 46th Anniversary Luncheon at O'Hara's Pub in Newton Highlands. It was not the opulent dining emporium Alice was accustomed to orchestrating for such occasions. But it was an Irish pub and Alice did have an affinity for Irish pubs!

During this stage of Alice's illness, when she spoke, she spoke her mind, and she was completely uninhibited. During our luncheon at O'Hara's, I cautioned Alice about eating too fast and not chewing her food thoroughly. Alice looked at Anne Marie and Katie and, in a matter-of-fact tone of voice said, "Pay no attention to him; he's just an old crab." For me, the honesty from her heart of hearts conveyed a recognition of love and her tone of voice conveyed an element of forgiveness for my anti-social limitations. All three of us laughed raucously at Alice's spontaneity and her unrestrained honesty. She was, one again...STILL ALICE!

Initially, when I would wake Alice up in the morning to visit Julia-Ruth's, she preferred to stay in the friendly confines of her bed as she emphatically stated, "I'm not going to Julia's today." I made several attempts to redirect her focus with suggestions such as, "it's time to brush our teeth" or "its breakfast time and we are having scrambled eggs, etc." But none of my alternative suggestions seemed to be effective in re-directing her mind-set. So, per usual, I resorted to lying. "It's Sunday Alice and we have to go to Mass." Amazingly, the Sunday Mass line worked like a charm! It was not a big lie, I did bring her to the 9:00 am daily Mass at Saint Bart's.

Whenever we attended a church, the first thing Alice did was locate the placement of the Tabernacle so she could genuflect in that direction. Saint Bart's was no different. She searched the sanctuary and then reverently genuflected and took her favorite seating location 8 to 10 rows from the altar.

Unfortunately, attending morning Mass at Saint Bart's meant Alice would be an hour late for Julia's, but the motivational aspect of morning Mass was of overriding significance. Directly after Mass we were on Route 128 heading to Westwood. When Alice spotted the first Westwood sign on the side of the road, she directed me to "get-off here, get-off here."

Evidently, she was motivated to prove to herself that she knew the route and was more than willing to assist me with directions. I responded, "You're exactly right Alice, that is an exit for Westwood, but there will be less traffic if we take the next Westwood exit." When we arrived at the next Westwood exit, once again, she repeated the same, "get-off here, get-off here" directive to me. I replied, "Good idea Alice, let's get-off here."

Shortly after Alice became a guest at Julia-Ruth's, her misconception that the Catholic Church was still in compliance with Pre-Vatican II regulations dissipated. Thankfully, her unwillingness to receive Holy Communion because she hadn't fasted was now in the rear-view mirror. Whether it was because she forgot Pre-Vatican II regulations or because she forgot she ate breakfast, I don't know. Obviously, forgetfulness of some sort should be credited with Alice receiving Holy Communion again.

Now that she was once again comfortable in receiving Holy Communion, she wanted to receive Communion more often, like five minutes later. After Mass concluded, she refused to leave the pew and said, "I'm not leaving until I receive Communion." She was unconvinced when I tried to explain both of us did receive Communion. She emphatically said, "I'm not leaving until I receive Communion." Ultimately, I assured her we would come back in the afternoon to receive Holy Communion (another white lie).

My modus operandi was never to correct Alice; I looked for opportunities to accentuate the positive and ignore the negative. If that strategy failed, I of course resorted to lying, which was the tactic most often employed.

Another effective method that proved to be effective in convincing her to accompany *me* to Julia's was, "We are meeting Katie and your new friends for breakfast." Instantly, she became cooperation personified. As Happy Alice exited the car to meet Katie and her new friends for breakfast, I assured her, "This will make Katie and your friends so happy; you're going to have so much fun today." Of course, by the time we reached Julia-Ruth's front door, Alice's focus was re-directed to her new-found friends; obstreperousness forgotten.

When I picked Alice up at the end of her Julia-Ruth day, she was generally participating in one type of activity or another—playing bingo with her friends, helping the person next to her with their bingo card, batting a foam ball back and forth or singing with the Julia-Ruth Chorale. Even though I was delighted to see Alice so happy, the reality of seeing her in that environment was difficult. Often, I couldn't constrain tears—tears of sadness and tears of joy. I was sad she was a societal member in a "new group of friends," yet joyful in watching a reinvigorated Alice renew her interest in helping others.

Yes, she was...still Alice, but now Alice was in the company of so many other "Alices." .... *A time to laugh... a time to dance... a time to weep...* (Ecclesiastes 3:4)

ALICE LOVED PARTIES

On Saturday, March 8, 2014, on "International Women's Day (secondarily, my birthday)," the kids, along with Alice, participated in devouring, a "de-licious" (Alice's vernacular) chocolate birthday cake recognizing both auspicious occasions. Alice joined in with the kids in singing "Happy Birthday." At the conclusion of the song, Alice verbalized a post-script, "HAPPY BIRTHDAY to...my caretaker." Even though Alice confused the word 'taker' with the word 'giver,' it was the thought that counted. Alice was always a "caregiver" and now she saw me in a similar light. At this challenging period in her life, to identify me, as her *caretaker* was the best birthday present I could have received.

Since the onset of her illness, I did not deem it beneficial to inform Alice she was in the throes of a long and arduous battle. In addition, I didn't ever identify myself as a helper or as a caregiver. Alice's remark conveyed comprehension that I didn't realize she still possessed.

The first opportunity for Alice to experience Julia-Ruth's holiday atmosphere was their St. Patrick's Day Celebration. Alice joined her newfound friends singing and dancing in an enthusiastic recognition of Patrick, the Patron Saint of Ireland and, the Patron Saint of the Archdiocese of Boston. For the occasion, I made certain Alice was dressed appropriately in festive greenery; she looked like a little leprechaun!

As we pulled into Julia's parking area that morning, Alice sprinted spryly to Julia-Ruth's front door, bearing a loaf of Irish soda bread containing a favorite of hers—caraway seeds. She was so pleased to display her Kelly-green slacks, Donegal woolen sweater (purchased, of course, on her trip to County Donegal and...at a bargain price). She looked like a little colleen dancing through emerald green grass in the Fields of Athenry; she was thrilled with herself! With her colorful outfit and beautiful blue Irish eyes, she was a cross between Maureen O'Hara and the Rose of Tralee!

A JULIA-RUTH FAVORITE

...you have given my heart more joy. (Psalm 4:8)

Alice's perpetual smile, combined with her inherent Gift of Gladness, was in full view as she greeted her new friends at the Julia-Ruth House that March. Without exception, the entire staff, including Julia herself, and the guests, loved Alice. Not only was her beautiful smile infectious, her genuine interest in caring for others was obvious to all.

Anne Marie, who loved to buy clothes for her mother, wanted her to have something new to wear to Julia-Ruth's. She went shopping and purchased a beautiful corduroy outfit for Alice. One day, Alice wore her new outfit to Julia's, and we agreed to meet in the Big Y parking lot so Anne Marie could see Alice in the new ensemble.

It was fortuitous the meeting was arranged on the property of the Big Y. In 1936, the Big Y grocery store was established in a small village in western Mass by Paul D'Amour, a personal friend of Alice's mother.

As soon as Alice saw Anne Marie in the Big Y parking lot, unlike her now-reticent self, she bounced out of the car and, like a little girl, she began twirling around in the middle of the parking lot, as if to say, "Pretty spiffy, huh?" It was so unlike the unpretentious Alice we used to know.

When Anne Marie saw her mother's parking lot pirouettes, she said, "You look great Mom." Alice smiled as she kept spinning around, then she took a little bow and immediately returned to the car. There was no encore;

her performance was over. Alice was obviously delighted to model her new outfit for Anne Marie, but once that was accomplished, she was back in the car and it was "let's go" time. In short order, we were on-the-road again.

The enthusiasm she displayed in publicly modeling her new outfit for Anne Marie demonstrated the depth of Alice's gratitude. Seldom did she purchase clothes for herself, unlike many women who shop 'til they drop, Alice was not a shopper. Whenever she did shop, it was for the kids, not for herself. Only when it was absolutely necessary did Alice shop for Alice.

The only other time Alice seemed pleased with her appearance was after she had her hair done. In the later stages of her illness, I would bring her to Newton for a hair-do by her favorite beautician, Mitten from Turkey. Never did I think I would be sitting in a beauty parlor with a half a dozen women under enormous electrical helmets, after which each complimented the other on their beautiful hair. I was so tempted to say to one of the women, "Your hair doesn't look that great; if I were you, I wouldn't pay for it." Fortunately, I overcame the temptation; I knew bloodletting in a beauty parlor would not be good for Mitten's business.

Alice was ecstatic as she looked admiringly at herself in the beauty parlor mirror and, similar to the Big Y parking lot, she proceeded to demonstrate her patented pirouette. She beamed from ear-to-ear when other patrons applauded.

A GOOD FIT FOR ALL

Whether it was a festive occasion or just a routine day, Alice fit in well at Julia-Ruth's. She participated in batting foam balls and playing bingo, and was often the center of the activity, but also found herself helping friends. In a bingo game, she not only played her own card, she also played the cards for the people sitting on either side of her. Even though her mind was no longer sharp, she was still capable of assisting her new-found friends. Alice could quickly process whether the number called by the staff member was on her card and/or on the card of her friends seated on either side. Elaine, a staff member, once told me, "Alice is such a delightful person, always smiling, always happy, but most of all she goes out of her way to help the other guests. She is more like a member of our staff than a guest!" STILL ALICE!

Pick-up time at Julia-Ruth's was 4:00 o'clock, and most of the drivers congregated in the sitting room to wait for their spouse. Not me. I went directly to the dining room where Julia's guests were participating in various activities. Without fail, as soon as Alice, who was sitting at the dining room table with the other guests, saw me, she would greet me with a big smile. I mean a BIG SMILE! I would always make a big thing of seeing her; with an enthusiastic tone and a huge smile, I would gleefully sing out; "HELLO ALICE! HELLO ALICE! You look so pretty, Alice!"

SMILES EMANATE FROM THE HEART

As Alice's beautiful smile slowly drifted into the rearview mirror of her life, she communicated joy through other means. Somehow her now, expressionless face appeared to radiate an effervescence; a transcendent communication derived from the depth of her soul! Much like the gesture of silent love she displayed in the morning when she gently tugged on my hair as I stooped down to tie her shoelaces; she didn't have to speak. Her beautiful eyes conveyed love. At this point in her cognitive diminishment, words were no longer necessary to transmit LOVE. In her own way, even though unable to speak, Alice did communicate through acts of love.

During her time at Julia-Ruth's, Alice certainly had a positive impact on other guests. One woman in particular, Marcia, who was several years older than Alice, was always looking after Alice. When I arrived at the conclusion of the day, Marcia would rush over to me and say, "Thank you sir, thank you for taking such good care of my *forever friend*, Alice." Marcia's phraseology was repeated every time she saw me, indicating she believed it was her obligation to watch-over Alice until I came to relieve her. In Marcia's mind I was, to an extent, sharing in her responsibilities to care for Alice. Without a doubt, Marcia's parlance of piety was reflective of the love Alice had extended to her. (FOA—Friend of Alice.)

One of Alice's Julia-Ruth friends, Marcia, gives Alice a kiss on her birthday.

After some time, Alice was no longer capable of assisting other guests at Julia's. She herself was now dependent and in need of assistance. Still, her unsmiling face displayed a pleasant look; never did she scowl or look cantankerous. The staff and guests at Julia's were kind and solicitous as Alice became more dependent on others. The assistance from Julia-Ruth's staff and the love conveyed to her by other guests in a time of need was phenomenal. In a sense, I perceived her decline to be an opportunity—an opportunity to be of more help. Selfishly, the look of gratitude in Alice's beautiful blue eyes for simply wiping her nose, putting on lipstick, or tying her shoes was more than gratifying; it was exhilarating. Truly, the privilege of helping helpless Alice was a magnificent gift—a Gift from God.

In spite of various tortuous turns and the complexity of challenges we experienced, my pal, the now Silent Alice and I enjoyed every minute of our blessed 17,498 days of marriage. At the time of Judgment, regardless of the Justice ascribed to me, it is my intention to thank Jesus for the Gift of Alice in my life and the Gift of Caring for Alice in her time of need. Truth be told: I received a far greater gift in caring for her than any benefit she may have derived from my oft-times inadequate therapeutic attempts.

As smiles and words continued to elude her, when I arrived to pick her up she would motion for me to sit next to her, and then she would slide a plate of snacks to me and motion for me to eat! Without a doubt, communication does not necessarily require words.

There I sat, amidst the guests, munching on snacks and checking bingo numbers. The fact that Alice was happy at the Julia-Ruth House was underscored when she saw me and wanted me to join her in the fun. In her heart of hearts, she wanted me to share in that same joy. Deo Gratias.

Initially, when I was at Julia Ruth's I witnessed a group of non-verbal people suffering from comparable illnesses, some totally taciturn, others struggling to speak. Others spoke, but unintelligibly; it was so sad. When Alice and I began to leave, some of guests appeared upset their friend Alice was leaving and would holler, "Don't leave Alice. Where are you going Alice? I don't want you to take my best friend away from me; please let her stay with me." Susan, a woman much younger than Alice who was recuperating from a severe brain injury, often said, "Alice is my forever friend and I don't want her to leave."

In the past, quick-witted Alice would have been prepared with a witty response to their queries, but now she was unable to formulate an appropriate retort. Still, her friends were looking for an explanation. At the risk of being obtrusive, on Alice's behalf I proffered a stimulating response, hoping to spark a reaction.

Excitedly and enthusiastically, I would verbalize whatever bizarre, mostly stupid thought that popped into my mind. "Alice and I are going bungee-jumping." Other times, I suggest, "We're going snorkeling, para-gliding, white river rafting, etc."

With this approach, my intent was twofold. First, I sought to stimulate their minds and put a little levity into their thought processes. Second, I wanted to compare their diminishment of skills to Alice's regression. Some of the guests laughed. Some said, "no way." Others remained expressionless. At this stage of her illness, it appeared to me that Alice would be categorized in the third group. Even though Alice's verbal skills and facial expressions were in decline, the possibility remained that the mind may absorb more than facial expressions indicate.

SEEMINGLY FORGOTTEN, YET SURPRISINGLY RECALLED

This I recall to my mind; therefore, I have hope. (Lamentations 3:21)

During this time frame, Alice's primary interest was watching, not necessarily comprehending, religious TV programs on CTV and EWTN. It was apparent she sensed a connection with long-ago memories of the Sisters of Notre Dame, who taught in Holy Name School in Chicopee; the Sisters of Saint Joseph, who taught in Saint Thomas School in West Springfield; or priests commiserating with bereaved families at the Charles J. Haggerty Funeral Home. It was obvious that watching television and viewing Mother Angelica, who Alice met in 1998, revived past recollections. In some way, Mother Angelica's presence on television seemed to provide a reflection of Christ to Alice. I doubt the content of the program resonated, but the presence of priests and nuns were certainly beneficial. She was comfortable going for car-rides and she was comfortable watching religious programs.

When Pope Francis appeared on the television screen, she seemed particularly entranced with him. Selfishly, when she would dose-off for a few minutes, I changed channels and watched an inning or two of the Red Sox games. As soon as she awakened, I switched back to the religious channel. That in and of itself was a role reversal. In previous years, I would switch from the religious channel I was watching to a channel Alice preferred. At that time, it was not religious TV.

An ancillary benefit for a caregiver of a dementia patient is that the caregiver has absolute control of the TV remote. If I wanted to watch a baseball game, a football game, Fox news, or local news, it made no difference to Alice. Hallelujah!

At one point during the summer of 2014, I noticed a picture of Pope Francis on the cover of *Columbia* magazine (a Knights of Columbus periodical). In an effort to stimulate Alice's mind, I pointed to the picture of Pope Francis and asked, "Alice, do you know who this is?" At a time when Alice's speech was sporadic, she stared at the picture for a second or two and then slowly, in a hesitatingly subdued tone of voice, said, "That's...my friend!"

It was of course, thrilling for me to hear her vocalize a response. She associated a familiar face with someone she saw on CTV and EWTN. In addition, she identified the familiar face as her friend. From the onset of Pope Francis's pontificate on March 13, 2013, his intent was to manifest friendship to everyone. Alice's pronouncement that Pope Francis was her friend affirmed that accomplishment. As often happens during this debilitating illness, a most unlikely, unanticipated, and profound pronouncement was emitted from a cognitively depleted mind.

EXPRESSION DOES NOT NECESSARILY NEGATE COMPREHENSION

As Alice's verbal skills eroded and her facial expressions faded, occasionally a semblance of recognition seemed to spark a glimmer in her eyes and the semblance of a smile on her face. If a neighbor or a friend stopped in for a visit, she seemed to display a look of recognition. When Jackie came home from Connecticut, Alice seemed transfixed; when he sat next to her, she appeared to be trying to smile. If he moved across the room, she didn't take her eyes off him; she followed his every move. Although there was no visible change of facial expression, Alice was obviously processing fond memories of Jackie as she watched his every move.

Whether they were memories in years past, or whether it was a maternal instinct and a mother's love for her son, I don't know. But unquestionably, she was pleased to see Jackie. Possibly, she associated Jackie with the back-rubs he used to give; could she have been expecting another back-rub from him?

Often when Alice appeared placid and uninvolved while watching TV, she would abruptly sit-up from the security of her living room couch. As she sat-up, with a bland look on her face, she would glance around the living room, then quizzically look at me, and subsequently flop back down on the couch. It was as if she awakened from a dream and couldn't determine where she was or what she wanted to do. Every hour or two, the same routine would be repeated; she woke up with a startled yet blank look. To assuage her restlessness, I would say, "I know just what you would like Alice," and head to the freezer. When I returned with a small ice cream cone, she would devour the ice cream, but not the bottom of the cone; she always handed me the bottom of the cone. Whether she thought she was sharing or whether she wanted me to dispose of the tail end of her treat, I don't know.

As Alice's verbalization diminished, her silence became more conspicuous. Our daily car-rides were now in solitude, with the exception of the car-radio and Frank Patterson's Irish CD. Nary a word was spoken. When I thought that her silence connoted incomprehension, on an occasional basis, I was proved wrong. In a barely audible voice and in unison with Frank Patterson, Alice would murmur, not sing, the title word, "Tipperary" at the appropriate point in the song. I loved to hear Alice chime in; it was so soft that it was difficult to hear, but her voice made my heart melt. The melody must have been etched in her mind; she comprehended exactly when the word was about to be sung.

CONFISCATION and ACQUITTAL

It is God who acquits. (Romans 8:33)

As Alice's illness progressed, food on other people plates became much more enticing than food on her own plate. Within an instant, Alice would reach her hand across the table and grab a fistful of food from my plate. Whether we were consuming cereal in the morning or mashed potatoes in the evening, food on the other person's plate was fair game. Believe it or not, Honorable Al was stealing food—and stealing it in broad daylight!

When Alice ravenously stuffed the misappropriated food into her mouth, my reflex reaction was automatic. "You don't have to do that Alice, you have your own bowl of cereal," I said. Then I added, "If you prefer, you can have my bowl." As Alice devoured my cereal (her bowl of preference) I would ask, "How did that taste Alice?" Now that her verbal skills were all but non-existent, her favorite response "DEE-LICIOUS," albeit inaudible, was great for me to hear.

The only items Alice rejected when devouring her—or anyone else's—bowl of cereal were blueberries and the small, packaged, bite-sized strawberries. She would take a handful of cereal in the morning, but she would not touch the cut-up strawberries.

During the early stage of Ali's illness, she constantly reminded me to place napkins adjacent to our dinner settings; every meal, without fail, she would say, "salt and pepper." Even when she became less vocal, I would adhere to her former admonitions of "napkin…salt…and pepper." Now, not only was she not reminding me of dinner etiquette, she was also engaged in the criminal activity of stealing food! As William Bendix used to say on an old-time radio program called *The Life of Reilly*, "What a revolting development this is."

EATING HEALTHY; DEVOURING FRUIT

To celebrate Alice's birthday in August 2014, she and I went to Maine to visit Eleanor and Emil in their seaside community of Ogunquit. We were pleasantly surprised to find that Bill and June St. Lawrence were also visiting El and Emil on the same day. They too were delighted to see Alice. For her part, Alice was so happy that she greeted everyone with her newly discovered means of communicating affection—rubbing her nose against their noses.

"Alice hasn't changed," said Cousin Bill. "She was always affectionate. She simply loved people. More importantly, she never said a disparaging word about anyone; she focused on the positive."

Our lunch was Classic Eleanor—it was delightful. She served corn on the cob, clam chowder and lobster rolls, replete with a frequently replenished, huge bowl of fresh strawberries. Everyone, especially Alice, was anxious to dig into the scrumptious array of food.

For all intents and purposes, Alice was non-verbal, but her dinner table reach was still extensive. I wasn't surprised to see her suddenly snatch food from plates within arm's reach, but it was bemusing for the others. I must admit it was a shock to me, when in public, Alice reached into the communal bowl of strawberries and grabbed a fistful!

When I suggested she use the ladle, Eleanor said, "Pay no attention to him Al, you can take as many as you like; use both hands if you want." (It is such a blessing to have sisters.) Everyone loved seeing Alice and she enjoyed visiting with the family she loved.

I couldn't understand why Alice was so opposed to eating strawberries with her breakfast cereal, yet in Maine, she reached into a bowl and grabbed handfuls of strawberries. Strange! I theorized it might be attributable to the large size and/or the bright color of the fresh strawberries.

From that day forward, I decided to put the reddest, largest (uncut) strawberries and the bluest of blueberries onto her morning cereal. Yes, the strategy worked. Large red strawberries became a big breakfast hit! Thank you, Eleanor!

DEALING WITH DEATH IN A UNIQUE WAY

As I suggested previously, an aspect of Alice's illness that periodically emerged was a perplexing difficulty in dealing with death. In September of 2014, another family member died and I was concerned news of her death may add unnecessary confusion for Alice. After a three-year battle, Darby, the daughter of my cousin Patty Burke Stott, died of cancer. Darby and her brother Jed were close in age to our kids, and they were more like brother or sister than cousins. When Danny entered St. John's Seminary in 2001, Darby was ecstatic and she prayed for him faithfully.

Since the onset of Alice's cognitive diminishment, which coincided with Danny's death, she seemed incapable of comprehending "death." From my perspective, I felt news of Darby's death may add to Alice's inability to compute the concept of death. Consequently, neither I, nor anyone else, mentioned Darby's death in Alice's presence.

On the morning of Darby's funeral, I brought Alice to the Julia-Ruth House, and then drove directly to Our Lady of Victory Church in Centerville for Darby's funeral Mass. After spending an hour or so with Darby's family, at the post-funeral reception I drove back to Westwood to pick Alice up at the conclusion of her Julia-Ruth day.

That evening, as Alice was in the process of eating her dinner, in a most unusual move she abruptly stood up from her chair and pointed to the sink or the windowsill. At that time, even though her ability to speak was significantly restricted, I would still ask questions in hopes she would respond. So I continued to ask, "Would you like a glass of water Alice?" No visible acknowledgement.

As Alice continued to walk around the kitchen while pointing to various other items—the calendar, the clock, the refrigerator—I couldn't interpret what she was trying to convey. So without success, I continued to query what she wanted. Eventually, when she pointed to a picture, I said, "Would you like to look at some pictures Alice? Why don't we look at some pictures?"

After guiding her into the living room, I brought out an album of family pictures, which we hadn't viewed since the album was assembled many years ago. Alice and I were not accustomed to sitting down and roaming through family albums, so for us this was an anomaly.

The two of us sat on the living room couch and browsed through the album. In turning page after page, Alice scrutinized the pictures and point to a group picture and say, "He would like this." Then, as she continued to turn pages in the album, she pointed to other pictures and said, "Give him this." Eventually, I realized the person in the group picture to whom she was pointing, the "he" or the "him," was Danny! An interesting display of recognition, especially on the day of Darby' funeral, Danny's close cousin.

What prompted Alice's interest in looking at family pictures on the day of Darby's funeral? What motivated her to point to Danny in the family pictures? Why Danny, who she hadn't mentioned in over six years? Through the Grace of God, by not mentioning Danny in years, she was spared the unimaginable grief of lamenting the death of her priest-son. She was the recipient of a God-given GIFT OF FORGETFULNESS.

The following day as Alice and I were concluding our daily car-ride, I decided to call Darby's mother to see how she was doing in the aftermath of Darby's wake and funeral. At the time, Alice and I were stopped at a traffic light in Wellesley, and while I was commiserating with Patty Stott over the telephone, I noticed the identification number of a Wellesley School Bus that had stopped in front of us—#116.

I immediately associated the number on the school bus with Danny as his birthday was, January 16th (116). At that point I lost cell-phone connection, so I decided to drive directly to Needham and re-dial.

As Alice and I approached Needham Center once again we were stopped at traffic light and, surprisingly, I noted the Identification Number on back door of a truck stopped in front of us; #127. That number was also of significance to me; January 27th was the date Danny died!

Within a 24-hour period, the confluence of three events seemed to manifest a mysterious connection with Danny. First, Alice's determination to see pictures of Danny. Second, a school bus in Wellesley bearing #116. Third, minutes later in another town, a vehicle in Needham bore #127. Two different towns, two different vehicles, and two different identifications numbers that related to the alpha and the omega of Danny's earthly life.

Whether there is meaning to these coincidences is subject to conjecture. What I choose to believe is these three incidents were, in some way, interconnected. I suspect that Alice, unaware of Darby's death, may have, unknowingly, been a conduit in bringing to mind memories of Danny.

JULIA-RUTH HOUSE: FUN AND GAMES FOR EVERYONE!

...A person finds joy in giving... (Proverbs 15:23).

By nature, Alice loved people, so it was natural for her to reciprocate with an expression of love. One of Alice's newfound daily duties at Julia's was rubbing her nose against other people's noses. She also went through a stage when she told everyone, "You're the best." Everyone at Julia-Ruth's loved that expression. In tune with Alice's obsession of telling people "they were the best," Katie always managed to find greeting cards for Alice that said, "You, are the BEST."

When I first met Alice Haggerty at Shaker Farms Country Club in Westfield, she radiated joy and gladness. Now, forty-five years later, those Gifts from God were still on display at the Julia-Ruth House in Westwood.

As Alice's illness progressed, affection remained, but gradually she began to exhibit a trait she never manifested in her entire life—fear! This onset of trepidation was in evidence when we visited Dr. Finn's office and his nurse began to prepare her arm for a blood test. When the kind and gentle nurse produced a needle, which must have looked foreboding to Alice, she became extremely agitated. I attempted to reassure Alice that the nurse wouldn't hurt her, but she was so troubled I told the nurse, "No more blood tests until I review her fear with Dr. Finn." Alice also became frightened when the nurse put the blood pressure cuff around her arm, so I told the nurse to refrain from conducting that test as well. Alice looked relieved and, appreciatively, rubbed her nose against my nose.

When Dr. Finn came into the examination room, I explained, "Both the blood test and the blood pressure test have become upsetting for Alice; are they essential?" He agreed to dispense with future blood tests but said from now on he would take her blood pressure because that was essential. Obviously, Alice recognized Dr. Finn as a friend, so as he loosely wrapped the cuff around her arm, assuring Alice it would not hurt. Alice relaxed and the blood pressure test was completed without any discomfort. Alice's blood pressure never became an issue; it was consistently in the range of 125/75.

SURPRISE, SURPRISE....RECOGNITION REVIVAL

On a Sunday evening in September of 2014, as Alice lay comfortably on the couch watching Catholic TV. She was presumably oblivious to the content and the logo of the Diocese of Springfield TV Series, "Real to Reel." The first segment of the program displayed a picture of an elderly priest with the caption, "95th Birthday Party!"

Alice, who no longer reacted to auditory comments and presumably could no longer read captions, immediately sat up and shouted, "That's Bishop Maguire, that's Bishop Maguire!"

I couldn't believe what I was witnessing—she instantaneously recognized what I thought was an unrecognizable person. Tears of joy ran down my cheeks as I marveled at Alice's momentary lucidity.

This was a reversal of an incident that occurred, as I mentioned previously, many years ago on a hot summer night at a parish mission at Holy Trinity Church in West Harwich. As dusk was setting in and people were standing in line waiting to enter the church, a man several feet ahead of where Alice was standing and recognized a familiar voice. He turned around and said, "Is that Alice Kennedy I hear?" The man who identified Alice by the sound of her voice on that evening in West Harwich was Bishop Joseph F. Maguire! Now, on a cold September evening at our home in Needham in 2014, it was Alice who identified the same man on TV—Bishop Maguire.

Alice's moment of lucidity was so moving I couldn't keep from shedding a few morsels of tears; it was a powerful moment. Alice was well along in her battle with dementia and Bishop Maguire certainly did not resemble the man we knew years ago; he definitely looked 95, yet Alice recognized him.

Shortly afterward, I sent an email to the Diocese of Springfield relating the emotional moment that occurred as Alice and I were watching "Real to Reel." The following morning, I received a response from the Diocese of Springfield assuring me Bishop Maguire would be informed of Alice's surprising recognition. For another glorious moment, she was...STILL ALICE! Deo Gratias!

A RELENTLESS ILLNESS INTENSIFIES

Alice's relentless requests to-go-home were in the distant past. Although she was still wandering around the house during the nights and spending time looking at her yearbook, those activities now occurred less often. I still continued to believe independence was important and wandering around the house aided and abetted her self-esteem. Every morning, it was reassuring for me to know that Alice was still in Wanderland!

One of the medications designed to alleviate fear and anxiety was successful in reducing Alice's hyperactivity, which had been of a concern. I was not a staunch believer in medications. However, since she began taking the new medication, she was much more manageable. In addition to a lessening of anxiety, she became frail and weakened. Thus—contrarianism became a distant memory.

Alice's loss of stamina was obvious when Christmas season arrived; gone were the days when Alice would strategically place her precious Byers carolers around the house. She expressed little interest in decorating the tree. Christmas was no longer of paramount interest.

Patti did manage to convince her to sit down and write Christmas cards to a few of her friends. Surprisingly, with Patti's perseverance, Alice addressed several Christmas cards. Writing cards had always been my responsibility. So, "writing" Christmas cards in 2014 was a first, and a last, for Alice.

As 2015 began, evidence was mounting; Alice's cognitive depravation was accelerating. Our February anniversary was a non-event and, in March, St. Patrick's Day for Alice was just another *day at the office.* I didn't want to disregard her love for St. Patrick's Day, so I went shopping for a Saint Patrick's Day outfit at Talbot's in Wellesley. The clerk, Ellie Devlin, a long-time friend of Alice's, suggested a green and gold floral print blouse (comparable to the azure floral print dress she wore on our first date). The new blouse went well with her Kelly green slacks and Donegal Irish sweater.

Just as in the past, the staff at Julia's made a big thing of Alice's Saint Patrick's Day outfit and, most importantly, for someone who was never overly conscious of her attire, Alice was delighted!

In view of the pleasure she derived from wearing her new Saint Patrick's Day outfit, I made it a point to dress her in a new outfit on every subsequent day of importance. On Independence Day, she was adorned with a new red and white blouse with navy blue slacks. On Halloween, she donned an orange and black ensemble. I wanted Alice to feel special and to be the recipient of recognition from her family and her friends at Julia-Ruth's.

Alice's ability to carry on a conversation had begun to diminish, and now that she transited to the advanced stage of her illness, her ability to speak was all but non-existent. For someone like Alice who communicated so well, this must have been frustrating. It was also obvious that she was beginning to lose her beautiful smile, which everyone at Julia-Ruth's loved to see. Also, long gone were her incessant chants to "go-for-a-ride."

Gone also was her proclivity to rub noses with anyone and everyone, nor did we hear her say "you're the BEST" to anyone who helped her. As time went on, Alice's ability to walk became more like a shuffle. Combined with the absence of her beautiful smile, she no longer looked on the exterior like she was the same person. Nevertheless, to those who knew her, she was...STILL ALICE!

Happy Birthday Alice
Love, all your friends at the
Julia Ruth House

Alice's friends at the Julia-Ruth House joined in
celebrating her August 22nd birthday.

Alice began to display difficulty extricating herself from chairs, so we moved an armchair from the dining room into the kitchen so it would be easier for her to propel herself out of the chair. We also placed another armchair on the side of the dining room table so she could easily get up after perusing her high school yearbook.

BRIDGING LIVES: A CELEBRATION

The 2014 legislative session of the Massachusetts General Court passed a bill identifying a bridge in Needham to be dedicated in memory of Father Daniel J. Kennedy. The legislation was filed by Massachusetts State Senator Michael F. Rush and was signed into law in December by Governor Deval Patrick.

The date of dedication was intended to occur in March 2015, but it was difficult to coordinate a date that was convenient for everyone, so the exact date of the ceremony was delayed. My hope was to select a date significant with an event in Danny's life or a date of religious or historical significance. Unfortunately, none of those prospective dates were compatible with the availability of various individuals who wished to be in attendance.

Ultimately, in browsing through "Butler's Lives of the Saints," I was pleasantly surprised to learn that June 15th is the Feast Day of Saint Alicia, a nun from Belgium! I never knew, nor do I believe Alice knew, there was a Saint Alicia. Fortunately, June 15th proved to be a date of communal convenience for many.

On June 15, 2015, the Father (Lt.) Daniel J. Kennedy Memorial Bridge, spanning Interstate 95 in Needham, was dedicated to our son Danny. I assumed a degree of spousal poetic license and identified the date of dedication, June 15th as the Feast Day of Saint Alice. We were honored to learn the Archbishop of Boston, Cardinal Sean O'Malley, would be in attendance at the bridge dedication ceremony.

Prior to the commencement of the program, Cardinal Sean greeted Alice with the warmth of a true shepherd as he graciously blessed her. Unfortunately, Alice's inability to speak prevented her from engaging in conversation with the convivial cardinal. I was so happy for Alice. Unlike 46 years ago at Saint Patrick's Day Mass in Holyoke when the Cardinal-Archbishop of Boston, Richard Cardinal Cushing, stopped two feet from distributing Holy Communion to Alice at Saint Jerome's Church in Holyoke, the current Cardinal-Archbishop of Boston knew her as the *mother of a Boston priest.*

In his Invocation, Cardinal Sean stated, "In just 247 days Father Dan 'built' many bridges between God and God's people." During her entire adult life, Father Dan's mother also built bridges between people. Alice, a lifelong peacemaker, worked non-stop to bridge relationships, reconcile fractured alliances, always emphasizing shared similarities and de-emphasizing dis-similarities.

The Cardinal-Archbishop of Boston Cardinal Sean Patrick O'Malley, OFM Cap greets Alice at the Dedication of the Father Daniel J. Kennedy Memorial Bridge as her children Jack and Katie, along with her sister Betsy, share the moment.

In addition to the Cardinal-Archbishop of Boston, there were several Commonwealth of Massachusetts officials in attendance at the ceremony: Secretary of Transportation Stephanie Pollack, Senator Michael F. Rush, Mo Handel, Chairman of the Needham Board of Selectman, and Father Matthew J. Westcott, seminary classmate of Father Dan.

Senator Michael F. Rush served as the master of ceremonies; Father Westcott blessed the Father Daniel J Kennedy Bridge; and Father Dan's brother, Jackie, was the keynote speaker. Though the day was damp, dark, and downcast, the spirit was alive and ebullient; excitement reigned! Many Boston priests, relatives, and friends of Father Dan's braved the inclement weather, brightening a dull day.

In blessing the bridge, Father Matt specifically referred to Father Dan's interest in promoting vocations to the priesthood. Jackie assured everyone that Danny would be honored to have a bridge in his hometown that was named in his honor. With the exception of two individuals, everyone stood in silence as Senator Rush unveiled the Memorial Bridge plaque. The two exceptions who did not stand? The mother of her priest-son reclined comfortably in a borrowed wheelchair while, at the same time, his nephew Daniel Francis Russell, frolicked inattentively in his baby carriage.

Alice and her family rejoice in the Dedication of the
Father Daniel J. Kennedy Memorial Bridge.

After the dedication of the Memorial Bridge, the Father Daniel J. Kennedy Council (#1611) of the Knights of Columbus hosted a reception at its hall on Highland Ave in Needham, where many of Danny's friends had an opportunity to visit and reminisce. Although Alice was in attendance at the reception, she was only passively present. Unlike her life of active participation in memorable events, she was sedentary at a celebration for her son, though she was...STILL ALICE!

Whenever Anne Marie brought baby Daniel Francis to Needham to see Nana, it was always a thrill to see the unique reaction when they saw each other, and the bridge dedication was no exception. Although Alice was unable to smile at this point, her eyes beamed brighter when she saw baby Daniel at the Knights of Columbus hall in Needham. Daniel responded, beaming right back at Alice as he excitedly grabbed her nose. It was a mutually shared moment of excitement.

ALICIA MARIA

Fear not I have redeemed you; I have called you by name: you are mine.
(Isaiah 43:1)

After Alice's death in 2016, I obtained her Baptismal Certificate from the Church of the Holy Name of Jesus in Chicopee, which affirmed that a girl, born to Mr. and Mrs. Charles Joseph Haggerty on August 22, 1939, was baptized Alicia Maria Haggerty on September 10, 1939. Shockingly, my wife of 49 years, who I knew as Alice Marie, was baptized *Alicia Maria!*

Alicia was actually Alice's true name. This strange turn of events brings to mind a question; should I have been referring to the song "Alice Blue Gown" as "Alicia Blue Gown?"

Interestingly, at a later date I discovered one of the more popular wines in Chile is Santa Alicia Wine! *Alicia Maria Kennedy* would have loved to sip a glass of Santa Alicia Wine.

DANIEL STEALS THE SHOW FROM DANIEL

On one of Anne Marie's initial visits to Needham with baby Daniel, she encouraged Mom—a.k.a. Nana—to push Daniel in his carriage up and down the driveway. Alice was thrilled! Alice had become accustomed to watching several little kids playing across the street, but now she associated

Daniel as one of those little kids. Eventually, when Nana became tired from pushing her grandson carriage, she turned to Anne Marie and said, "Now shove him back across the street." Apparently, Alice thought all little kids belonged across the street.

In the weeks that passed, whenever Alice and I drove over the bridge, I slowed the car and pointed to the placard on the bridge and asked if she could read the sign, hoping she would connect with either the name Daniel or Kennedy; she did not. At various times, after idling the car for a moment or two she would voice one word, "bridge." Disappointed as I was when Danny's name did not resonate with her, it was consistent with Alice's indifference whenever her first-born son's name was mentioned.

CHAPTER 11

THE FINAL STANZA

*"You changed my mourning into danc-
ing." (Psalm 30:12)*

A s Alice's ability to negotiate stairs became more and more challenging, we began to attend Mass at Saint Bartholomew's Church
in Needham, where there are fewer steps to negotiate. One Sunday, as both
of us were in line to receive Holy Communion, Alice abruptly refused to
open her mouth to receive the Sacred Host. I attempted to persuade her to
receive the Eucharist, but failed. It seemed inconceivable to me that someone
with such a high regard for Holy Communion would refuse to consume the
Host. Not only did this incident reflect her further cognitive deterioration,
I was also alarmed that Alice's spirituality may be eroding.

"Don't feel badly Dan," Marty Cunniffe remarked after the Liturgy.
"I distribute Holy Communion at Briarwood Nursing Home and often
dementia patients are fearful of receiving Communion." Thankfully, Marty's
consoling words mitigated my concerns. In effect, June 15, the Feast Day of
St. Alicia, was the most appropriate date to dedicate the bridge.

On another occasion, after Mass at "St. Bart's," a woman named Mary
who came to know Alice through hockey came up to me and said, "Years
ago as Alice and I were watching our sons play in the Needham Youth
Hockey program, I mentioned to her that I hadn't been to Mass in over

25 years. Without batting an eye, she suggested we meet for coffee. After a few morning coffee-breaks, Alice convinced me that I would be pleased if I returned to the church; I did and I am." Another FOA—Friend of Alice.

HELP IS AVAILABLE; HELP IS CLOSE AT HAND

Several neighbors reached out and offered to help Alice during this challenging period in her life. Traci McLaughlin brought various items to assist in caring for Alzheimer's patients and Barbara Tierney often brought muffins or turkey dinners. Many of Saint Joseph's stalwarts were always available to assist Alice. Among the many were Frances Gallagher, Pat McNamara, Ann Cosgrove, Mary Hegarty, Ginny Topham, Rita Bailey, Mary Lou Bonasia, and Katie Whyte, whose husband Paul provided a handicap designed toilet seat that was a major help for Alice.

There was a common thread expressed by all her friends.

"Alice has been so good to me; I want to do something for her."

"She was always helping somebody."

"I love Alice, she was so much fun."

Her kindnesses and her upbeat personality obviously had a positive impact on many people. Rita Bailey expressed it well when she said, "Alice had a perpetual smile on her face, she was always happy; you would think she didn't have a care in the world even though she did."

As Alice's decline accelerated, her children came to the forefront time and time again; all of whom would drop whatever they might be doing to help their mother. Ashley also pitched in with expertise that she acquired at the Epoch Nursing Home in Harwich.

Alice's out-of-town family was also an indispensable component in helping her face the challenge of her life. Alice's sisters Eleanor and Betsy were also anxious to help their sister Al Marie. In addition, friends such as Loraine Salois, Margaret Dunlap, and Mary Beth Ash called, offered prayers, or sent flowers just to let Alice know they cared.

Even though Alice was unable to express her happiness, when Jack arrived from Connecticut, the joy in her beautiful blue eyes was obvious; they sparkled as she watched Jackie's every move. The poignant Irish ballad, "A Mother's Love is a Blessing" often came to mind. It stated, "...love her as in childhood, though feeble old and gray, you'll never miss a Mother's love 'til she's buried beneath the clay." The tune and lyrics were embedded deep in our hearts, 24/7.

When the kids were young and we were living in Westfield, every Saturday morning the radio station was turned to our weekly staple, "The Irish Hour." Whenever "A Mother's Love is a Blessing" was played, Katie, Anne Marie, Danny, and Jackie seemed indifferent to the sentimentality of the lyrics, but not Patti. She took the typical elements of an Irish song to heart. Patti pondered the lyrics, and remonstrated at the disturbing theme. Whenever "A Mother's Love is a Blessing" was played, Patti would cry and ask me to turn-off the radio.

My father often said, "'A Mother's Love is a Blessing' is my favorite Irish song!" As a young boy, it was commonplace to see my father listening and singing as his favorite song played incessantly on our Victrola. My father's mother died when he was young. Consequently, when he heard that song, he listened with nostalgia; Patti listened to the song prospectively with apprehension.

Even at a young age, Patti didn't want to contemplate the sadness of losing her mother. Coincidentally, or perhaps, not so coincidentally, Patti was the only person with her mother when she died.

ENERGY DEFICIENCY

On the morning of July 30, 2015, as I was preparing Alice for a day at Julia-Ruth's I sensed she may be more lethargic than usual. But I wasn't absolutely certain my observation was accurate, so I was anxious for an unbiased assessment. With that thought in mind, when I brought Alice to Julia's that morning, I purposely did not mention my concern to the staff.

When I picked Alice up in the afternoon, I posed my customary inquiry about Alice's day. Julia's assistant director, Anne Marie, informed me that Alice seemed to be unusually listless; she thought Alice might not have slept well the previous evening. Predicated on Anne Marie's affirmation of my morning observation, I drove directly to the emergency room at the Beth-Israel Deaconess Hospital (BIDH) in Needham.

After an extensive examination, the doctor informed me Alice was dehydrated, and her condition warranted overnight admittance. The nurse inquired as to whether she drank much water, to which I explained Alice has difficulty swallowing. In response to her suggestion to provide her with a straw, I informed her Alice bites the straw, thus her primary source of liquids was from consuming watermelon and cantaloupe.

Alice's evening at the BIDH remedied the de-hydration issue and she was released the following day, July 31, 2015—the Feast Day of Saint Ignatius Loyola. Although Alice was released from BIDH, she wasn't discharged; the Visiting Nurse Association (VNA) will conduct an at-home evaluation and would subsequently discharge Alice.

Within 24 hours, a Visiting Nurse Association representative was at our front door. In the course of four weeks, we saw a steady stream of VNA personnel: nurses, therapists, and health care aides. The care she received from the VNA representatives was extraordinary, and she was she eventually discharged.

DID SOMEONE SAY....PARTY?

In the later part of August, a few days before Alice's 76th birthday, Katie, our other August 22nd birthday girl, drove her mother to Ogunquit, Maine to celebrate their birthdays with sisters Betsy (another August birthday girl) and Eleanor. As soon as they arrived at Eleanor's house, Alice spotted the living room couch and, in a moment of verbal revival, said, "That looks like a good place to flop." Alice was in her comfort zone.

After Alice rested, the three Haggerty Sisters and Katie went to Alice's favorite Perkin's Cove restaurant, Barnacle Billy's. As might be expected, Betsy and Eleanor were entertaining their sister with not only a traditional water view, there was the added excitement of watching boats coming in and out of Perkins's Cove.

Eleanor wanted Alice to have a bird's-eye view of the boats transiting in and out of the Cove, so she reserved a table on the outside deck of Barnacle Billy's. Apparently, Alice was fearful when she looked down at the water and suggested changing tables (several times). Alice's lifelong love for a water-view was relegated to secondary status, as she preferred the confined quarters of the dining room. Alice's two sisters are always upbeat and enthusiastic; everyone enjoyed the birthday celebration—especially Alice and Katie!

RECOLLECTION RECALL

The Lord is close to the brokenhearted, and saves those whose spirit is crushed. (Psalm 34:19)

It was a week or so after Columbus Day when Alice and I took a ride to Saint Mary's Cemetery in Westfield. Alice of course derived great comfort in car-rides and a 90-mile trek on the Massachusetts Turnpike would certainly pass the 'comfort test.' Most importantly, the serenity of the cemetery was never a threatening experience for Alice.

Since the onset of her illness, whenever Alice wanted to extricate herself from an uncomfortable situation, she would plead, "let's go, let's go." Interestingly, she never expressed an urgency to leave Saint Mary's Cemetery. When I returned to the car after visiting Danny's grave, Alice would be perfectly content to continue sitting silently staring at the gravestone. She didn't speak, even when she had the ability to speak. Neither did she display any discernable fear from the deafening sound of thundering F-15 Fighter Jets roaring overhead on flight patterns to and from nearby Barnes Air Base.

Did Alice receive solace while sitting silently in the car gazing at Danny's stone? Did she intuitively believe Danny was at peace? Was the Blessed Mother comforting a grieving mother's heart?

On that brisk autumn day in October 2015, after parking the car a short distance from the gravesite as was my custom, I asked, "Would you like to visit Danny's grave Alice?" I was absolutely shocked when she nodded her head affirmatively. Never before did Alice express interest in visiting Danny's grave. I was euphoric as we walked slowly, ever so slowly, hand-in-hand, across the well-manicured emerald green grass of Saint Mary's Cemetery. I was beyond delighted; completely unaware of the momentous moment that was about to transpire.

As we reached the grave, Alice looked at the stone momentarily. Then, after months of silence, she began to speak. "You were such a good boy Danny. I love you Danny." I couldn't believe what I was witnessing. Alice's face was expressionless, her voice strong and confident. She was speaking from the depths of her maternal heart. Without hesitation she continued, "I miss you Danny; you are with God Danny, and you are happy. Good-bye Danny." After an absence of several years, Alice's visceral love for her son Danny poignantly surfaced at Saint Mary's Cemetery.

As the two of us walked hand-in-hand back to the car, she remained stoic, devoid of emotion. The magnitude of that moment was surreal. For at least the previous six months, Alice was nonverbal, including an inability to speak with Cardinal Sean O'Malley during the June Dedication of the Father Daniel J. Kennedy Memorial Bridge in Needham. Now, on a brisk autumn day in a desolate cemetery in Westfield, Mass, Alice was gifted with the ability to speak, and speak she did. She spoke from the depths of her maternal heart, with a mystical love that was infused into the soul of a grieving mother.

From the cradle to the grave, "A Mother's Love is truly a Blessing...."

FACIAL CHANGE OR A FACIAL MIRAGE?

A few days later, in assisting Alice with her dinner, I thought the left side of her face appeared to be slightly distorted. Without revealing my concern, I asked grand-daughter Ashley for evaluation of Nana's appearance. Without hesitation, Ashley said, "Nana's mouth looks distended." Ashley's opinion affirmed my concern and I ceased feeding her and focused completely on any future facial contortion that I did not detect. If I perceived any subsequent abnormality, facially or otherwise, I was prepared to dial 911. I did not note any subsequent variance and gradually her face returned to normal.

In the morning, as I prepared her breakfast, which consisted primarily of watermelon, cantaloupe, and oatmeal, thankfully there was no discernable indication of the distortion that I perceived the previous evening. "It's going to be a fun-day for you Alice, a fun-day at Julia's. It's really, really, going to be a fun-day at Julia's!" I said as we sauntered toward the car.

When I picked Alice up in the afternoon, Elaine, a member of Julia's staff, who, like other staff members exuded a genuine interest in Alice, informed me that Alice was *pocketing her food* at lunchtime. Realizing Alice's recent inclination to steal food from someone else's plate, I presumed she meant Alice was stuffing her pockets with ill-gotten mashed potatoes. Since her illness, Alice had a proclivity to stuff items into her pockets, but in the past those items were napkins not edibles.

Elaine provided an explanation: "*Pocketing,* in a medical context, is a term used to describe the storage of food between teeth and cheek." It was my epiphany; the distorted look I observed on Alice's face the previous evening was evidence she was *pocketing food.*

Elaine, the staff-nurse at Julia-Ruth's, recommended I purchase mouth swabs specifically designed to remove pocketed food from a person's mouth. Resultantly, our evening menu going forward consisted primarily of Gerber's Baby Food, clear soup, pureed foods, cottage cheese, mashed potatoes, puddings, watermelon, ice cream and a supply of mouth swabs. The Bill of Fare in the morning menu consisted of oatmeal, soft boiled eggs, and watermelon, enabling her to consume liquids since she was prone to biting straws. In view of Alice's rapid regression, the menu was one thing, but consumption was significantly more challenging. Alice's inability to swallow prevented her from consuming even puree-type foods; thankfully she was able to munch on watermelon.

AS CURIOUSITY ABATES, WANDERING CEASES

Signs of Alice's further deterioration continued. There were no longer indications that Alice had been wandering during the night. There were no 'X' marks on her classmate's pictures. She did not rip out yearbook pages, and there was no indication she doodled on scrapes of paper. As I told Dr. Finn, "Alice is not consuming much food; she is becoming quite feeble." "Continue as best you can to have her consume puree foods and liquids; if she can't swallow solids, keep trying purees and liquids. Come back in three days and we will discuss home care options."

Not only was Alice no longer wandering during the night, when I came downstairs during the night and in the morning, she was in exactly the same position on the living room couch as when I tucked her in at night. In effect, she was immobile.

I was convinced God would continue to provide us with instincts to adequately care for Alice. In essence, the Grace our family received in caring for Alice was comparable to the Grace that Alice received in caring for her children. In essence, just as God provides prayerful parents with the Gift of Caring for their children, so too will He provide the Gift of Caring to family members who minister to disabled family members.

Even though at this point Alice was presumably incommunicado, I continued to proceed with our customary suppertime musical interlude. I would still sing our old-time favorite songs; the only difference was that Alice was now emotionless; she just sat and stared.

THE BEST LAID PLANS....

"Plans are in the heart of a man the decision of the Lord endures."
(Proverbs 19:21)

After one of our customary late-afternoon car-rides, as the sun was setting on a brisk autumn Saturday, I left Alice in the comfort of the warm car while I went into the house to prepare her dinner and set the table.

Alice's ability to walk and to climb stairs was limited so, when I returned from setting the table, I developed a little sing-song to encourage her to walk to the front door. It was a stupid little ditty designed to engage her cooperation in transiting from car to house. "Pick your feet up Alice; peddle those piggies Alice...peddle those piggies Alice..." resounded as we proceeded along the sidewalk and up the front steps. I assisted Alice in lifting her feet as she slowly ascended the front steps but, just as we were approaching the stoop, one of her legs weakened. I assisted her in picking-up the weakened leg but unfortunately that applied too much weight to the stronger leg which subsequently buckled and Alice began to fall.

Thankfully, I was able to cushion her fall and she wasn't seriously injured. She was, however, in a contorted position teetering precariously on the edge of the stoop and I couldn't risk leaving her in that position for fear she might tumble down the steps. Furthermore, I couldn't access my cell phone; it was in the car!

As dusk began to encroach upon daylight, Alice and I were marooned, perhaps for 5 or 10 minutes before a passer-bye came to our assistance. The stranger was able to support Alice on the stoop while I retrieved my cell phone and called 911.

When four burly Needham Firefighters arrived, they began quizzing Alice as to whether or not she was injured. I responded, "No, she is not injured; we need you to help in up-righting her."

"Please sir, we want the lady to respond, not you; are you hurt Mam?" said the firefighter. In a hushed voice, so Alice wouldn't hear, I said, "My wife has dementia and is unable to respond; please just put her in a vertical position." After the firefighters up-righted Alice, they assisted her into the comfort of her kitchen chair. Other than a slight bruise on her leg, thankfully Alice was uninjured.

Alice's resilience in rebounding from a near disaster was most impressive. Although the physical consequence was minimal, lying in a prone position on the front stoop, precariously close to cascading down the concrete steps, would be emotionally upsetting to most everyone. But it seemed to be a non-event to Alice.

Certainly, her indifference to a calamitous situation was diametrically different than recent reactions for her dementia-based, fearful frame of mind. I don't know whether her nonchalance was attributable a late-stage dementia placidity or to her innate courageousness. At any rate, Alice's encounter with a platform plunge did not unduly upset her.

Evidently this near disaster was God's way of prompting me to take remedial action and provide preventive protection for Alice, now quite frail. Once she was safely in bed, I called Tom Gallagher, a contractor and the husband of Alice's friend Frances Gallagher, and asked him if he would install an additional handrail on our front steps.

The following morning as Alice and I returned from Sunday Mass, Tom was constructing an additional handrail. When Alice saw Tom, she recognized him immediately and managed a slight smile; Ali always liked Tom and often referred to him as an "Irish Divil," which of course was the kettle calling the pot black. Her description of Tom Gallagher defined the two of them; both were "Irish Divils."

The new handrail was definitely helpful, but after a week or two, I realized Alice's inability to pick-up her feet necessitated installing a ramp to our front door. I called Chuck Mangini, whose wife Sandy, a counting team member from Saint Joseph's and a good friend of Alice, and asked Chuck if he would build a ramp for Alice so she wouldn't have to climb our front steps. Within 24 hours, Chuck constructed a custom-made ramp, covered with an Astro-turf-like material, so Alice wouldn't slip in the upcoming winter season. Chuck also constructed a mini-ramp from the concrete stoop to the front-hall threshold.

Thankfully, the minimal upward grade of the mini-ramp negated the need for Alice to lift her legs; initially, she was apprehensive about using the ramp, so I informed her, "This is our new ski slope Alice," prompting me to coin another stupid motivational jingle.

"Climb that ski slope, Ali; climb that ski slope, Ali; pick those piggies up, Ali; pick those piggies up, Ali." When Alice thought she was on a ski-slope, gone was her recently acquired reticence; she did pick-up her piggies and she pranced right up the ramp—so proud of herself.

ON-SITE MEDICAL INTERVENTION—A GODSEND

During Alice's October appointment, Dr. Finn detected significant deterioration. First, Alice's weight was dropping precipitously; second, she was unable to respond verbally and most significantly, she was decidedly weaker. Dr. Finn assured me that although Alice was declining, she didn't appear to be in imminent danger. He suggested that I continue feeding her baby food, puddings, popsicles, puree foods, and watermelon.

"With Alice's comfort as our primary focus, I would recommend contacting VNA Hospice Care and discuss Home Visitation," the doctor said. I agreed. Dr. Finn informed me that a VNA Representative would be in touch with me shortly; he also offered to meet with family members to discuss care for Alice. Dr. Finn conjectured, "Alice's tortuous journey might conclude in two or three months." The good news: Alice should be with us for Christmas 2015!

Shortly after our appointment, a VNA Hospice Care representative visited our home to assess Alice's needs. After a thorough evaluation, the VNA representative concurred that Alice's cognitive skills were significantly impaired, which would qualify her for the VNA Home Hospice program.

The VNA representative also recommended I relinquish a portion of my time with Alice, so our children could become more actively involved in caring for their mother. Evidently, caregiver burn-out was a concern, and I may have been susceptible.

I did not agree. In my mind, taking care of Alice was a privilege, not an exasperating experience. Why would I want reprieve from a privilege? I was capable of attending to Alice's needs and, truly believed everything was under control.

Subsequently, in accord with the VNA recommendation, I suggested to Katie, Patti, Anne Marie and Jackie that "Mom would love to have each of you help her; let's work out a schedule so you can private time with her."

All four of her children were most anxious to experience the joy of helping their mother in time of need; soon, each of them was *caring for Mom*.

I also concurred with the recommendation that Alice had reached the stage where a hospital bed and a wheelchair would be of benefit. I did inform the VNA representative there wasn't a need for Alice to avail herself to the VNA's offer to provide a Spiritual Counselor. Danny's priest friends were frequent visitors and they administered Sacraments to Alice.

Alice's face glowed whenever Danny's priest friends, Father(s) Matt Westcott, Bob Blaney, Daniel Hennessey, Bill Lohan, Paul Sullivan, and Dermot Roach stopped to see her. When Father Bob Blaney visited, he played several beautiful pieces on our living room piano and Alice's attention was riveted on the lightening-like fingers of a professional pianist. Danny always referred to his Saint John's Seminary friend, a former star in Broadway Musicals as, "Broadway Bob." True to his moniker, Broadway Bob entertained his friend's dying mother with a private concerto on our family piano!

Lastly, the VNA representative informed us that if Alice's condition should warrant extraordinary care, Assisted Living Facilities might be a future consideration. Without hesitation, Katie emphatically exclaimed, "We are not interested in outside facilities; we intend to keep our mother at home!" THANK YOU, KATIE!

Shortly after our discussion with the VNA representative, the doorbell rang and it was the Hospice Nurse/Coordinator Kelly Hart. As soon as Kelly walked into our home, and saw Alice, she was beaming with an ear-to-ear smile, provoking a reciprocal response from Alice. She too displayed an ear-to-ear smile; yes, Alice and Kelly clicked!

Resultantly, Alice was unafraid when Kelly took her blood pressure, a completely different reaction than when other nurses did. Kelly's effervescence was obviously endearing to Alice.

During Kelly's "getting to know you" session, she unpacked her laptop and began to feverishly schedule visits with a health aide, Carlotta and, coincidentally, Alice's previous physical therapist, Jeff Crompton.

It was obvious that Carlotta's caring nature resonated with Alice; she was genuinely interested in developing a personal relationship with Alice. After assisting with hygiene, she sat with Alice at the dining room table patiently and lovingly enticing Alice to consume a snack— Carlotta was truly the personification of the Corporal Works of Mercy.

Jeff was shocked at Alice's drastic decline since his last visit three months prior. He was, however, pleased a hospital bed was on order and, which would provide her greater security and more comfort. He also provided Alice with a foam cushion for her chair to assist me in transporting her. Not only was Alice more comfortable sitting on the foam cushion, the additional elevation assisted me in transporting her out of the chair.

As a consequence of her immobility, she never ostensibly demonstrated any discernable concern with aluminum brackets on the hospital bed, as she was well beyond the point where might try to climb over the aluminum brackets. This vibrant woman, the embodiment of limitless energy, the manifestation of courageousness, was now completely helpless and totally devoid of any motor skills and was no longer capable of getting out of bed on her own.

COMSUMPTION: AN ACUTE PROBLEM

As a consequence of Alice's swallowing difficulties, her weight continued to plummet. Oatmeal, watermelon, cottage cheese, and Gerber's Baby Food were nutritious but paltry consumption continued to precipitate weight loss.

Dementia patients are susceptible to aspiration issues, whether it be consuming solids or liquids. Consequently, the VNA recommended adding a drink thickener to create more substance to liquids, thus lessening the likelihood of a choking issue. I was extremely careful with drink thickened liquids—just a drop or two of water or cranberry juice.

I was reminded of an expression often voiced by my mother; "It's as broad as it is long." Translation: In all probability, the end result will inevitably be the same. If a person fails to eat, the body will die; if a person with dementia attempts to eat, the throat may constrict and the body will die. Consequently, I was ultra-careful in administering solid foods or liquids.

On Thanksgiving Day, November 26, we maintained our annual tradition. Just as Alice always orchestrated, on Thanksgiving morning all inhabitants of 45 Woodlawn Ave would wake-up to the savory smell of a fresh turkey from Owens Turkey Farm roasting in our oven. Thanksgiving 2015 was no different. All of us were delighted with the aroma, hopeful that Alice's sense of smell was functional, and she too would be aware of a house filled with a succulent, mouth-watering, savory smell of a turkey roasting in her kitchen. We anticipated a "de-licious" turkey dinner.

Unfortunately, her ability to swallow was significantly impaired, preventing her from consuming the "de-licious" turkey. She did however get a taste of turkey on Turkey Day— Gerber's turkey!

A TIME TO REMEMBER IN EARLY DECEMBER

On long weekends Alice scoured the paper seeking the time and place of parades and fireworks; she loved holiday celebrations. Never did she or the kids miss a parade; whether it was a 4th of July Parade, a Memorial Day Parade, or a Saint Patrick's Day Parade, they were present and they were waving flags. Now that she was growing weaker by the day, I needed to create a stimulant to motivate her when we were transiting from the kitchen to the living room; why not "parade"' from one room to another?

With a firm grip under both of Alice's arms, instead of walking, we *paraded* from the kitchen to the living room as Monotone Dan sang familiar marching tunes, such as "I Love A Parade," "McNamara's Band" and, of course, the Notre Dame Victory March. Even though Alice wasn't able to vocally respond, she was motivated to move her feet as we shuffled-off to the living room. Intermittingly, I would intersperse supplemental verses, including "pick up those piggies ALICE, pick up those piggies..." My little pal and I were *marching along together.*

When we reached our destination, my strategy of enlisting her cooperation continued. As I placed one of her favorite caps on her head (most often a Catholic Memorial High School hockey cap), I sang a self-composed little ditty: "Sit down, Alice; pick your feet up, Alice; put your face on the pillow, Alice." I guided her through the process so the right-side of her face would be positioned on the pillow facing the television set. As this procedure concluded, she would clasp her hands together in a prayerful manner between her cheek and the pillow as if in prayer. At that point, I covered her with her County Kerry kelly-green blanket (appropriated from one of our Aer Lingus flights).

As she lay peacefully and contentedly on the couch, I would often say, "You are not only important to me Alice, you are really important in the eyes of God; you are the mother of a priest!" It may have been wishful thinking on my part, but I thought I detected a glimmer of joy in her ever-so blue eyes as she contemplated being the mother of a priest. As I said a Hail Mary or two, she would close her eyes and fall asleep.... counting her blessings!

For several months our nightly bedtime ritual worked flawlessly until, it no longer worked flawlessly. One evening, for some unexplainable reason, Alice's face was not positioned on the pillow. Unexpectedly, the back of her head was on the pillow, which prevented her from viewing the television set. The bewildered look on her face was disturbing to me as she lay staring up at the snow-white plaster ceiling. The most effective method to position her properly was to repeat the process. Unfortunately, the re-enactment was no different; the back of her head was on the pillow and she peered perplexedly at the ceiling.

It was disturbing to witness the bewilderment on Alice's face. As tears began to well-up in my eyes, wistfully I murmured, "I'm so sorry Alice dear, I can't seem to position you properly to watch television."

With the same expressionless face, with which we were all too familiar, she looked forlornly into my tear-filled eyes, ostensibly devoid of comprehension. Then, after what seemed to be an eternity, slowly, ever so-slowly, she raised her left hand and gently rubbed my cheek. Somehow Alice deduced my dejection and conveyed my compassion. In the stillness of Alice's world of silence, her message spoke and, spoke resoundingly. "Don't cry Dan, it's all right. Don't cry." Yes, *The Heart of Our Home* was...STILL ALICE!

My eyes will always moisten whenever I recall that moment of extraordinary Grace. Without a doubt, it was a message of reassurance for me, a message transmitted through the silent world of Alice. Deo Gratias. *"The Lord will fight for you while you remain silent" (Exodus 14:14).*

O HOLY NIGHT...

"Do not be afraid.... I proclaim to you good news of great joy...." (Luke 2:10)

The girls and Jackie decorated the house exactly as Alice would have liked. Her sister Eleanor, as usual, brought a tray of delicious homemade cookies and desserts. Her granddaughter Ashley placed Baby Jesus in the manger while everyone sang Christmas carols.

In a sense, Christmas 2015 was unlike, yet similar to, all the Christmas celebrations Alice and I enjoyed in Westfield and in Needham. Unlike other Christmas's, Alice's weakened condition made it impossible for her to laugh, to sing and to physically rejoice. It was similar to other Christmas's in that her soul experienced the Love of the Christ Child which, as always, she transmitted to her family.

Even though Alice's facial expressions were staid, her eyes appeared alert. Those beautiful blue eyes followed the movements of her loving family as they doted over her, trying to build her spirits by engaging her with laughter, stories of past Christmases and, joyfully singing her favorite Christmas carols.

Alice was the recipient of many hugs and kisses from her entire family; everyone showered her with an abundance of attention and a continuum of love. Although speech was a distant memory, Alice appeared pleased to sit silently in her wheelchair and enjoy the excitement of the day. Yes, Christmas 2015 was twice as nice as other Christmases. Not only did "Mom" enjoy watching her children open their gifts, this Christmas she was the center of attention and joy was on the faces of her children as they opened gifts for their mother!

CALLED BY GOD......HOSPICE CAREGIVERS

Initially, Kelly and Carlotta visited Alice three days a week, but after Christmas, as Alice's incapacitation accelerated, it was necessary to increase the frequency of their visits; soon they were administering to Alice five days a week. In order to meet Alice's weekend needs, Carlotta instructed Katie and me on the intricacies of flipping a patient lying prostate in a hospital bed, and Kelly provided us with medications and an at-home blood pressure kit.

Carlotta trained Katie and me in the method of "turning" a prone patient by tugging on an extra sheet, which gently turns a patient on their side. For Carlotta, it was a simple, one-person process, but for Katie and me, the procedure necessitated a father/daughter Tugging Team.

Not only did Carlotta provide Alice with excellent hygienics, she seemed to sense what Alice might like to eat. When Alice was able to consume a morsel of food, Carlotta would talk lovingly with Alice and rhetorically say, "Alice dear, you love strawberries don't you?" Expressionless Alice would just look at Carlotta with her beautiful blue eyes replicating the same love Carlotta extended to her.

Carlotta spoke to Alice in such a loving way it was obvious Alice appreciated her kindnesses. Carlotta informed me she was formerly a chemical engineer but decided she would rather help people in the final stages of illness, so she resigned her position and became a home health care aide. If that isn't dedication, I don't know the meaning of the word! Obviously, Carlotta, and others who help the dying are special human beings. It is unquestionably a Gift from God—providing care for the dying, they are often the last earthlings patients see before entering eternity.

Although now in a weakened condition, Alice was still comfortable sitting in her customary chair at the dining room table. In place of high school yearbook, she was watching videos on Katie's iPad. Even Alice's electronically illiterate husband could manage to find a few old sit-coms on the iPad, and soon I stumbled on one of Alice's all-time favorites: a British Broadcasting Company (BBC) sitcom, *Ballykissangel*.

When we lived in Westfield, every Saturday night Alice and I watched Ballykissangel, which depicted a typical small town in Ireland replete with hardworking, joyful people, a catholic church, priests, and of course, an Irish Pub! Years later, in our Needham dining room, Alice was glued to the iPad watching replays of *Ballykissangel*.

As background music played, she sat transfixed, watching the characters, intrigued with their brogues and the admonitions of the parish priest. Perhaps it was the quaintness of the town, the songs, and merriment that renewed a residue of long-forgotten memories. Watching the BBC sitcom *Ballykissangel* on the iPad was, unquestionably, a pleasure-filled time for Alice. In a sense, she was watching a moment of Irish lore—*"The Sun Go Down on Galway Bay"* from the cocktail lounge at the Great Southern Hotel.

Now, in reality, she was watching the sun set but it was not setting on Galway Bay or Cape Cod Bay; it was setting on Alice Blue Gown!

Alice was so enthralled with *Ballykissangel* that every evening at suppertime I struggled to find the *Ballykissangel* video on the iPad. I did as Alice would have done in her mechanically proficient days—I tapped links, swiped images, double clicked and dragged icons, but nothing worked. Alice waited patiently for the family klutz to figure out what her former self could have resolved in seconds. After numerous unsuccessful attempts to find Ballykissangel, for some unexplainable reason, the monitor screen was suddenly full of unrelated record albums, none of which would have allowed me to access sit-com videos. As Alice sat silently, seemingly unperturbed, my exasperation was mounting exponentially!

Just as I was about to close out the irrelevant record album screen, my eyes focused on an icon promoting Hit Songs of the 1950s. The artist pictured on the icon was a popular recording artist familiar to most people in our generation—Joni James! Shockingly, the album her picture promoted was Alice Blue Gown! Neither Alice nor I mentioned that song in many, many, years and now, mysteriously, it popped-up on the iPad amidst a plethora of unwanted albums.

I clicked on the Alice Blue Gown icon, and as Alice I sat side by side, we nostalgically listened to Joni James sing "My Sweet Little Alice Blue Gown." At this point in Alice's illness, she seemed captivated by videos and music. To what degree the song may or may not have revived her memory, I do not know. I do know she was riveted to the iPad and, attentively sat in silence and stared as the song played repeatedly. I have absolutely no idea what I did to access the "Alice Blue Gown" icon; it was without a doubt, another Godsend. From that day on it was, good-bye *Ballykissangel* and hello ALICE BLUE GOWN!

Rather than risk another self-inflicted miscue, I saved the Joni James CD on the iPad Favorites List so, every afternoon before what was presumably

Alice's dinner, the Joni James CD played over and over and Alice watched and watched. The fact that Alice was visually incapable of expressing happiness and joy, yet stoically attached to the video was of course emotional for me. Her intense interest in the song she and her mother loved so much seemed to belie her veneer of vagueness. In the deep recesses of her mind, could familiarity restore remembrance? Did she recall happy days when she and her mother enjoyed singing Alice Blue Gown?

As we sat at the dining room table, side by side, day after day, listening to Alice Blue Gown, I would intersperse stories of the past and refresh Alice's memories—Christmas Eve celebrations, trips to Ireland, the kid's birthday parties, West Springfield High School, Cape Cod, Maine, lobster rolls, etc. I was hoping against hope that Alice would recall happier days.

Unfortunately, most often Alice would just look at me with a blank expression. However, there were times when, wishfully, I would think she displayed what I perceived to be *eyes of remembrance*. I also chose to believe her beautiful blue eyes mirrored the beautiful eyes of her soul. *Praise the Lord!*

A MID-WINTER NIGHT'S DREAM

Shortly after New Year's Day 2016, during a typical January in New England, I had a dream! I don't often dream, and if I do dream, the dream is soon forgotten. In this instance I vividly recalled the dream.

In my dream, Alice forgot something at a ski lodge in Vermont and asked me to drive from Needham to Vermont to retrieve the missing item. When we reached the snow-capped Vermont mountain, she directed me to park in front of a three-story ski-lodge. It was a typical ski resort; groups of skiers plodding through the snow while others milled around with ski poles in one hand and hot chocolate in the other.

As my dream continued, Alice informed me the item she wished to retrieve was on the roof of the three-story ski-lodge so, while she remained seated in the warmth of the car, I trudged through the snow-packed parking lot into the lodge and proceeded to climb a steep and narrow flight of darkened stairs to roof of the lodge. As I climbed what seemed like an endless number of stairs, I thought, "Was this trip to Vermont necessary?" Eventually, I reached the top of the treacherous staircase, only to encounter a trap-door leading to the roof. The trap-door was securely affixed to roof joists, proving to be much too difficult for me to dislodge it. After several futile attempts, I decided to descend the steep stairs and ask Alice if she would be willing to assist me in prying open the trap-door.

As I proceeded back to the car, I passed many skiers milling around, half expecting to see Alice among them. But she was not there, and neither was she seated in front seat of our car! Realizing Alice's penchant for resourcefulness, I presumed she must have found an alternate means of accessing the roof of the lodge and was undoubtedly on the roof waiting to help me unlatch the trap-door. Once again, I climbed the steep set of threatening stairs and, once again, attempted to access the roof. After exerting considerable force, somehow, the trap-door dislodged, and I climbed onto to the roof anticipating Alice would be there to greet me. She was not there, nor was there any forgotten item on the snow-covered roof.

Assuming Alice repossessed the forgotten item, I secured the trap-door, descended the stairs, and returned to the car with great expectation that Alice would be seated comfortably and proudly displaying the forgotten item; she was not in the car nor was she milling around with skiers. Alice was gone!

When I awoke the following morning, in my somewhat somnambulant state of mind, the dream predominated my thought process. I concluded that Alice was not only gone in my dream but soon she will be gone—gone to meet Jesus!

The Vermont ski-loft dream also reminded me of Jacob's Dream, in which he encountered messengers, going up and down a stairway, and the Lord said, *"Know that I am with you; I will protect you..." (Genesis 28:15)*

Consequently, I felt assured Jesus would protect Alice.

ALICE'S DECLINE GAINS MOMENTUM

When Kelly and Carlotta visited Alice on Friday, January 8, 2016, they were disappointed to detect drastic deterioration in Alice's bodily functions. Although Kelly was, to a degree, apprehensive, she felt Alice was not in imminent danger. She provided Katie and me with the VNA emergency hotline number when we noted signs of decline in Alice's condition. Armed with the hotline as a backup, Katie and I were confident that we could provide Alice with top-shelf weekend family care.

Bright and early on Saturday morning Katie arrived and, between the two of us, we were able to administer Carlotta's hygienic instructions. We wet Alice's lips with a taste of water and watermelon juice. It was a privilege for both of us to care for the closest human being in our lives—a mother and a wife!

Before anyone could snap their fingers, Alice was sitting pretty on her cushioned chair in the dining room, listening to and staring at the Alice Blue Gown icon on the iPad while our customary Saturday morning Irish Music played softly, maybe not so softly, on the radio.

Sunday was another opportunity for Katie and me to swing into caregiver action and, once again, it wasn't long before Alice was sitting pretty on her foam cushion at the dining room table. It was a day like all days, with one exception—Katie found another video on the iPad, which she knew Alice would love: "THE BELLS OF SAINT MARY'S," starring Bing Crosby as Father O'Malley and Ingrid Bergman as Sister Superior!

Regardless of Alice's rapidly advancing incapacitation, she continued to be completely immersed in religious programs, whether on television or on an iPad. "The Bells of St. Mary's" was certainly no exception! The legendary 1945 American drama introduced an ever-popular song that was sung every year at Saint Mary's School Christmas Pageant in Westfield. Alice was absolutely mesmerized as she sat in front of the iPad and watched Bing Crosby and Ingrid Bergman from her cushioned dining room chair.

In spite of the length of the video (two hours) she sat stoically, captivated by the depiction of priests, nuns, and children's voices as they periodically sang "THE BELLS OF SAINT MARY'S, I hear they are calling..." As the two of us sat, side-by-side, engrossed in the travails of Father O'Malley and Saint Mary's School Choir, tears trickled down my face. But Alice sat silently, spared of the emotional drama of the movie.

Alice never failed to find comfort whenever she saw anyone affiliated with the Catholic Church; and now, obviously she felt secure in the presence of someone she deemed to be a Friend of Christ. Watching "The Bells of Saint Mary's" on the last Sunday of her life affirmed the serenity, the solace, and the peacefulness she must have experienced as a young girl deeply impacted by the Sisters of Notre Dame at Holy Name of Jesus School in Chicopee, and the Sisters of Saint Joseph at Saint Thomas the Apostle School in West Springfield. It was as if, in watching "The Bells of Saint Mary's," the Lord bestowed one more blessing on our little Alice Blue Gown.

When Carlotta arrived on Monday, January 11th, once again she was appalled with Alice's rapid deterioration, "What happened to you my pretty Alice? What happened dear Alice?" Carlotta wasn't playing a role and falsely proclaiming concern; Carlotta genuinely loved Alice. In her weakened and presumably incommunicative malaise, somehow Alice's eyes seemed to convey recognition of Carlotta. In Carlotta's mind and in my mind, Alice silently reciprocated her love for Carlotta.

Soon, Nurse Kelly arrived and she too detected a drastic decline in Alice, which was corroborated with extremely low blood pressure, an indication of obvious weakness. Kelly alerted the VNA that we may need back-up support for the next few days and she put Katie in touch with the VNA's on-duty nurse to monitor Alice's condition.

Thankfully, Alice spent a relative tranquil night on Monday January 11th, but on Tuesday Kelly reported to her superiors that Alice was deemed to be permanently bed-ridden and subsequently, instructed Katie on the method to administer morphine if authorized by the VNA hotline nurse.

We alerted Anne Marie and Jackie of Alice's declining condition, assuring them we were receiving excellent support from the VNA. Patti and Ashley were of course on the scene and immediately proceeded to speak reassuringly to Alice as they held her hand and wiped her forehead with cool cloths. Later on, Katie's husband, Max, arrived and the five of us took shifts ministering to Alice during the night.

We sat with her, wiped her face, prayed, and assured Alice of our presence. Katie updated the 24-hour VNA hotline nurse on Alice's diminishing condition, and when she exhibited signs of congestion, Katie received authorization to administer morphine which, thankfully, alleviated throat congestion and allowed Alice to rest peacefully through the night.

JANUARY 13, 2016

On Wednesday morning, I sat with Alice as she lay motionless, a mere facsimile of her former vibrant self, I couldn't help but think that just three days ago, side by side, she and I watched "The Bells of Saint Mary's." Now, in a matter of days, she lay comatose, in the familiar confines of her own living room.

I continued to gaze at Alice's stillness and thought of her approaching encounter with Jesus, hopeful that Alice's faith in God, love for her children and for others would be pleasing to Him. Certainly, her love for our family enriched our marriage and mystically united our souls—the ultimate blessing God bestows on a husband and wife. As flawed human beings, most of us, by virtue of our humanity, are ego-oriented. Alice was not among those mortals; she was altruistic. In her mind, she was secondary to others.

Assured Alice was resting comfortably, I decided to take a quick trip to the Santander Bank and procure the Sacred Linen used at Danny's ordination. Unbeknown to me, that would be the last time I saw Alice, body and soul.

Thank you, Lord, for the gift of Alice Marie Haggerty. She was THE BEST!

APPENDIX

HAPPENINGS AFTER JANUARY 13, 2016

- A few days after Alice passed away, I was on a mission to purchase chia seeds at a local supermarket. As I proceeded to examine a packet of chia seeds, another customer approached me and said, "Excuse me sir, are you purchasing chia seeds?" I replied, "I am." He said, "Take my advice and don't buy chia seeds, buy flaxseeds." I just smiled and continued to read the label on the chia seed packet. The stranger was not easily dissuaded and replied, "I'm 79 years old, and I'm telling you not buy chia seeds, purchase flaxseeds." Incredulous; a total stranger volunteering his age? I responded, "You don't look 79 years of age and I'm certain all in those years of you have acquired considerable knowledge about flaxseeds. However, I am also 79 years of age and I'm here to purchase chia seeds." The persistent supermarket stranger was undaunted and said, "My wife just died and she always told me to buy flaxseeds." I responded, "I'm sorry to learn of your wife's death and I'm certain her allegiance to flax seeds is important to you. However, my wife just died and she told me to buy chia seeds!"

- What are the chances of a total stranger initiating a conversation in which he divulged his age and laments his recently deceased wife? We're exactly the same age and both recent widowers.

- I must have spent 10 to 15 minutes listening to the nostalgic Supermarket Stranger regal me with exploits of his multi-talented wife, who he proudly proclaimed to be a professional singer turned housewife. At that point, similarities ended; Alice was not a professional singer; nor was she ever accused of being a singer! Supermarket coincidence?

- A week or two later, Jack and a few of his friends, including Paul Finigan, dropped-in on their way to a New England Patriot's football game. During our conversation, Katie urged me to tell Paul about my Vermont ski-lodge dream. After I recounted the dream that sparked Paul's recollection and he told me his Vermont ski-lodge story. After Danny and Matt were ordained in 2007, they attended a golf academy in Stratton Vermont, which was not far from Paul's 3rd floor condominium. So Paul offered them accommodations while they were attending the golf school. Paul went on to explain: Danny lost the key to the 3rd floor condo and, rather than admit to Paul he lost the key, Danny climbed on the roof of the Ski-lodge, reached down and proceeded to pry open an unlocked 3rd floor window and gained entrance. Correlation to my Vermont Ski-lodge dream?

- Shortly after the Fourth of July, near our front steps I noticed what appeared to be a small weed, probably two or three inches in height, and made a mental note to pull it out at a later date. A day or two later, I bent down to pull out the weed but thought to myself, "This may not be a weed," and decided to let it grow a few more days. A week later, there was no longer any doubt; it wasn't a weed. It was a fledgling tomato plant! Every year since Alice and I were married, I planted a vegetable garden in our backyard and my primary crop was tomato plants. Now, mysteriously growing on the precise spot where Alice's wheelchair ramp resided was a tomato plant. Assuming a bird must have dropped a tomato seed I concluded the fine feathered friend must have been confused by summer holidays. In order to avoid the on-set of autumn weather and yield tomatoes prior to Labor Day, tomato plants must be in the ground by Memorial Day. In spite of the probability of a premature tomato plant terminus, my strategy was to nurture the plant and extend its life expectancy. Every night, before I went to bed, I covered the plant with Alice's coat and poured warm water around the roots, hoping to trick the plant into believing it was still summer. Thankfully, the strategy worked; Alice's tomato plant lived until December 1, 2016 and, on Christmas Day, we served pickle-lily from Alice's front yard tomato plant. Coincidence?

- On Saturday August 6, 2016, I drove to western Mass to meet Jackie and his two children, Jack and Celia, for a 9:30 a.m. breakfast. My intention was, to stop en route to attend an early morning Mass, which I determined would be Saint Thomas the Apostle Church in West Springfield. As I parked the car in front of the church, nostalgia began to set-in; 49 years ago, Alice and I were married in Church of Saint Thomas the Apostle. During Mass I realized it was the Feast Day of the Transfiguration; another nostalgic moment. In the Holy Land, at The Church of the Transfiguration on Mount Tabor, Alice was prevented from entering the holy site because the security guard considered her shorts to be "too short." They were not. Lastly, the Scriptural reading during that Mass referred to a *myriad of angels*. When that Scriptural passage was proclaimed, I was taking particular note of the word *myriad*. My mind focused on a sympathy card I received, just days before, from a summertime guest at Dennis Seashores who belatedly learned of Alice's death. Bill Early from Branford, Connecticut penned a beautiful note describing Alice's unique abilities in which he aptly stated, "Alice was able to skillfully handle a myriad of personalities and resolve volatile situations to everyone's satisfaction." As I contemplated these coincidental occurrences, I commenced to believe Alice's spirit was pleased I attended

Mass at the church where we were married, on The Feast Day of the Transfiguration. Coincidence?

- On August 22, a hot and humid night, we had a small birthday cake for Katie at our Woodlawn Ave home. Katie and Alice shared the same birthday, so this was the first year Alice's name was not inscribed on the cake. After singing "Happy Birthday," Katie, who was seated in Alice's customary kitchen chair, was about to blow-out the candles. Suddenly, a gust of wind blew through the kitchen window and extinguished every candle. Immediately, Katie said, "Thanks' Mom." I added, "Your mother must be annoyed we didn't sing Happy Birthday to her." We relit the candles and sang, "Happy Birthday Alice." Katie's husband Max was videoing the festivities, so we have a video of the Mysterious Extinguishment. Coincidence?

- In November of 2016, I received a letter from a young man who I did not know. In the letter he explained that in 2008, when he was in the 8th grade at a local high school, he came across and article about a young Boston priest who died shortly after his ordination. He was particularly struck by a quotation in the article attributed to the young priest's mother, "My son loved the Boston Red Sox, the Boston Bruins, and the New England Patriots, but most of all he loved Christ and his people." This young man went on. "After reading that article, I began to ponder the possibility of becoming a priest. Subsequently, I completed four years of high school, four years of college, and that image of a mother's remembrance of her priest-son never left my mind. Eight years later, I applied to St. John's Seminary in Brighton, and I am currently a First Year Pre-Theology student," said Patrick O'Connor. Not only was I delighted to learn of another young man studying for the priesthood at Saint John's Seminary, I was particularly pleased he attributed Alice's synopsis of Danny's call to the priesthood as the most significant aspect of the article. DEO GRATIAS!